International Directory of Museum Training

Heritage: Care–Preservation–Management
Editor-in-chief Andrew Wheatcroft

Architecture in Conservation: *Managing development at historic sites*
James Strike

The Development of Costume
Naomi Tarrant

Forward Planning: *A handbook of business, corporate and development planning for museums and galleries*
Edited by Timothy Ambrose and Sue Runyard

The Handbook for Museums
Gary Edson and David Dean

Heritage Gardens: *Care, conservation and management*
Sheena Mackellar Goulty

Heritage and Tourism: *in the global village*
Priscilla Boniface and Peter J. Fowler

The Industrial Heritage: *Managing resources and uses*
Judith Alfrey and Tim Putnam

Museum Basics
Timothy Ambrose and Crispin Paine

Museum Exhibition
David Dean

Museum Security and Protection: *A handbook for cultural heritage institutions*
ICOM and ICMS

Museums 2000: *Politics, people, professionals and profit*
Edited by Patrick J. Boylan

Museums and the Shaping of Knowledge
Eilean Hooper-Greenhill

Museums and their Visitors
Eilean Hooper-Greenhill

Museums without Barriers: *A new deal for disabled people*
Fondation de France and ICOM

The Past in Contemporary Society: *Then/Now*
Peter J. Fowler

The Representation of the Past: *Museums and heritage in the post-modern world*
Kevin Walsh

Towards the Museum of the Future: *New European perspectives*
Edited by Roger Miles and Laura Zavala

International Directory of Museum Training

Gary Edson

London and New York

First published 1995
by Routledge
11 New Fetter Lane, London EC4P 4EE

Simultaneously published in the USA and Canada
by Routledge
29 West 35th Street, New York, NY 10001

© 1995 Gary Edson and ICOM

Typeset in Sabon and Univers by
Florencetype Ltd, Stoodleigh, Nr Tiverton, Devon

Printed and bound in Great Britain by T J Press Ltd,
Padstow, Cornwall

British Library Cataloguing in Publication Data
A catalogue record for this book is available from
the British Library

Library of Congress Cataloguing in Publication Data
A catalogue record for this book is available.

ISBN 0-415-12257–0

"The person who can bring to an 'ordinary' profession a sense of dedicated vocation, restores to that profession its genius."
Janet Flanner (Genêt)

Contents

————•◆•————

Illustrations

———•◆•———

Biographical note

—•◆•—

Gary Edson is an active member of the American Association of Museums (AAM). He serves as chair of the AAM standing professional Committee on Museum Professional Training (COMPT), is chair of the United States Committee on Museology (US-ICOFOM), and is secretary of the International Committee for Training of Personnel (ICTOP). Currently he is executive director of the Museum of Texas Tech University, Director of the Museum Science Program, and Professor of Museum Science. Edson has an MFA degree from Tulane University and has been involved in academic teaching and administration for twenty-six years. He has worked and taught in Mexico, Korea, and Ecuador as well as the United States. Publications include *The Museum Handbook* co-authored with David K. Dean.

Foreword

———•◆•———

[There] is a clear and growing demand in many parts of the world today that museums increasingly should become crucibles in which culture is forged. In other words, they should be places in which past cultures emerge from the shadows to illuminate the present and to cast a finger to the light over the future.[1]

In most parts of the world there is also an increasing interest in the developments associated with the museum profession. Newly formed museum studies programs are preparing students for entry into the museum community and those persons already working in museums are seeking ways to improve their knowledge, skills, and technical capabilities. Recognizing the evolving nature of the museum profession, training is an ongoing process that does not stop with completion of a formal education. It is a career-long process calculated to develop the full potential of a person and to assure the greatest benefit for the individual, the museum community and society.

Considering the importance of museum training, the sixteenth General Assembly of ICOM, meeting in The Hague, The Netherlands recommended the following:

1   Existing training courses be reinforced and new ones established for personnel at all levels of museum employment;
2   Training programmes be developed which ensure an understanding of all aspects of the museum operation, having regard to the rapid development of new technologies and the increasing number of skills involved;
3   Particular consideration be given to training needs in natural science preparation and conservation of biological specimens;
4   Research be encouraged into all aspects of the museum operation and its technology.[2]

To add to the complexity of training requirements, most museums are being transformed from traditional, object-oriented institutions to dynamic, public-oriented institutions in the service of society. With this change, museums are attempting to anticipate developments and the evolving expectations of society rather than reflecting a historic perspective of sociological conditions. Meeting this public-oriented concept requires open-minded, creative, and professionally trained personnel eager to assume a leadership role in the museums of the next century.

During the last two decades, an increasing number of professions have recognized that continuous updating of skills and practices is a necessity. It is essential that all museum personnel, regardless of their work, educational background, and experience have the opportunity to improve their museological skills. Those persons in or entering the museum field have both a basic right and an obligation to receive appropriate professional training.

> Members of the museum profession require appropriate academic, technical, and professional training in order to fulfill their important role in relation to the operation of the museum and the care for the heritage.[3]

Before beginning a training or retraining program, the first step should be to determine individual goals, professional expectations, and the nature and scope of available museum training programs. This publication is intended to assist with all three of these concerns. It gives detailed information so prospective students can compare training program requirements, curriculum, financial aid, and program size when determining which training opportunity meets their particular needs.

Piet J.M. Pouw
Chairman, ICTOP Amsterdam
The Netherlands

Notes

1   Blokhuis, S. (1991) *ICOM '89 Museums: Generators of Culture*, The Hague: ICOM, p. 11.
2   Ibid., p. 70.
3   International Council of Museums (1990) *Code of Professional Ethics*, (revised) Paris: ICOM, pp. 25–6.

Acknowledgments

———•◆•———

The International Directory of Museum Training is the result of a coordinated effort involving several people and agencies. It is sponsored by the International Council of Museums (ICOM), the International Committee for Training of Personnel (ICTOP), and the Museum of Texas Tech University.

The reader should realize that this book is the latest of a number of publications sponsored either totally or in part by ICOM, and designed to provide training information for persons either entering the museum profession or continuing their quest for the highest level of skill and knowledge related to museological activities. One of the earliest of these books was titled *La Formation du personnel des musées*. It had an introduction by S. Dillon Ripley and a chapter titled, "Répertoire des cours de muséologie dans le monde" compiled by Anita Sabourin. This section, published only in French, listed seventy-six training programs. Hopefully the present volume will serve the museum community as well as the earlier contributions.

A number of people helped to make this book possible. Of particular importance are the members of the ICTOP Board and Dr Piet Pouw, the Committee Chair. Without their endorsement and support there would have been no beginning to this endeavor. Thanks are due to Dr Saroj Ghose, President, and Elisabeth des Portes, Secretary General, for the support of ICOM. I have benefited from the help and encouragement of Professor Patrick Boylan and Jane Glaser, who compiled and edited the last edition of the *Directory*. (Earlier editions of this publication were titled *Museum Studies International*. However, in an effort to define more clearly the content and purpose of the book, the current title, *International Directory of Museum Training*, was selected.) I wish also to acknowledge the Smithsonian Institution for providing data generated as part of the previous publication, and Jane Sledge, Chief of the UNESCO/ICOM Museum Information Center, for allowing me the use of the Documentation Center.

My gratitude goes to Nicky Olson for providing photographs, to

Rebecca Hinrichs for helping with photo processing, to Linda Lamb and Cora Kolander for clerical assistance, and to all those training administrators who took the time to complete the survey that is the information source for the section on training programs.

Finally, a major thank you goes to M, my wife and collaborator. She read and reread the text, offered suggestions, (gentle) criticism, and (thoughtful) comments. For the most part she did the job willingly, and the other times she allowed a small amount of coercion to renew her enthusiasm. As always she was there when needed. *¡Mil gracias!*

In the end, as with all publications, the responsibility for content lies with the author, or in this case with the compiler/editor. The information came from several sources. It has been compiled and edited to document the museum training being offered worldwide. No institution responding to the questionnaire was intentionally excluded (except by their request) and no great liberty was taken with the descriptive material provided. In some cases, the writing was edited to fit the allowed space or reorganized to accommodate an established format. I hope the next edition of *The International Directory of Museum Training* will include more programs from more of the world so the international community of museums and museum workers can be better served.

Gary Edson
Secretary, ICTOP
Executive Director, Museum of Texas Tech University
Lubbock, Texas
USA

Abbreviations

—•◆•—

A.B.   Artium Baccalaureus
A.M.   Artium Magister
B.A.   Bachelor of Arts
B.F.A.   Bachelor of Fine Arts
B.Litt.   Bachelor of Letters
B.S.   Bachelor of Science
D.Phil.   Doctor of Philosophy
M.A.   Master of Arts
M.F.A.   Master of Fine Arts
M.Litt.   Master of Letters
Ph.D.   Doctor of Philosophy

PART I

Plate 1 Exhibits Preparator Michael Nickell hanging framed work in exhibit (photograph by Gary Edson)

ONE

Introduction to museum training

—•◆•—

The term "museum" has changed over time. It is a word that has acquired special meaning in different places and among different people. In 1727, Caspar F. Neickel of Hamburg wrote in *Museographia*: [Museum] "a chamber of treasures – rarities – objects of nature – of art and of reason." A few years later in 1755, Dr Samuel Johnson's *Dixonary* identifies a museum as "a Repository of learned Curiosities." More than two hundred years later, in 1970, the American Association of Museums defined a museum as: "an organized and permanent nonprofit institution, essentially educational or aesthetic in purpose, with professional staff, which owns and utilizes tangible objects, cares for them and exhibits them to the public on some regular schedule."

The ICOM definition of a museum is: "[A] non-profit making, permanent institution in the service of society and of its development, and open to the public, which acquires, conserves, researches, communicates, and exhibits, for purposes of study, education, and enjoyment, material evidence of people and their environment."[1]

The word "museum" as currently used is associated with the Greek word *mouseion*, which designates a place of contemplation, a philosophical institution or temple of the Muses.[2] The Romans made similar application of the word to describe a place for philosophical discussion.[3] The *World Heritage Dictionary* defines "museum" as "An institution for the acquisition, preservation, study, and exhibition of works of artistic, historical, or scientific value."[4] The latter definition has been generally accepted since the eighteenth century in most of the western world.

G. Ellis Burcaw writes about an early museum in Alexandria, Egypt, established as a center of learning dedicated to the Muses in about 290 BC.[5] Prior to that time, 1504–1450 BC, Tuthmosis III was reported to have formed a fine collection of Asian flora and fauna gathered during military campaigns. In the Babylonian Empire, the Kings Nebuchadrezzer (605–562 BC) and Nabonidus (*c.* 555–539 BC) were collectors and archeologists in that they excavated and restored parts of their city of Ur.[6]

The concept of museums has always had worldwide implications. As defined by Alma Wittlin,[7] the gathering of objects with magical importance is one of the primary motives for collecting. With the rise of Islam in the current era, objects were collected for mainly religious motives. These treasures were associated with the tombs of Muslim martyrs.[8] One of the best known of these tombs (shrines) is in Iran and still a location to which pilgrims go. According to Geoffrey Lewis, the idea or principle of giving property, in perpetuity, for the public good and religious benefit was formalized as a concept by Muhammad.[9]

In the Far East both China and Japan venerated the past and collected objects of antiquity from very early times. During the Shang dynasty (*c.* 1600–1025 BC) collections of gold and bronze artifacts were assembled. These objects were found during excavations in Honan Province. An extraordinary collection of terracotta warriors and horses from the Qin dynasty were found in Shanxi Province near Xi'an.[10] There are also reports of individual collectors and treasure houses in China. Collections in Japan were often housed in temples, particularly those maintained by Buddhists. An example of this is the Shoso-in that was constructed to house the collection of the widow of Emperor Shomu.[11]

In Europe, a significant change in museums came as the result of the shift in attitude that fostered the Renaissance in Italy. The focus of human thinking changed to place humanity at the center of the universe. The seat of influence, at least regionally, rested in Italy. The Fourth Crusade at the beginning of the fourteenth century resulted in the capture of Constantinople. The occupation of that city marked the beginning of the decline of the Byzantine era of artistic influence that had lasted for over five hundred years. The Renaissance was a time of experimentation, observation, and exploration. Humankind became interested in the things that surrounded them. This interest led to the formation of natural history collections and other materials relating to science and investigation. The first herbarium came into existence during this time in the Italian city of Padua. It was also an age in which collections of objects of art and curiosities flourished. Collectors like Cosimo de' Medici (1389–1464) and his grandson Lorenzo collected manuscripts, prints, gem stones, tapestries, and icons as well as paintings and sculptures. Reportedly the first modern use of the word "museum" was to describe a collection of objects assembled by Lorenzo de' Medici. The de' Medici collections eventually became a part of what we know today as the Uffizi Museum established in 1582.

It is interesting to note that the first documented attempts to restrict exportation of national patrimony in the form of antiquities and art occurred in 1534, when the Pope tried to ban this export trade. The prohibition was unsuccessful.[12]

In other parts of Europe other collections were being formed. Often these objects were housed in locations designated as "galleries," "cabinets of curiosities," *Kabinetts*, and *Kammer*. The latter two words of Germanic origin normally had a prefix attached to give a more precise description of the collection.

There is a correlation between those establishments defined as museums and the institutions of learning called the academy. The learning process and the exchange of information are primary functions of both. Museums provided the ideal venue for creating an awareness of national consciousness by providing information about the legacy of the land and people. Research, interpretation, and communication evolved from the early days of the nineteenth century and with that development came a gradual awareness of responsibility. The pursuit of the highest level of achievement in museum training, skill development, and intellectual growth is a challenging task. The requirements of museum work must go beyond the academy and the traditional limits of the institution to include the broadest concept of social interaction. "A hallmark of museums is intellectual rigor, a tradition that must continue to be applied in the context of a wider public dimension."[13]

The study of museology as the science of museums is an overview of the theories associated with the practices of museums. Included are the history and philosophy of museums and the attitudes promoted by persons actively involved in developing museum understanding. Museology is not limited to the history of museums or a listing of their functions.[14] Traditional museology is accepted as referring to a body of practical knowledge as it relates to museums.[15]

> Museology is museum science. It has to do with the study of the history and background of museums, their role in society, specific systems for research, conservation, education and organization, relationship with the physical environment, and the classification of kinds of museums. In brief, museology is the branch of knowledge concerned with the study of the purposes and organization of museums.[16]

According to the International Committee for Museology 1986/87, the word "museology" is defined to mean: "the study of the specific relation of man [humankind] to reality that is expressed by his [or her] collecting, preserving and documenting activities related to this reality, and by communicating knowledge about it to others."[17]

Museography is defined as being: "the body of techniques related to museology. It covers methods and practices in operating museums, in all their various aspects."[18]

In 1965, the seventh General Conference of ICOM, held in New York, devoted significant time to issues about museum training. At the end of the Conference the General Assembly adopted four resolutions that remain relevant to museum training. They are:

1　It is vital that museum personnel of all categories should have a status corresponding to that of the academic profession, since the required qualifications and responsibilities are similar.
2　With equal qualifications and years of service, a member of the staff of a museum should have the same status and salary as professionals in the teaching world or other learned institutions.
3　A candidate for the post of museum curator should have a university degree. Exceptions may be made for candidates of unusual merit. Curators for all types of museums should receive a postgraduate training in a university or technical school covering museology in general. This training should include both theory and practice. Training may be undertaken by museums in the form of internships. This may include such subjects as field research, scientific examination of works of art, and technical studies pertaining to a candidate's own specialty. These postgraduate studies should receive the sanction of a diploma.
4　Curators and other trained museum personnel should be provided with the necessary facilities and time to carry on research and scientific work independent of their regular museum duties. They also should have opportunities to increase their knowledge through study in other museums in their country and abroad, and to participate in seminars and conferences at home and abroad.

Since that time, several changes have taken place. One example of change occurred in 1968 when the General Conference of ICOM, held in Cologne and Munich, approved the creation of a new International Committee for the Training of Personnel with Raymond Singleton, director of Museum Studies at Leicester University in the UK, as chair.[19] One of the first projects of the new committee was a series of regional museum training surveys and teaching visits in various parts of the world. The results of this investigation were eventually published in 1970, as *Training of Museum Personnel (La Formation du personnel des musées)*, by ICOM with help from the Smithsonian.

The new committee held its first major Museology Symposium at the University of Leicester in July 1969. At that meeting the committee adopted a total of ten resolutions which form the basis of the Training Committee's objectives. Included in the resolutions are these recommendations:

that the authorities responsible for museums and for universities, in every country, should immediately recognize museology as a discipline of academic status and value, et cetera;
that technical training should be obtained from museography;
that the necessity for providing advanced and refresher courses for personnel already practicing in the profession be reaffirmed;

that in every country having a museology center, the diplomas granted by these centers be officially recognized as, or equivalent to, university diplomas and that they give access to the profession at a certain level, providing that they guarantee studies of sufficient length and quality in all fields of museology.

Other recommendations encourage establishing an ICOM model syllabus for museum training.

The ICOM Committee for the Training of Personnel (ICTOP) adopted a Common Basic Syllabus for Professional Museum Training during the ninth General Conference of ICOM in 1971 and made revisions that were adopted in 1979. That Syllabus has nine primary instructional headings to be included in professional museum training programs. These are:

1 introduction to museology: history and purpose of museums;
2 organization, operation and management of museums;
3 architecture, layout, equipment;
4 collections: origin, related records, set-up and movement;
5 scientific activities;
6 preservation and care of collections;
7 presentation: exhibitions;
8 the public;
9 cultural and educational activities of the museum.

This committee and the resulting report were prompted in part by the Belmont Report published in October 1968. In the report there is a statement that in part speaks of understaffing:

A contributing factor is a shortage of trained people. The solution, museum professionals agree, is more in-service training for workers now on museum staffs and more museum training opportunities in colleges and universities for prospective museum personnel.

Museums themselves, for lack of funds, have been able to do no more than scratch the surface of this field. Though some 60 museums and universities offer museum training courses, the number of fellowships available is severely limited, as is the size of each stipend. No doubt more fellowships and more adequate stipends would be offered if museum salaries and working conditions were improved.[20]

To attempt to establish one criterion for museum training is an impossible task. There is no unanimously supported vision of the content, sequence, or method of training for museum personnel. There are those who advocate academic-based training with a theoretical base. Others endorse an informal approach with a primary emphasis on applied practices, a form of on-the-job training. A third possibility, one endorsed for a number of years, is subject discipline-based. Each may have merit in a given situation. The success of any program depends on a balance of technique and theory.

Museums have existed in an identifiable form for over two thousand years and in a configuration not unlike today's for over three hundred years. By contrast, museum training can be measured in decades. At the turn of the twentieth century museum training was almost unknown. Most museums were continuing the traditional practice of warehousing objects in an open storage fashion. Objects were gathered, identified, processed, and deposited in publicly accessible storage cases, offering a static, under-interpreted, and marginally informational view to the visiting public. Curators, normally academics, gathered the material and stored it for future reference. Guards patrolled the galleries and custodial personnel kept the area clean. No other museum staff was required.

In early museums, curators provided most of the collections-related services. Field work, object selection, and identification were the responsibility of the curator with research, documentation, care, and exhibition. As the collections diversified and the public orientation of museums changed, the role and responsibility of the museum worker changed also. Specialization has added conservators, exhibits designers, fabricators, public relations persons, education specialists, and information scientists to undertake duties once assigned to curators.[21]

Many of the first museum training programs, particularly those located in universities, were subject discipline electives. They offered insight into basic museum practices as a career option, but generally provided minimal study of museology.[22]

There are a number of important professional museum studies courses in the world. Each has its special focus and/or emphasis. Probably the most important issues to face museum studies programs in the future will be alignment. There must be working arrangements between museum studies programs to share faculty and curriculum for the betterment of the students and the museum profession.

At the 1989 General Conference of ICOM in The Hague, Resolution No. 2 addresses the training of museum personnel. It states:

> Considering the lack of trained museum personnel in many parts of the world and the changing social, cultural and economic situations in which museums increasingly are expected to contribute:
> Having regard to the precedents already created by UNESCO and UNDP to contribute to the funding of training and the priority given by UNESCO to training;
> Noting that in certain countries the employer is expected to contribute not less than a fixed percentage of employee costs for training purposes;

Recognizing that bilateral agreements and the twinning of cities can provide a framework in which the exchange and training of personnel can be provided;

Wishing to recognize the role that ICOM's National and International Committees and Regional Agencies can play in fostering and contributing to museum training programmes;

Bearing in mind the need for training to have regard to the socio-cultural requirements of the student, and preferably to be done at the regional level.

In planning for the future, the museum profession must look beyond the traditional strength of the collections and recognize the value of the human resource. Knowledgeable curators, educators, and presentation staff, as well as docents, guards, and volunteers in all areas are essential for transforming collections into substantive exhibits and programs. The concept of the museum as not only a collection of objects but as a collection of professionals dedicated to protecting, using, and interpreting the objects for the purposes for which they were brought together is an imperative element of proper stewardship. The professional museum worker also requires adequate care and training to guarantee the correct and appropriate response to collection and constituency needs.

A well-trained staff is necessary if museums are to provide the leadership to "promote a greater knowledge and understanding among people."[23]

Notes

1 ICOM (1990) *Statutes*, Article 2 – Definitions, Paris: ICOM, p. 3.
2 Lewis, G. (1984) "Museums and their precursors, a brief world survey," in J.M.A. Thompson (ed.) *Manual of Curatorship* (2nd edition, 1992), Oxford: Butterworth-Heinemann, p. 5.
3 Ibid.
4 *American Heritage Electronic Dictionary*, Version 1.1, Macintosh edition (1991), Houghton Mifflin Company (Word Star International Inc., 1992).
5 Burcaw, G. (1975) *Introduction to Museum Work*, Nashville: American Association of State and Local History, p. 17.
6 Lewis, "Museums and their precursors, a brief world survey," p. 5.
7 Wittlin, A. (1970) *Museums: In Search of a Usable Future*, Cambridge, Mass.: MIT Press.
8 Lewis, "Museums and their precursors, a brief world survey," p. 6.
9 Ibid., p. 7.
10 Ibid., p. 7.
11 Ibid., p. 7.
12 Ibid., p. 8.

13 Pittman, B. (chair, AAM Task Force on Education) (1991) *Excellence and Equity, Education and the Public Dimension of Museums*, Washington, D.C.: American Association of Museums, p. 8.

14 Sola, T. (1987) "The concept and nature of museology," *Museum (UNESCO)*, Vol. XXXIX, No. 1: pp. 45–9.

15 Ibid.

16 Burcaw, *Introduction to Museum Work*, pp. 12–13.

17 Sofka, V., definition included in unpublished paper titled "Contemporary museology – concept, role and trends," presented at the ICTOP Annual Meeting in Rio de Janeiro, 1993.

18 Burcaw, *Introduction to Museum Work*, pp. 12–13.

19 Papageorge, M. (1978)"A world view of museum studies," *Museum News*, November/December, pp. 7–9.

20 American Association of Museums (1969) *America's Museums: The Belmont Report*, Washington, D.C.: American Association of Museums, p. 5.

21 Lewis, G. (1987) "Editorial: Who trains museum staff?", *Museum (UNESCO)*, No. 156 (Vol. XXXIX No. 4): pp. 219–20.

22 Singleton, R. (1987) "Museum training: status and development," *Museum (UNESCO)*, Vol. XXXIX No. 4: pp. 221–4.

23 "Preamble (c)," *Statutes – Code of Professional Ethics* (1987), Paris: ICOM, p. 15.

Plate 2 Museum Studies student Shannan Faulk conducting inventory of clothing collection artifacts (photograph by Gary Edson)

T W O

Museum training in a changing world

—•◆•—

The current pace of socio-economic, cultural, and scientific development far exceeds all previous times. As part of this process of change, every museum and museum worker has a growing number of responsibilities. Each new report defines an additional critical need that must be addressed by the museum community either singly or collectively. The role and mission of the museum worker is shifting due to greater attention being focused on worldwide museum issues. Specialized training for the museum workforce is necessary if positive care and use of the common wealth of humanity is to be realized. There can be little doubt that museum personnel training and the ideals of museum professionalism are worldwide concerns. The responsibility for active information exchange with museum colleagues is an essential element of museum professionalization.

In many parts of the world emerging and established nations are aggressively collecting, conserving, and researching the objects and specimens that represent their country's cultural and scientific heritage. In Mexico, Central and South America, across Africa, the Middle East, and the Orient, governments have built and continue to build museums to house the treasures of the land and people.[1] Many countries have spent large amounts of money on museum-related projects to instill pride and self-identity in the people. In some cases the museums serve to further a particular ideology. In others, they meet alternative educational needs. Usually the limiting factors are identifying the role of museums and training of museum personnel.

Conceptually the basic components of museums have not changed; they remain objects and people. It may be argued that the order has been reversed or that the proportion of each ingredient has been altered. In reality it is probably the working relationship of the two basic elements that has changed. The amalgam of interpretation, presentation, use, and care of objects has been altered.

Museum professionals all over the world must work to solve problems common to all people, while conforming to existing national and regional conditions. These activities are vividly illustrated in the dynamics of professional museum training interests and reinforced by the supposition that the main mission of museums is education and through that process cultural enlightenment.

At three different museum-sponsored workshops in Africa during 1991, four general and overlapping themes emerged. They are:

1   autonomy for museums;
2   collaboration between regional museums;
3   training of museum workers;
4   implications for the future.[2]

In all three workshops, attention was given to the critical issue of specialized training for museum workers. Three separate training needs were identified: training of technicians, training of curators, and training of museum educators.

Unfortunately, worldwide inequities in museum training, museum development, and professional achievement cannot be resolved as easily as they are identified. Differences in individual nations limit the ability to meet many of the basic needs of the museum workforce. If museum training needs were limited to one people, society, or nation, it might be described as an unfortunate though understandable situation. However, if reports from around the world are to be believed, many societies are experiencing the same circumstances. Partly in response to this need, museum training is a rapidly growing area of individual concern. It is also a major focus for professional museum associations.

At a meeting of Latin American and Caribbean museum representatives in Santiago, Chile, the participants "agreed that retraining of existent [museum] personnel should be carried out at the national and regional levels. They also endorsed the idea that training in foreign countries should be facilitated."[3]

The museum community has tremendous responsibilities in view of extraordinary changes that affect the traditions and practices of the past as well as the entire future of humankind.

Economically limited or decentralized nations have not historically had the ways and means of collecting and maintaining the objects of their cultural heritage. In many instances they have been hostage to the good intentions of endowing entities that have neither the ethnic pride nor personal knowledge to give adequate recognition and meaning to the objects. Current conditions not only allow but encourage the development of specialized collections and museums with a focus on service.

Information and materials are being gathered to form new collections and museums that will give a redefined perspective to historic people, events, and even the environment. Many of these new "museums" do not fit the accepted description as places that collect, preserve, and study objects and specimens. Eco-museums, museums without walls, site museums, and non-collection galleries fall into this group. Preservation of historic buildings in the original setting can endow the structure with greater meaning. This is also true of archeological excavations, many of which have been formalized with self-guided tour trails, overlooks, and interpretative centers. The excavation becomes a working museum for research, interpretation, and education.

"The legacy of the past and the shape of the future put museums at the beginning of an era of considerable opportunity and challenge."[4] This statement from *Museums for a New Century*, written over a decade ago, was never more true than it is today. As the desire for greater international exchange accelerates, the issues and concerns of museums in one country will inevitably have an impact on the museums of another. Questions about repatriation, traveling exhibits, conservation, ecology, and most of all personnel training draw the world museum community together. The idea of the common wealth of humanity crossing political boundaries in quest of responsible museum workers draws attention to the need for museum training on a broad scale.

Looking to the future and considering the needs of the global museum community, collaboration offers new challenges and new opportunities. Museum training is a shared responsibility. It is a dialogue where the trainer and trainee are equal contributors as each learns from the other. The giving and receiving of information is a mutually supportive process based on common respect – a partnership. Training in the international arena is a challenging and complex process that requires time, resources, and commitment.

Except those provided by ICOM, there are few models on which to base international training programs. By the nature of the organization, ICOM is involved with multinational training and cross-cultural information exchange. Almost from the beginning, ICOM regarded the study and promotion of all aspects of museum training as a central part of its work. As early as 1958, the ICOM Secretariat noted that three levels of museum training were needed: basic training, general training in museology, and specialized or advanced training in museology.

In 1979 the training committee of ICOM:

> agreed that far greater opportunities for the international and regional exchange of teachers of museology and other experienced museum professions were needed as an essential part of the improvement of the training of museum personnel at all levels throughout the world.[5]

Ten years later, in 1989, the sixteenth General Assembly of ICOM, meeting in The Hague, recommended that:

1   existing training courses be reinforced and new ones established for personnel at all levels of museum employment;
2   training programmes be developed that insure an understanding of all aspects of the museum operation, having regard for the rapid development of new technologies and the increasing number of skills involved;
3   particular consideration be given to training needs in natural science preparation and conservation of biological specimens;
4   research be encouraged into all aspects of the museum operation and its technology.[6]

Under the auspices of ICOM, the International Committee for Training of Personnel and national committees, the responsibility for implementation of this plan must fall to those of us currently working in museums and museum training programs. The luxury of postponement vanished with the acceptance of public trust and the stewardship of the common wealth. Newly emerging and historically sound nations, including our own, are struggling with new forms of expression, cultural awareness, and social and environmental accountability. The concept of international training may be valid in our own communities as embodied in a pluralistic society. Museum development and the preservation and interpretation of the world's heritage are validation for the museum professionalism whether across town or across continents.

In the book, *New Approach to Continuing Education for Business and the Professions*, P. M. Nowlen describes three models of continuing professional education.[7] They are: the *update model* that emphasizes keeping up with a profession's knowledge and skills base; the *competence model* that adds analysis of job functions and preparation for new roles within professional practices; and last, the *performance model* that includes the previous factors and allows for consideration of the environmental, professional, and personal contexts within which professionals practice. Nowlen suggests that continuing professional education should be based on a performance model that is, according to him, "likely to generate the richest assortment of needs and responses." Nowlen also emphasizes that this model encourages, is enhanced by, and requires collaboration among providers.

One primary question for trainers of museum workers revolves around the difference between defining and assessing a learning experience by the knowledge that has been gained or by the competence achieved. Should museum training programs consist primarily of the acquisition of theoretical knowledge and analytical skills that the recipient then applies to a work situation or should the training focus on dealing with practice-based circumstances that include a mix of concepts and methodology? Should the training process be primarily deductive or inductive? Should the instruction be theory or practice? Or should there be a balance, and if so, what is the proper balance?

As a partial answer to the question of balance, you must consider that knowledge and skills go together. Knowledge informs the skills required to execute professional tasks. Because continuing professional education should be geared toward improving performance, emphasis must be placed on relating knowledge and skills to practice. Expansion of knowledge alone is not enough to affect practice substantially.[8] Knowledge and skill are also important factors in assessing the goal of the training program. The differences between assessment of educational needs and competency assessment are substantial. Educational needs assessment is designed to discriminate between broad knowledge, skill, and practice levels across a range of content areas. Competency assessment determines the ability of a person or persons to practice a particular activity or profession.

There are three primary factors impacting the quality of professional work: (1) knowledge (information); (2) competence (ability); (3) condition (circumstance).

There are two factors impacting the delivery of professional training that must be considered: (1) affordability; (2) availability.

No matter what the design or content, if the programs are not affordable and available they will go unused. Museum training is a spiral, not a circle. It should not be a repetitive recycling of the same data but a cumulative process of theory, information, skill enhancement, and projection.

Professional museum training must be a focused program extending the preparatory curriculum and expanding through the career stages of professional practice. To do this, it must go beyond individual learning activities to include development of learning agendas specifically designed to meet professionals' practice-oriented needs.

If museum training is to improve or enhance the collective performance of the international workforce, it must relate to practice. Training must build on previous education. It must address the entire scope of museum practice, and offer opportunities to improve performance, update knowledge, and clarify the role and responsibility of museums in the context of human need.

Episodic museum training in which practitioners may choose isolated activities throughout their careers simply is not adequate to achieve a well-rounded learning program that will enhance professional practice.

One of the dangers of standardizing museum practices and procedures is the perpetuation of past norms without consideration of current needs. The museum community is dynamic. The changing role of museums requires creative and innovative solutions to processes of preserving and interpreting the world's cultural heritage.

* * *

The ICOM common basic syllabus for professional museum training

Prepared by the ICOM Training Unit and the International Committee for the Training of Personnel, the syllabus was adopted during the ninth General Conference of ICOM, Paris and Grenoble, France, 1971, and incorporates revisions adopted by the committee in plenary session, Leicester, UK, 1979 (reproduced in this publication with the permission of ICOM and ICTOP).

1 Introduction to museology: history and purpose of museums

1.1 General principles: museology and museography.
1.2 General history of museums and collections.
    1.2.1 National history of museums and collections.
1.3 Role and function of museums in the modern world.
    1.3.1 Professional ethics; general principles of ethics (cf. 2.2.3; 4.1.1).
    1.3.2 Museums and the national heritage; cultural and natural properties (cf. 4.3).
    1.3.3 Museums and research (cf. 5).
    1.3.4 The public and its needs (cf. 8.1.2).
        1.3.4.1 Individuals.
        1.3.4.2 Groups.
        1.3.4.3 Specialists.
    1.3.5 General policy.
1.4 Various types of museums and study of certain current trends (museums and environment, etc.).
1.5 Main types of legislation concerning museums in the whole world; international law, relevant national and local law.
1.6 Cooperative ties between museums.
    1.6.1 National and professional associations, organizations, meetings, publications, exchanges, etc.
    1.6.2 International level (world and regional) organizations: Unesco, ICOM, etc.: meetings, publications, exchanges, etc.

2 Organization, operation, and management of museums

2.1 Legal status and administrative framework.
    2.1.1 Administrative unit or authority under which the museum is established.
    2.1.2 Administrative boards; trustees.

2.1.3   Operating committees (membership, etc.)
2.2   Management problems.
    2.2.1   Policy and work planning (cf. 1.3.5; 3.2; 8.1).
    2.2.2   Administrative set-up of services and departments.
    2.2.3   Collections: general considerations and policy of acquisitions (cf. 4.1).
    2.2.4   Insurance.
2.3   Budget; financial resources of museums.
    2.3.1   Modes of financing.
        2.3.1.1   Regular operating budget.
        2.3.1.2   Subsidies.
        2.3.1.3   Donations and bequests.
        2.3.1.4   Friends and members of the museum (cf. 9.1.1).
        2.3.1.5   Fund-raising and other campaigns.
        2.3.1.6   Admission fees.
        2.3.1.7   Other resources.
    2.3.2   Estimates and allocation of expenditure.
    2.3.3   Control of budget; audit.
2.4   Personnel: selection and allocation.
    2.4.1   In-service training of personnel.
    2.4.2   Volunteers.
    2.4.3   Labor problems.
2.5   General maintenance (cf. 6.8).
2.6   General problems of supervision, safety, custody, etc.
2.7   Public relations (cf. 9.1).
2.8   Evaluation of performance and statistics (cf. 8.6).

3   Architecture, layout, equipment

3.1   History of museum buildings (cf. 1.2).
3.2   Project work (devised according to the program of the museum); location; use of space; design (cf. 1.3.5).
3.3   Special problems.
    3.3.1   Building and layout according to types of museum.
    3.3.2   Building and layout according to climate (cf. 6.2).
    3.3.3   Adaptation and use of old buildings (whether or not of historic interest).
    3.3.4   Air conditioning.
    3.3.5   Lighting.
    3.3.6   Safety (cf. 2.6).
3.4   Circulation of visitors, staff, collections (cf. 8.4.2).
3.5   Layout and furniture in the various departments (according to the special requirements of their own particular operations).

3.6   Audio-visual aids.

4   Collections: origin, related records, set-up, and movement

4.1   General principles (cf. 2.2.2).
    4.1.1   Ethic of acquisitions (cf. 1.3.1).
    4.1.2   Acquisition policy.
    4.1.3   Special problems.
        4.1.3.1   Terms and conditions.
        4.1.3.2   Forgeries.
        4.1.3.3   Copies, replicas, reproductions.
4.2   Modes of acquisition.
    4.2.1   Field collecting.
    4.2.2   Purchase.
    4.2.3   Donations.
    4.2.4   Bequests.
    4.2.5   Loans (articles received on loan).
    4.2.6   Deposits.
    4.2.7   Exchanges.
4.3   National and regional parks and nature reserves and their geological and biological features.
4.4   Data and documents related to items in collections.
    4.4.1   Elementary technology: descriptive terminology of certain categories of objects or specimens.
    4.4.2   Identification at the time of acquisition.
        4.4.2.1   Survey questionnaires and acquisition forms.
        4.4.2.2   Field notes.
        4.4.2.3   Techniques for identification, dating processes, etc.; use of audio-visual means.
    4.4.3   Registration; inventory.
    4.4.4   Numbering and marking of articles and specimens.
    4.4.5   Cataloging and classification.
        4.4.5.1   Descriptive and scientific catalogs (cf. 5.5.1).
        4.4.5.2   Guides and forms used by catalogs (cf. 4.4.2.1).
        4.4.5.3   Types of cards.
            4.4.5.3.1   Visual and mechanical types of appliances.
    4.4.6   Automatic retrieval: computers, current research.
    4.4.7   Types of classifications suitable to museum collections.
    4.4.8   Technical files relating to collections and/or separate items.
        4.4.8.1   Confidential information.
        4.4.8.2   Restrictions derived from copyright.

5   Scientific activities

6   Preservation and care of collections

6.2.3   Light.
6.4   Pollution.
6.5   Set-up and operation of workshops and technical and scientific laboratories.
    6.5.1   Examination of articles; equipment, products, techniques.
    6.5.2   Treatment; decontamination, hot chambers, etc.
        6.5.2.1   Treatment of collections according to their nature and their constitutive materials (A to Z of the Unesco-ICOM Museum Classification Scheme).
6.6   Rehabilitation and repair (follow the same schedule).
    6.6.1   Restoration.
6.7   Workshops for the preparation and mounting of the collections (molding, models, dioramas).
6.8   Main principles and special rules for the maintenance of collections (cf. 2.5).
6.9   Records of data concerning the treatment of collections: cards and files; photographic and microphotographic data, samples (cf. 4.4.9.1).
    6.9.1   Liaison with outside laboratories and workshops: regional, national, international, private (cf. 5.3).
    6.9.2   Liaison with national or foreign agencies or departments concerned with architecture, historical monuments, etc.

7   Presentation: exhibitions

7.1   General theory of communication.
    7.1.1   General principles of presentation.
    7.1.2   Programming of exhibitions.
    7.1.3   Preparation and layout; roles of curator and designer.
    7.1.4   Main techniques and basic equipment (cf. 2).
7.2   Various types of exhibitions.
    7.2.1   Permanent exhibitions.
    7.2.2   Temporary exhibitions.
    7.2.3   Circulating and touring exhibitions (cf. 4.8.2).
    7.2.4   Various types of didactic and outside exhibitions.
7.3   Presentation of related information: main principles (cf. 4.7).
    7.3.1   Graphic aids: labels, etc.
    7.3.2   Audio-visual (cf. 3.6; 4.5).
    7.3.3   Guiding processes (cf. 8.4.4).
7.4   Operation and evaluation.

8 The public

8.1 The museum as a public facility: general principles.
    8.1.1   Educational and cultural responsibility of the museum personnel (at all levels) (cf. 2.4).
    8.1.2   Knowledge of the community (cf. 1.3.4).
8.2 Visitors; their behaviour (cf. 8.6).
8.3 Organization of the facilities and services geared to the public.
    8.3.1   Incoming visitors: access, parking facilities, etc.
    8.3.2   Circuit of visitors (cf. 3.5).
    8.3.3   Direction signing, etc., within the museum (cf. 4.7; 7.3; 9.5.1).
    8.3.4   Information to visitors; guiding (cf. 3.7; 4.7; 7.3).
        8.3.4.1   Written information.
        8.3.4.2   Guided tours.
        8.3.4.3   Automatic guiding.
        8.3.4.4   Audio-visual aids.
8.4 Various facilities for public use.
    8.4.1   Sale counters (guides, folders, pamphlets, reproductions, postcards, color slides, etc.).
    8.4.2   Auditorium, projection room, movie theatre.
    8.4.3   Lecture room (cf. Library: 4.6).
    8.4.4   Workshops available to the public (cf. 9.4.6).
    8.4.5   Comfort of visitors.
        8.4.5.1   Seats, benches, etc.
        8.4.5.2   Bar, coffee shop, restaurant.
        8.4.5.3   Lounge, restrooms, cloakrooms; day nursery.
        8.4.5.4   Facilities for handicapped visitors.
8.5 Method of analysis of the visitors' behaviour (cf. 8.3).
8.6 Statistics (cf. 2.8).

9 Cultural and educational activities of the museum

9.1 Public relations (cf. 2.7).
    9.1.1   The Society of Friends of the Museum (cf. 2.3.1.4).
9.2 Induced activities and leaders or organizers; educational activities.
    9.2.1   Cooperation between the museum educational personnel and outside instructors.
9.3 The museum educational personnel, role and training.
    9.3.1   Pedagogy for an educational department: principles, methods, equipment.
    9.3.2   Activities designed for children and youth (cf. 8.4.5).
        9.3.2.1   Schools and teachers.

          9.3.2.2   Cooperation with specialists in the field of education.

9.3.3   Activities designed for the country people (cf. 9.6.3).

9.3.4   Activities designed for illiterates.

9.4   Special exhibitions and programs for young people or adults.

    9.4.1   Demonstrations.

    9.4.2   Lectures, projections, discussions.

    9.4.3   Concerts, plays.

    9.4.4   Participation in events, celebrations, etc., interesting to the community.

    9.4.5   Clubs.

    9.4.6   Applied work (cf. 8.5).

9.5   Publicity: general principles.

    9.5.1   External signs.

    9.5.2   Press.

    9.5.3   Publications.

    9.5.4   Radio broadcasts.

    9.5.5   Television shows.

    9.5.6   Promotion and marketing.

9.6   Outside departments and museum extension (cf. 9.5.4).

    9.6.1   Museums and tourism.

    9.6.2   Museums and industries.

    9.6.3   Traveling museums; mobile museum units (cf. 9.3.3).

    9.6.4   Loan services.

    9.6.5   Outside facilities (buildings, cases, etc.).

9.7   The museum's influence on creative activities.

* * *

Regardless of syllabus, faculty, or facility, not all museum training programs are for all people. As with all educational endeavors, students should assume the responsibility of determining the most appropriate museum training to meet their individual goals. In this case, "student" refers to all those entering or already in the museum workforce. As with most "professions," museum training and information gathering is an ongoing process that requires a continuous investment of time and energy. In-service, mid-career, or special topic seminars should be available to all persons working in museums regardless of their job, position, or title.

> Mid career programs must provide this additional training to develop the potential of a person to assure the highest benefit for the individual, the museum and the society. . . .The employer as well as the employee has an ethical responsibility for training and retraining.[9]

Most potential students decide to enter a museum training program without a clear idea of what they want to do, or what options are available to them. Often they have a fascination with museum work in general but have given only minimal thought to the position or role they may wish to pursue. It is important for persons considering a career in museums to learn as much as possible about the range of activities involved in museum practice. With a clearer vision of personal goals, the beginning student as well as the experienced museum worker will be better equipped to make training and skill development decisions.

Notes

1   Anders, C. *et al.* (1988) "Museums, a global view," *Museums News*, Washington, D.C.: American Association of Museums, Vol. 67, No. 1: 22–47.
2   ICOM, (1982) "What museums for Africa? Heritage in the future," *ICOM News*, Paris: ICOM, Vol. 45, No. 2: 5–7.
3   Astudillo, L. (1990) *An Overview of the Needs for Museum Training in Latin America and the Caribbean*, Proceedings from the ICOM Committee for the Training of Personnel annual meeting, Washington, D.C.: Smithsonian Institution.
4   Bloom, J. and Powell, E. (1984) *Museums for a New Century*, Washington, D.C.: American Association of Museums, p. 27.
5   Boylan, P. (1989) "Museum training in an international perspective," in P. van Mensch (ed.) *Professionalising the Muses*, Amsterdam: AHA Books.
6   Blokhuis, S. (ed.) (1991) "Museums: Generators of Culture," Reports and comments from the ICOM 1989 General Conference, The Hague: ICOM.
7   Nowlen, P. (1988) *New Approach to Continuing Education for Business and the professions*, New York: Macmillan, NUCEA, and American Council on Education.
8   Nowlen, P. (1988) "A new approach to continuing education for business and the professions," unpublished paper.
9   Pouw, P. (1993) "Editorial," *ICOM News*, Paris: ICOM, Vol. 46, No. 4: 1.

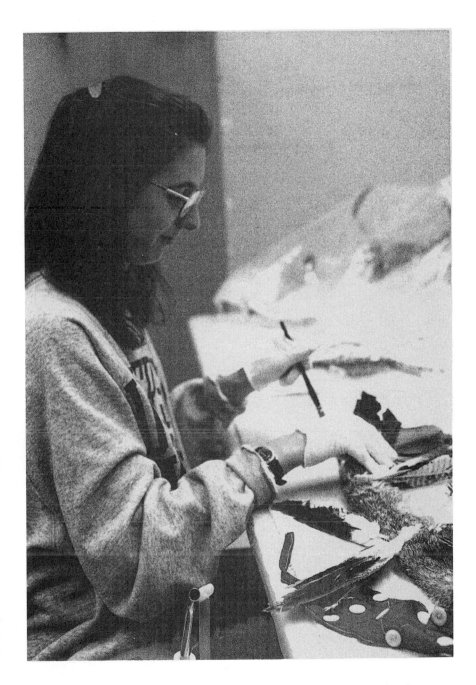

Plate 3 Museum Studies student Tanya Fisher evaluating ethnology collection artifact (photograph by Gary Edson)

THREE

Museum work today

——•◆•——

With the changes in museums, it is reasonable to believe that the roles and duties of museum personnel have also changed. Who does what? One of the most often asked questions, for those entering the museum profession and those considering further training is: what job should I be training for? Predictions for the future are general at best. Traditional jobs, titles, and roles in the museum are being re-evaluated and redefined.

Training programs cannot be formulated without "first considering the nature of the museums profession and the profession is absolutely determined by the basic purpose of museums."[1] Although this comment was written in 1969, it continues to be true today. As part of the attitude of public service, museums have proliferated. They are formed around special collections to reflect the interests and beliefs of the communities in which they were founded.[2] Museums have attempted to address a growing number of issues by developing or evolving programs to explain, justify, or illuminate a variety of social and cultural phenomena.

> The sense of community among museums and their common identity as pluralistic institutions continue to evolve. As the open, democratic nature of museums becomes more emphatic, the relationship of museums to the rest of society – institutions and individuals alike – becomes even stronger."[3]

As the complexities of contemporary society are compounded, so also are the needs and requirements of the museum profession. Efforts to achieve and maintain diversity among trustees, staff, and volunteers while reinforcing the professionalism of the museum community is a formidable task. The only viable way of achieving that goal is through both formal and informal training opportunities.

Traditionally, museums have been characterized by the kind of objects they maintain. Early museums often reflected the social, economic, or professional status of the donor/collectors around whose collection the museum was formed. Collections served the collector as a didactic and professional resource.[4] Examples of this kind of museum are: the Ashmolean Museum at the University of Oxford, a purpose-built institution to house the collections of Elias Ashmole; the Louvre, or the Musée Central des Arts as it was first called, based on the royal collections;[5] and the National Museum of Indonesia at Jakarta established to house the collections of the learned society, Batavia Society of Arts and Sciences.[6] The list might continue to include most of the early museums in all parts of the world.

Historically, the primary division in the museum community appears to be between art museums and all other kinds.[7] The division is assumed to be the result of a philosophical difference in the methods of collecting, maintaining, exhibiting, and interpreting the various collections. Whatever the reasoning, the schism has narrowed. Museums have been divided by collection classification. As the museum community attempts to reflect the totality of human experience, the previously clear divisions based on collection content merge to reflect common experience. Museums are also becoming more aware of their connection with each other and the encompassing role of transmitters of culture.

There are a number of associated types of museums dealing with non-living collections. The collection areas of art, history, and science defined the limitations of traditional museums (see Figure 3.1). In addition, there

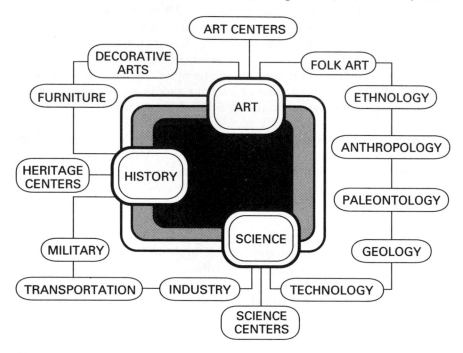

Figure 3.1 Museums as related to the traditional scheme

are those museums dealing with living collections. Zoos, aquariums, botanical gardens, and arboreta are examples of a further extension of what was previously a fairly compact selection of institutional types. The divisions and sub-divisions increase almost daily. Ecomuseums fit no particular type as they differ, one from the other, depending on location, mission, and evolving constituent need.

> Museums perform their most fruitful public service by providing an educational experience in the broadest sense: by fostering the ability to live productively in a pluralistic society and to contribute to the resolution of the challenges we face as global citizens.[8]

There are new and differing definitions of museums as institutions of public service and education. The role and physical environment of museums differ to reflect local, regional, and national needs. "The mission of museums as institutions grows out of tradition and is shaped by public need."[9] In the book *Starting Right*, there is a basic organizational structure[10] that locates the museum staff in relation to the external entities that impact the museum (see Figure 3.2).

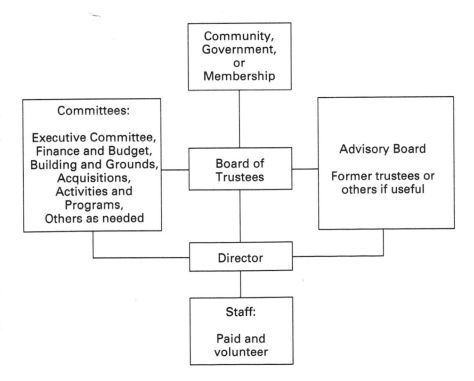

Figure 3.2 Basic organizational structure

The common factor is the founding authority of the museum – community, government, or membership. This source of creation and perpetuation differs from the earlier methodology where collections preceded museums and where mission was formed around personal preference. Current trends in museums endorse participation in the social and cultural continuum, rather than the detached attitude of observation and reaction.[11]

The philosophical, social, cultural, or economic motivations of a museum or museums establish the foundation, but it is the staff who transfer that rationale into practice. The complex challenges of the international museum community can best be addressed by well-trained professionals who are resourceful and determined to reinforce the public dimension of museums.

Problems can occur in museum operations when the process becomes confused. Very often it is the process rather than the personnel that causes difficulty in the transfer of information from one part of the museum structure to another. Where possible, elements of the museum should have clearly defined roles and functions to allow the separation of both authority and responsibility. When the staff is small, the duties of individuals often overlap. However, some functions, such as the role of the trustees and the duties of the museum director, should not be mingled to a point where clarity of role becomes confused or arbitrary. The governing body (trustees) establishes policy, oversees funding, hires and evaluates the director, and verifies compliance with the mission of the museum including the maintaining of public trust. The administration (director) advises the governing body, supervises the expenditure of funds, oversees the daily operations of the museum, directs, hires, and evaluates the staff, and is responsible for fulfilling the mission of the museum. The implementation element (staff) includes all those persons assigned duties by the director of the museum (see Figure 3.3). Their role is to do the jobs outlined by their job descriptions, comply with museum policy, and contribute to the goals of the museum as defined by the mission statement.

Museums, depending on the size, mission, and collections, may have positions with several titles and job descriptions. Personnel from chief executive officer to guard should have special training in the requirements

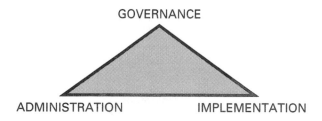

GOVERNANCE

ADMINISTRATION   IMPLEMENTATION

Figure 3.3 Basic museum governance model

and expectations of museum operations. All members of the museum workforce should have a clearly defined role in accomplishing the goals of the institution. The following list includes some position titles common to the museum community. A number of the titles may describe the same work responsibility, and in smaller museums one person may have the duties of more than one position. Typical examples of this duality would be: Director/Development Officer/Public Relations Officer, Curator/Director, Curator/Registrar, Exhibits Designer/Technician/Preparator. Every job should have a description that explains both the responsibility and the authority of that position.

Chief Executive Officer	Chief Curator
Executive Administrator	Keeper of Collections
Executive Director	Curator of Collections
Director	Curator
Deputy Director	Associate Curator
Associate Director	Assistant Curator
Assistant Director	Assistant Keeper
Curator/Director	Curatorial Assistant
Facilities Manager	Collections Manager
Development Officer	Education Manager
Public Relations Officer	Program Manager
Personnel Officer	Exhibits Designer
Business Manager	Publications Director
Leisure Services Officer	Display Officer
Registrar	Exhibits Technician
Conservator	Artist/Draftsperson
Archivist	Carpenter (Cabinet Maker)
Astronomer	Zoo Keeper
Librarian	Preparator
Teacher (Docent/Guide)	Photographer
Research Assistant	Lighting Specialist
Editor	Model Maker
Shop Manager	Guard (Warden)

It is also important to note that the roles within the museum are changing. As in institutions of higher education and business, different positions are assuming different duties. Curators as collection research specialists are also fund raisers, technical advisors, consultants, and public relations persons speaking for a particular project, exhibition, or even the institution. Registrars are becoming computer technicians, and education managers are multimedia specialists. Guides, wardens, and security personnel are becoming very much a part of the public relations team.

In the typical institutional flow chart, the number of positions and the

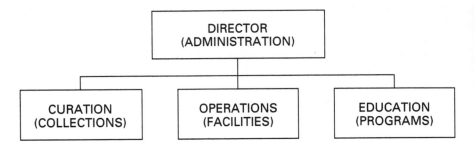

Figure 3.4 Basic staff structure

names may vary but the basic concept is the same (see Figure 3.4). One person is placed in a position of administrative responsibility with multiple layers below. A less workable example is where everyone reports to the chief administrator. For small museums with a limited number of staff the reporting line is less of an administrative factor.

An example of the duties associated with each of the four primary organizational components is as follows:

- Administration
  Staff of administrative departments
    Personnel
    Accounting/business
    General services
    Public relations
    Fund raising
    Membership
- Curation
  Staff of curatorial departments
    Collection care
    Collection maintenance
    Collection documentation
    Conservation
    Research
- Operations
  Staff of operational departments
    Exhibits technicians
    Preparators
    Security personnel
    Custodians
    Safety and compliance
    Facilities

- Education
    Staff of education departments
        Public education
        Program instructors
        Workshop leaders
        Technical services
        Exhibitions
        Docents

It is not only the job descriptions that are being changed, it is the entire structure of museums. The vertical or pyramid structures of the past are giving way to lateral team approaches to everything from administration to collection management and program design (see Figure 3.5). Museums have begun to experiment with new structures to stimulate better coordination between the collections-related functions of the museum and the public programs.[12] Other museums have developed new structural models that place greater emphasis on programming, education, fund raising, and community service. In the international community, museums have gained greater recognition as repositories and presenters of cultural and national heritage.

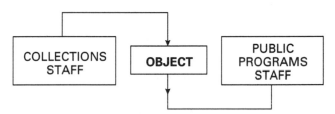

Figure 3.5 A program–oriented model

Assuming the current direction in museums continues, and there is every reason to expect it to increase rather than decrease, there will be a greater dependence on personnel. In the historic paradigm the objects served as the primary means of interaction with the public. Once on display the object maintained a life of its own with a minimal amount of interpretation. The new paradigm continues to recognize the object as a central part of the museum's purpose while expanding the programmatic component. Programming requires trained, dedicated, and intellectually responsive personnel.

Defining the requirements and expectations of museum positions is a difficult undertaking. Defining positions appropriate to one country or region may exclude a significant requirement of another. The same may be true from institution to institution. Job or placement descriptions are included in this publication as a reference.

* * *

37

Museum personnel job descriptions

Before beginning the hiring process, existing job descriptions should be reviewed and updated. Careful consideration should be given to the needs of the institution. The greatest difficulty in hiring is the inability to know or determine the requirements of the position. The second difficulty arises when the position is changed to accommodate the skills of a preselected individual. Both can be difficult and compromising situations that can be avoided with a carefully considered, preapproved job description.

The following job descriptions are intended to give general direction in nature and content for positions in museums. Some were included (in part) in the Smithsonian Institute/ICOM International Committee on Training of Personnel publication, *Museum Studies International* (1988). The descriptions have been modified to reflect recent thinking. Entry requirements have become more inclusive, world-oriented, and sensitive to public and community service. Many of the most critical issues facing museums as elements of service cannot be delineated in a position description. All persons entering the museum profession should be expected to comprehend the museological ideal and have the practical means of implementing that ideal.

Museum director

The director provides conceptual leadership through specialized knowledge of the discipline of the museum and is responsible for policy making and funding (with the governing board), planning, organizing, staffing, directing and/or supervising and coordinating activities through the staff. The director is responsible for professional practices such as acquisition, preservation, research, interpretation, and presentation, and may be responsible for financial management. All museum positions report directly or indirectly to the director. Many museum directors are spending more of their time as a spokesperson for the museum including: public relations, fund raising, marketing, and public service. The director is expected to foster the ideals of museum professionalism.

The director reports to the governing board and is responsible for the supervision of administrative and technical personnel.

Typical work performed

- Develop, recommend, and implement strategic plans for the museum.
- Insure the collection is well maintained and used to further the mission of the museum.

- Provide organizational vision and leadership for museum growth and development.
- Select, develop, and maintain a highly qualified and motivated professional team of museum workers, researchers, and scholars.
- Work to cultivate and maintain relations with donors and other funding sources.
- Maintain a programmatic balance between the scholarly, educational, and recreational activities of the museum to address the needs of the culturally diverse public served.
- Coordinate museum goals and activities with those of the support organization.
- Cultivate gifts and bequests from donors to insure the growth of the collections as appropriate to the mission of the museum.
- Perform required duties in a safe manner giving consideration to objects, colleagues, and the environment.

Knowledge, abilities, and skills

- Broad-based knowledge of museum administration and philosophy.
- Specialized knowledge in at least one area of the museum's governing collection or in the management of a particular type of museum.
- Ability to implement the policy established by the museum's governing body and encourage the active participation of the governing body, the museum staff, and the public in realizing the goals of the museum.
- Demonstrated knowledge of financial management.
- Knowledge of the legal aspects of museum operations.
- Demonstrated commitment to the ethical standards established by the national and international museum community.
- Fund-raising skills.

Education

- Advanced degree in an area of the museum's specialization. Coursework and evidence of participation in museum management and administration are requirements. Specialized training in business administration, marketing, fund raising, and/or public relations is necessary.

Experience

- Five years of management experience in a museum or related cultural institution. Additional administrative experience in a related field is desirable.

Museum curator

The curator is a specialist in a particular academic discipline relevant to the museum's collections. The curator is directly responsible for the care and academic interpretation of all objects, materials, and specimens belonging or lent to the museum; recommendations for acquisition, de-accession, attribution, and authentication, and research on the collections and the publication of the results of that research. The curator also may have administrative and/or exhibition responsibilities and should be sensitive to sound conservation practices.

The curator reports to the director, chief executive officer, or head of collections.

Typical work performed

- Plan and coordinate the long-range activities in area of specialization and communicate those plans to the director of the museum.
- Conduct appropriate field work with sensitivity to laws, rules, and local custom.
- Identify and catalog collection items and materials.
- Conduct research related to collections and exhibits.
- Perform public relations activities related to area of specialization.
- Participate in special museum events and public programs.
- Train appropriate personnel, both volunteer and paid, to work in collections area.
- Perform related work as required.
- Perform required duties in a safe manner giving consideration to objects, colleagues, and the environment.

Knowledge, abilities, and skills

- Specialized knowledge (connoisseurship) in one area of the museum's collections.
- Ability to interpret the collections and to communicate knowledge relevant to the collections.
- Knowledge of the techniques of selection, evaluation, preservation, restoration, and exhibition of objects.
- Knowledge of the current market, collecting ethics and current customs regulations in the area of specialization.

Education

- Advanced degree with a concentration in a discipline related to an area of the museum's specialization.

Experience

- Three years of experience in a museum or related educational or research organization.
- Evidence of scholarly research and writing.

Museum educator

The museum educator develops, implements, evaluates, and/or supervises the museum's educational programs with the goal of enhancing public access to and understanding and interpretation of the collections and resources. The programs, which may employ a variety of media and techniques, may encompass educational exhibitions, printed materials such as self-guides, demonstrations, classes, tours, films, lectures, special events, workshops, teacher training programs, school or other outreach programs as well as docent/guide training. The educator may have administrative responsibilities.

The museum educator reports to the director or chief executive officer.

Typical work performed

- Develop and present informative and educational programs for the public.
- Develop and present curriculum-related programs for elementary and secondary students.
- Develop and present complementary and supplementary programs for adult learners.
- Supervise training of volunteers and part-time staff members for educational and general programs in the museum.
- Prepare for distribution, descriptive and promotional materials for scheduled functions.
- Provide in-service teacher training for elementary and secondary teachers as appropriate.
- Serve as a resource person and information officer for educational programming for the public.
- Supervise and organize division budget.
- Perform other education-related duties as may be assigned by the director of the museum.
- Perform required duties in a safe manner giving consideration to objects, colleagues, and the environment.

Knowledge, abilities, and skills

- Ability to devise and carry out education programs, including the preparation and use of publications and exhibitions.

- Knowledge of museum education techniques and resources.
- Knowledge of the learning characteristics of museum audiences.
- Skill in oral and written communication techniques appropriate to various educational levels and objectives.
- Knowledge of the goals, curricula, and operation of school systems and other educational institutions.
- Knowledge in the area of the museum's collections.
- Skill in using research techniques.
- Knowledge of education evaluation methods.

Education

- Advanced degree in education, and area of the museum's specialization, or museum studies with a concentration in museum education.

Experience

- Two years in a museum education department or other educational institution.

Museum registrar

The museum registrar is responsible for creating, organizing, and maintaining orderly forms, legal documents, files, and retrieval systems associated with the following: acquisition, accessioning, deaccessioning, cataloging, loans, packing, shipping, inventory, insurance, and storage, pursuant to the care, custody, and control of the objects in perpetuity. A museum registrar organizes, documents, and coordinates all aspects of borrowing and lending objects, which include responsibility for the handling and/or packing of objects, negotiating insurance coverage, processing insurance claims, making shipping arrangements, arranging for security, handling customs procedures, processing incoming and outgoing loans, and processing requests for object use and reproductions. The museum registrar organizes data so that facts and ideas may be usefully extracted.

The registrar reports to the museum director or the head of collections (chief curator, curator of collections, keeper of collections).

Typical work performed

- Supervise assignment and management of accession numbers and associated data for all incoming and outgoing objects.
- Coordinate insurance and transportation arrangements for all incoming and outgoing collections materials.

- Coordinate the public relations and staff activities associated with the acquisition and deaccession of museum objects and related material.
- Coordinate the photo documentation of collections.
- Supervise computerization of all registration records.
- Verify compliance with laws, restrictions, and ethical practices as related to the acquisition and deaccession of all collection and loan materials.
- Perform required duties in a safe manner giving consideration to objects, colleagues, and the environment.

Knowledge, abilities, and skills

- Knowledge of accepted museum registration techniques.
- Knowledge of conservation and storage practices.
- Knowledge of legal matters related to the collections, copyright laws and policies governing rights and reproductions.
- Knowledge of records management and data processing systems.
- Knowledge of insurance requirements for the collections, packing techniques and transportation methods.
- Knowledge of the museum's collections.

Education

- Master's degree in museum science (studies) or area of museum's specialization or in liberal arts.

Experience

- Three years in a museum registration department or in a museum position in which registration was an ongoing responsibility.

Conservator of museum collections

The conservator, on a scientific basis, examines museum objects, works to prevent their deterioration, and treats and repairs them when necessary. The conservator sees that objects are fumigated, kept at proper levels of temperature and relative humidity, and protected from air pollutants and exposure to damaging light intensities and wave lengths. The conservator usually has the specialized knowledge to treat a certain class of objects, such as paintings, sculpture, textiles, ceramics, glass, metals, furniture and woodwork, books and art on paper, and should know where to refer materials that cannot be treated in the museum laboratory. To keep his or her knowledge current, the conservator may belong to a professional conservation organization that expects adherence to a code of ethics.

The conservator reports to the museum director or the head of collections (chief curator, curator of collections, keeper of collections).

Typical work performed

- Review and evaluate collection care and maintenance and recommend means for preventing deterioration or damage to objects.
- In cooperation with curators, recommend and supervise appropriate non-invasive treatment for collection objects.
- Evaluate damaged objects and recommend appropriate care, treatment, restoration, or deaccessioning.
- Perform appropriate treatment of objects as determined in consultation with curators and director.
- Perform required duties in a safe manner giving consideration to objects, colleagues, and the environment.

Knowledge, abilities, and skills

- Manual skill in the treatment of materials.
- Knowledge of the technology and materials of artistic, historic, scientific, and technological objects and of the chemical and physical processes of their deterioration.
- Knowledge of the procedures relating to the examination and preventive and corrective treatment of objects and specimens.
- Ability to write thorough and effective treatment reports.
- Knowledge of environmental requirements and controls for handling, storage, exhibition, and travel of objects and specimens.
- Ability to communicate the required participation of other staff in the implementation of approved conservation practices throughout the institution.
- Knowledge of conservation and other relevant literature to assure knowledge of new technology.
- Ability to plan a basic or specialized conservation laboratory and to implement its development.

Education

- Graduate-level training in a recognized conservation program comprising two or more years' work on the theory, principles, and practice of conservation, including a year's training in the principles of general material conservation and a minimum of one year's training or internship in a specialized field or equivalent training by apprenticeship with one or more qualified practitioners. Undergraduate training should include courses in cultural or art history, scientific studies (chemistry, physics, material science, biology), studio arts and manual skills.

Experience

- Two years of postgraduate on-the-job experience (beyond academic training or apprenticeship), under the supervision of a qualified conservator.

Museum exhibits designer

The exhibits designer translates curatorial and educational staff ideas into permanent, temporary, or circulating exhibitions through renderings, drawings, scale models, lighting and arrangement of objects and signage. The exhibits designer may supervise the production of exhibitions and have administrative responsibilities.

The exhibits designer reports to the director, assistant director for operations, curator of education or head of collections. Museums with large staffs also may have a program director to coordinate all public programming.

Typical work performed

- Propose design for exhibitions based on information provided by the curators.
- Consult with curators from specializations other than the primary curator to obtain their input or verification of information contained in the exhibition.
- Prepare work requests for proposed exhibits, coordinate purchasing, facility, construction, and curatorial needs.
- Supervise the organization and maintenance of the exhibits workshop including areas for design, drafting, photography, and construction.
- Establish work schedules and project deadlines.
- Perform required duties in a safe manner giving consideration to objects, colleagues, and the environment.
- Perform related work as required.

Knowledge, abilities, and skills

- Ability to conceptualize exhibition designs appropriate to the aims and style of the institution.

- Ability to make refined esthetic judgments.
- Ability to specify designs in drawings and written instruction.
- Ability to supervise fabrication and installation of exhibits.
- Knowledge of security and conservation requirements and practices.
- Knowledge of lighting systems.
- Knowledge of tools and techniques for exhibition preparation, shop practices, mechanical drawing, and the use of planning models and mock-ups.
- Knowledge of estimating, budgeting, bidding, and accounting practices.
- Knowledge of the state of the art in exhibition design and related fields.
- Knowledge of communication media and materials.
- Knowledge of the nature and the materials to be displayed.

Education

- Degree or certificate in museum science (studies), graphic design, industrial design, commercial art or communication arts, or in architecture, interior design, theater design or studio arts.

Experience

- Experience in exhibition design, preferably in or for a museum. Additional experience in exhibit production, model making or in media (graphics, advertising, illustration, audio-visual presentations) may be desirable.
- Portfolio of current and past work.

Museum collections manager

The collections manager is responsible for supervising, numbering, cataloging, and storing the specimens within each department or division and may perform the combined functions of registrar and curatorial assistant.

The collections manager reports to the curator.

Typical work performed

- Coordinate with appropriate personnel the management of collection-related items including field notes, catalogs, scientific permits, accessions, loan and computer records, supplies and equipment necessary for the collection, preparation, preservation, and storage of objects (artifacts or specimens), and documentation.

- Coordinate and oversee all loans of objects (artifacts or specimens), and documentation.
- Assist in maintenance of acceptable museum practices.
- Work with director and curators to set priorities for collection care and management.
- Assist in acquisition, identification, preparation, conservation, cataloging, registration, storage, maintenance, installation, and disposal of collections and related materials.
- Perform required duties in a safe manner giving consideration to objects, colleagues, and the environment.
- Perform related work as required.

Knowledge, abilities, and skills

- Ability to coordinate personnel and plan and administer programs for collections management, including financial planning and budget preparation.
- Knowledge of the organization, arrangement, and nomenclature of specimens and objects in the relevant academic field.
- Knowledge of file and information management techniques used in museum registration and record keeping.
- Ability to accurately identify specimens and objects within the context of the museum's collections.
- Ability to handle objects appropriately with knowledge of the basic principles of conservation, security, and environmental controls.

Education

- Master's degree in museum science (studies) or area of museum's specialization.

Experience

- Three years of experience in a museum registration department or a museum position in which the main functions are the technical duties relating to collections management, such as the handling, storage, preservation, and cataloging of objects and specimens.

* * *

Some assume that non-skilled or non-technical personnel in the museum need not have specialized training. This is far from the truth; in fact, every member of the museum workforce should not only be given the opportunity to gain greater information and skill relating to the job – it should be required. Guides, custodians, security personnel, and shop sales persons are a part of the team. Often they are the only persons encountered by the visitor. The more knowledge they have about museums and museum work the more they feel a part of the institution and the better they can represent the interests of the museum. Trained personnel will recognize both positive and negative situations and respond according to established procedures.

As already stated, the museum workforce is changing. The higher cost for persons with specialized training has caused many museums to rely on contract personnel. Conservators, exhibit designers, public relations specialists and fund raisers are examples of services provided from outside the traditional ranks of the museum profession. Some museums are also using contract custodians, shop personnel, and security services. The logic is basic – to acquire the greatest skill at the least cost. The missing factor in most contract-provided services is dedication to the institution and a sense of fiduciary responsibility to the constituency of the museum.

Notes

1 Singleton, R. (1969) "The purpose of museums and museum training," *Museum Journal*, Vol. 69, No. 3: 133.
2 Edson, G. and Dean, D. (1993) *Handbook for Museums*, London: Routledge.
3 Bloom, J. and Powell, E. (1984) *Museums for a New Century*, Washington, D.C.: American Association of Museums, p. 27.
4 Impey, O. and MacGregor, A. (eds) (1985) *The Origins of Museums*, Oxford: Clarendon Press, p. 6.
5 Thompson, J. (ed.) (1992) *Manual of Curatorship* (2nd edition), Oxford: Butterworth-Heinemann, p. 10.
6 Ibid., p. 14.
7 Burcaw, G. (1975) *Introduction to Museum Work* (2nd edition 1983), Nashville: American Association of State and Local History, p. 31.
8 Pitman, B. (Chair, AAM Task Force on Museum Education) (1991) *Excellence and Equity*, Education and the Public Dimension of Museums, Washington, D.C.: American Association of Museums, p. 6.
9 Bloom, J. and Powell, E. (1984) *Museums for a New Century*, Washington, D.C.: American Association of Museums, p. 75.
10 George, G. and Sherrell-Leo, C. (1989) *Starting Right*, Nashville: American Association of State and Local History, p. 141.
11 Bloom, J. and Powell, E. (1984) *Museums for a New Century*, Washington, D.C.: American Association of Museums, p. 28.
12 Ibid., pp. 61–3.

PART II

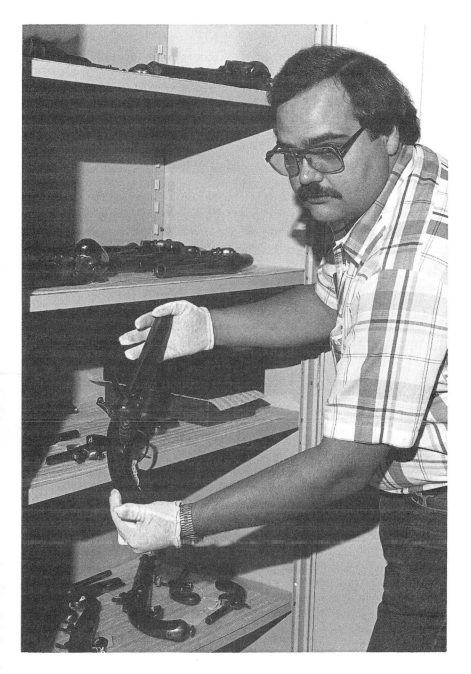

Plate 4 Collection Manager Robert Tucker rehousing history collection artifact (photograph by Nicky L. Olson)

Training programs
reference guide

———•◆•———

To assist users in comparing training programs, the information has been organized in two ways. The first is a quick reference guide that gives a one-line view of each agency's offerings (see Table 5.1). In this way users can compare programs and determine which agenda most closely meets their needs. The first entry on each line is the name of the host agency. In some cases there are multiple entries from one host. This has been done when the programs being offered are so different that including them in one listing would cause confusion. By using the categories at the top of the page, users can follow the entries across and down the page to determine program offerings in several areas.

The second listing is in Chapter 5, Training programs directory. The directory gives detailed information about programs and includes a narrative statement provided by the program representative. All responding agencies were given the opportunity to answer to the same survey questions. The directory includes the survey questions and the answers. The listing also notes the name of the program coordinator and the mailing address. Requests for additional programmatic information should be addressed to the sponsoring agency.

Table 5.1, Reference guide and programs directory, lists the information in the same order. It is organized alphabetically by (1) country; (2) state, province, or territory; (3) city. The first entry is University of Canberra, Australia, and the last is University of Belgrade, Yugoslavia. Both lists are drawn from the same database.

Table 5.1 Reference guide and programs directory

INSTITUTION NAME	Training Level							Training Areas										Specializations of Training															Training Schedule		Other			
	Course work	Workshops	Internships	Certificate	Diploma	Bachelor's Degree	Graduate Degree	Collection Management	Administration	Public Programming	Exhibit Design	Arch. Preservation	Curatorship	Education	Conservation	Field Methods	Info. Technology	Anthropology	Archaeology	Archeology	Architecture	Archives	Clothing	Decorative Arts	Ethics	Ethnology	Fine Arts	History	Material Culture	Museology	Paleontology	Natural Science	Full-time Study	Part-time Study	Lecture/Seminar	Training in Museums	International Students	Financial Assistance
University of Canberra							•	•	•	•	•	•	•	•	•	•	•	•		•										•	•	•			•	•	•	
University of Canberra/NCCHSS			•			•	•	•	•	•	•	•	•	•	•	•	•	•																	•	•	•	•
University of Sydney						•	•	•	•	•	•	•	•	•	•	•	•	•		•									•	•	•	•			•	•	•	•
University of Sydney					•	•		•		•	•	•	•	•	•	•	•	•		•									•	•	•	•			•	•	•	•
James Cook University	•	•				•		•	•	•	•	•	•	•	•	•	•	•	•	•						•			•	•					•	•	•	•
James Cook University						•		•	•	•	•	•	•	•	•	•	•	•	•	•						•			•	•						•	•	•
James Cook University					•			•	•	•	•	•	•	•	•	•	•	•	•	•						•			•	•						•	•	•
Deakin University, Rusden Campus					•			•	•	•	•		•	•			•													•	•				•	•	•	•
Deakin University, Rusden Campus								•	•	•	•		•	•			•													•	•				•	•	•	•
Deakin University, Rusden Campus					•	•		•	•	•	•		•	•			•													•	•				•	•	•	•
Deakin University, Rusden Campus						•	•	•						•															•	•					•	•	•	•
Academy of Fine Arts, Vienna						•	•																	•			•			•							•	
Ministère de L'Education Nationale																•																					•	
University of Rio de Janeiro	•					•	•	•	•	•	•	•	•	•	•		•		•	•										•	•	•			•	•	•	•
Instituto de Museologia de São Paulo	•			•				•	•	•	•	•	•	•	•	•	•		•		•							•	•	•	•	•			•	•	•	•
University of Calgary						•	•	•		•	•		•	•	•		•		•																•	•	•	•
University of Alberta			•	•		•	•	•	•	•	•	•	•	•	•	•	•	•	•	•						•	•	•		•	•	•			•	•	•	•
Alberta Museums Association	•	•						•	•				•	•	•			•											•	•					•	•	•	•
Grant MacEwan Community College		•	•	•				•	•				•	•																			•		•	•	•	•
University of British Columbia	•	•	•					•	•	•	•		•	•	•		•	•	•	•				•	•	•	•	•	•	•		•	•		•	•	•	•
University of Victoria	•	•			•			•	•	•	•		•	•	•				•					•	•	•	•	•	•	•		•	•		•	•	•	•
Manitoba Museum of Man and Nature		•	•			•		•	•	•	•		•	•	•		•	•	•	•		•	•	•	•	•	•	•	•	•	•	•			•	•	•	•
Manitoba Museum of Man and Nature		•	•			•		•	•	•	•		•	•	•		•	•	•	•		•	•	•	•	•	•	•	•	•	•	•			•	•	•	•
The Beaverbrook Art Gallery								•	•	•	•		•	•	•		•										•								•	•	•	•
Memorial University of Newfoundland	•	•		•				•	•	•	•		•	•		•			•										•						•	•	•	•
Queen's University	•	•		•		•	•	•	•	•	•		•	•		•			•								•	•		•					•	•	•	•
University of Western Ontaria	•	•		•		•		•	•	•	•		•	•		•			•								•	•	•	•					•	•	•	•
Algonquin College	•			•	•			•	•	•	•		•	•		•			•								•	•	•	•			•	•	•	•	•	•
York University	•				•	•		•	•				•	•					•								•	•	•	•			•	•	•	•	•	•
University of Ottawa	•																				•						•	•	•	•				•	•	•	•	•
Interpretation Canada	•	•	•	•		•		•	•	•			•	•					•											•					•		•	•
Canadian Conservation Institute	•	•	•		•			•	•			•		•	•															•					•	•	•	•
National Archives of Canada	•	•						•	•	•	•		•	•	•												•	•	•	•					•	•	•	•
Ontario Association of Art Galleries	•	•						•	•	•	•		•	•	•												•	•	•	•					•		•	•

Table 5.1 Continued

Column group structure (diagonal headers):

- **Training Level:** Course Work · Workshops · Internships · Certificate · Diploma · Bachelor's Degree · Graduate Degree
- **Training Areas:** Administration · Collection Management · Exhibit Design · Public Programming · Arch. Preservation · Curatorship · Education · Conservation · Field Methods · Info. Technology
- **Specializations of Training:** Anthropology · Archeology · Architecture · Archives · Clothing · Decorative Arts · Ethics · Ethnology · Fine Arts · History · Material Culture · Museology · Paleontology · Natural Science
- **Training Schedule:** Full-time Study · Part-time Study
- **Other:** Lecture/Seminar · Training in Museums · International Students · Financial Assistance

INSTITUTION NAME
Ministry of Culture, Tourism and Recreation
Ontario Museum Association
University of Toronto
The Ontario Historical Society
Concordia University
Laval Université
Museums Association of Saskatchewan
University of Zagreb
University of Zagreb
Masaryk University
Masaryk University
CENTROMIDCA
Finnish Museums Association
Ecole du Louvre
Ecole Nationale du Patrimoine
Deutsches Historisches Museum
German National Museum
Rheinisches Museumsamt
Hungarian National Museum
Hungarian National Museum
Hungarian National Museum
Maharaja Sayajirao University of Baroda
Prachya Niketan
National Research Laboratory
National Research Laboratory
ICCROM
Massey University
Centre for Museum Studies – Jos
University of Maiduguri
School of Field Archaeology
Fudan University
Nankai University
Nicholas Copernicus University

Table 5.1 Continued

INSTITUTION NAME	Training Level							Training Areas										Specializations of Training														Training Schedule		Other			
	Course work	Workshops	Internships	Certificate	Diploma	Bachelor's Degree	Graduate Degree	Administration	Collection Management	Exhibit Design	Public Programming	Arch. Preservation	Curatorship	Education	Conservation	Field Methods	Info Technology	Anthropology	Archeology	Architecture	Archives	Clothing	Decorative Arts	Ethics	Ethnology	Fine Arts	History	Material Culture	Museology	Paleontology	Natural Science	Full-time Study	Part-time Study	Lecture/Seminar	Training in Museums	International Students	Financial Assistance
University of Stellenbosch				●				●	●		●		●	●	●	●	●	●		●	●		●	●	●	●	●	●	●					●		●	●
Göteborg University		●	●			●		●	●		●	●	●	●	●	●	●	●			●		●			●	●	●	●					●		●	●
Riksutställningar		●	●					●	●	●	●																							●	●	●	●
Kungliga Husgerådskammaren											●		●			●																		●			
Umeå University		●	●		●			●	●		●	●	●	●		●		●			●		●			●	●	●	●					●		●	●
Université de Neuchâtel		●	●					●	●		●		●	●	●	●	●						●		●		●	●	●					●		●	●
University of Leiden		●	●					●	●		●		●	●	●	●	●		●		●		●			●	●	●	●					●		●	●
University of Amsterdam		●	●					●	●		●		●	●	●	●	●						●			●	●	●	●					●		●	●
Reinwardt Academie				●		●		●	●		●		●	●	●	●	●						●	●	●	●	●	●	●					●		●	●
University of Cambridge					●			●	●		●		●			●		●	●				●			●	●	●	●					●		●	●
University of Cambridge			●				●	●	●		●		●			●			●															●		●	●
University of Cambridge					●			●	●		●		●		●	●			●															●		●	●
University of Durham								●	●		●		●	●		●			●				●				●							●		●	●
University of Leicester			●	●	●			●	●		●		●	●		●													●					●		●	●
University College London					●			●	●		●		●		●	●		●	●	●	●		●				●		●					●		●	●
City University			●					●	●		●		●	●		●	●			●									●					●		●	●
University of Manchester		●	●		●			●	●		●		●	●		●				●					●		●		●					●		●	●
University of Newcastle upon Tyne		●	●		●			●	●		●		●	●	●	●			●	●							●		●					●		●	●
Ulster Museum		●	●					●	●		●		●	●	●	●													●					●		●	●
Textile Conservation Centre			●		●			●	●						●							●												●		●	●
Birmingham Museum of Art				●				●	●		●		●	●		●							●			●	●							●		●	●
Arizona State University							●	●	●		●		●	●		●			●								●							●		●	●
Arkansas State University			●					●	●		●		●	●		●			●								●							●		●	●
Arkansas Historical Society		●	●					●	●		●		●	●		●											●							●		●	●
University of California at Berkeley		●	●					●	●		●		●	●		●		●	●								●							●		●	●
Museum of Anthropology								●	●		●		●	●		●		●	●															●		●	●
California State University at Long Beach			●	●				●	●		●		●	●		●						●	●	●			●		●					●		●	●
University of Southern California			●	●				●	●		●		●	●		●	●						●	●			●		●					●		●	●
J. Paul Getty Museum			●					●	●		●		●			●							●											●		●	●
John F. Kennedy University			●		●		●	●	●		●		●	●		●			●					●					●					●		●	●
California State University – San Bernardino			●	●				●	●		●		●	●		●	●	●	●								●		●			●	●	●		●	●
University of San Diego			●	●				●	●		●		●	●		●			●	●			●				●		●		●	●	●	●		●	●
San Francisco State University			●	●				●	●		●		●	●		●		●	●	●			●	●			●		●		●	●	●	●		●	●

Table 5.1 Continued

INSTITUTION NAME	Course work	Workshops	Internships	Certificate	Diploma	Bachelor's Degree	Graduate Degree	Administration	Collection Management	Exhibit Design	Public Programming	Arch. Preservation	Curatorship	Education	Conservation	Field Methods	Info. Technology	Anthropology	Archeology	Archaeology	Architecture	Archives	Clothing	Decorative Arts	Ethics	Ethnology	Fine Arts	History	Material Culture	Museology	Paleontology	Natural Science	Full-time Study	Part-time Study	Lecture/Seminar	Training in Museums	International Students	Financial Assistance
University of Colorado	•			•		•		•	•	•	•	•	•	•	•	•		•	•	•	•							•			•	•	•				•	•
University of Colorado	•			•	•			•	•	•	•	•	•	•	•	•			•	•												•	•				•	•
Colorado History Museum				•				•	•	•	•	•	•	•	•	•			•	•	•					•		•		•			•			•	•	•
Denver Museum of Natural History			•					•	•	•	•	•	•	•	•	•			•	•	•					•			•	•	•	•	•			•	•	•
University of Denver	•		•	•	•			•	•	•	•	•	•	•	•	•	•		•	•	•					•			•	•		•	•	•	•		•	•
Birdcraft Museum and Sanctuary	•		•	•				•	•		•	•	•	•	•	•								•					•			•	•		•		•	•
Wadsworth Athenaeum			•					•	•	•	•	•	•	•	•									•			•			•			•			•	•	•
Smithsonian Institution		•		•				•	•	•	•		•	•	•																		•			•	•	•
Corcoran Gallery of Art			•	•				•	•	•	•	•	•	•										•			•						•				•	•
National Museum of African Art				•				•	•	•	•		•	•							•	•		•				•					•			•	•	•
National Air and Space Museum								•	•	•			•																	•			•			•	•	•
US Army Center of Military History	•		•					•	•	•	•		•		•				•	•								•		•			•	•		•	•	•
The George Washington University	•	•		•				•	•	•	•		•	•	•															•			•	•	•			
National Trust for Historic Preservation				•				•	•	•	•	•	•	•							•												•			•	•	•
US/ICOMOS			•					•	•		•	•	•	•		•			•	•	•	•								•			•	•			•	•
National Endowment for the Arts	•	•		•				•	•		•		•	•																			•			•	•	•
Smithsonian Institution				•				•	•	•	•		•	•	•																		•			•	•	•
Smithsonian Institution		•						•	•		•		•	•	•																		•			•	•	•
Washington Conservation Guild	•		•	•				•	•		•		•		•									•									•			•	•	•
Marine Corp Historical Center				•				•	•	•	•		•	•		•																	•			•	•	•
Smithsonian Institution				•				•	•	•	•		•	•	•																		•			•	•	•
Smithsonian Institution				•				•	•	•	•		•	•	•				•	•													•			•	•	•
The George Washington University							•	•	•	•	•		•	•	•				•	•	•	•		•	•	•	•	•	•	•			•	•	•	•	•	•
The George Washington University							•	•	•	•	•		•	•	•					•	•	•		•	•		•	•	•	•			•	•	•	•	•	•
Smithsonian Institution		•	•	•				•	•	•	•		•	•	•																		•			•	•	•
Smithsonian Institution		•	•	•				•	•	•	•		•	•	•																		•			•	•	•
Smithsonian Institution		•		•				•	•	•	•		•	•	•																		•			•	•	•
Smithsonian Institution				•				•	•	•	•		•	•	•																		•			•	•	•
University of Delaware	•			•			•	•	•	•	•		•	•	•	•				•	•	•		•	•		•	•	•	•			•	•	•	•	•	•
University of Delaware	•			•			•	•	•	•	•		•	•	•	•				•	•	•		•	•		•	•	•	•			•	•	•	•	•	•
University of Delaware	•		•	•				•	•	•	•		•	•	•	•				•	•	•		•	•		•	•	•	•			•	•	•	•	•	•
University of Delaware/Winterthur Museum	•		•	•			•	•	•	•	•		•	•	•	•				•	•	•		•	•		•	•	•	•			•	•	•	•	•	•

Table 5.1 Continued

INSTITUTION NAME	Training Level							Training Areas										Specializations of Training														Training Schedule		Other			
	Course work	Workshops	Internships	Certificate	Diploma	Bachelor's Degree	Graduate Degree	Administration	Collection Management	Exhibit Design	Public Programming	Arch. Preservation	Curatorship	Education	Conservation	Field Methods	Info. Technology	Anthropology	Archeology	Architecture	Archives	Cloning	Decorative Arts	Ethics	Ethnology	Fine Arts	History	Material Culture	Museology	Paleontology	Natural Science	Full-time Study	Part-time Study	Lecture/Seminar	Training in Museums	International Students	Financial Assistance
Historical Society of Delaware			•					•	•	•	•	•	•	•	•												•	•	•	•						•	•
Henry Francis duPont Winterthur Museum							•	•	•	•	•	•	•	•	•												•	•	•					•		•	•
Museum of Science and History			•						•	•	•	•	•	•	•				•	•							•	•		•					•		•
Georgia Museum of Art			•					•	•	•	•	•	•	•	•											•								•		•	•
Atlanta History Center			•						•	•	•	•	•	•	•												•	•		•				•		•	•
Emory University	•			•					•	•	•	•	•	•	•	•							•				•	•			•			•		•	•
The Columbus Museum			•						•	•	•	•	•	•	•	•					•		•											•		•	•
Museum of Arts and Sciences			•								•	•	•															•						•		•	•
University of Hawaii at Manoa	•			•					•							•		•						•			•		•	•				•		•	•
Southern Illinois University			•				•		•		•	•	•	•	•	•											•		•					•	•	•	•
Krannert Art Museum			•				•					•	•	•	•						•					•			•					•		•	•
Eastern Illinois University			•									•		•																				•		•	•
Field Museum of Natural History	•	•																													•			•		•	•
Society of American Archivists			•					•	•			•	•	•	•		•				•							•						•	•	•	•
Campbell Center	•	•																																•	•	•	•
Illinois State Museum			•						•		•	•	•	•				•									•		•		•			•	•	•	•
University of Illinois			•				•		•	•		•	•	•	•	•		•						•		•	•		•					•	•	•	•
Indiana University			•				•		•	•		•	•	•		•								•			•		•					•	•	•	•
University of Iowa			•										•	•												•	•		•	•				•	•	•	•
University of Kansas			•													•		•	•					•			•		•	•				•	•	•	•
Old Cowtown Museum	•			•					•		•	•	•	•	•	•			•								•							•		•	•
University of Kentucky Art Museum			•						•				•													•			•			•		•		•	•
J. B. Speed Art Museum			•						•				•																					•		•	•
Louisiana Arts and Science Center			•						•				•	•																				•		•	•
Historic New Orleans Collection			•						•		•	•	•	•						•	•						•		•					•		•	•
Portland Museum of Art			•						•				•													•			•					•		•	•
The Walters Art Gallery			•						•				•	•										•		•			•					•		•	•
Baltimore City Life Museums			•						•				•	•													•		•					•		•	•
The Baltimore Museum of Art			•						•		•		•	•										•		•								•		•	•
The Walters Art Gallery			•						•				•	•																				•		•	•
Smithsonian Institute		•															•																	•		•	•
Goucher College							•																									•		•		•	•
Boston National Historical Park	•								•	•	•	•	•	•	•				•								•		•	•				•			•

Table 5.1 Continued

Table 5.1 (continued): Matrix of institutions by Training Level, Training Areas, Specializations of Training, Training Schedule, and Other.

INSTITUTION NAME	Course work	Workshops	Internships	Certificate	Diploma	Bachelor's Degree	Graduate Degree	Administration	Collection Management	Exhibit Design	Public Programming	Arch. Preservation	Curatorship	Education	Conservation	Field Methods	Info. Technology	Anthropology	Archeology	Architecture	Archives	Clothing	Decorative Arts	Ethics	Ethnology	Fine Arts	History	Material Culture	Museology	Paleontology	Natural Science	Full-time Study	Part-time Study	Lecture/Seminar	Training in Museums	International Students	Financial Assistance
Wheelock College	●	●		●			●				●	●	●	●		●	●	●									●	●								●	●
Boston Athenaeum	●	●	●	●				●	●		●	●	●	●	●	●	●			●							●	●	●						●	●	●
Boston University	●	●		●			●	●			●	●	●	●	●	●	●			●							●	●	●					●	●	●	●
Brockton Art Museum	●	●	●							●	●	●	●		●	●	●																				
Harvard University	●	●		●			●			●		●	●	●	●	●	●	●		●							●					●			●	●	●
Lesley College			●		●			●		●			●	●	●	●	●																			●	●
Historic Deerfield, Inc.	●	●	●	●	●						●	●	●	●	●	●	●						●				●	●	●				●		●	●	●
Chesterwood	●	●		●				●	●	●	●	●	●	●	●	●							●				●	●	●							●	●
Old Sturbridge Village			●									●	●	●																							
Williams College	●	●	●	●						●	●	●	●	●	●	●	●	●		●			●			●	●							●		●	●
Williamstown Regional Art Conservation												●		●	●	●	●																	●		●	●
Henry Ford Museum and Greenfield Village		●						●	●	●	●	●	●	●	●	●	●		●	●		●	●	●			●	●	●				●		●		●
Michigan State University Museum	●		●	●										●	●	●	●		●											●	●				●	●	●
Central Michigan University	●		●	●				●	●	●	●	●	●	●	●	●	●		●	●		●	●	●			●	●	●	●	●	●			●	●	●
University of Michigan	●		●	●				●				●	●	●	●	●	●	●		●							●			●	●		●		●	●	●
Walker Art Center			●							●				●		●	●																				
The Minneapolis Institute of Arts			●							●			●	●		●	●											●									
Minnesota State Arts Board			●					●								●	●																				
Minnesota Museum of Art			●	●					●							●	●																				
University of Mississippi			●					●	●			●	●	●	●	●	●		●																	●	●
University of Missouri – Columbia		●	●						●			●	●	●	●	●	●	●																	●	●	●
Harry S. Truman Library		●	●													●	●											●	●						●		●
Kansas City Museum		●	●					●								●	●																		●		●
Exhibits USA							●																												●		
The Saint Louis Art Museum			●					●								●	●		●	●		●	●	●			●	●	●				●		●	●	●
University of Nebraska – Lincoln		●	●					●	●			●	●	●	●	●	●	●	●	●		●	●	●			●	●	●	●	●		●			●	●
Joslyn Art Museum		●	●													●	●											●	●				●		●	●	●
University of Nevada – Reno			●									●	●	●	●	●	●	●	●	●		●	●	●			●	●	●	●	●	●			●	●	●
Science Center of New Hampshire		●	●													●	●																		●	●	●
Rutgers University			●			●	●							●		●	●																●		●	●	●
Institute of American Indian Arts	●	●	●	●					●		●	●	●	●	●	●	●		●			●	●	●			●	●	●	●	●	●			●	●	●
The New York Botanical Garden	●	●	●	●	●									●		●	●														●	●	●		●	●	●
State University College at Buffalo		●	●	●						●				●		●	●		●										●						●		●

Table 5.1 Continued

INSTITUTION NAME	Course work	Workshops	Internships	Certificate	Diploma	Bachelor's Degree	Graduate Degree	Administration	Collection Management	Exhibit Design	Public Programming	Arch. Preservation	Curatorship	Education	Conservation	Field Methods	Info. Technology	Anthropology	Archaeology	Architecture	Archives	Clothing	Decorative Arts	Ethics	Ethnology	Fine Arts	History	Material Culture	Museology	Paleontology	Natural Science	Full-time Study	Part-time Study	Lecture/Seminar	Training in Museums	International Students	Financial Assistance
Cooperstown Graduate Program								•	•	•	•	•	•	•	•	•	•	•	•				•	•	•	•	•	•	•					•		•	•
New York University			•	•			•	•	•	•	•	•	•	•	•	•	•	•	•	•			•			•	•	•	•					•	•	•	•
American Numismatic Society	•		•																															•	•		•
City University of New York	•		•				•	•	•	•	•	•	•	•	•	•	•	•	•	•	•		•			•	•	•	•					•	•	•	•
American Museum – Hayden Planetarium	•		•		•				•		•		•	•		•	•	•	•		•									•	•			•		•	•
New York University			•	•				•	•	•	•	•	•	•	•	•	•	•	•	•			•		•	•	•	•	•					•	•	•	•
Bank Street College							•	•	•	•	•	•	•	•	•	•	•	•					•			•	•	•	•					•	•	•	•
New York University, FAS	•		•			•	•	•	•	•	•	•	•	•	•	•	•	•	•	•			•			•	•	•	•					•	•	•	•
Parsons School of Design	•		•					•	•	•	•	•	•	•	•	•	•						•			•	•	•						•	•	•	•
Bard College				•				•	•	•	•	•	•	•	•	•	•	•					•	•	•	•	•	•	•					•		•	•
Bank Street College							•	•	•	•	•	•	•	•	•	•	•	•					•	•	•	•	•	•	•					•		•	•
Bank Street College								•	•	•	•	•	•	•	•	•	•	•						•	•	•	•	•	•					•		•	•
Hartwick College	•		•	•		•		•	•	•	•	•	•	•	•	•	•	•	•	•			•			•	•	•	•					•		•	•
State University of New York	•		•	•		•		•	•	•	•	•	•	•	•	•	•	•	•	•			•			•	•	•	•					•	•	•	•
Rochester Museum and Science Center			•		•													•	•											•	•			•			•
Rochester Museum and Science Center		•	•					•	•	•	•		•	•		•	•	•					•				•		•		•			•			•
George Eastman House			•		•			•	•	•	•		•	•	•	•	•				•		•			•	•	•	•					•			•
Syracuse University				•				•	•	•	•	•	•	•	•	•	•	•	•		•		•		•	•	•	•	•					•	•	•	•
Rensselaer County Historical Society			•	•				•	•	•	•	•	•	•	•	•	•	•					•		•	•	•	•	•					•	•		•
North Carolina Aquarium on Roanoke Island			•					•			•			•		•		•	•												•			•	•		•
North Carolina State University			•					•	•	•	•	•	•	•	•	•	•	•	•							•	•	•	•		•			•		•	•
Reynolda House, Museum of American Art		•	•					•	•	•	•	•	•	•									•			•	•	•						•			•
Cincinnati Zoo and Botanical Garden			•					•			•			•				•											•		•			•			•
The Cleveland Museum of Art			•					•	•	•	•	•	•	•	•		•						•			•	•	•	•					•			•
Case Western Reserve University			•	•				•	•	•	•	•	•	•	•	•	•	•	•				•			•	•	•	•					•	•	•	•
National Audubon Society			•					•			•			•		•															•			•			•
University of Oklahoma			•			•		•	•	•	•	•	•	•	•	•	•	•	•		•		•			•	•	•	•		•			•	•	•	•
Lehigh University					•																													•			•
Independence National Historial Park		•																																•	•		•
CIGNA Museum and Art Collection	•	•									•												•			•	•							•		•	•
American Law Institute – American Bar Association																																		•		•	•
Duquesne University								•	•		•		•	•		•	•				•		•			•	•	•	•					•		•	•

Table 5.1 Continued

Training Level / Training Areas / Specializations of Training / Training Schedule / Other

Column headers:

- **Training Level:** Course work, Workshops, Internships, Certificate, Diploma, Bachelor's Degree, Graduate Degree
- **Training Areas:** Administration, Collection Management, Exhibit Design, Public Programming, Arch. Preservation, Curatorship, Education, Conservation, Field Methods, Info. Technology
- **Specializations of Training:** Anthropology, Archeology, Architecture, Archives, Clothing, Decorative Arts, Ethics, Ethnology, Fine Arts, History, Material Culture, Museology, Paleontology, Natural Science
- **Training Schedule:** Full-time Study, Part-time Study
- **Other:** Lecture/Seminar, Training in Museums, International Students, Financial Assistance

INSTITUTION NAME

- Penn State University
- Roger Williams University
- Brown University
- American Association for State and Local History
- Texas Historical Commission
- University of Texas
- University of Texas at Austin
- Panhandle-Plains Historical Museum
- Texas A & I University
- Texas Tech University
- Baylor University
- Office of Historic Alexandria
- Virginia Commonwealth University
- Virginia Commonwealth University
- Mary Baldwin College
- The Colonial Williamsburg Foundation
- Colonial Williamsburg Foundation
- Colonial Williamsburg Foundation
- College of William and Mary
- National Park Service
- University of Wisconsin – Madison
- University of Wisconsin – Milwaukee
- The John Michael Kohler Arts Center
- University of Belgrade

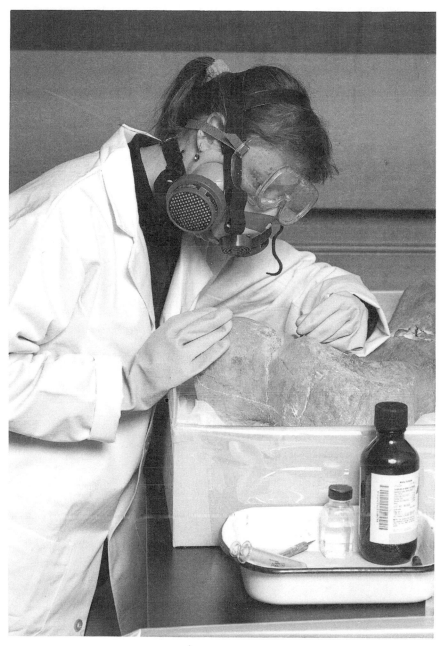

Plate 5 Conservator treating collection object (photograph by Nicky L. Olson)

Training programs directory

———•◆•———

The information included in this program directory was gathered through a direct mail survey. Institutions were asked to complete the survey, write a brief description of their program, and return it for inclusion in this publication. The survey asked for specific information about the program of instruction. Approximately 50 percent of the institutions responded and of that number several indicated that either their agency has discontinued the museum training program or their offerings have been reduced substantially. In the latter case, they asked that their agency not be listed.

As there is no international standard for museum training programs, all those responding have been included in the listing. The idea is to provide potential students with as much information as possible so that they can make an informed decision about which program offers the kind of training they need to meet their career objectives.

Issues that should be considered by the student when evaluating museum training programs are numerous. The following are a few of the questions that should be asked.

How long does it take to complete the program?
The issue of program length is only a part of the equation. Whether the program is short or long, the student should consider the amount of time required to gain a particular outcome (degree, diploma, certificate, or program objective). It is advisable to compare program offerings and the time required to achieve a defined goal. In the United States undergraduate degree programs normally require four years to complete. The time needed in other countries may vary. Graduate-level programs demand one or two years of course work plus a thesis, internship, and/or examination. Diploma and certificate programs may be of any length. Students should request a description of the time needed to complete the program of study and the requirements for successful completion.

Is the program full-time, part-time, correspondence, seminar, workshop or lecture?
Degree programs in the United States are normally full-time and based on academic semesters or quarters of study. Other countries may base their programs on units of instruction that are concentrated in shorter sequenced periods. As with seminars and workshops, diploma and certificate programs may be of any length and require a predetermined format and time.

Is the training offered in a museum/gallery or classroom setting?
The type of training being offered should dictate the environment in which it is presented. A non-museum classroom may be appropriate for theoretical course work, group discussions, topic-specific seminars, or general information exchange. The museum is often the preferred location for collection- or exhibition-related activities allowing a "hands-on" experience. Some programs supplement classroom training with practicums and internships. Seminars and workshops may require instruction-specific equipment.

Is the program focused on a single aspect of museum work or is it flexible and/or broad based?
Discipline-related museum training programs, such as those in anthropology, history, or fine art, combine academic training in a specific area with museology and museography. On completing the program, the student may have a degree in the discipline with a certificate in museology. Broad-based programs focus on museum training with the academic discipline as a supplemental or supporting role. The degree is in Museum Studies, Museum Science, or Museology with collateral training in a support area. Both concepts are valid. However, students should carefully consider their career objectives before deciding which kind of program they will pursue. Workshops or seminars are most often focused on a single element of museum work due to the limitations of time and audience interest.

How many students have successfully completed the program?
Critical mass is a factor in most training programs. A large number of graduates over a short period of time may indicate large classes and impersonal instruction. A few graduates over a long period of time may be due to either an inactive program or a minimal commitment by the host institution or organization. A small number of graduates also may indicate a specialized program for which only a few are interested or qualified.

Is financial aid available?
Financial assistance may be available for all forms of museum training. Workshop, seminar, and professional meeting registration may be waived

for persons requesting help. Travel grants are sometimes provided for persons traveling long distances to attend training programs. College and university degree programs often have grants, scholarships, assistantships, loans, and tuition waivers for deserving students or those with high academic or standardized test scores. Many countries provide subsidized training for students enrolled in degree programs. The form of the subsidy may vary.

Do the faculty have museum experience?
Persons not involved in the daily activities of the profession may not keep up with the rapidly changing role and responsibility of the museum community. As procedures, techniques, and attitudes change to meet professional needs and expectations, active participation in a museum role is one means of maintaining proficiency. However, employment by itself does not confirm expertise or knowledge of current practices.

Do students get practical experience in museography?
This experience may be working in a museum as part of the instructional program, an internship, or a practicum. Depending on the seminar or workshop topic, application of skills and techniques may be a part of the program.

No museum training program should be judged on the answer to any one question. Each question and response should be calculated to give the student a better understanding of the training program being reviewed and what a participant in that program should expect. Training may vary greatly in quality and content and careful investigation is the responsibility of the student. Delivery of advertised programming is the responsibility of the provider.

The single most important question for any student to ask is: "What does the training program offer that will help me in achieving my educational goal and enhancing my role as a museum professional?"

* * *

The information in the program directory is arranged alphabetically by (1) country; (2) state, province, or territory; (3) city. Each entry has a directory number located above the name of the institution. The number can be used for the Museum Training Indices. Requests for additional information should be addressed to the institution offering the program of interest.

Those using this publication should realize that inclusion in this directory does not constitute endorsement by the International Council of Museums, the International Committee on Training of Personnel, the editor, or the publisher.
The directory is for information.

Australia

1

Cultural Heritage Management
University of Canberra
PO Box 1
Belconnen, ACT 2616
Australia

The program began in: *1989*
Time required to complete program: *Varies*
Level of training provided: *Diploma, Graduate degree, Bachelor degree*
Areas of study: *Administration, Collection management, Public programming, Curatorship, Education, Conservation, Architectural preservation*
Areas of specialization: *Anthropology, Material culture, History, Museology*
Instructional opportunities provided: *Full-time study, Part-time study*
Is museum ethics a regular part of the program? *Yes*
Is the program open to international students? *Yes*
The primary language of instruction is: *English*
Is financial assistance available for students? *No*
The program is affiliated with: *University(ies)*
Is instruction given in a museum? *Yes*
Do students work in a museum collection as part of the program of study? *Yes*
Do program instructors have museum experience? *Yes*
How many students begin the program each year? *18*
How many students have completed the program since it began? *32*
Are the majority of the beginning students already employed by museums? *No*
What percentage of the students completing this program enter or return to museum work? *25% to 50%*
Contact person: *Linda Young*
Description of program: *Bachelor's degree, Master's degree Diploma*

The Cultural Heritage Management Program brings together the professional fields of heritage objects and sites, training students in curatorship, interpretation, preservation, and management. It has a particular focus on Australian Aboriginal culture and history, and seeks to serve Aboriginal students. The sister programs in Conservation of Cultural Materials, and

Resource and Environmental Science, also give Cultural Heritage Management students access to specialist training in conservation and/or park management. An active program of local museum/site placements guarantees substantial professional exposure.

2

Conservation of Cultural Materials
University of Canberra/NCCHSS
PO Box 1
Belconnen, ACT 2616
Australia

The program began in: *1978*
Time required to complete program: *Varies*
Level of training provided: *Diploma, Graduate degree, Bachelor degree*
Areas of study: *Conservation*
Areas of specialization: *Archives, Fine arts, Conservation*
Instructional opportunities provided: *Full-time study, Part-time study*
Is museum ethics a regular part of the program?   *No*
Is the program open to international students?   *Yes*
The primary language of instruction is: *English*
Is financial assistance available for students?   *No*
The program is affiliated with: *Museum(s), Gallery(ies), University(ies), Science Center(s)*
Is instruction given in a museum?   *No*
Do program instructors have museum experience?   *Yes*
How many students begin the program each year?   *30*
How many students have completed the program since it began?   *130*
Are the majority of the beginning students already employed by museums?   *Yes*
What percentage of the students completing this program enter or return to museum work?   *25% to 50%*
Contact person: *Robert C. Morrison*
Description of program: *Diploma, Bachelor's degree, Master's degree*

Associate Diploma in Applied Science Course – Conservation of Cultural Materials specialization: the first year introduces scientific methods and the science of conservation. The second and final year of study introduces artifact preservation, conservation philosophy, and ethics. Also, the final year provides some of the basic preservation theories in paper, painting, and objects conservation. This gives students an overview of the preser-

70

vation of cultural artifacts and the skill and knowledge to work as a conservation technician.

The degree of **Bachelor of Applied Science – Conservation of Cultural Materials** specialization: the first year of the course teaches scientific methods and the science of conservation. There is emphasis on the technological history of cultural artifacts and what causes their deterioration. The second year of study introduces artifact preservation, conservation philosophy, and ethics. Students elect a major at this time: painting, paper, or objects. The final year of the course offers advanced theory and a refinement of practical skills in the specialist area.

The degree of **Master of Applied Science – Conservation of Cultural Materials** specialization: this program gives a student the opportunity to do advanced study in paintings, paper, or objects conservation. Students graduate by passing an examination of their dissertation. To qualify for the degree of Master of Applied Science, a student completes 48 credit points of study. Students must earn the 48 credit points in one of the following ways: (1) a dissertation with a 48 credit point value; (2) a dissertation with a 36 credit point value and 12 credit points of class work; (3) a dissertation with a 24 credit point value plus an additional 24 credit points of class work.

3

Centre for Museum Studies
University of Sydney
Sydney, New South Wales 2006
Australia
Telephone: (02) 692 2209 or (02) 692 3800
Fax: (02) 692 0656

The program began in: *1976*
Time required to complete program: *Varies*
Level of training provided: *Diploma*
Areas of study: *Administration, Collection management, Exhibit design, Public programming, Curatorship, Education, Information technology, Conservation*
Areas of specialization: *Material culture, Museology*
Instructional opportunities provided: *Full-time study, Part-time study*
Is museum ethics a regular part of the program?   *Yes*
Is the program open to international students?   *Yes*

The primary language of instruction is: *English*
The program is affiliated with: *University(ies)*
Is instruction given in a museum?   *Yes*
Do students work in a museum collection as part of the program of study?   *Yes*
Do program instructors have museum experience?   *Yes*
How many students begin the program each year?   *20*
How many students have completed the program since it began?   *200*
Are the majority of the beginning students already employed by museums?   *No*
What percentage of the students completing this program enter or return to museum work?   *50% to 75%*
Contact person: *John Hodge, Senior Lecturer*
Description of program: *Diploma*

Diploma in Museum Studies: the course of study is designed to provide students with the necessary skills and theoretical knowledge to prepare them for professional museum work. It aims to encourage a critical response and a constructive contribution to the changes that are occurring in museums throughout the world. The program includes museum management, collections management, internships, and two of the following: exhibition management or museums and the public and material culture studies or art and the museum. The course lasts one academic year (full-time) or two years (part-time).

4

Centre for Museum Studies
University of Sydney
Sydney, New South Wales 2006
Australia
Telephone: (02) 692 2209 or (02) 692 3800

The program began in: *1991*
Time required to complete program: *Varies*
Level of training provided: *Graduate degree*
Areas of specialization: *Material culture, Museology, Cultural heritage*
Instructional opportunities provided: *Part-time study*
Is museum ethics a regular part of the program?   *Yes*
Is the program open to international students?   *Yes*
The primary language of instruction is: *English*
Is financial assistance available for students?   *Yes*

72

Financial assistance is available in the following ways: *Scholarships*
The program is affiliated with: *Museum(s), University(ies)*
Is instruction given in a museum? *No*
Do program instructors have museum experience? *Yes*
How many students begin the program each year? *2*
How many students have completed the program since it began? *1 (new)*
Are the majority of the beginning students already employed by museums? Yes
What percentage of the students completing this program enter or return to museum work? *More than 75%*
Contact person: *Shar Jones*
Description of program: *Master's degree*

M.Litt. in Museum Studies: this is a higher degree by course work and short thesis. Students who wish to apply for this degree should have qualified for the award of the Diploma in Museum Studies or an equivalent Museum Studies qualification from another university. Students are required to undertake a one-semester course in either Material Culture Studies or Museums and Cultural Heritage, a case study on a specified area of museum practice and a 20,000-word thesis/long essay.

5

Material Culture Unit
James Cook University
JCU Post Office
Townsville, Queensland 4811
Australia
Telephone: (077) 81 4334, Fax: (077) 81 4045

The program began in: *1978*
Time required to complete program: *1 year*
Level of training provided: *Diploma*
Areas of study: *Administration, Collection management, Exhibit design, Curatorship, Conservation, Field methods, Information technology*
Areas of specialization: *Anthropology, Ethnology, Fine arts, Material culture, Decorative arts, Ethics, Museology*
Instructional opportunities provided: *Full-time study, Part-time study, Scheduled lectures/seminars*
Is museum ethics a regular part of the program? *Yes*
Is the program open to international students? *Yes*

The primary language of instruction is: *English*
Is financial assistance available for students? *Yes*
Financial assistance is available in the following ways: *Scholarships*
The program is affiliated with: *University(ies)*
Is instruction given in a museum? *Yes*
Do students work in a museum collection as part of the program of study? *Yes*
Do program instructors have museum experience? *Yes*
How many students begin the program each year? *Varies*
How many students have completed the program since it began? *55*
Are the majority of the beginning students already employed by museums? *No*
What percentage of the students completing this program enter or return to museum work? *25% to 50%*
Contact person: *Barrie Reynolds, Director*
Description of program: *Diploma, Graduate Diploma of Museum Curatorship*

This program offers the student the opportunity to train for a museum career in museums of human history, natural science, and art. The student has the advantage of working in a museum environment within a university, in well-equipped laboratories, and with full access to a collection of approximately 7000 objects. A small but well-furnished gallery, a conservation laboratory, and a darkroom provide specialized facilities in which students undertake practical work. Applicants should possess a Bachelor's degree in an appropriate subject.

6

Material Culture Unit
James Cook University
JCU Post Office
Townsville, Queensland 4811
Australia
Telephone: (077) 81 4334, Fax: (077) 81 4045

The program began in: *1990*
Time required to complete program: *Varies*
Level of training provided: *Courses, Workshops*
Areas of study: *Administration, Collection management, Exhibit design, Curatorship, Education, Conservation, Information technology*
Areas of specialization: *Ethics, Museology*

Instructional opportunities provided: *Scheduled lectures/seminars, Correspondence study*
Is museum ethics a regular part of the program? *Yes*
Is the program open to international students? *Yes*
The primary language of instruction is: *English*
Is financial assistance available for students? *No*
The program is affiliated with: *University(ies)*
Is instruction given in a museum? *Yes*
Do students work in a museum collection as part of the program of study? *No*
Do program instructors have museum experience? *Yes*
How many students begin the program each year? *15–30*
Are the majority of the beginning students already employed by museums? *Yes*
What percentage of the students completing this program enter or return to museum work? *More than 75%*
Contact person: *Helen Tyzack*
Description of program: *Certificate, Diploma*

The **Graduate Certificate in Community Museum Management** is a one-year course and the **Graduate Diploma** normally takes two years. Applicants are required to have a Bachelor's degree or substantial experience in museum work. These courses offer a unique opportunity within Australia for the many volunteer staff of community museums throughout the country to study by correspondence through the open learning mode. Students are required to attend some subjects on campus, which offers them the opportunity to meet and exchange ideas.

7

Material Culture Unit
James Cook University
JCU Post Office
Townsville, Queensland 4811
Australia
Telephone: (077) 81 4334 or (077) 81 4045

The program began in: *1992*
Time required to complete program: *2 years*
Level of training provided: *Graduate degree*
Areas of study: *Administration, Collection management, Exhibit design,*

Public programming, Curatorship, Education, Information technology,
Conservation, Field methods
Areas of specialization: *Anthropology, Material culture, Ethics,
Museology*
Instructional opportunities provided: *Correspondence study*
Is museum ethics a regular part of the program? *No*
Is the program open to international students? *Yes*
The primary language of instruction is: *English*
Is financial assistance available for students? *Yes*
Financial assistance is available in the following ways: *Scholarships*
The program is affiliated with: *University(ies)*
Is instruction given in a museum? *Yes*
Do program instructors have museum experience? *Yes*
How many students begin the program each year? *New program*
Are the majority of the beginning students already employed by
    museums? *Yes*
Contact person: *Barrie Reynolds, Director*
Description of program: *Graduate degree*

The **Master's degree** program involves a minimum of one year's study;
however, students normally take two years to complete their research and
prepare the thesis of 50,000 to 60,000 words. Applicants must possess a
course work Master's or a Bachelor's degree with honors (or equivalent).
Prior museum experience is essential. The program is designed for students
wishing to undertake higher degree research in the fields of material culture
or museology.

The **Doctorate** program involves a minimum of two years' study; however,
students normally take three to four years to complete their research and
prepare the thesis of 80,000 to 100,000 words. Applicants must possess
a Master's or Bachelor's degree with high honors (or equivalent). Prior
museum experience is essential. The program is designed for students
wishing to undertake higher degree research in the fields of material culture
or museology and involves a substantial field work component.

8

Museum Studies
Deakin University, Rusden Campus
662 Blackburn Road
Clayton, Victoria 3168
Australia
Telephone: (03) 805 3333
Fax: (03) 544 7413

The program began in: *1979*
Time required to complete program: *1 year*
Level of training provided: *Diploma*
Areas of study: *Administration, Collection management, Exhibit design, Public programming, Curatorship, Education, Conservation, Field methods, Information technology*
Areas of specialization: *Multidisciplinary study, Ethics, Museology*
Instructional opportunities provided: *Full-time study, Part-time study*
Is museum ethics a regular part of the program? *Yes*
Is the program open to international students? *Yes*
The primary language of instruction is: *English*
Is financial assistance available for students? *Yes*
Financial assistance is available in the following ways: *Scholarships*
The program is affiliated with: *University(ies)*
Is instruction given in a museum? *Yes*
Do students work in a museum collection as part of the program of study? *Yes*
Do program instructors have museum experience? *Yes*
How many students begin the program each year? *25*
How many students have completed the program since it began? *260*
Are the majority of the beginning students already employed by museums? *No*
What percentage of the students completing this program enter or return to museum work? *More than 75%*
Contact person: *Roger Trudgeon, Senior Lecturer*
Description of program: *Diploma*

The Graduate Diploma in Museum Studies program is designed to give students a comprehensive introduction to museum work in Australia. Students intending to work in museums and those already employed in museums are encouraged to participate. The course consists of eight units covering collections management, museum management, public programs, marketing and public relations, and a research project. Units in the course balance theory with practice in the museum context. Students also complete two museum placements. The diploma program can be completed in one year full-time or two years part-time. Applicants for the course are expected to have a relevant degree or diploma and preferably should have gained some museum experience through employment or volunteer programs.

9

Environmental and Heritage Interpretation
Deakin University, Rusden Campus
662 Blackburn Road
Clayton, Victoria 3168
Australia
Telephone: (03) 805 3333, Fax: (03) 544 7413

The program began in: *1991*
Time required to complete program: *1 year*
Level of training provided: *Certificate*
Areas of study: *Administration, Public programming, Exhibit design, Education, Information technology*
Areas of specialization: *Ethics, Museology, Interpretation*
Instructional opportunities provided: *Part-time study*
Is museum ethics a regular part of the program?   *Yes*
Is the program open to international students?   *Yes*
The primary language of instruction is: *English*
Is financial assistance available for students?   *Yes*
Financial assistance is available in the following ways: *Scholarships*
The program is affiliated with: *University(ies)*
Is instruction given in a museum?   *Yes*
Do students work in a museum collection as part of the program of study?   *Yes*
Do program instructors have museum experience?   *Yes*
How many students begin the program each year?   *30*
How many students have completed the program since it began?   *50*
Are the majority of the beginning students already employed by museums?   *Yes*
What percentage of the students completing this program enter or return to museum work?   *More than 75%*
Contact person: *Rachel Faggetter, Lecturer in Interpretation*
Description of program: *Certificate*

The Graduate Certificate in Environmental and Heritage Interpretation course is designed for all those working in cultural institutions who are involved in communicating with the public. It focuses on the art of effective public programming. Students in the course come from national and metropolitan parks, zoos, museums, historic houses, and sites. There are four units in the course: Introduction to Interpretation, Natural and Cultural Heritage Resources, Techniques of Interpretation, and a research project. It is possible to complete the course part-time in one year. Applicants should normally have a relevant degree; however, special entry provisions are available for those employed in the field without formal tertiary qualifications.

10

Museum Studies Program
Deakin University, Rusden Campus
662 Blackburn Road
Clayton, Victoria 3168
Australia
Telephone: (03) 805 3333 or (03) 544 7413

The program began in: *1992*
Time required to complete program: *2 years*
Level of training provided: *Internships, Graduate degree*
Areas of study: *Administration, Collection management, Exhibit design, Public programming, Curatorship, Education, Conservation, Field methods, Information technology*
Areas of specialization: *Anthropology, Clothing, Ethnology, Fine arts, Material culture, Natural science, Archeology, Architecture, Decorative arts, Ethics, History, Museology, Paleontology*
Instructional opportunities provided: *Full-time study*
Is museum ethics a regular part of the program? *Yes*
Is the program open to international students? *Yes*
The primary language of instruction is: *English*
Is financial assistance available for students? *Yes*
Financial assistance is available in the following ways: *Scholarships*
The program is affiliated with: *University(ies)*
Is instruction given in a museum? *Yes*
Do students work in a museum collection as part of the program of study? *Yes*
Do program instructors have museum experience? *Yes*
How many students begin the program each year? *6*
How many students have completed the program since it began? *5*
Are the majority of the beginning students already employed by museums? *Yes*

What percentage of the students completing this program enter or return
to museum work? *More than 75%*
Contact person: *Roger Trudgeon, Senior Lecturer*
Description of program: *Graduate degree*

Master of Applied Science (Museum Studies): the Master's by course work
program in Museum Studies consists of a year of course work followed
by the completion of a research methodology unit, a museum practicum,
and a minor thesis. The course takes two years to complete, commencing
students enrolling in the graduate diploma units in the first year. In the
second year, students complete a fifteen-week museum-based practicum
preferably conducted in areas of direct relevance to the 15,000-word thesis.
Applicants holding a Graduate Diploma in Museum Studies are eligible
for advanced standing toward the first year of the Master's program.

Austria

11

Master School for Restoration and Conservation
Academy of Fine Arts Vienna
Schillerplatz 3
Vienna, 1010
Austria
Telephone: 84 72 185

The program began in: *1934*
Time required to complete program: *5 years*
Level of training provided: *Magister Artium (M.A.), Graduate degree*
Areas of study: *Conservation*
Areas of specialization: *Fine arts, Natural science, Museology*
Instructional opportunities provided: *Full-time study, Scheduled
lectures/seminars*
Is museum ethics a regular part of the program? *No*
Is the program open to international students? *Yes*
The primary language of instruction is: *German*
Is financial assistance available for students? *No*
The program is affiliated with: *University(ies)*

Is instruction given in a museum? *No*
Do program instructors have museum experience? *Yes*
How many students begin the program each year? *5*
How many students have completed the program since it began? *245*
Are the majority of the beginning students already employed by
   museums? *No*
What percentage of the students completing this program enter or return
   to museum work? *25% to 50%*
Contact person: *Hans Mayerl*
Description of program: *Master's degree*

Applicants for this **Master of Arts program** have to undergo an entrance
exam where their artistic skills and physical aptitude are assessed.
Successful candidates are taught the theory, methodology, and history of
conservation as well as the practical application of methods on projects.
Instruction focuses on basic studies in natural science, documentation
techniques and preservation of cultural objects, museology, photographic
documentation, historical technology and sources. The practical work
includes conservation and restoration of easel paintings, painted objects
and polychrome sculpture as well as graphic works of art. The diploma
includes a practical and theoretical project, written and photographic documentation. Degree granted: Magister Artium (M.A.).

Belgium

12

Institut Royal du Patrimoine Artistique
Ministère de l'Education Nationale
Parc du Cinquantenaire 1
Brussels, B-1040
Belgium
Telephone: (02) 735 41 60

Time required to complete program: *8 months*
Areas of study: *Conservation*
Areas of specialization: *Fine arts, Archeology, Sculpture, Metals*
Instructional opportunities provided: *Scheduled lectures/seminars*

Is the program open to international students?   *Yes*
The primary language of instruction is: *French, Dutch, and English*
Is financial assistance available for students?   *Yes*
Financial assistance is available in the following ways: *Lodging, Grants*
The program is affiliated with: *Museum(s)*
Is instruction given in a museum?   *Yes*
Do students work in a museum collection as part of the program of study?   *Yes*
Do program instructors have museum experience?   *Yes*
Contact person: *Liliane Masschelein-Kleiner, Ph.D., Director*
Description of program: *Training Program*

Advanced practice in conservation for young professional conservators of easel paintings, polychromed sculpture, textiles and occasionally archeological objects in metal with priority to museum personnel. Training is a combination of practice with lectures, demonstrations, and seminars. The program lasts from early October to late May. Participants are expected to benefit from a grant to cover their travel and living expenses.

Brazil

13

School of Museology
University of Rio de Janeiro
Rua Xavier Sigaud, 290/s 610 – Urca
Rio de Janeiro RJ 22.290
Brazil

The program began in: *1932*
Time required to complete program: *More than 2 years*
Level of training provided: *Bachelor degree*
Areas of study: *Administration, Collection management, Exhibit design, Education, Information technology, Conservation, Architectural preservation*
Areas of specialization: *Anthropology, Archives, Ethnology, Fine arts, Material culture, Archeology, Decorative arts, History, Museology, Textiles, Numismatics*
Instructional opportunities provided: *Full-time study*

Is museum ethics a regular part of the program?   *No*
Is the program open to international students?   *Yes*
The primary language of instruction is: *Portuguese*
Is financial assistance available for students?   *Yes*
The program is affiliated with: *University(ies)*
Is instruction given in a museum?   *No*
Do program instructors have museum experience?   *Yes*
How many students begin the program each year?   *100*
How many students have completed the program since it began?   *400*
Are the majority of the beginning students already employed by
     museums?   *No*
What percentage of the students completing this program enter or return
     to museum work?   *25% to 50%*
Contact person: *Mário de Souza Chagas*
Description of program: *Bachelor's degree*

Bachelor's degree in Museology: courses selected from four major areas
of study – history, science, fine art, and museology – form the basis of
this program. Additional courses, selected from among such related
subjects as numismatics, heraldry, and decorative arts, are also part of
the degree requirements. The museology sequence is comprehensive in
nature and covers educational and cultural activities, public relations,
organization and administration, and collections management. Practical
training assignments complete the program. The final year is comprised
of two major projects, each lasting one semester. First, students design
and install an exhibition of a professional caliber and second, they
conclude their academic studies by serving as interns in museums in and
around Rio de Janeiro.

14

Museology
Instituto de Museologia de São Paulo
Rua Jesuino Pascoal, 51
São Paulo, SP CEP: 01224-050
Brazil
Telephone: (55 11) 222 9680

The program began in: *1992*
Time required to complete program: *2 years*
Level of training provided: *Diploma, Workshops, Certificate*
Areas of study: *Administration, Collection management, Exhibit design,*

Curatorship, Education, Conservation, Information technology, Field methods, Architectural preservation

Areas of specialization: *Anthropology, Archives, Clothing, Ethnology, Material culture, Natural science, Architecture, Decorative arts, Ethics, Museology, Documentation, History, Museum pedagogy*

Instructional opportunities provided: *Part-time study, Short-term lectures on request, Scheduled lectures/seminars*

Is museum ethics a regular part of the program? *Yes*

Is the program open to international students? *Yes*

The primary language of instruction is: *Portuguese*

Is financial assistance available for students? *No*

The program is affiliated with: *Museum(s)*

Is instruction given in a museum? *Yes*

Do students work in a museum collection as part of the program of study? *No*

Do program instructors have museum experience? *Yes*

How many students begin the program each year? *20*

Are the majority of the beginning students already employed by museums? *Yes*

Contact person: *Roberto Haidar, Director, or Ivani Kotait*

Description of program: *Diploma, Certificate, Workshops*

The Instituto de Museologia de São Paulo, IMSP, is sponsored by the Fundação Escola de Sociologia e Política de São Paulo (FESP-SP), and offers, on a post-graduate level, courses in advanced museology. The course of instruction includes the following subjects: museology, museography, documentation, conservation and restoration of cultural assets, museum pedagogy, scientific research methodology, and dissertation.

The course of instruction requires eighteen months, four hours per day, for a total of 1000 hours. The course is designed for persons with a Bachelor's degree in social sciences, natural history, architecture, tourism, administration, archeology, library science, plastic arts, communications, and other related areas.

Canada

15

Department of Archaeology
University of Calgary
2500 University Drive
Calgary, Alberta T2N 1N4
Canada

The program began in: *1966*
Time required to complete program: *More than 2 years*
Level of training provided: *Bachelor degree*
Areas of specialization: *Archeology, Museology*
Instructional opportunities provided: *Full-time study, Part-time study*
Is museum ethics a regular part of the program? *No*
Is the program open to international students? *Yes*
The primary language of instruction is: *English*
Is financial assistance available for students? *Yes*
Financial assistance is available in the following ways: *Loans*
The program is affiliated with: *University(ies)*
Is instruction given in a museum? *No*
Do students work in a museum collection as part of the program of
  study? *No*
Do program instructors have museum experience? *Yes*
Are the majority of the beginning students already employed by
  museums? *No*
What percentage of the students completing this program enter or return
  to museum work? *Less than 25%*
Contact person: *Jane H. Kelley*
Description of program: *Course*

A one-semester **course on general museology.**

16

Division of Recreation and Leisure Studies
University of Alberta
Edmonton, Alberta T6G 2H9
Canada
Telephone: (403) 432 3111

The program began in: *B.A. 1962; M.A. 1979*
Time required to complete program: *More than 2 years*
Level of training provided: *Graduate degree, Bachelor degree*
Areas of study: *Administration, Public programming, Education, Conservation*
Areas of specialization: *Anthropology, Natural science, History*
Instructional opportunities provided: *Full-time study, Part-time study*
Is the program open to international students? *Yes*
The primary language of instruction is: *English*
Is financial assistance available for students? *Yes*
Financial assistance is available in the following ways: *Scholarships, Loans*
The program is affiliated with: *University(ies)*
Is instruction given in a museum? *No*
Do program instructors have museum experience? *No*
How many students begin the program each year? *50 B.A.*
How many students have completed the program since it began? *1300 B.A., 45 M.A.*
Are the majority of the beginning students already employed by museums? *No*
Contact person: *Guy S. Swinnerton, Director*
Description of program: *Bachelor's degree, Master's degree*

Heritage interpretation is available through four **undergraduate courses** taught jointly between the Division of Recreation and Leisure Studies and Forest Science.

17

Training Program
Alberta Museums Association
Suite 40, 9912-106 Street
Edmonton, Alberta T5K 1C5
Canada
Telephone: (403) 424 2626
Fax: (403) 425 1679

The program began in: *1988*
Time required to complete program: *Varies*
Level of training provided: *Workshops*
Areas of study: *Administration, Collection management, Exhibit design, Public programming, Curatorship, Conservation, Information technology*

Areas of specialization: *Museology*
Instructional opportunities provided: *Scheduled lectures/seminars*
Is museum ethics a regular part of the program?   *Yes*
Is the program open to international students?   *Yes*
The primary language of instruction is: *English*
Is financial assistance available for students?   *Yes*
Financial assistance is available in the following ways: *Individual training grants*
The program is affiliated with: *Museum(s)*
Is instruction given in a museum?   *Yes*
Do students work in a museum collection as part of the program of study?   *No*
Do program instructors have museum experience?   *Yes*
How many students begin the program each year?   *10*
How many students have completed the program since it began?   *19*
Are the majority of the beginning students already employed by museums?   *Yes*
Contact person: *Dianne Smith or Adriana Davies*
Description of program: *Workshops*

The Alberta Museums Association provides a multilevel training program in museum practice: the **Citation Program in Basic Museum Practice – Levels I and II**, and the **Professional Development Series**.

The Citation Program in Basic Museum Practice – Levels I and II is a series of workshops focusing on hands-on, skills-oriented training in basic museum practice. Four Level I and five Level II workshops are offered each year in museums around the province.

The Professional Development Series is an intermediate/advanced-level training program for museum workers with a strong grounding in museum practice. The focus is on management topics and issues of ongoing and current concern to museum managers and staff.

18

Arts Administration
Grant MacEwan Community College
Jasper Place, 10045 156 Street
Edmonton, Alberta T5P 2P7
Canada
Telephone: (403) 483 2359

The program began in: *1980*
Time required to complete program: *10 months*
Level of training provided: *Courses, Internships, Certificate*
Areas of study: *Administration, Collection management, Education, Public programming*
Instructional opportunities provided: *Full-time study*
Is museum ethics a regular part of the program?   *Yes*
Is the program open to international students?   *Yes*
The primary language of instruction is: *English*
Is financial assistance available for students?   *Yes*
Financial assistance is available in the following ways: *Loans*
Is instruction given in a museum?   *No*
Do program instructors have museum experience?   *No*
How many students begin the program each year? *25 Arts Administration and 6–10 Museums and Gallery*
Are the majority of the beginning students already employed by museums?   *No*
What percentage of the students completing this program enter or return to museum work?   *Less than 25%*
Contact person: *Denise Roy, Chair*
Description of program: *Certificate*

This ten-month **certificate program** covers the basics of marketing and publicity, financial management, fund raising, microcomputer applications, advocacy and lobbying, and personnel management. In addition, the program offers an elective course in museum/gallery management. Students are required to complete a three-month placement with a visual or performing arts organization before graduation.

19

Museum of Anthropology
University of British Columbia
6393 N.W. Marine Drive
Vancouver, British Columbia V6T 1Z2
Canada
Telephone: (604) 822 5052
Fax: (604) 822 2974

Time required to complete program: *Varies*
Level of training provided: *Courses, Internships, Graduate degree, Workshops, Bachelor degree*

Areas of study: *Administration, Collection management, Exhibit design, Public programming, Curatorship, Education, Conservation, Information technology, Field methods*

Areas of specialization: *Anthropology, Archives, Ethnology, Fine arts, Material culture, Archeology, Ethics, Museology*

Instructional opportunities provided: *Full-time study, Part-time study, Scheduled lectures/seminars*

Is museum ethics a regular part of the program? *Yes*

Is the program open to international students? *Yes*

The primary language of instruction is: *English*

Is financial assistance available for students? *Yes*

Financial assistance is available in the following ways: *Scholarships, Student work program, Internships, Challenge grants, Work-study*

The program is affiliated with: *Museum(s), University(ies)*

Is instruction given in a museum? *Yes*

Do students work in a museum collection as part of the program of study? *Yes*

Do program instructors have museum experience? *Yes*

Are the majority of the beginning students already employed by museums? *Yes*

What percentage of the students completing this program enter or return to museum work? *50% to 75%*

Contact person: *Jennifer Webb, Program Assistant*

Description of program: *Courses*

Credit courses in museum theory and practice are offered as components of both graduate and undergraduate degree programs in anthropology. This training is also available to students of other related disciplines such as Asian studies, classics, history, or fine arts by arrangement with the relevant departments. In addition to course work there is a limited number of internships and student assistantships available to students who meet university and course requirements. Individuals working in the museum community or those who want to upgrade knowledge and skills without entering a degree program can attend Anthropology 431 (Museum Principles and Methods) and Anthropology 541 (Advanced Seminar in Museum Studies), as unclassified students or auditors. Other courses offered by the Department of Anthropology and Sociology that contribute to the Museum Studies program include Conservation of Organic/ Inorganic Materials, the Anthropology of Art, and Material Culture, as well as a variety of courses in ethnography and archeology.

20

Cultural Resource Management Program
University of Victoria
PO Box 3030
Victoria, British Columbia V8W 3N6
Canada
Telephone: (604) 721 8462
Fax: (604) 721 8774

The program began in: *1983*
Time required to complete program: *More than 2 years*
Level of training provided: *Courses, Internships, Diploma, Certificate*
Areas of study: *Administration, Collection management, Exhibit design,*
    Public programming, Curatorship, Education, Information technology,
    Conservation, Field methods, Architectural preservation
Areas of specialization: *Museology*
Instructional opportunities provided: *Part-time study, Short-term lectures*
    on request, Correspondence study
Is museum ethics a regular part of the program?   *Yes*
Is the program open to international students?   *Yes*
The primary language of instruction is: *English*
Is financial assistance available for students?   *Yes*
Financial assistance is available in the following ways: *Loans*
The program is affiliated with: *University(ies)*
Is instruction given in a museum?   *Yes*
Do students work in a museum collection as part of the program of
    study?   *Yes*
Do program instructors have museum experience?   *Yes*
How many students begin the program each year?   *10–12*
How many students have completed the program since it began?   *40*
Are the majority of the beginning students already employed by
    museums?   *Yes*
What percentage of the students completing this program enter or return
    to museum work?   *More than 75%*
Contact person: *Joy Davis, Program Coordinator*
Description of program: *Courses, Diploma, Certificate*

This program provides **courses in museum studies, heritage conservation, and cultural management** in an eight-day on-campus immersion format, to enable professionals in the heritage community in Canada and the United States to study on a part-time basis while continuing with their professional commitments. Participants can take individual courses as unclassified or non-credit students, or they can complete a series of courses in a structured, part-time credit program leading to a Diploma in Cultural Conservation. The program offers its core courses in museum studies and heritage conservation in a distance education format to professionals across North America and abroad.

21

Internship Program
Manitoba Museum of Man and Nature
190 Rupert Avenue
Winnipeg, Manitoba R3B 0N2
Canada
Telephone: (204) 988 0655

The program began in: *1972*
Time required to complete program: *1 year*
Level of training provided: *Certificate*
Areas of study: *Administration, Collection management, Exhibit design, Public programming, Curatorship, Education, Conservation, Information technology, Field methods*
Areas of specialization: *Anthropology, Archives, Clothing, Ethnology, Material culture, Natural science, Archeology, Decorative arts, Ethics, History, Museology, Paleontology*
Instructional opportunities provided: *Short term lectures on request, Lectures/seminars, Correspondence study*
Is the program open to international students? *No*
The primary language of instruction is: *English*
Is financial assistance available for students? *Yes*
The program is affiliated with: *Museum(s), Science center(s)*
Is instruction given in a museum? *Yes*
Do students work in a museum collection as part of the program of study? *Yes*
Do program instructors have museum experience? *Yes*
How many students begin the program each year? *2*
How many students have completed the program since it began? *55*
Are the majority of the beginning students already employed by museums? *Yes*
What percentage of the students completing this program enter or return to museum work? *50% to 75%*
Contact person: *Doug Leonard, Chief Curator, Human History Division*
Description of program: *Internships*

The Museum Internship Program is designed to provide hands-on experience in all aspects of museum work plus skill development related to specific career goals. Training includes on-the-job experience, lectures, demonstrations, assigned readings, special projects, and a secondary internship of up to three months at another institution. Open to individuals who are currently working in a Canadian museum as paid staff or volunteers. Two trainees are selected annually. This is a paid position.

22

Aboriginal Internship Program
Manitoba Museum of Man and Nature
190 Rupert Avenue
Winnipeg, Manitoba R3B 0N2
Canada
Telephone: (204) 988 0655

The program began in: *1992*
Time required to complete program: *1 year*
Level of training provided: *Certificate*
Areas of study: *Administration, Collection management, Exhibit design, Public programming, Curatorship, Education, Conservation, Information technology, Field methods*
Areas of specialization: *Anthropology, Archives, Clothing, Ethnology, Material culture, Natural science, Archeology, Decorative arts, Ethics, History, Museology, Paleontology*
Instructional opportunities provided: *Short-term lectures on request, Scheduled lectures/seminars, Correspondence study*
Is the program open to international students? *No*
The primary language of instruction is: *English*
Is financial assistance available for students? *Yes*
Financial assistance is available in the following ways: *Paid position*
The program is affiliated with: *Museum(s), Science center(s)*
Is instruction given in a museum? *Yes*
Do students work in a museum collection as part of the program of study? *Yes*
Do program instructors have museum experience? *Yes*
How many students begin the program each year? *1*
How many students have completed the program since it began? *New program*

Are the majority of the beginning students already employed by
     museums?   *No*
Contact person: *Doug Leonard, Chief Curator, Human History Division*
Description of program: *Aboriginal internship*

The Aboriginal Internship Program is designed to provide an Aboriginal
person with essential skills, practices, and principles of current museology
related to the management and interpretation of native heritage collections. Training includes hands-on experience, lectures, workshops, assigned
readings, and special projects. Open to Aboriginal people coming from
either an academic or community-based background who have demonstrated interest in this field as a career path. This is a paid position. One
intern is selected annually.

23

Visual Literacy for Teachers
The Beaverbrook Art Gallery
PO Box 605
Fredericton, New Brunswick E3B 4X7
Canada
Telephone: (506) 455 6551

The program began in: *1991*
Time required to complete program: *6 months or less*
Level of training provided: *Workshops*
Areas of study: *Education*
Areas of specialization: *Fine arts*
Instructional opportunities provided: *Scheduled lectures/seminars*
Is museum ethics a regular part of the program?   *No*
Is the program open to international students?   *No*
The primary language of instruction is: *English*
Is financial assistance available for students?   *Yes*
Financial assistance is available in the following ways: *Tuition waiver*
Is instruction given in a museum?   *Yes*
Do students work in a museum collection as part of the program of
     study?   *No*
Do program instructors have museum experience?   *Yes*
How many students begin the program each year?   *10–12*
How many students have completed the program since it began?   *24*
Are the majority of the beginning students already employed by
     museums?   *No*

Canada

Contact person: *Caroline Walker*
Description of program: *Workshops*

A program of **workshops** designed to provide experience in different aspects of art gallery operations.

24

**Memorial University of Newfoundland
Art Gallery
St John's, Newfoundland A1C 5S7
Canada
Telephone: (709) 737 8209**

The program began in: *1982*
Time required to complete program: *1 year*
Level of training provided: *Internships*
Areas of study: *Administration, Exhibit design, Education, Public programming, Curatorship*
Areas of specialization: *Fine arts*
Instructional opportunities provided: *Correspondence study*
Is museum ethics a regular part of the program? *Yes*
Is the program open to international students? *No*
The primary language of instruction is: *English*
Is financial assistance available for students? *Yes*
Financial assistance is available in the following ways: *Grant-funded salary*
The program is affiliated with: *Gallery(ies)*
Is instruction given in a museum? *Yes*
Do students work in a museum collection as part of the program of study? *Yes*
Do program instructors have museum experience? *Yes*
How many students begin the program each year? *1*
How many students have completed the program since it began? *4*
Are the majority of the beginning students already employed by museums? *Yes*
What percentage of the students completing this program enter or return to museum work? *More than 75%*
Contact person: *Patricia Grattan, Director*
Description of program: *Internship*

This twelve-month **curatorial internship** includes on-the-job training and a course of study on various aspects of gallery operations. The program varies depending on the gallery's exhibition schedule and the intern's area of interest. The training moves the intern through most areas of gallery work but emphasizes curation. A key benefit is the program's flexibility. The program is open to individuals with a degree in fine arts and some art gallery experience.

25

Conservation Program
Queen's University
Art Centre Extension
Kingston, Ontario K7L 3N6
Canada
Telephone: (613) 545 2156
Fax: (613) 545 6889

The program began in: *1974*
Time required to complete program: *2 years*
Level of training provided: *Courses, Internships, Graduate degree, Workshops, Lab work, Seminars*
Areas of study: *Collection management, Exhibit design, Conservation, Field methods, Information technology*
Areas of specialization: *Anthropology, Archives, Ethnology, Fine arts, Material culture, Archeology, Decorative arts, Ethics, Museology, Ethnology, Textiles, Mural painting*
Instructional opportunities provided: *Full-time study, Short-term lectures on request, Scheduled lectures/seminars*
Is museum ethics a regular part of the program?   *Yes*
Is the program open to international students?   *Yes*
The primary language of instruction is: *English*
Is financial assistance available for students?   *Yes*
Financial assistance is available in the following ways: *Scholarships, Loans, Tuition waiver, Student work program, Fellowships and tuition bursaries*
The program is affiliated with: *Museum(s), Gallery(ies), University(ies), Science center(s)*
Is instruction given in a museum?   *No*
Do program instructors have museum experience?   *Yes*
How many students begin the program each year?   *12*
How many students have completed the program since it began?   *180*

Are the majority of the beginning students already employed by
museums?   *Yes*
What percentage of the students completing this program enter or return
to museum work?   *More than 75%*
Contact person: *Ian Hodkinson*
Description of program: *Master's degree*

The **Master of Art Conservation Program** at Queen's University is a
program of theoretical studies and practical work in the restoration and
conservation of historic and artistic works. There are four areas of specialization. These are: 1) Artifacts, which includes archeology, ethnography,
and decorative arts; 2) Paintings, including paintings on canvas, wood,
walls, and other supports; 3) Paper objects, archives, including works of
art on paper and library materials; 4) Scientific research in the conservation of cultural property.

Entrance requirements include: a four-year Honors degree in humanities or sciences with an appropriate spread of courses relevant to the area
of specialization, specified courses in general and organic chemistry, and
demonstrated manual skills. The program is of two years' duration
including four terms on campus at Queen's and two summer internships
in established conservation laboratories in Canada or abroad. Successful
completion of the program leads to the granting of a Master's degree.

26

Honors Degree in Visual Arts
University of Western Ontario
Department of Visual Arts
London, Ontario N6A 5B7
Canada
Telephone: (519) 661 3440, Fax: (519) 661 2020

The program began in: *1972*
Time required to complete program: *More than 2 years*
Level of training provided: *Courses, Internships, Workshops, Bachelor
degree*
Areas of study: *Exhibit design, Curatorship, Education, Information
technology*
Areas of specialization: *Fine arts, Museology*
Instructional opportunities provided: *Full-time study, Scheduled
lectures/seminars*
Is museum ethics a regular part of the program?   *Yes*

Is the program open to international students? *Yes*
The primary language of instruction is: *English*
Is financial assistance available for students? *Yes*
Financial assistance is available in the following ways: *Scholarships,*
Student work program, Loans
The program is affiliated with: *Museum(s), Gallery(ies), University(ies)*
Is instruction given in a museum? *Yes*
Do students work in a museum collection as part of the program of
study? *Yes*
Do program instructors have museum experience? *Yes*
How many students begin the program each year? *20*
How many students have completed the program since it began? *100*
Are the majority of the beginning students already employed by
museums? *No*
What percentage of the students completing this program enter or return
to museum work? *25% to 50%*
Contact person: *A. Mansell, Chair, Department of Visual Arts*
Description of program: *Bachelor's degree*

Bachelor of Fine Arts, and Honors, Art History and Criticism: program requires studio, theory, and history courses that have formal museological components. The focus is on understanding how different museums, galleries, and collections function through a study of theory and development projects such as preparation and analysis of exhibitions documents (catalogs). Students will be able to participate in cooperative projects with experts in the National Gallery of Canada, the Power Plant, the Art Gallery of Ontario, London Regional Art and Historical Museum, and the McIntosh Gallery.

27

Museum Technology Program
Algonquin College
1385 Woodroffe Avenue
Nepean, Ontario K2G 1V8
Canada
Telephone: (613) 727 7612

The program began in: *1972*
Time required to complete program: *More than 2 years*
Level of training provided: *Internships, Diploma*
Areas of study: *Administration, Collection management, Exhibit design,*

Public programming, Curatorship, Education, Conservation, Information technology, Field methods
Areas of specialization: Archives, Ethnology, Material culture, Natural science, Decorative arts, Ethics, History, Museology, Paleontology
Instructional opportunities provided: Full-time study, Correspondence study, Part-time study
Is museum ethics a regular part of the program? Yes
Is the program open to international students? Yes
The primary language of instruction is: English
Is financial assistance available for students? No
The program is affiliated with: Museum(s), Gallery(ies)
Is instruction given in a museum? No
Do program instructors have museum experience? Yes
How many students begin the program each year? 44
How many students have completed the program since it began? 500+
Are the majority of the beginning students already employed by museums? Yes
What percentage of the students completing this program enter or return to museum work? More than 75%
Contact person: J. Patrick Wohler
Description of program: Diploma

Museum Technology Diploma: this three-year program provides students with a sound background in museum work and the technical areas common to all museums. Students study registration, exhibit preparation, conservation, restoration, and regional museum operations. The program has three components: academic studies, workshops, and field placements.

28

Program in Arts and Media Administration
York University
4700 Keele Street
North York, Ontario M3J 1P3
Canada
Telephone: (416) 736 5082, Ext. 77905
Fax: (416) 736 5687
BITNET: AS000076@ORION,YORKU.CA

The program began in: 1970
Time required to complete program: 2 years
Level of training provided: Graduate degree

Areas of study: *Public programming, Information technology, Administration*
Areas of specialization: *Media management, General arts*
Instructional opportunities provided: *Full-time study*
Is museum ethics a regular part of the program? *No*
Is the program open to international students? *Yes*
The primary language of instruction is: *English*
Is financial assistance available for students? *Yes*
Financial assistance is available in the following ways: *Research assistantships*
The program is affiliated with: *University(ies)*
Is instruction given in a museum? *No*
Do program instructors have museum experience? *Yes*
How many students begin the program each year? *12–15*
How many students have completed the program since it began? *125*
Are the majority of the beginning students already employed by museums? *No*
What percentage of the students completing this program enter or return to museum work? *Less than 25%*
Contact person: *Prof. Joseph G. Green, Director*
Description of program: *Graduate degree*

The **Master of Business Administration** is a graduate degree program in business administration with a concentration in arts and media management. It includes intensive theoretical and applied research in the arts and communications media. The program combines practical study with an internship. Open to individuals who meet university entry requirements plus some background and practical experience in the arts.

29

Visual Arts Department
University of Ottawa
100 Laurier East
Ottawa, Ontario K1N 6N5
Canada
Telephone: (613) 564 6588

Time required to complete program: *Two semesters*
Level of training provided: *Courses*
Areas of specialization: *Fine arts, Photography, History of arts*
Instructional opportunities provided: *Full-time study, Part-time study*

Is museum ethics a regular part of the program?   *No*
The primary language of instruction is: *English and French*
The program is affiliated with: *University(ies)*
Is instruction given in a museum?   *No*
Do students work in a museum collection as part of the program of study?   *No*
Contact person: *Diane Daniel, Academic Assistant*
Description of program: *Course*

Introduction to Museology: an analysis of theoretical problems related to functions of museums and art galleries including collections, conservation, and exhibitions. It is an undergraduate credit course offered as an option in the third or fourth year. The duration of the course of study is two semesters. Instruction is offered in English and French.

30

Interpretation Canada
Box 2667, Station D
Ottawa, Ontario K1P 5W7
Canada

The program began in: *1974*
Time required to complete program: *1 to 5 days*
Level of training provided: *Workshops, Certificate*
Areas of study: *Collection management, Exhibit design, Education, Public programming, Information technology, Field methods*
Areas of specialization: *Interpretative technology, Interpretation*
Instructional opportunities provided: *Scheduled lectures/seminars*
Is museum ethics a regular part of the program?   *Yes*
Is the program open to international students?   *Yes*
The primary language of instruction is: *English*
Is financial assistance available for students?   *No*
Is instruction given in a museum?   *Yes*
Do students work in a museum collection as part of the program of study?   *Yes*
Do program instructors have museum experience?   *Yes*
How many students begin the program each year?   *250*
Are the majority of the beginning students already employed by museums?   *Yes*
What percentage of the students completing this program enter or return to museum work?   *More than 75%*

Description of program: *Workshops, Certificate*

A series of **workshops** on topics relating to various aspects of interpretation and interpretative techniques are held as part of the annual meeting. Each year the meeting is hosted by a different region. The regional sections also sponsor workshops throughout the year. Workshops are open to members and non-members.

31

Conservation Training Program
Canadian Conservation Institute
1030 Innes Road
Ottawa, Ontario K1A 0C8
Canada
Telephone: (613) 998 3721, Fax: (613) 998 4721

The program began in: *1977*
Time required to complete program: *Varies*
Level of training provided: *Internships, Workshops*
Areas of study: *Conservation*
Areas of specialization: *Ethnology, Fine arts, Archeology, Art on paper, Furniture, Textiles*
Is museum ethics a regular part of the program? *No*
Is the program open to international students? *Yes*
The primary language of instruction is: *English and French*
Is financial assistance available for students? *No*
The program is affiliated with: *Museum(s), Gallery(ies)*
Is instruction given in a museum? *No*
Do program instructors have museum experience? *Yes*
How many students begin the program each year? *7 Interns and 7 Fellowships*
Are the majority of the beginning students already employed by museums? *No*
Contact person: *Ainsley (Joe) Dorning, Chief Extension Services*
Description of program: *Internships, Workshops*

Seminar Program: a program of basic-level seminars on the care of the museum, archival, and art collections are offered in various regions throughout Canada in collaboration with provincial or territorial museum associations. The seminars are available on request and last from one to three days. They are open to museum workers.

Conservation Education Program: advanced technical conferences, workshops, and symposia on different aspects of conservation are organized on a regular basis or by request. Duration: one to five days.

Internships: in response to the diverse training requirements of the conservation community, an extensive program of internships is offered.
1   Curriculum Internship. For students enrolled in a recognized conservation training program requiring practical experience as part of the course requirement. The duration varies but normally a minimum of three months.
2   Specialized Technique Internships. For conservators, assistant conservators and conservation technicians who have a minimum of three years' relevant prior conservation experience and desire specialized and intensive training in one particular conservation treatment or technique.
3   Professional Development Internship. For graduates of recognized conservation training programs and for conservators, assistant conservators, and conservation technicians with relevant prior conservation experience wishing to gain further practical experience in their area of specialization.
4   Conservation Research Internship. For scientists, conservation scientists and graduates of conservation science training programs desiring practical conservation science research experience within their area of specialization.

Conservation Fellowship Program: CCI fellowships are designed to give further experience to the graduates of a conservation program. Fellowships will encompass work in laboratories at the Canadian Conservation Institute as well as participation in CCI services in museums, art galleries, and related institutions. Fellowships may be offered in archeology, ethnology, works on paper, furniture and wooden objects, fine arts, textiles, and conservation sciences. Preference for fellowships is normally given to Canadian citizens or landed immigrants.

32

National Archives of Canada
395 Wellington Street
Ottawa, Ontario K1A 0N3
Canada
Telephone: (613) 996 1579, Fax: (613) 995 2267

The program began in: *1976*
Time required to complete program: *6 months or less*
Level of training provided: *Workshops, Certificate*
Areas of study: *Administration, Collection management, Curatorship, Public programming, Information technology, Conservation*
Areas of specialization: *Archives*
Instructional opportunities provided: *Scheduled lectures/seminars*
Is museum ethics a regular part of the program? *Yes*
Is the program open to international students? *Yes*
The primary language of instruction is: *English*
Is financial assistance available for students? *No*
Is instruction given in a museum? *Yes*
Do students work in a museum collection as part of the program of study? *Yes*
Do program instructors have museum experience? *Yes*
How many students begin the program each year? *20*
How many students have completed the program since it began? *120*
Are the majority of the beginning students already employed by museums? *Yes*
What percentage of the students completing this program enter or return to museum work? *More than 75%*
Contact person: *Sam Kula, Course Administrator*
Description of program: *Course*

The National Archives of Canada offers **courses in the theory, practice, and general administration of archives.** Instructors are senior archivists and technical specialists on the staff of the National Archives of Canada and from institutions across North America.

Course participants must have worked in an archives for at least one year and have some understanding of archival theory and some familiarity with the basic literature.

The courses will be limited to twenty participants. Candidates should write to the Course Administrator providing details of their education and work experience and a paragraph on why they feel the course will be beneficial.

33

Ontario Association of Art Galleries
489 King Street W., Suite 306
Toronto, Ontario M5V 1K4
Canada
Telephone: (416) 598 0714, Fax: (416) 598 4128

Level of training provided: *Workshops*
Areas of study: *Administration, Collection management, Exhibit design, Public programming, Curatorship, Education, Conservation*
Areas of specialization: *Public art galleries*
Instructional opportunities provided: *Scheduled lectures/seminars*
Is museum ethics a regular part of the program?   *No*
Is the program open to international students?   *Yes*
The primary language of instruction is: *English*
Is financial assistance available for students?   *No*
Is instruction given in a museum?   *No*
Are the majority of the beginning students already employed by museums?   *Yes*
Contact person: *Anne Kolisuyk, Executive Director*
Description of program: *Workshops*

The Ontario Association of Art Galleries (OAAG) was formed as the provincial non-profit organization representing public art galleries in the province of Ontario. Institutional membership includes approximately eighty-four public art galleries, exhibition spaces, and arts-related organizations. Activities include **professional development seminars and workshops.**

34

Museological Training for Community Museums
Ministry of Culture, Tourism and Recreation
77 Bloor Street West
Toronto, Ontario M7A 2R9
Canada
Telephone: (416) 314 7151, Fax: (416) 314 7175

The program began in: *1980*
Time required to complete program: *1/2 to 3 days*
Level of training provided: *Workshops*
Areas of study: *Administration, Collection management, Education, Public programming, Curatorship, Conservation*
Areas of specialization: *Material culture, Museology, Conservation*
Instructional opportunities provided: *Short-term lectures on request*
The primary language of instruction is: *English*
Is financial assistance available for students?   *No*
Is instruction given in a museum?   *Yes*
Do program instructors have museum experience?   *Yes*

Are the majority of the beginning students already employed by
 museums? *Yes*
Contact person: *John C. Carter, Museum Advisor*
Description of program: *Seminars, Workshops*

Seminars and workshops on museum management, conservation, interpretation and education, exhibit design, master planning, audience
development, and public relations are available to client institutions upon
demand.

These sessions are designed to meet specific needs of staff in community
museums, and to assist in upgrading to meet recognized museological
standards. Several of these seminars are run in conjunction with the
Ontario Museum Association and the Ontario Historical Society.
Workshops for regional museum collaboratives are also offered.

Museum Notes, a series of printed reference materials, is available.
Museum advisors and conservators conduct site visits and offer conser-
vation assessments and artifact treatment. Publications are in English and
French.

35

Professional Development Programs
Ontario Museum Association
50 Baldwin Street
Toronto, Ontario M5T 1L4
Canada
Telephone: (416) 348 8672
Fax: (416) 348 8689

The program began in: *1980*
Time required to complete program: *More than 2 years*
Level of training provided: *Courses, Workshops, Certificate*
Areas of study: *Administration, Collection management, Exhibit design,
 Public programming, Education, Conservation, Information technology,
 Curatorship, Architectural preservation*
Areas of specialization: *Material culture, Museology*
Instructional opportunities provided: *Part-time study, Short-term lectures
 on request, Correspondence study, Scheduled lectures/seminars*
Is museum ethics a regular part of the program? *No*
Is the program open to international students? *No*
The primary language of instruction is: *English*
Is financial assistance available for students? *Yes*

Financial assistance is available in the following ways: *Tuition waiver*
The program is affiliated with: *Museum(s)*
Is instruction given in a museum? *Yes*
Do students work in a museum collection as part of the program of study? *Yes*
Do program instructors have museum experience? *Yes*
How many students begin the program each year? *50*
How many students have completed the program since it began? *130*
Are the majority of the beginning students already employed by museums? *Yes*
What percentage of the students completing this program enter or return to museum work? *More than 75%*
Contact person: *Mary Anne Neville, Coordinator*
Description of program: *Courses, Workshops, Certificate*

The Ontario Museum Association is the professional association for museums and museum workers in Ontario. The Association conducts a series of nine basic-level courses comprising every aspect of the museum operation and leading to a **Certificate in Museum Studies**.

Other professional development opportunities are offered in the form of seminars, symposia, and workshops on a comprehensive range of museological topics for workers with varying levels of expertise and experience. A series of seminars is conducted in collaboration with regional museum groups throughout the province. Outreach training is also available through audio-visual materials. An annual conference is held.

36

Museum Studies Program
University of Toronto
Robarts Library, 130 St George Street
Toronto, Ontario M5S 1A1
Canada
Telephone: (416) 978 4211, Fax: (416) 978 8821

The program began in: *1969*
Time required to complete program: *2 years*
Level of training provided: *Courses, Internships, Graduate degree, Workshops*
Areas of study: *Administration, Collection management, Exhibit design, Public programming, Curatorship, Education, Information technology, Conservation, Field methods, Architectural preservation*

Areas of specialization: *Anthropology, Archives, Clothing, Ethnology, Fine arts, Material culture, Natural science, Archeology, Architecture, Decorative arts, Ethics, History, Museology, Paleontology*

Instructional opportunities provided: *Full-time study, Part-time study, Scheduled lectures/seminars*

Is museum ethics a regular part of the program?   *Yes*

Is the program open to international students?   *Yes*

The primary language of instruction is: *English*

Is financial assistance available for students?   *Yes*

Financial assistance is available in the following ways: *Scholarships, Loans, Tuition waiver*

The program is affiliated with: *Museum(s), Gallery(ies), University(ies), Science center(s)*

Do students work in a museum collection as part of the program of study?   *Yes*

Do program instructors have museum experience?   *Yes*

How many students begin the program each year?   *12–14*

How many students have completed the program since it began?   *300*

Are the majority of the beginning students already employed by museums?   *Yes*

What percentage of the students completing this program enter or return to museum work?   *More than 75%*

Contact person: *J. Lynne Teather, Graduate Coordinator*

Description of program: *Master's degree*

The aim of the **University of Toronto Museum Studies Program** is to provide students with both a comprehensive knowledge of the function of museums in the broader social and cultural context and a methodology for research in museology. Thus, the program is both academic and professional: the theoretical body of scholarship in museology and its practical application in the museum environment are examined in a variety of core courses. Moreover, students will have ample opportunity to pursue special interests within this generalist program. Students will further develop their practical skills through individual projects and internships in museums.

Graduates of this program have found employment in virtually every area of museum work, both in Canada and abroad. In addition to curatorial and management positions in community museums, alumni are employed as educators, program coordinators, exhibition organizers, and collections managers in a wide variety of types and sizes of museums and galleries. Still others hold administrative and advisory positions in museum associations and government. Furthermore, the Museum Studies Program constitutes a useful adjunct to advanced graduate studies in many academic disciplines for those who wish to pursue curatorial research positions with larger museums and galleries.

37

Workshop Series
The Ontario Historical Society
5151 Yonge Street
Willowdale, Ontario M2N 5P5
Canada
Telephone: (416) 226 9011
Fax: (416) 226 2740

The program began in: *1980*
Time required to complete program: *Varies*
Level of training provided: *Courses, Workshops*
Areas of study: *Collection management, Exhibit design, Education, Conservation, Public programming, Field methods, Architectural preservation*
Areas of specialization: *Archives, Clothing, Material culture, Architecture, Decorative arts, Ethics, History, Museology, Social history*
Instructional opportunities provided: *Short-term lectures on request, Scheduled lectures/seminars*
Is museum ethics a regular part of the program? *Yes*
Is the program open to international students? *Yes*
The primary language of instruction is: *English and French*
Is financial assistance available for students? *No*
The program is affiliated with: *Museum(s), Gallery(ies)*
Is instruction given in a museum? *Yes*
Do students work in a museum collection as part of the program of study? *Yes*
Do program instructors have museum experience? *Yes*
How many students begin the program each year? *Varies*
Are the majority of the beginning students already employed by museums? *Yes*
Contact person: *Lorraine Lowry, Workshop Coordinator*
Description of program: *Courses, Workshops*

Ontario Historical Society Workshop Series: a series of training workshops are held throughout the year at various locations in the province on historical and museum-related topics. This is a basic workshop/seminar program, offered approximately forty times each year in approximately forty different locations. The registrants range from newcomers to the field to seasoned curators. Attendance ranges from twelve to 112 persons at each program.

In addition, a three day-conference is organized in conjunction with the annual meeting. Workshops are open to members and non-members.

38

DIA/DSA Programs
Concordia University
1455 boul. de Maisonneuve O.
Montreal, Quebec H3G 1M8
Canada
Telephone: (514) 848 2718, Fax: (514) 848 8645

Time required to complete program: *Varies*
Level of training provided: *Internships, Diploma, Graduate degree*
Areas of study: *Administration*
Areas of specialization: *Archives, Fine arts, Ethics*
Instructional opportunities provided: *Full-time study, Part-time study*
Is museum ethics a regular part of the program? *No*
Is the program open to international students? *Yes*
The primary language of instruction is: *English*
Is financial assistance available for students? *Yes*
Financial assistance is available in the following ways: *Loans, Student work program, Tuition waiver*
The program is affiliated with: *Museum(s), University(ies)*
Is instruction given in a museum? *No*
Do program instructors have museum experience? *Yes*
How many students begin the program each year? *10*
How many students have completed the program since it began? *50*
Are the majority of the beginning students already employed by museums? *Yes*
What percentage of the students completing this program enter or return to museum work? *50% to 75%*
Contact person: *Joycelyn Jones or Clarence Bayne*
Description of program: *Diploma*

The **Graduate Diploma in Institutional Administration** (DIA) program provides training in the basic body of administrative and managerial knowledge needed to become an administrator/manager in not-for-profit, cultural, and public sector organizations.

The graduate program is housed in the Faculty of Commerce and Administration drawing from the rich international multicultural background of the professors, many of whom are consultants in the industry. The internship gives students the practical experience to apply classroom concepts in the working environment. A research paper is possible for part-time students.

The minimum entry requirement is an undergraduate degree. Applicants can study on a full-time or part-time basis.

39

Faculté des Lettres
Laval Université
Pavillon Charles-De Koninck
Quebec City, Quebec G1K 7P4
Canada
Telephone: (418) 656 3877, (418) 656 3080

Time required to complete program: *Varies*
Level of training provided: *Graduate degree*
Areas of study: *Administration, Collection management, Exhibit design,*
  Public programming, Curatorship, Conservation
Areas of specialization: *Museology*
Instructional opportunities provided: *Full-time study*
Is museum ethics a regular part of the program? *Yes*
Is the program open to international students? *Yes*
The primary language of instruction is: *French*
The program is affiliated with: *Museum(s), University(ies)*
Contact person: *Secrétariat des 2e et 3e cycles*
Description of program: *Graduate degree*

The program of study awards a **diploma of the second cycle in muse-ology (Master's degree)**. The primary purpose of the program is to prepare specialists in the functions of museums and in conservation and education. The particular techniques and methods of museology have various applications: works of art in conjunction with daily life, as keepers of the ecosystem, and for the many other aspects of shaping society and culture. Also important to museology are conservation and education. The curriculum includes six courses and three practical internships. These courses are the foundation for this graduate program.

The program is offered to those professionals already working in museums or other organizations devoted to interpretation, and those who have obtained a minimum of a diploma at the baccalaureate level in a discipline that includes courses in museography and museology. A good understanding of English is required.

40

Education Programming
Museums Association of Saskatchewan
1808 Smith Street
Regina, Saskatchewan S4P 2N3
Canada
Telephone: (306) 359 9769

Time required to complete program: *1 and 2 days*
Level of training provided: *Workshops, Certificate*
Areas of study: *Administration, Collection management, Exhibit design,*
  Public programming, Education,Conservation, Information technology
Areas of specialization: *Museology*
Instructional opportunities provided: *Scheduled lectures/seminars*
Is museum ethics a regular part of the program?   *No*
Is the program open to international students?   *Yes*
The primary language of instruction is: *English*
Is financial assistance available for students?   *No*
The program is affiliated with: *Museum(s)*
Is instruction given in a museum?   *Yes*
Do students work in a museum collection as part of the program of
  study?   *No*
Do program instructors have museum experience?   *Yes*
How many students begin the program each year?   *20 per seminar*
Are the majority of the beginning students already employed by
  museums?   *Yes*
Contact person: *Patricia Fiori*
Description of program: *Certificate, Workshops, Seminars*

Certificate Program in Museum Studies: a five-course program of study
at the introductory level in governance, collections care and management,
exhibit design, and education.

Skill Development Workshops: this program is designed to improve
museum skills at the basic to intermediate levels. Three topics are chosen
annually based on identified needs.

Special Interest Workshops and Discussion Groups: a wide variety of topics
are offered annually at the intermediate to advanced levels as proposed
by the Special Interest Groups within the Association.

Financial Assistance Program: short-term study grants ($750 maximum)
and the museum studies bursary ($5000) are available to Saskatchewan

residents working in the museum field who wish to attend education programs not offered by the Association.

Seminars are held in different locations around the province and are open to both members and non-members.

Croatia

41

Faculty of Philosophy
University of Zagreb
D. Salaja 3
Zagreb 41000
Croatia
Telephone: (38 0 41) 620 111
Fax: (38 0 41) 513 834

The program began in: *1988*
Time required to complete program: *More than 2 years*
Level of training provided: *Bachelor degree*
Areas of study: *Administration, Collection management, Exhibit design, Public programming, Curatorship, Education, Conservation, Information technology*
Areas of specialization: *Clothing, Ethnology, Archeology, History*
Instructional opportunities provided: *Full-time study*
Is museum ethics a regular part of the program? *Yes*
Is the program open to international students? *Yes*
The primary language of instruction is: *Croatian*
Is financial assistance available for students? *No*
The program is affiliated with: *Museum(s) Gallery(ies)*
Is instruction given in a museum? *Yes*
Do students work in a museum collection as part of the program of study? *No*
Do program instructors have museum experience? *Yes*
How many students begin the program each year? *5*
How many students have completed the program since it began? *4*
Are the majority of the beginning students already employed by museums? *No*

What percentage of the students completing this program enter or return to museum work? *50% to 75%*
Contact person: *Ivo Maroevic, Ph.D.*
Description of program: *Bachelor's degree, Study program*

Basic Study in Informatology/Museology Bachelor's degree: students enrolled in any of the social-humanistic sciences (history, art history, ethnology, archeology, etc.) can also enter the study of informatology. After two years of study, students can choose museology. During the following two years, a comprehensive program of museological study is offered. The program includes: introduction to museology, history of museums and museology, collection management, care of collections, museum institutions and management, exhibition and presentation, communication with museum users, trends, tendencies, and the future of museums.

Supplementary Study of Museology: students enrolled in any course at the University of Zagreb on entering the third year of study, as well as those with a Bachelor's degree, may undertake this program. It is equivalent to the last two years of the Bachelor's degree in Museology.

42

Faculty of Philosophy
University of Zagreb
D. Salaja 3
Zagreb 41000
Croatia
Telephone: (38 0 41) 620 111
Fax: (38 0 41) 513 834

The program began in: *1988*
Time required to complete program: *Varies*
Level of training provided: *Graduate degree*
Areas of study: *Administration, Collection management, Exhibit design, Public programming, Curatorship, Education, Conservation, Information technology*
Areas of specialization: *Anthropology, Ethnology, Fine arts, Natural science, Archeology, Architecture, History, Paleontology*
Instructional opportunities provided: *Full-time study*
Is museum ethics a regular part of the program? *Yes*
Is the program open to international students? *Yes*

The primary language of instruction is: *Croatian*
Is financial assistance available for students?   *No*
The program is affiliated with: *Museum(s), Gallery(ies)*
Is instruction given in a museum?   *Yes*
Do students work in a museum collection as part of the program of study?   *No*
Do program instructors have museum experience?   *Yes*
How many students begin the program each year?   *15*
How many students have completed the program since it began?   *10*
Are the majority of the beginning students already employed by museums?   *No*
What percentage of the students completing this program enter or return to museum work?   *50% to 75%*
Contact person: *Ivo Maroevic, Ph.D.*
Description of program: *Master's degree, Doctor of Philosophy*

Department of Information Sciences Master's degree: individuals with a Bachelor's degree in museological studies or in any appropriate study program may pursue a two-year sequence of postgraduate informatology training. The museological part of the program aims to widen museological knowledge in at least two special museological fields. Written diploma work is required.

Doctor of Philosophy: without a special program, it is possible to obtain a Ph.D. degree in the museological field. A Ph.D. thesis is required. Individuals who possess a Bachelor's and Master's degree in museology can enter this program. Those with other backgrounds must pass a general examination in museology.

Czech Republic

43

International Summer School in Museology
Masaryk University
Zerotínovo námestí 9
Brno 60177
Czech Republic

The program began in: *1986*
Time required to complete program: *1 month*
Level of training provided: *Certificate*
Areas of study: *Administration, Collection management, Exhibit design, Public programming, Curatorship, Education, Conservation, Information technology*
Areas of specialization: *Museology*
Instructional opportunities provided: *Part-time study*
Is museum ethics a regular part of the program? *Yes*
Is the program open to international students? *Yes*
The primary language of instruction is: *English and French*
Is financial assistance available for students? *Yes*
Financial assistance is available in the following ways: *Scholarships, Travel allowance*
The program is affiliated with: *Museum(s), Gallery(ies)*
Is instruction given in a museum? *Yes*
Do students work in a museum collection as part of the program of study? *No*
Do program instructors have museum experience? *Yes*
How many students begin the program each year? *20*
How many students have completed the program since it began? *20*
Are the majority of the beginning students already employed by museums? *Yes*
What percentage of the students completing this program enter or return to museum work? *More than 75%*
Contact person: *Zbynek Z. Stránsky, Director*
Description of program: *Certificate*

The **International Summer School of Museology** (ISSOM) has operated since 1986 on the basis of a resolution of the UNESCO General Conference. UNESCO also supports the School. Each year, the School has a one-month session (usually in July), providing general information on the theoretical basis of museology as a scientific discipline. Instruction is in English and French simultaneously. It is intended for university graduates working in museums or having a perspective in this area. The faculty of ISSOM includes leading figures of international museology. The School closely collaborates with ICOM and especially with ICOFOM. ISSOM graduates get a certificate attesting to their participation in the program.

44

Department of Museology
Masaryk University
Arne Nováka 1
Brno 66088
Czech Republic
Telephone: (42 5) 750050 Ext. 134
Fax: (42 5) 753050

The program began in: *1965*
Time required to complete program: *More than 2 years*
Level of training provided: *Diploma, Graduate degree, Bachelor degree*
Areas of study: *Administration, Collection management, Exhibit design, Public programming, Curatorship, Education, Conservation, Information technology, Architectural preservation*
Areas of specialization: *Museology*
Instructional opportunities provided: *Full-time study, Part-time study*
Is museum ethics a regular part of the program? *Yes*
Is the program open to international students? *Yes*
The primary language of instruction is: *Czech*
Is financial assistance available for students? *Yes*
Financial assistance is available in the following ways: *Scholarships, Travel allowance, Lodging*
The program is affiliated with: *Museum(s), Gallery(ies)*
Is instruction given in a museum? *Yes*
Do students work in a museum collection as part of the program of study? *Yes*
Do program instructors have museum experience? *Yes*
How many students begin the program each year? 25 diplomas and 20 degrees
How many students have completed the program since it began? *18*
Are the majority of the beginning students already employed by museums? *Yes*
What percentage of the students completing this program enter or return to museum work? *More than 75%*
Contact person: *Zbynek Z. Stránsky, Director*
Description of program: *Diploma, Bachelor's degree, Graduate degrees*

Beginning in the school year 1993/4, a **full-time curriculum of museology** in free combination with other disciplines from natural sciences or humanities is available. The B.A. study lasts three years and ends with the state examination I and the degree of Bachelor. The M.A. study requires five years and ends with the final state examination and the Master's degree.

M.A. graduates may apply for a doctoral study program lasting three years concluding with a doctorate examination and the Ph.D. degree.

Post-graduate study. This program of museological study began in 1965. It is intended for university graduates working in museums. It lasts three years and is based on monthly consultations of three days' duration. The program content is discipline-specific – museology. Graduation implies the presentation of a thesis and completion of the state examination in museology.

Dominican Republic

45

Archivo General de la Nación
CENTROMIDCA
Calle Modesto Díaz No. 2
Santo Domingo
Dominican Republic
Telephone: 532 2508 or 532 2509

The program began in: *1976*
Time required to complete program: *6 months or less*
Level of training provided: *Internships, Diploma, Workshops, Certificate*
Areas of study: *Public programming, Curatorship, Conservation*
   Architectural preservation
Areas of specialization: *Archives, Material culture, Natural science*
Instructional opportunities provided: *Full-time study, Part-time study,*
   Scheduled lectures/seminars
Is museum ethics a regular part of the program?   *No*
Is the program open to international students?   *Yes*
The primary language of instruction is: *Spanish*
Is financial assistance available for students?   *No*
Is instruction given in a museum?   *No*
Do students work in a museum collection as part of the program of
   study?   *No*
Do program instructors have museum experience?   *No*
How many students begin the program each year?   *25*

How many students have completed the program since it began? *325*
Are the majority of the beginning students already employed by
  museums? *Yes*
What percentage of the students completing this program enter or return
  to museum work? *Less than 25%*
Contact person: *Lic. Carlos Velez Pacheco*
Description of program: *Internships, Diploma, Workshops, Certificates*

**Centro interamericano de microfilmacion y restauracion de documentos,
libros y fotografias:** classes detailing the history of graphic documents as
well as the characteristics of cultural property serve as an introduction to
restoration and preservation processes. This program is for qualified
personnel from archives and libraries in the Dominican Republic and other
Caribbean countries.

Finland

46

**In-Service Training Program
Finnish Museums Association
Annankatu 16 B 50
Helsinki SF-00120
Finland
Telephone: 90 649 001**

The program began in: *1923*
Time required to complete program: *1, 2, or 3 days*
Level of training provided: *Courses, Workshops, Certificate*
Areas of study: *Administration, Collection management, Exhibit design,
  Public programming, Curatorship, Education, Information technology,
  Conservation, Field methods, Architectural preservation*
Areas of specialization: *Museology*
Instructional opportunities provided: *Scheduled lectures/seminars*
Is museum ethics a regular part of the program? *Yes*
Is the program open to international students? *Yes*
The primary language of instruction is: *Finnish*
Is financial assistance available for students? *No*

The program is affiliated with: *Museum(s), University(ies), Science center(s)*

Is instruction given in a museum? *Yes*

Do students work in a museum collection as part of the program of study? *No*

Do program instructors have museum experience? *Yes*

How many students begin the program each year? *20 to 100 entrants per course*

How many students have completed the program since it began? *600 annually*

Are the majority of the beginning students already employed by museums? *Yes*

Contact person: *Anja-Tuulikki Huovinen*

Description of program: *In-service training*

The purpose of the training activities of the Finnish Museums Association is to supplement and expand the professional knowledge and skills of the individuals working in the museum sector and to provide current information on international developments in the field.

The Association arranges **yearly courses and symposiums** for museum staff, elected officials, and amateurs in the field. Fifteen to eighteen training courses are implemented annually.

France

47

Muséologie Ecole du Louvre
36 quai du Louvre
Paris 75001
France
Telephone: (1) 40 70 00 67
Fax: (1) 47 20 85 53

The program began in: *1985*

Time required to complete program: *1 year*

Level of training provided: *Diploma, Graduate degree*

Areas of study: *Administration, Collection management, Education, Information technology, Public programming, Conservation*

Areas of specialization: *Ethnology, Fine arts, Material culture,*
   Archeology, Decorative arts, Ethics, Museology
Instructional opportunities provided: *Full-time study*
Is museum ethics a regular part of the program?   *Yes*
Is the program open to international students?   *Yes*
The primary language of instruction is: *French*
Is financial assistance available for students?   *Yes*
Financial assistance is available in the following ways: *Scholarships*
The program is affiliated with: *Museum(s), Gallery(ies), University(ies)*
Is instruction given in a museum?   *Yes*
Do students work in a museum collection as part of the program of
   study?   *Yes*
Do program instructors have museum experience?   *Yes*
How many students begin the program each year?   *100–150*
How many students have completed the program since it began?   *1000*
Are the majority of the beginning students already employed by
   museums?   *Yes*
What percentage of the students completing this program enter or return
   to museum work?   *50% to 75%*
Contact person: *Marie-Clarté O'Neill*
Description of program: *Diploma, Master's degree*

The second cycle of the Ecole du Louvre, is called the **"year of museology."**
It is exclusively for the study of available knowledge of the history of art,
ethnology, or archeology. It is composed of six principal modules of instruction organized as required and optional courses. Modules are as follows:
(1) The History of Museums and Patrimony; (2) Initiatives in Research
(instruction in methods); (3) Examination of Works (comprehension of the
restoration of objects); (4) Administration and Development of Museum
and Patrimony; (5) Museography; (6) Patrimony and the Public.
   The diversity of instruction in core courses permits familiarization with
a variety of patrimonial functions and acquaints the students with the
different museological disciplines.

48

Ecole Nationale du Patrimoine
117 Boulevard Saint-Germain
Paris 75006
France
Telephone: (1) 44 41 16 41
Fax: (1) 44 41 16 76

The program began in: *1991*

Time required to complete program: *18 months*

Level of training provided: *Courses, Internships, Workshops*

Areas of study: *Administration, Collection management, Exhibit design, Public programming, Curatorship, Education, Information technology, Conservation, Architectural preservation*

Areas of specialization: *Anthropology, Archives, Ethnology, Fine arts, Archeology, Museology, Law*

Instructional opportunities provided: *Full-time study, Short-term lectures on request, Scheduled lectures/seminars*

Is museum ethics a regular part of the program? *Yes*

Is the program open to international students? *Yes*

The primary language of instruction is: *French*

Is financial assistance available for students? *No*

The program is affiliated with: *Museum(s), University(ies)*

Is instruction given in a museum? *Yes*

Do students work in a museum collection as part of the program of study? *Yes*

Do program instructors have museum experience? *Yes*

How many students begin the program each year? *25–35*

How many students have completed the program since it began? *100*

Are the majority of the beginning students already employed by museums? *Yes*

What percentage of the students completing this program enter or return to museum work? *More than 75%*

Contact person: *Bruno Pons*

Description of program: *Courses, Internships, Workshops*

Created in 1990, the Ecole Nationale du Patrimoine is a school dedicated to the highest standards. It is situated under the supervision of the Minister of Culture and responds to the needs of current and future professionals in the field of cultural heritage.

The responsibility for the conservation of cultural heritage is entrusted to those persons who after receiving an education of the highest standards in history, archeology, and the history of art are faced from the beginning of their careers with the management of cultural heritage (identification, protection, conservation, restoration) and the administration of services.

The Ecole Nationale du Patrimoine provides a **professional foundation in conservation** in six specialties: archeology, archives, libraries, general inventory, museums, and historical monuments.

Germany

49

Deutsches Historisches Museum
Zeughaus, Unter den Linden 2
Berlin 0-1086
Germany
Telephone: (030) 215 02 0

The program began in: *1987*
Time required to complete program: *More than 2 years*
Level of training provided: *Technical training, Courses*
Areas of study: *Conservation*
Areas of specialization: *Material culture, Archeology, History, Book restoration*
Instructional opportunities provided: *Full-time study*
The primary language of instruction is: *German*
The program is affiliated with: *Museum(s)*
Is instruction given in a museum?   *Yes*
Do program instructors have museum experience?   *Yes*
How many students begin the program each year?   *Limited*
Contact person: *Regina Seegardel, Chief of Administration*
Description of program: *Technical training*

Specialized studies in the conservation and restoration of prehistorical cultural assets and those from early history, restoration of archeological excavations, restoration of books and cultural materials are combined with general studies in chemistry, social science, and basic art techniques. Knowledge of a trade or manual skill is essential. A limited number of students are accepted to this four-year program each year.

50

Institute for Fine Arts Technology and Conservation
German National Museum
Postfach 9580
Nuremberg 11-8500
Germany
Telephone: (0911) 20 39 71

Time required to complete program: *More than 2 years*
Level of training provided: *Courses, Internships, Technical training*
Areas of study: *Conservation*
Areas of specialization: *Clothing, Fine arts, Archeology, Textiles, Musical instruments*
Instructional opportunities provided: *Full-time study*
Is the program open to international students?   *Yes*
The primary language of instruction is: *German and English*
The program is affiliated with: *Museum(s)*
Is instruction given in a museum?   *Yes*
Do program instructors have museum experience?   *Yes*
Contact person: *Thomas Brachert*
Description of program: *Technical training*

Restorers-in-Training: applicants must be high school graduates, with a pass mark on the final examination required of all German students finishing high school, and with one of the following requirements: knowledge of a trade, or three years' experience in a field relevant to the program, or completion of a research project of a scientific or artistic nature. Participants study the techniques employed in the restoration of textiles, sculpture, painting, musical instruments, craftwork, archeology, and furniture. Practical exercises are part of the curriculum, as is an internship which is undertaken in a museum or similar organization in Germany or abroad. The program lasts four years.

51

Training Institute for Museum Personnel
Rheinisches Museumsamt
Ehrenfriedstr. 19
Pulheim 2-5024
Germany
Telephone: (02234) 805 300

The program began in: *1981*
Time required to complete program: *3 days*
Level of training provided: *Courses, Workshops*
Areas of study: *Administration, Collection management, Exhibit design, Public programming, Curatorship, Conservation, Information technology*
Areas of specialization: *Ethnology, Fine arts, Material culture, Archeology, Decorative arts, Museology*

Instructional opportunities provided: *Scheduled lectures/seminars*
Is museum ethics a regular part of the program?   *Yes*
Is the program open to international students?   *Yes*
The primary language of instruction is: *German*
Is financial assistance available for students?   *No*
The program is affiliated with: *Museum(s), University(ies), Science center(s)*
Is instruction given in a museum?   *Yes*
Do students work in a museum collection as part of the program of study?   *Yes*
Do program instructors have museum experience?   *Yes*
How many students begin the program each year?   *150*
How many students have completed the program since it began?   *2000*
Are the majority of the beginning students already employed by museums?   *Yes*
What percentage of the students completing this program enter or return to museum work?   *50% to 75%*
Contact person: *Alfons W. Biermann, Ph.D. or Hartmut John, Ph.D.*
Description of program: *Workshops*

These **workshops** are open to museum directors, scientific and technical staff, and conservators. Six or seven programs are offered each year, providing instruction on many museum-related topics. Each workshop lasts three days. The programs are primarily designed for qualified personnel from German museums; however, applicants from other countries will be considered and admitted on a space available basis.

Hungary

52

Academy of Fine Arts Program for Object Conservation
Hungarian National Museum
Training Section, Pf. 124
Budapest, IX
1450 Hungary
Telephone: 138 2122

The program began in: *1974*
Time required to complete program: *More than 2 years*
Level of training provided: *Diploma*
Areas of study: *Information technology, Conservation*
Areas of specialization: *Archives, Clothing, Fine arts, Material culture, Natural science, Archeology, Decorative arts, Ethics, History, Museology*
Instructional opportunities provided: *Part-time study*
Is museum ethics a regular part of the program? *Yes*
Is the program open to international students? *Yes*
The primary language of instruction is: *Hungarian*
Is financial assistance available for students? *No*
The program is affiliated with: *Museum(s), Gallery(ies), University(ies), Science center(s)*
Is instruction given in a museum? *No*
Do program instructors have museum experience? *Yes*
How many students begin the program each year? *14*
How many students have completed the program since it began? *125*
Are the majority of the beginning students already employed by museums? *Yes*
Contact person: *Ágnes Tímár-Balázsy, Ph.D., Head of Training*
Description of program: *Diploma*

Academic Training Program for Object Conservators: this part-time training program by the Hungarian Academy of Fine Arts and the Hungarian National Museum is for conservators already employed in collections. The training takes five academic years. First study year: conservation of siliceous objects. Second study year: conservation of metal objects. Third study year: conservation of organic objects (wood, paper, textile, and leather). Fourth and fifth study years allow specialization in one of five areas: (1) restoration of siliceous objects; (2) restoration of metal-goldsmiths objects; (3) restoration of wooden objects and furniture; (4) restoration of textile and related leather objects; or (5) restoration of paper and related leather objects. The study ends with restoration of an object and documentation as diploma work.

53

Hungarian National Museum
Training Section, Pf. 124
Budapest, IX
1450 Hungary
Telephone: 138 2122

The program began in: *1963*
Time required to complete program: *1 year*
Level of training provided: *Certificate*
Areas of study: *Information technology, Conservation*
Areas of specialization: *Material culture, Natural science, Ethics,*
  Museology
Instructional opportunities provided: *Part-time study*
Is museum ethics a regular part of the program? *Yes*
Is the program open to international students? *Yes*
The primary language of instruction is: *Hungarian*
Is financial assistance available for students? *No*
The program is affiliated with: *Museum(s)*
Is instruction given in a museum? *No*
Do program instructors have museum experience? *Yes*
How many students begin the program each year? *14*
How many students have completed the program since it began? *586*
Are the majority of the beginning students already employed by
  museums? *Yes*
Contact person: *Gábor Séd*
Description of program: *Certificate*

Basic course in Conservation: a part-time training program for conservators employed in a collection. A basic training in active conservation of ceramic and metal objects, especially in an archeological context. Training in preventive conservation of organic museum objects. The study ends with a project including documentation and an examination. The certificate is provided by the Hungarian Ministry of Culture.

54

Hungarian National Museum
Training Section, Pf. 124
Budapest, IX
1450 Hungary
Telephone: 138 2122

The program began in: *1992*
Time required to complete program: *1 year*
Level of training provided: *Certificate*
Areas of study: *Information technology, Conservation*
Areas of specialization: *Clothing, Material culture, Natural science,*
  Archeology, Decorative arts, Ethics, History, Museology

Instructional opportunities provided: *Part-time study*
Is museum ethics a regular part of the program? *Yes*
Is the program open to international students? *Yes*
The primary language of instruction is: *Hungarian*
Is financial assistance available for students? *No*
The program is affiliated with: *Museum(s), University(ies), Science center(s)*
Is instruction given in a museum? *No*
Do program instructors have museum experience? *Yes*
How many students begin the program each year? *36*
How many students have completed the program since it began? *New program*
Are the majority of the beginning students already employed by museums? *Yes*
Contact person: *Ágnes Tímár-Balázsy, Ph.D., Head of Training*
Description of program: *Certificate*

High-level courses in Conservation: part-time training program for conservators already employed in a collection. Prerequisite for admission is a certificate from the basic course in conservation. Six different high level courses on conservation and restoration are offered: (1) metal objects; (2) siliceous objects; (3) wooden objects; (4) textile objects; (5) paper objects; (6) leather objects. The training takes one year and ends with a project that includes documentation and an examination. The certificate is provided by the Hungarian Ministry of Culture.

India

55

Faculty of Fine Arts
Maharaja Sayajirao University of Baroda
Department of Museology
Baroda, Gujarat 390002
India
Telephone: 64510

The program began in: *1952*

Time required to complete program: *Varies*
Level of training provided: *Diploma, Graduate degree, Certificate*
Areas of study: *Administration, Collection management, Exhibit design, Public programming, Curatorship, Education, Conservation*
Areas of specialization: *Museology*
Instructional opportunities provided: *Full-time study*
Is museum ethics a regular part of the program?   *Yes*
Is the program open to international students?   *Yes*
The primary language of instruction is: *English*
Is financial assistance available for students?   *No*
The program is affiliated with: *Museum(s), University(ies)*
Is instruction given in a museum?   *Yes*
Do students work in a museum collection as part of the program of study?   *Yes*
Do program instructors have museum experience?   *Yes*
How many students begin the program each year?   *12*
How many students have completed the program since it began?   *189*
Are the majority of the beginning students already employed by museums?   *Yes*
What percentage of the students completing this program enter or return to museum work?   *More than 75%*
Contact person: *R. P. Shah, Head*
Description of program: *Graduate degree, Postgraduate diploma, Certificate*

Course of instruction designed to give extensive **training in museology**. Museology and museography classes are conducted in the Department of Museology. Practical training is conducted in the Museum and Picture Gallery in Baroda. Students are given six weeks practical experience in museums outside Baroda every year.

56

Center of Advanced Studies in Indology and Museology
Prachya Niketan
Birla Museum, PO Satpura
Bhopal, Madhya Pradesh 462 004
India
Telephone: 551 388

The program began in: *1971–2*
Time required to complete program: *1 year*

Level of training provided: *Diploma*

Areas of study: *Administration, Exhibit design, Curatorship, Education, Conservation, Field methods, Architectural preservation*

Areas of specialization: *Clothing, Material culture, Archeology, Architecture, History, Museology*

Instructional opportunities provided: *Full-time study, Short-term lectures on request, Scheduled lectures/seminars*

Is museum ethics a regular part of the program? *Yes*

Is the program open to international students? *Yes*

The primary language of instruction is: *English and Hindi*

Is financial assistance available for students? *No*

The program is affiliated with: *Museum(s)*

Is instruction given in a museum? *Yes*

Do students work in a museum collection as part of the program of study? *Yes*

Do program instructors have museum experience? *Yes*

How many students begin the program each year? *10*

How many students have completed the program since it began? *140*

Are the majority of the beginning students already employed by museums? *Yes*

What percentage of the students completing this program enter or return to museum work? *More than 75%*

Contact person: *Manjushri Rao, Ph.D.*

Description of program: *Diploma*

Postgraduate Diploma in Museology: students are given training in maintenance and conservation of art objects and monuments. Computerized documentation of antiquities is another feature of the program. Students visit ancient sites in the vicinity of Bhopal for an expanded and comparative knowledge of Indian art, iconography, and architecture. Students study various aspects of museology in New and Old Delhi where exhibit methods and collections are the most comprehensive. Birla Museum functions as an attached laboratory for students to study art iconography, architecture, numismatics, and epigraphy. Seminars on Indological, museological, and archeological subjects are held yearly at Prachya Niketan at both the national and international levels.

57

Conservation of Cultural Property
National Research Laboratory
E/3, Aliganj Scheme
Lucknow, U.P. 226020
India

The program began in: *1978*
Time required to complete program: *6 months or less*
Level of training provided: *Certificate*
Areas of study: *Conservation*
Areas of specialization: *Archives, Clothing, Archeology, Museology,*
   Conservation of art objects
Instructional opportunities provided: *Full-time study*
Is museum ethics a regular part of the program?   *Yes*
Is the program open to international students?   *Yes*
The primary language of instruction is: *English*
Is financial assistance available for students?   *Yes*
Financial assistance is available in the following ways: *Scholarships,*
   Materials/supplies, Tuition waiver
The program is affiliated with: *Museum(s)*
Is instruction given in a museum?   *Yes*
Do students work in a museum collection as part of the program of
   study?   *Yes*
Do program instructors have museum experience?   *Yes*
How many students begin the program each year?   *10*
How many students have completed the program since it began?   *104*
Are the majority of the beginning students already employed by
   museums?   *Yes*
What percentage of the students completing this program enter or return
   to museum work?   *More than 75%*
Contact person: *M. V. Nair, Ph.D., Director*
Description of program: *Training courses*

Conservation specialization: after a group study of basic subjects, participants are assigned, according to individual and academic qualifications, to specific departments within the laboratory. Instruction emphasizing conservation techniques is offered as well as training of a more scientific nature for students with science degrees. The opportunity to study at other advanced technical institutions in India is also available. Field trips to excavation sites, monuments, and museums are a part of the educational process. The program is of six months' duration. Applicants must be residents of South or Southeast Asia. A graduate degree is also required. Ten participants are chosen for the course that begins in September of each year. Applicants employed in the field of conservation will be given preference.

58

Conservation of Cultural Property
National Research Laboratory
E/3, Aliganj Scheme
Lucknow, U.P. 226020
India

The program began in: *1980*
Time required to complete program: *10 days*
Level of training provided: *Certificate*
Areas of study: *Conservation*
Areas of specialization: *Care and maintenance of objects*
Instructional opportunities provided: *Full-time study*
Is museum ethics a regular part of the program?   *Yes*
Is the program open to international students?   *Yes*
The primary language of instruction is: *English*
Is financial assistance available for students?   *Yes*
Financial assistance is available in the following ways: *Lodging, Tuition waiver*
The program is affiliated with: *Museum(s)*
Is instruction given in a museum?   *No*
Do program instructors have museum experience?   *Yes*
How many students begin the program each year?   *15*
How many students have completed the program since it began?   *162*
Are the majority of the beginning students already employed by museums?   *Yes*
What percentage of the students completing this program enter or return to museum work?   *More than 75%*
Contact person: *M.V. Nair, Ph.D., Director*
Description of program: *Certificate*

The **Orientation workshop** has been designed for museum directors, curators, and others who administer art collections. Preventive care is emphasized during the ten-day program: lighting and climate control techniques are examined and packing and transportation methods are discussed. Fifteen participants are selected.

Italy

59

Training Courses in Conservation/Restoration
ICCROM
Via di San Michele 13
Rome 00153
Italy
Telephone: (6) 589 2622

The program began in: *1966*
Time required to complete program: *6 months or less*
Level of training provided: *Workshops, Certificate*
Areas of study: *Collection management, Education, Conservation, Field methods, Information technology, Architectural preservation*
Areas of specialization: *Ethnology, Fine arts, Material culture, Architecture, Ethics, Paper conservation, Preventive conservation*
Instructional opportunities provided: *Full-time study*
Is museum ethics a regular part of the program? *Yes*
Is the program open to international students? *Yes*
The primary language of instruction is: *English and French*
Is financial assistance available for students? *Yes*
Financial assistance is available in the following ways: *Scholarships*
The program is affiliated with: *Museum(s), University(ies)*
Is instruction given in a museum? *Yes*
Do students work in a museum collection as part of the program of study? *Yes*
Do program instructors have museum experience? *Yes*
How many students begin the program each year? *75*
How many students have completed the program since it began? *1800*
Contact person: *Cynthia Rockwell, Training Secretary*
Description of program: *Courses*

The International Center for the Study of the Preservation and the Restoration of Cultural Property offers **training courses in conservation/restoration** open to architects, urban planners, archeologists, art and architectural historians, engineers, librarians, and museum conservators, curators, and administrators. Programs in architectural conservation, the conservation of mural paintings, and the scientific principles of conservation last for four to five months. For all courses, preference is given to those who have at least four years of provisional experience in the field and are actively participating in the preservation and conservation programs of their country. Instruction is provided in both English and French. Conversational ability in Italian is recommended. Scholarships are available from several sources.

ICCROM publishes a complete listing of conservation training programs throughout the world.

New Zealand

60

Museum Studies Program
Massey University
Private Bag Palmerston North
New Zealand

The program began in: *1989*
Time required to complete program: *Varies*
Level of training provided: *Diploma, Graduate degree*
Areas of study: *Administration, Collection management, Exhibit design, Public programming, Curatorship, Education, Conservation*
Areas of specialization: *Ethics, Museology, Museums and indigenous peoples*
Instructional opportunities provided: *Full-time study, Correspondence study, Part-time study*
Is museum ethics a regular part of the program? *Yes*
Is the program open to international students? *Yes*
The primary language of instruction is: *English*
Is financial assistance available for students? *Yes*
Financial assistance is available in the following ways: *Scholarships, Loans, Assistance for New Zealand students only*
The program is affiliated with: *Museum(s), Gallery(ies), University(ies)*
Is instruction given in a museum? *Yes*
Do students work in a museum collection as part of the program of study? *Yes*
Do program instructors have museum experience? *Yes*
How many students begin the program each year? *25 part-time and 5 full-time*

How many students have completed the program since it began? *20*
Are the majority of the beginning students already employed by
museums? *Yes*
What percentage of the students completing this program enter or return
to museum work? *50% to 75%*
Contact person: *David J. Butts*
Description of program: *Diploma, Master's degree*

Postgraduate Diploma in Museum Studies requires one year of study.
Master's degree in Museum Studies requires two years of study.

Nigeria

61

Museum Studies Program
Centre for Museum Studies – Jos
P.M.B. 2031
Jos
Nigeria
Telephone: (073) 535 16

The program began in: *1963*
Time required to complete program: *1 year*
Level of training provided: *Internships, Certificate*
Areas of study: *Administration, Collection management, Exhibit design,
Public programming, Curatorship, Education, Conservation, Information
technology, Field methods, Architectural preservation*
Areas of specialization: *Anthropology, Ethnology, Material culture,
Natural science, Archeology, Architecture, History, Museology*
Instructional opportunities provided: *Full-time study, Short-term lectures
on request, Scheduled lectures/seminars*
Is museum ethics a regular part of the program? *Yes*
Is the program open to international students? *Yes*
The primary language of instruction is: *English*
Is financial assistance available for students? *Yes*
Financial assistance is available in the following ways: *Scholarships*
The program is affiliated with: *Museum(s)*

Is instruction given in a museum? *Yes*
Do students work in a museum collection as part of the program of study? *Yes*
Do program instructors have museum experience? *Yes*
How many students begin the program each year? *15*
How many students have completed the program since it began? *360*
Are the majority of the beginning students already employed by museums? *Yes*
What percentage of the students completing this program enter or return to museum work? *More than 75%*
Contact person: *Jide Famuyiwa, Principal*
Description of program: *Certificate*

Training offered covers museum technicians and middle-level museum staff. In certain cases courses are designed to meet the training needs of graduate curators.

Courses offered include conservation, documentation, exhibition and display techniques, photography, preservation of architecture and historic buildings, natural heritage, museology, museum education, museum administration, library science, introduction to archeology, and African history. There is also a one-month attachment to a museum. The duration of the program is ten months.

62

Department of Creative Arts
University of Maiduguri
P.M.B. 1069
Maiduguri, Borno State
Nigeria

The program began in: *1983*
Time required to complete program: *More than 2 years*
Level of training provided: *Courses, Bachelor degree*
Areas of study: *Collection management, Exhibit design, Conservation*
Areas of specialization: *Museology, Museography*
Instructional opportunities provided: *Full-time study*
Is museum ethics a regular part of the program? *No*
Is the program open to international students? *Yes*
The primary language of instruction is: *English*
Is financial assistance available for students? *No*
The program is affiliated with: *University(ies)*

Is instruction given in a museum?   *No*
Do program instructors have museum experience?   *Yes*
How many students begin the program each year?   *Varies*
How many students have completed the program since it began?   *10*
Are the majority of the beginning students already employed by
   museums?   *No*
What percentage of the students completing this program enter or return
   to museum work?   *Less than 25%*
Contact person: *W. Seidensticker, Head of Department*
Description of program: *Undergraduate degree*

The Department of Creative Arts offers a **Bachelor's degree with an optional specialization in art history and museology.** Included is a study of the history and classification of museums, primarily African, with specific reference to museums in Nigeria. Classes in museum techniques provide students with an understanding of the tasks involved in managing collections. Basic conservation and exhibition methods are also explored.

63

Field Archaeology
School of Field Archaeology
P.M.B. 2031
Jos, Plateau State
Nigeria

The program began in: *1990*
Time required to complete program: *1 year*
Level of training provided: *Diploma*
Areas of study: *Administration, Conservation, Field methods*
Areas of specialization: *Archeology*
Instructional opportunities provided: *Full-time study*
Is museum ethics a regular part of the program?   *No*
Is the program open to international students?   *Yes*
The primary language of instruction is: *English*
Is financial assistance available for students?   *No*
The program is affiliated with: *Museum(s), University(ies)*
Is instruction given in a museum?   *Yes*
Do students work in a museum collection as part of the program of
   study?   *Yes*
Do program instructors have museum experience?   *Yes*
How many students begin the program each year?   *5*

How many students have completed the program since it began?   *8*
Are the majority of the beginning students already employed by
   museums?   *Yes*
What percentage of the students completing this program enter or return
   to museum work?   *More than 75%*
Contact person: *Yashim Isa Bitiyong, Principal*
Description of program: *Diploma*

Postgraduate diploma in field archeology: the program of study is designed
to provide advanced training in professional field techniques; to prepare
participants to qualify for recognition by law as professional archeologists
who can be granted excavation permits to conduct archeological research;
and to supplement undergraduate technical training for graduates
intending to become professional archeologists.

The twelve-month program includes instructional components in the
following areas: research design, environmental studies, reconnaissance,
surveying, excavation, conservation, technology of artifacts, audio-visuals,
drafting, reporting, exhibitions, general administration, and French. The
method of instruction includes lectures, seminar/tutorials, survey/exca-
vation, and excursion sessions of twenty hours per week. Individual
performance in field work and written assignments is assessed on a continuous basis.

People's Republic of China

64

Institute for Museology
Fudan University
Shanghai
P. R. China

The program began in: *1986*
Time required to complete program: *Varies*
Level of training provided: *Internships, Diploma, Graduate degree,
   Bachelor degree*
Areas of study: *Administration, Collection management, Exhibit design,
   Curatorship, Education, Conservation, Field methods*

Areas of specialization: *Anthropology, Archives, Ethnology, Fine arts, Material culture, Natural science, Archeology, Decorative arts, Ethics, History, Museology*

Instructional opportunities provided: *Full-time study, Short-term lectures on request, Part-time study, Scheduled lectures/seminars*

Is museum ethics a regular part of the program? *Yes*

Is the program open to international students? *Yes*

The primary language of instruction is: *Chinese and English*

Is financial assistance available for students? *Yes*

Financial assistance is available in the following ways: *Scholarships, Tuition waiver, For Chinese students only*

The program is affiliated with: *Museum(s), Gallery(ies), University(ies), Science center(s)*

Is instruction given in a museum? *Yes*

Do students work in a museum collection as part of the program of study? *Yes*

Do program instructors have museum experience? *Yes*

How many students begin the program each year? *30*

Are the majority of the beginning students already employed by museums? *Yes*

What percentage of the students completing this program enter or return to museum work? *More than 75%*

Contact person: *Professor Zhuang, Xi-Chang*

Description of program: *Bachelor's degree, Master's degree*

The programs of the Institute for Museology are co-sponsored by the Shanghai Museum, Shanghai, PRC. The **conservation/restoration program** is given in its laboratories. It was established as a regional center for museology. The **degree programs** (B.A. and M.A.) are accredited by the State Administrative Bureau for Museum and Archeology Data, Beijing.

In addition to full-time students, the institute annually receives a number of museum personnel for in-service training.

International students may contact: Dr. Alfonz Lengyel, Fudan Museum Foundation, 1522 Schoolhouse Road, Ambler, Pennsylvania 19002, telephone: (215) 699 6448

65

Museum Studies Program, History Department
Nankai University
94 Weijin Road
Tianjin City 300071
P. R. China
Telephone: 33 1640 5 581

The program began in: *1980*
Time required to complete program: *More than 2 years*
Level of training provided: *Internships, Diploma, Graduate degree, Workshops, Certificate, Bachelor degree*
Areas of study: *Administration, Collection management, Exhibit design, Curatorship, Education, Conservation, Field methods, Architectural preservation*
Areas of specialization: *Anthropology, Material culture, Archeology, Architecture, History, Museology, Western museum history and theory*
Instructional opportunities provided: *Full-time study, Short-term lectures on request, Scheduled lectures/seminars*
Is museum ethics a regular part of the program? *Yes*
Is the program open to international students? *Yes*
The primary language of instruction is: *Chinese*
Is financial assistance available for students? *Yes*
The program is affiliated with: *Museum(s), Gallery(ies), University(ies)*
Is instruction given in a museum? *Yes*
Do students work in a museum collection as part of the program of study? *Yes*
Do program instructors have museum experience? *Yes*
How many students begin the program each year? *15–20*
How many students have completed the program since it began? *277*
Are the majority of the beginning students already employed by museums? *Yes*
What percentage of the students completing this program enter or return to museum work? *More than 75%*
Contact person: *Prof. Fumei, Director, and Jia Jianming, Lecturer*
Description of program: *Bachelor's degree, Master's degree*

Bachelor's degree in Museology: this four-year undergraduate program consists of courses in museology, history of material culture, basic curatorship and archeology. Students also enroll in Chinese antiquities studies, a course that involves the examination of objects made of bronze, ceramics, and jade. An examination and thesis are required before the degree is conferred.

Master's degree in Museology: the three-year graduate program incorporates the study of museology with courses in art history, cultural anthropology, comparative studies of eastern and western cultures, ethnology, and numismatics. All students must pass a written examination and submit a thesis on an approved topic.

A comprehensive program of vocational training and research is provided by the Museum Studies Program, History Department of Nankai University. Founded in 1980, the program is the first of its kind in China. The Program has considerable flexibility. It provides systematic courses on both museology and the special areas of bronzes, pottery, and porcelain, jades, stone carving, traditional painting, and paleography. It offers opportunities for those wishing to enter the museum profession and those already in museum posts wishing to qualify and undertake post-experience work. Those wishing to pursue advanced study leading to a higher degree may undertake study on a full-time basis.

Poland

66

Institute for Preservation and Conservation of Works of Art
Nicholas Copernicus University
Sienkiewicza 30/32
Torun PL-87-100
Poland
Telephone: (056) 249 77

The program began in: *1969*
Time required to complete program: *More than 2 years*
Level of training provided: *Graduate degree*
Areas of study: *Collection management, Exhibit design, Curatorship,
   Conservation, Information technology*
Areas of specialization: *Archives, Fine arts, Archeology, Decorative arts,
   History, Museology, Documentary drawing and photo*
Instructional opportunities provided: *Full-time study*
Is museum ethics a regular part of the program?   *No*
Is the program open to international students?   *Yes*

The primary language of instruction is: *Polish*
Is financial assistance available for students? *Yes*
Financial assistance is available in the following ways: *Social stipends for Polish students only*
The program is affiliated with: *Museum(s), Gallery(ies)*
Is instruction given in a museum? *No*
Do program instructors have museum experience? *Yes*
How many students begin the program each year? *10–15*
How many students have completed the program since it began? *170*
Are the majority of the beginning students already employed by museums? *No*
What percentage of the students completing this program enter or return to museum work? *25% to 50%*
Contact person: *Zygmunt Wazbinski, Director*
Description of program: *Master's degree*

The **Master's degree program** is unique among those offered by Polish universities in that it deals with museum-related problems at the university level. Primarily devoted to art collecting and art museums, the course of instruction can be described as art history complemented by museology. Contrary to conventional art history programs, the program offers more contact with objects, both fine and decorative arts. This connoisseurship approach is enhanced by museum apprenticeships, documentary drawing, and technology of photography, archival introduction, exhibition design study, and museum information training.

South Africa

67

Department of Museology
University of Stellenbosch
Private Bag
Stellenbosch 7600
Republic of South Africa
Telephone: (02231) 772390

The program began in: *1976*

Time required to complete program: *1 year*
Level of training provided: *Diploma*
Areas of study: *Administration, Collection management, Exhibit design, Public programming, Curatorship, Education, Conservation, Information technology, Field methods, Architectural preservation*
Areas of specialization: *Material culture, Archeology, Decorative arts, Museology, Cultural history*
Instructional opportunities provided: *Full-time study*
Is museum ethics a regular part of the program?   *Yes*
Is the program open to international students?   *Yes*
The primary language of instruction is: *English and Afrikaans*
Is financial assistance available for students?   *No*
The program is affiliated with: *Museum(s), University(ies)*
Is instruction given in a museum?   *Yes*
Do students work in a museum collection as part of the program of study?   *Yes*
Do program instructors have museum experience?   *Yes*
How many students begin the program each year?   *5*
How many students have completed the program since it began?   *90*
Are the majority of the beginning students already employed by museums?   *No*
What percentage of the students completing this program enter or return to museum work?   *More than 75%*
Contact person: *H. van der Merioe*
Description of program: *Diploma program*

Postgraduate Diploma in Museology: applicants must have a Bachelor's degree from a recognized university with a major in a museum-related discipline such as archeology, anthropology, fine arts, history, or cultural history. This year-long program includes lectures and seminars on museum purpose and development, research and documentation, and educational services. Students are expected to work two days a week in a museum environment for the duration of the course. Lectures are conducted in Afrikaans and English. The lecturers are bilingual. Written work and examinations may be done in the language of the student's choice.

Sweden

68

Institute of Conservation
Göteborg University
Bastionsplatsen 2
Göteborg S-41108
Sweden
Telephone: (31) 773 4700
Fax: (31) 773 4703

The program began in: *1985*
Time required to complete program: *More than 2 years*
Level of training provided: *Internships, Graduate degree, Workshops, Bachelor degree*
Areas of study: *Collection management, Curatorship, Conservation, Field methods, Information technology*
Areas of specialization: *Archives, Clothing, Ethnology, Fine arts, Material culture, Natural science, Archeology, Architecture, Decorative arts, Ethics, History, Museology, Paleontology, Theory of conservation*
Instructional opportunities provided: *Full-time study*
Is museum ethics a regular part of the program? *Yes*
Is the program open to international students? *Yes*
The primary language of instruction is: *Swedish*
Is financial assistance available for students? *Yes*
Financial assistance is available in the following ways: *Loans, Swedish study loans, Materials/supplies*
The program is affiliated with: *Museum(s), University(ies), Science center(s)*
Is instruction given in a museum? *No*
Do program instructors have museum experience? *Yes*
How many students begin the program each year? *15*
How many students have completed the program since it began? *60*
Are the majority of the beginning students already employed by museums? *No*
What percentage of the students completing this program enter or return to museum work? *More than 75%*
Contact person: *Jan Rosvall or Lars Eric Olsson*
Description of program: *Graduate degree, Undergraduate degree, Courses*

Ph.D. Program/Degree in Conservation: the program accepts applicants with a full degree in conservation, integrated conservation or museum studies/museology. The program is four years including a Ph.D. thesis and courses. Program of study includes required courses as well as electives.

Master of Arts in Museology Program (M.A.): the program provides preparation for a career as curator or other relevant cultural position in management. Focus on both theoretical and methodological study of museology. The program consists of two semesters. A Bachelor's degree is a prerequisite. Students can specialize in their fields of interest. The program is concluded with a thesis. Five to ten students begin the program each year.

Conservation Program/Degree (B.A.): a degree program of three years leading to competence as a scientifically educated conservator/restorer. The first year is mainly theoretical, based on courses in documentation, ethics, principles of conservation, chemistry, and humanities. The specialization begins after the second year when students choose between conservation in painting, textiles, paper, stone, wood, metal, archeological material, or natural history. Fifteen students begin the program each year. The program is concluded with a diploma project and scientific thesis.

Integrated Conservation of Built Environments Program/Degree (B.A.): the three-year program leads to competence in conservation and preservation of historic buildings and constructed environments principally as a planner with a humanistic and historical approach. The students study all aspects of the constructed environments from theoretical approach to practical exercises in restoration. Twenty-five students enter the program each year. A large field work project is included and the program concludes with a diploma project and scientific thesis.

Preventive Conservation Course. A theoretical course of factors of importance when handling, storing, keeping, and conserving works of art, antiquities, and other kinds of cultural resources. Twenty students are admitted each year.

69

The Swedish Traveling Exhibitions
Riksutstallninger
PO Box 4715
Stockholm S-116 92
Sweden
Telephone: (8) 644 9720

The program began in: *1986*
Time required to complete program: *Varies*
Level of training provided: *Courses, Workshops*
Areas of study: *Exhibit design, Education, Field methods, Information technology*
Areas of specialization: *Production and use of exhibitions*
Instructional opportunities provided: *Part-time study, Short-term lectures on request, Scheduled lectures/seminars*
Is museum ethics a regular part of the program? *No*
Is the program open to international students? *Yes*
Is financial assistance available for students? *No*
The program is affiliated with: *Museum(s), University(ies)*
Is instruction given in a museum? *No*
Do program instructors have museum experience? *Yes*
How many students begin the program each year? *Varies*
Are the majority of the beginning students already employed by museums? *Yes*
What percentage of the students completing this program enter or return to museum work? *50% to 75%*
Contact person: *Bengt Skoog*
Description of program: *Courses, Workshops*

The Swedish Traveling Exhibitions, Riksutstallninger, a state-operated foundation, organizes exhibitions in collaboration with schools, societies, museums, municipal committees, and special interest groups.

Workshops and seminars dealing with such topics as exhibitions techniques, cultural policy, museology, and museum education are conducted throughout the year. All interested persons may apply.

70

Royal Collections
Kungliga Husgerådskammaren
Kungliga Slottet/The Royal Palace
Stockholm S-111 30
Sweden
Telephone: (8) 789 85 00, Fax: (8) 789 86 29

Time required to complete program: *Varies*
Level of training provided: *Courses, Internships, Individual training*
Areas of study: *Collection management, Conservation*
Areas of specialization: *Clothing, Material culture, Decorative arts, History, Furniture*

The primary language of instruction is: *Swedish*
Is financial assistance available for students? *No*
The program is affiliated with: *University(ies)*
Is instruction given in a museum? *Yes*
Do students work in a museum collection as part of the program of study? *Yes*
Do program instructors have museum experience? *Yes*
How many students begin the program each year? *Varies*
Contact person: *Anki Dahlin, Curator*
Description of program: *Courses, Internships*

Kungliga Husgerådskammaren/The Royal Collections is responsible for the administration and preservation of furniture, textiles, silver, and objects of applied art in the ten royal palaces and pavilions in Sweden. Each year one or more students are given the opportunity to gain **practical experience at the Royal Collections.** An individual program is designed for each student. The training area differs depending on the student and his or her education. The period of time also varies. Trainees in the field of conservation usually do their compulsory practice in more than one museum/workshop. Financial assistant is not provided.

Short theoretical courses are arranged for students in conjunction with Swedish universities.

71

Cultural Studies
Umeå University
Department of Museology
Umeå S-901 87
Sweden
Telephone: (090) 165000

The program began in: *1981*
Time required to complete program: *More than 2 years*
Level of training provided: *Workshops, Bachelor degree*
Areas of study: *Collection management, Exhibit design, Curatorship, Education, Public programming, Conservation, Architectural preservation*
Areas of specialization: *Ethnology, Archeology, Architecture, History, History of art, History of ideas*
Instructional opportunities provided: *Full-time study*

Is museum ethics a regular part of the program?   *Yes*
Is the program open to international students?   *No*
The primary language of instruction is: *Swedish*
Is financial assistance available for students?   *No*
The program is affiliated with: *University(ies)*
Is instruction given in a museum?   *Yes*
Do students work in a museum collection as part of the program of
   study?   *Yes*
Do program instructors have museum experience?   *Yes*
How many students begin the program each year?   *25*
How many students have completed the program since it began?   *250*
Are the majority of the beginning students already employed by
   museums?   *Yes*
What percentage of the students completing this program enter or return
   to museum work?   *50% to 75%*
Contact person: *Per-Uno Ågren*
Description of program: *Undergraduate degree*

A 3½-year program joins one year of museum-related courses with a major
area of two years of concentrated study of subjects selected among art
history, ethnology, history, archeology, and history of ideas. The introductory term on museology covers historical theory, human ecology, the
history and function of museums. The second term covers museography
and offers a five-week internship. The program is open to students from
the Scandinavian countries.

Switzerland

72

Institut d'ethnologie
Université de Neuchâtel
Rue Saint-Nicolas 4
Neuchâtel CH-2006
Switzerland
Telephone: (038) 24 41 20

The program began in: *1947*

Time required to complete program: *1 year*
Level of training provided: *Graduate degree*
Areas of study: *Collection management, Exhibit design, Education, Field methods*
Areas of specialization: *Ethnology, Fine arts, Material culture, Ethics, Museology*
Instructional opportunities provided: *Part-time study, Scheduled lectures/seminars*
Is museum ethics a regular part of the program? *Yes*
Is the program open to international students? *Yes*
The primary language of instruction is: *French*
Is financial assistance available for students? *No*
The program is affiliated with: *Museum(s), University(ies)*
Is instruction given in a museum? *Yes*
Do students work in a museum collection as part of the program of study? *Yes*
Do program instructors have museum experience? *Yes*
How many students begin the program each year? *15–30*
Are the majority of the beginning students already employed by museums? *No*
Contact person: *M. Roland Kaehr*
Description of program: *Training*

The **Museum Training program** is related to the field of social anthropology. The instruction focuses on curatorial methods.

The Netherlands

73

Department of Museology
University of Leiden
Dapperstraat 315
Amsterdam 1093 BS
The Netherlands

The program began in: *1983*
Time required to complete program: *1 year*

Level of training provided: *Courses, Internships, Workshops*
Areas of study: *Collection management, Exhibit design, Education, Conservation, Field methods*
Areas of specialization: *Museology*
Instructional opportunities provided: *Scheduled lectures/seminars*
Is museum ethics a regular part of the program?   *Yes*
Is the program open to international students?   *No*
The primary language of instruction is: *Dutch*
Is financial assistance available for students?   *No*
The program is affiliated with: *University(ies)*
Is instruction given in a museum?   *Yes*
Do students work in a museum collection as part of the program of study?   *Yes*
Do program instructors have museum experience?   *Yes*
How many students begin the program each year?   *80*
How many students have completed the program since it began?   *800*
Are the majority of the beginning students already employed by museums?   *No*
What percentage of the students completing this program enter or return to museum work?   *Less than 25%*
Contact person: *Olga Faber*
Description of program: *Courses, Workshops*

Graduate students enrolled in such diverse curricula as anthropology, art history, and science are eligible for this **two-part museology sequence**. Studies begin with a series of lectures and reading assignments that provide participants with a foundation in general, theoretical, and historical museology. Students successfully completing this segment proceed to more specialized study, pursuing either individual research, a project, or a full-time, three-month internship. Altogether, the program comprises one-fourth of graduate degree requirements. Qualified students from other Dutch universities may arrange to register for the museum studies program.

74

Museology/Anthropology of Material Culture
University of Amsterdam
Oudezijds Achterburgwal 185
Amsterdam 1012 DK
The Netherlands
Telephone: (020) 92 49 49

The program began in: *1969*
Time required to complete program: *6 months or less*
Level of training provided: *Courses, Internships, Graduate degree*
Areas of study: *Curatorship, Education*
Areas of specialization: *Anthropology, Ethnology, Material culture, Ethics, History, Museology*
Instructional opportunities provided: *Part-time study*
Is museum ethics a regular part of the program?   *Yes*
Is the program open to international students?   *No*
The primary language of instruction is: *Dutch*
Is financial assistance available for students?   *No*
The program is affiliated with: *Museum(s), University(ies)*
Is instruction given in a museum?   *Yes*
Do students work in a museum collection as part of the program of study?   *No*
Do program instructors have museum experience?   *Yes*
How many students begin the program each year?   *25*
How many students have completed the program since it began?   *500*
Are the majority of the beginning students already employed by museums?   *No*
What percentage of the students completing this program enter or return to museum work?   *Less than 25%*
Contact person: *G. van Beek, Ph.D., or H. Leyten, Ph.D.*
Description of program: *Courses*

The **study of museology,** as it applies to ethnographic museums, is the major focus of the program. Training is concentrated into six-month courses with classes in educational theories, display techniques, general museum history, and the history and societal role of ethnographic museums. Other related areas are also included. Undergraduate and graduate students may apply.

75

Department of Museology, Amsterdam School of the Arts
Reinwardt Academie
Dapperstraat 315
Amsterdam 1093 BS
The Netherlands
Telephone: (31 20) 6922111 or (31 20) 6926338
Fax: (31 20) 6926836 or (31 20) 6925762

The program began in: *1976*

Time required to complete program: *Varies*

Level of training provided: *Graduate degree, Bachelor degree*

Areas of study: *Administration, Collection management, Exhibit design, Public programming, Curatorship, Education, Conservation, Information technology, Field methods*

Areas of specialization: *Anthropology, Ethnology, Fine arts, Material culture, Archeology, Architecture, Ethics, History, Museology*

Instructional opportunities provided: *Full-time study*

Is museum ethics a regular part of the program? *Yes*

Is the program open to international students? *Yes*

The primary language of instruction is: *Dutch and English*

Is financial assistance available for students? *Yes*

Financial assistance is available in the following ways: *Scholarships*

The program is affiliated with: *Museum(s), Gallery(ies), University(ies), Science center(s)*

Is instruction given in a museum? *Yes*

Do students work in a museum collection as part of the program of study? *Yes*

Do program instructors have museum experience? *Yes*

How many students begin the program each year? *60*

How many students have completed the program since it began? *450*

Are the majority of the beginning students already employed by museums? *Yes*

What percentage of the students completing this program enter or return to museum work? *50% to 75%*

Contact person: *Piet J.M. Pouw, Ph.D., Director*

Description of program: *Undergraduate degree, Graduate degree*

The four-year **program in museology**, consisting of academic studies and practical training assignments, is open to Dutch students who possess a high school diploma. The curriculum is divided into three areas. Each area focuses on a specific aspect of museum work. The program begins with an introduction to the field, with basic instruction in museum management, registration techniques, exhibition design methods, and public relations. Following this segment, students participate in extended practical assignments, working two days per week for fourteen weeks and full-time for ten weeks on either a preservation or exhibition project. During the final segment, an area of specialization is selected, such as collections management, museum communications, or cultural management, and a final examination project is prepared based on this chosen specialization. A diploma is awarded upon satisfactory completion of all course requirements and an oral board examination.

Reinwardt also offers an international **Master's degree course in Museology**. The program consists of six basic courses dealing with the four fields of museum work: Operational Management, Collection Management, Research, and Communication. The six basic courses are: Management, Registration and Documentation of Collections, Conservation, Education (Communication), Visitor Surveys, and Exhibition Design. In addition, there are two coordinating and integrating courses: theoretical museology and methodology. The final stage of the Master's degree program is a written thesis.

The program is open to postgraduates of all universities, polytechnics, and higher vocational schools throughout the world. There is a full-time and part-time study program starting in September and in February.

United Kingdom

76

Department of Social Anthropology
University of Cambridge
Free School Lane
Cambridge CB2 3RF
United Kingdom
Telephone: (01223) 333514

The program began in: *1980/1*
Time required to complete program: *1 year*
Level of training provided: *Internships, Graduate degree, Workshops*
Areas of study: *Administration, Collection management, Exhibit design, Curatorship, Education, Conservation, Field methods, Information technology*
Areas of specialization: *Anthropology, Clothing, Ethnology, Material culture, History, Museology*
Instructional opportunities provided: *Full-time study, Scheduled lectures/seminars*
Is museum ethics a regular part of the program?   *Yes*
Is the program open to international students?   *Yes*
The primary language of instruction is: *English*
Is financial assistance available for students?   *Yes*
Financial assistance is available in the following ways: *Scholarships*

The program is affiliated with: *Museum(s), University(ies)*
Is instruction given in a museum?   *Yes*
Do students work in a museum collection as part of the program of
   study?   *Yes*
Do program instructors have museum experience?   *Yes*
How many students begin the program each year?   *3*
How many students have completed the program since it began?   *30*
What percentage of the students completing this program enter or return
   to museum work?   *25% to 50%*
Contact person: *Anita Herle*
Description of program: *Seminars*

Social Anthropology with Special Reference to the Work of a Museum
(Option B): Option B is a component within the Master of Philosophy
program in Social Anthropology. Students taking option B are required
to attend seminars in the four core areas: religion, politics, economics,
and kinship, and write a paper (final examination) in two of these areas.
Option B students also write a third paper on social anthropology with
special reference to the work of a museum and submit a thesis of 7,500
to 10,000 words that has special reference to material culture. Students
are also required to complete a six-week internship within a museum
selected in consultation with their supervisor.

The course of study has a three-fold aim. First, it is intended to allow
students to examine in some detail the relationship between material
and non-material aspects of culture and society. Second, to provide some
vocational training for anthropologists hoping to work in museums. Third,
to develop relations between social anthropology as a discipline and as a
museum enterprise. Much of the teaching takes place in the Cambridge
University Museum of Archaeology and Anthropology which has a
renowned collection of artifacts from around the world. Of particular
note are collections from the Pacific, Western Africa, and select areas
in North America and Southeast Asia. Students are encouraged to use
the Museum collections and involve themselves in its work as far as is
practicable.

77

Hamilton Kerr Institute
University of Cambridge
Mill Lane, Whittlesford
Cambridge CB2 4NE
United Kingdom
Telephone: (01223) 832040

The program began in: *1976*
Time required to complete program: *More than 2 years*
Level of training provided: *Internships, Diploma, Certificate*
Areas of study: *Conservation*
Areas of specialization: *Fine arts*
Instructional opportunities provided: *Full-time study*
Is museum ethics a regular part of the program?   *Yes*
Is the program open to international students?   *Yes*
The primary language of instruction is: *English*
Is financial assistance available for students?   *Yes*
Financial assistance is available in the following ways: *Scholarships*
The program is affiliated with: *Museum(s), University(ies)*
Is instruction given in a museum?   *Yes*
Do students work in a museum collection as part of the program of
   study?   *Yes*
Do program instructors have museum experience?   *Yes*
How many students begin the program each year?   *2*
How many students have completed the program since it began?   *23*
Are the majority of the beginning students already employed by
   museums?   *Yes*
What percentage of the students completing this program enter or return
   to museum work?   *50% to 75%*
Contact person: *Ian McClure, Director*
Description of program: *Certificate, Diploma*

Conservation of Easel Paintings: students are enrolled for a three-year
course in the conservation and restoration of easel paintings, followed by
an optional year of attachment either to the Institute's own studio in
London or to a conservation laboratory in the United Kingdom or abroad.
The practical and theoretical instruction is given by members of the staff
and by visiting lecturers. Additional theory is imparted in the studios as
part of the practical work. Applicants will normally be expected to hold
a first degree or equivalent qualification in subjects relevant to the course,
such as fine arts and crafts, history of art, physics, or chemistry, or a joint
degree including one or more of these subjects. Those who successfully
complete program requirements will be awarded a Certificate in the
Conservation of Easel Paintings. Students who have obtained this certificate will be eligible to proceed to a further year of conservation work in
an approved context, qualifying for the examination leading to the
Diploma in the Conservation of Easel Paintings.

78

Department of Archaeology
University of Cambridge
Downing Street
Cambridge CB2 3DZ
United Kingdom
Telephone: (01223) 337733, Fax: (01223) 333503
BITNET: CC43@PHX.CAM.AC.UK.

The program began in: *1990*
Time required to complete program: *1 year*
Level of training provided: *Graduate degree*
Areas of study: *Administration, Collection management, Exhibit design, Curatorship, Information technology, Education*
Areas of specialization: *Archeology*
Instructional opportunities provided: *Full-time study*
Is museum ethics a regular part of the program? *Yes*
Is the program open to international students? *Yes*
The primary language of instruction is: *English*
Is financial assistance available for students? *Yes*
Financial assistance is available in the following ways: *Scholarships*
The program is affiliated with: *Museum(s), University(ies)*
Is instruction given in a museum? *Yes*
Do students work in a museum collection as part of the program of study? *Yes*
Do program instructors have museum experience? *Yes*
How many students begin the program each year? *9*
How many students have completed the program since it began? *20*
Are the majority of the beginning students already employed by museums? *Yes*
What percentage of the students completing this program enter or return to museum work? *50% to 75%*
Contact person: *Christopher Chippindale, Assistant Curator*
Description of program: *Graduate degree*

Master of Philosophy Archaeology/Museums Program: a one-year program of study dealing with the physical relics of the past. It includes the methods for addressing those portable objects that are taken into museums, and the immovable sites that stay in the landscape. The course is taught jointly in the Department of Archaeology and in the Museum of Archaeology and Anthropology, so it benefits from both university and museum experience, expertise, and environment.

79

Department of Archaeology
University of Durham
46 Saddler Street
Durham DH1 3NU
United Kingdom
Telephone: (0191) 374 2000

The program began in: *1975*
Time required to complete program: *2 years*
Level of training provided: *Internships, Graduate degree*
Areas of study: *Conservation*
Areas of specialization: *Material culture, Archeology, Conservation of historic material*
Instructional opportunities provided: *Full-time study*
Is museum ethics a regular part of the program?   *Yes*
Is the program open to international students?   *Yes*
The primary language of instruction is: *English*
Is financial assistance available for students?   *No*
The program is affiliated with: *Museum(s), University(ies)*
Is instruction given in a museum?   *Yes*
Do students work in a museum collection as part of the program of study?   *Yes*
Do program instructors have museum experience?   *Yes*
How many students begin the program each year?   *6*
How many students have completed the program since it began?   *45 (diploma and M.A.)*
Are the majority of the beginning students already employed by museums?   *Yes*
What percentage of the students completing this program enter or return to museum work?   *More than 75%*
Contact person: *Chris Caple, Ph.D., Course Director*
Description of program: *Master's degree*

The Durham **conservation course**, previously a Postgraduate Diploma and now an M.A., is known for training conservators who specialize in cleaning, preserving, researching, and conserving archeological and historical artifacts.

The initial year of the course is spent on a full-time course of instruction in Durham University. After a summer of practical training in the conservation laboratories of the Department of Archaeology, students spend twelve months on a work placement (internship) in a conservation laboratory of a museum or national heritage agency within the United Kingdom.

80

Department of Museum Studies
University of Leicester
105 Princess Road East
Leicester LE1 7LG
United Kingdom
Telephone: (01533) 523 963
Fax: (01533) 523 960

The program began in: *1978*
Time required to complete program: *Varies*
Level of training provided: *Internships, Graduate degree, Workshops*
Areas of study: *Administration, Collection management, Exhibit design, Public programming, Curatorship, Education, Conservation, Information technology, Field methods, Architectural preservation*
Areas of specialization: *Anthropology, Clothing, Ethnology, Fine arts, Material culture, Natural science, Archeology, Decorative arts, Ethics, History, Museum management, Marketing, Museology*
Instructional opportunities provided: *Part-time study*
Is museum ethics a regular part of the program? *Yes*
Is the program open to international students? *Yes*
The primary language of instruction is: *English*
Is financial assistance available for students? *Yes*
Financial assistance is available in the following ways: *Scholarships*
Is instruction given in a museum? *Yes*
Do students work in a museum collection as part of the program of study? *Yes*
Do program instructors have museum experience? *Yes*
How many students begin the program each year? *40 diplomas and 40 degrees*
How many students have completed the program since it began? *263 diplomas and 203 degrees*
Are the majority of the beginning students already employed by museums? *Yes*
What percentage of the students completing this program enter or return to museum work? *More than 75%*
Contact person: *Gaynor Kavanagh, Admissions Tutor*
Description of program: *Diploma, Master's degree*

The Department of Museum Studies offers two postgraduate courses of study: one leads to the **Diploma in Museum Studies,** the other to a **Master's degree in Museum Studies.** These courses are taught jointly. The Master's degree has the additional element of a dissertation of 10,000 words.

Courses are of nine and twelve months' duration respectively. There are pre-sessional language courses for students without English as their first language.

The courses are taught on a modular basis. Core courses include: museum provision and professionalism; management; material culture – objects and collections; communication; and collection management. In addition, students study a special subject: archeology, art, history, museum education service, management and marketing, documentation and information technology, or sciences.

All students undertake an eight-week work experience in a museum during their third term. This is arranged by the department. Students are assessed on written work and on an oral examination.

Applicants are reviewed based on their individual merits. A good academic background, such as a relevant university degree, and clear vocational intent are considered important. Evidence of proficiency in the English language will be sought where necessary.

The department also offers opportunities to undertake original research leading to a higher degree in museum studies, either an M.Phil. or a Ph.D.

81

Institute of Archeology – Museum Studies
University College London
31–34 Gordon Square
London WC1H OPY
United Kingdom
Telephone: (0171) 387 7050 Ext. 4775

The program began in: *1987*
Time required to complete program: *1 year*
Level of training provided: *Graduate degree*
Areas of study: *Administration, Collection management, Exhibit design, Curatorship, Education, Conservation*
Areas of specialization: *Natural science, Archeology, History*
Instructional opportunities provided: *Full-time study*
Is museum ethics a regular part of the program?   *Yes*
Is the program open to international students?   *Yes*
The primary language of instruction is: *English*
Is financial assistance available for students?   *Yes*
Financial assistance is available in the following ways: *Scholarships*
The program is affiliated with: *Museum(s), Gallery(ies)*
Is instruction given in a museum?   *Yes*

Do students work in a museum collection as part of the program of
   study?   *Yes*
Do program instructors have museum experience?   *Yes*
How many students begin the program each year?   *20*
How many students have completed the program since it began?   *100*
What percentage of the students completing this program enter or return
   to museum work?   *50% to 75%*
Contact person: *Elaine Sansom*
Description of program: *Master's degree*

The **M.A. degree program** provides a broad academic and professional
training in museum work, with special reference to museums with human
history or natural science collections. The course consists of four main
parts: museum theory, museum practice, care of collections, and a dissertation. The course is intended for those wishing to enter the museum
profession as curators, but those already working in museums (e.g. conservators, designers, registrars, educators, etc.) who wish to improve their
museological knowledge and perspective will find it instructive and helpful
in their career development and improvement. The taught parts of the
course consist of lectures, seminars, and tutorials, and visits to museums
in and around London. The various aspects of the course are taught by
expert lecturers from museums and university staff. In addition to the
main courses, students may also attend optional courses.

   Applicants are usually required to have a first degree, but because of the
broad approach of the course, the nature of applicants' first degrees may
vary considerably. In some special cases (overseas or mature students), the
first degree requirement may be waived on evidence of suitable alternative
qualification or experience.

82

Department of Arts Policy and Management
City University
Frobisher Crescent, Barbican
London EC2Y 8HB
United Kingdom
Telephone: (0171) 477 8000, Fax: (0171) 477 8887

The program began in: *1985*
Time required to complete program: *1 year*
Level of training provided: *Graduate degree*
Areas of study: *Administration, Public programming, Education,*
   Information technology

Areas of specialization: *Human resources, Public policy*
Instructional opportunities provided: *Full-time study, Short-term lectures on request, Part-time study, Scheduled lectures/seminars*
Is museum ethics a regular part of the program?   *Yes*
Is the program open to international students?   *Yes*
The primary language of instruction is: *English*
Is financial assistance available for students?   *No*
The program is affiliated with: *University(ies)*
Is instruction given in a museum?   *No*
Do program instructors have museum experience?   *Yes*
How many students begin the program each year?   *30*
How many students have completed the program since it began?   *200*
Are the majority of the beginning students already employed by museums?   *Yes*
What percentage of the students completing this program enter or return to museum work?   *More than 75%*
Contact person: *Patrick J. Boylan, Head of Department*
Description of program: *Graduate program*

The **M.A. in Museum and Gallery Management** is one of the five post-graduate courses of the Department. It is the largest interdisciplinary postgraduate education and research center of arts, museums, and heritage policy and management in Europe (200 students, including 30 full- or part-time Ph.D. research – for which applications are also welcome).

This mid-career management program is for those with at least five years experience in museums, galleries, or a closely related field. Compulsory modules are Museums Framework and Museum and Gallery Management. Two additional modules are chosen from a wide range of options. The course is completed by researching and writing a substantial thesis.

83

Department of History of Art
University of Manchester
Manchester M13 9PL
United Kingdom
Telephone: (0161) 275 3312, Fax: (0161) 275 3331

The program began in: *1971*
Time required to complete program: *1 year*
Level of training provided: *Internships, Diploma, Graduate degree,*

Workshops, M.A. and M.Phil.

Areas of study: *Administration, Collection management, Exhibit design, Public programming, Curatorship, Education, Conservation, Information technology*

Areas of specialization: *Fine arts, Material culture, Decorative arts, Museology*

Instructional opportunities provided: *Full-time study*

Is museum ethics a regular part of the program?   *Yes*

Is the program open to international students?   *Yes*

The primary language of instruction is: *English*

Is financial assistance available for students?   *Yes*

Financial assistance is available in the following ways: *Government grants*

The program is affiliated with: *Museum(s), Gallery(ies)*

Is instruction given in a museum?   *Yes*

Do students work in a museum collection as part of the program of study?   *Yes*

Do program instructors have museum experience?   *Yes*

How many students begin the program each year?   *20*

How many students have completed the program since it began?   *400*

Are the majority of the beginning students already employed by museums?   *Yes*

What percentage of the students completing this program enter or return to museum work?   *More than 75%*

Contact person: *I. G. Wolfenden, Head of Gallery*

Description of program: *Diploma, Graduate degree*

The **Postgraduate course in Art Gallery and Museum Studies** is concerned with providing curatorial experience and expertise in administering and interpreting art gallery and museum collections. The diploma is currently recognized by the Museum Association of Great Britain and partially qualifies students for the diploma of the Association. Students examine the theoretical aspects of museum curatorship and also work in close contact with art galleries and museums in the Manchester region. A public exhibition is mounted annually in the University's Whitworth Art Gallery as an integral part of the course. The program has a strong arts bias.

The diploma requires one academic year of study. The M.A. also requires one full year. The M.Phil. can be completed in one year of full-time study or two years part-time.

84

Department of Archaeology
University of Newcastle upon Tyne
Kensington Terrace
Newcastle upon Tyne NE1 7RU
United Kingdom
Telephone: (0191) 22 27 419

Time required to complete program: *1 year*
Level of training provided: *Diploma, Graduate degree*
Areas of study: *Administration, Collection management, Education, Public programming, Curatorship, Conservation, Information technology*
Areas of specialization: *Ethnology, Fine arts, Natural science, Archeology, Decorative arts, Ethics, Museology*
Instructional opportunities provided: *Full-time study, Part-time study*
Is museum ethics a regular part of the program?   *Yes*
Is the program open to international students?   *Yes*
The primary language of instruction is: *English*
The program is affiliated with: *Museum(s), University(ies)*
Is instruction given in a museum?   *Yes*
Do students work in a museum collection as part of the program of study?   *Yes*
Do program instructors have museum experience?   *Yes*
Contact person: *Peter Davis, Course Organizer*
Description of program: *Diploma, Master's degree*

The **Museum Studies program** is based in the Department of Archaeology. There are four museums on the University of Newcastle upon Tyne campus. Their collections encompass the natural sciences, archeology, ethnology, fine arts, and decorative arts. These museums and their collections form the focal point for much of the course work.

This course of study has been developed in close association with Tyne and Wear Museums Service, the North of England Museums Service and the Museums Training Institute. The philosophy of the program is to give students a practical insight into how museums work, and much of the course will be delivered by museum professionals. Whenever possible, the course encourages a "hands-on" approach dealing with real objects and real situations.

The course of study is modular in structure, consisting of sixteen modules. Each module is equivalent to 100 hours of study. There are eight core modules, four specialist modules, and four research modules.

Successful completion of the core and specialist modules will gain students a Diploma in Museum Studies. The submission of a dissertation based on four modules of research will result in the award of a Master of Arts in Museum Studies.

85

Ulster Museum
Botanic Gardens
Belfast, Northern Ireland BT9 5AB
United Kingdom

The program began in: *1988*
Level of training provided: *Internships*
Areas of study: *Collection management, Curatorship, Education, Exhibit design, Public programming, Conservation, Information technology*
Areas of specialization: *Clothing, Ethnology, Fine arts, Material culture, Natural science, Archeology, Decorative arts, History, Paleontology, Irish history and culture*
Is museum ethics a regular part of the program? *Yes*
Is the program open to international students? *Yes*
The primary language of instruction is: *English*
Is financial assistance available for students? *No*
Is instruction given in a museum? *Yes*
Do students work in a museum collection as part of the program of study? *Yes*
Do program instructors have museum experience? *Yes*
How many students begin the program each year? *Varies*
How many students have completed the program since it began? *4*
Are the majority of the beginning students already employed by museums? *No*
What percentage of the students completing this program enter or return to museum work? *Less than 25%*
Contact person: *John C. Nolan*
Description of program: *Internship*

The **internship program** is not formal. It affords students (or professionals) an opportunity to work in the various departments of the Museum alongside professional staff in order that they may gain knowledge of the collections and an appreciation of working practices. Interns are expected to be self-motivated participants in practical work activities, and well read. Interns may work in more than one department.

86

Textile Conservation
Textile Conservation Centre
Apartment 22, Hampton Court Palace
East Molesey, Surrey KT8 9AU
United Kingdom
Telephone: (0181) 977 4943, Fax: (0181) 977 9081

The program began in: *1975*
Time required to complete program: *More than 2 years*
Level of training provided: *Internships, Diploma*
Areas of study: *Conservation*
Areas of specialization: *Clothing, Material culture, Decorative arts, Ethics, History of textiles*
Instructional opportunities provided: *Full-time study*
Is museum ethics a regular part of the program?   *Yes*
Is the program open to international students?   *Yes*
The primary language of instruction is: *English*
Is financial assistance available for students?   *Yes*
Financial assistance is available in the following ways: *Scholarships*
The program is affiliated with: *University(ies)*
Is instruction given in a museum?   *No*
Do program instructors have museum experience?   *Yes*
How many students begin the program each year?   *7*
How many students have completed the program since it began?   *70*
Are the majority of the beginning students already employed by museums?   *Yes*
What percentage of the students completing this program enter or return to museum work?   *More than 75%*
Contact person: *Nell Hoare, Director*
Description of program: *Diploma, Internship, Seminar*

Postgraduate Diploma course in Textile Conservation: the aim of the program is to provide students with the theoretical background and practical experience of textile conservation techniques. This three-year full-time course comprises lectures, seminars, practical projects, demonstrations, and field trips. Each year's curriculum is organized to meet specific goals. The purpose of the first year of study is to establish the relationship between the history of textile arts, conservation ethics, and science and technology. The second year consolidates and expands the first year by concentrating on practical work assignments. Students continue to work on textiles with a wide range of conservation problems during the third year and are responsible for the completion of a complex practical project plus a research/investigation project. The program is offered in conjunction with the Courtauld Institute of Art, University of London.

Yearly seminars are held for alumni.

Special arrangements are made for accredited observers – historians, scientists, and conservators – to study at the Textile Conservation Centre.

United States of America

87

Birmingham Museum of Art
2000 8th Avenue North
Birmingham, Alabama 35203-2278
USA
Telephone: (205) 254 2571

The program began in: *1982*
Time required to complete program: *6 months or less*
Level of training provided: *Internships*
Areas of study: *Collection management, Exhibit design, Curatorship, Education, Public programming*
Areas of specialization: *Fine arts, Decorative arts, Museology*
Is museum ethics a regular part of the program? *No*
Is the program open to international students? *Yes*
The primary language of instruction is: *English*
Is financial assistance available for students? *No*
The program is affiliated with: *University(ies)*
Is instruction given in a museum? *Yes*
Do students work in a museum collection as part of the program of study? *Yes*
Do program instructors have museum experience? *Yes*
How many students begin the program each year? *2–4*
Are the majority of the beginning students already employed by museums? *No*
What percentage of the students completing this program enter or return to museum work? *25% to 50%*
Contact person: *Jeffrey J. York, Curator of Education*
Description of program: *Internships, Work-study*

Undergraduate internship: a limited number of unpaid positions are available. Arrangements are made between the museum and universities to place students enrolled in art-related fields. Paid internships are available periodically through grants. Each intern is responsible for a specific research project and works for school credit only. The University of Alabama at Birmingham co-sponsors work-study assignments with the museum. These unsalaried positions are available in the registrar's offices, curatorial department, and education department; however, opportunities may exist in other areas.

88

Museum Studies Program
Arizona State University
Department of Anthropology
Tempe, Arizona 85287
USA
Telephone: (602) 965 6213

The program began in: *1978*
Time required to complete program: *More than 2 years*
Level of training provided: *Graduate degree, Certificate*
Areas of study: *Administration, Collection management, Exhibit design, Public programming, Curatorship, Education, Conservation, Field methods*
Areas of specialization: *Anthropology, Ethnology, Material culture, Archeology, Museology*
Instructional opportunities provided: *Full-time study, Part-time study*
Is museum ethics a regular part of the program?   *Yes*
Is the program open to international students?   *Yes*
The primary language of instruction is: *English*
Is financial assistance available for students?   *Yes*
Financial assistance is available in the following ways: *Student work program, Teaching Assistant and Research Assistant positions, Tuition waiver*
The program is affiliated with: *Museum(s), University(ies)*
Do students work in a museum collection as part of the program of study?   *Yes*
Do program instructors have museum experience?   *Yes*
How many students begin the program each year?   *4 degree/6–10 certificate*
How many students have completed the program since it began?   *14 degree/21 certificate*

Are the majority of the beginning students already employed by
museums? *Yes*
What percentage of the students completing this program enter or return
to museum work? *25% to 50%*
Contact person: *Ann Lane Hedlund, Director Museum Science*
Description of program: *Master's degree, Certificate*

Department of Anthropology, **Master of Arts in Anthropology with a
concentration/Certificate in Museum Studies**: the program prepares
students for careers in anthropology museums and covers the concepts
and theories of museum work, the organization and management of such
institutions, care of collections, and exhibition design and preparation.
Concurrently, degree students must acquire graduate-level competency in
anthropology. The degree program consists of a minimum of thirty-six
hours. Students must complete twelve hours in anthropology, twelve hours
in museum studies, plus a six-hour internship and six semester credit
thesis. Internships are done at local, regional, and national museums based
on 20–40 hours per week of practical work experience.

Certification involves twelve hours' course work in museum studies and
an internship.

89

Arizona Historical Society
Southern Arizona Division Internships
Arizona Historical Society
949 East Second Street
Tucson, Arizona 85719
USA
Telephone: (602) 628 5774

The program began in: *1980*
Time required to complete program: *Varies*
Level of training provided: *Internships*
Areas of study: *Administration, Collection management, Exhibit design,
Public programming, Education, Conservation*
Areas of specialization *Archives, Material culture, History*
Instructional opportunities provided: *Part-time study*
Is museum ethics a regular part of the program? *No*
Is the program open to international students? *Yes*
The primary language of instruction is: *English*

Is financial assistance available for students?   *No*
The program is affiliated with: *University(ies)*
Is instruction given in a museum?   *Yes*
Do students work in a museum collection as part of the program of
    study?   *Yes*
Do program instructors have museum experience?   *Yes*
How many students begin the program each year?   *2*
How many students have completed the program since it began?   *40*
Are the majority of the beginning students already employed by
    museums?   *No*
Contact person: *Gwen Harvey, Director of Education*
Description of program: *Work-study, Internships*

Work-study program through the University of Arizona. Funds awarded
through application for college work-study. Various positions available in
different museum departments.

Undergraduate or graduate internships can be arranged through a coop-
erating department (usually history, anthropology, or education) at the
University of Arizona. Interns work in one museum department such as
education, conservation, collections, library, archives, or administration.
Museum staff and student design program to suit educational needs.
Number of positions limited. No stipends or salaries.

90

ASU Museum
Arkansas State University
Museum, PO Box 490
State University, Arkansas 72467
USA
Telephone: (501) 972 2074

The program began in: *1983*
Time required to complete program: *6 months or less*
Level of training provided: *Courses*
Areas of study: *Collection management, Exhibit design, Curatorship,
    Education, Conservation*
Areas of specialization: *Clothing, Natural science, Archeology,
    Decorative arts, History*
Instructional opportunities provided: *Scheduled lectures/seminars*
Is museum ethics a regular part of the program?   *Yes*
Is the program open to international students?   *Yes*

The primary language of instruction is: *English*
Is financial assistance available for students?   *Yes*
Financial assistance is available in the following ways: *Scholarships, Student work program, Loans*
The program is affiliated with: *Museum(s), University(ies)*
Is instruction given in a museum?   *Yes*
Do students work in a museum collection as part of the program of study?   *Yes*
Do program instructors have museum experience?   *Yes*
How many students begin the program each year?   *10–15*
How many students have completed the program since it began?   *30*
Are the majority of the beginning students already employed by museums?   *No*
What percentage of the students completing this program enter or return to museum work?   *Less than 25%*
Contact person: *Charlott Jones, Ph.D., Director*
Description of program: *Courses*

Department of History. Upper-division undergraduates are introduced to museum work through **sessions on registration, exhibition planning, education,** and other topics. The course is taught in alternate years in the spring semester.

Independent study. Special projects are developed within the context of the Museum's collections. Graduate students are eligible for the three-credit course.

91

University Art Museum
University of California at Berkeley
2625 Durant Avenue
Berkeley, California 94720
USA
Telephone: (415) 642 1207

The program began in: *1992–3*
Time required to complete program: *6 months or less*
Level of training provided: *Courses, Internships*
Areas of study: *Administration, Collection management, Exhibit design, Public programming, Curatorship, Education, Conservation*
Areas of specialization: *Film and video studies, Fine arts*
Instructional opportunities provided: *Part-time study*

Is museum ethics a regular part of the program? *Yes*
Is the program open to international students? *Yes*
The primary language of instruction is: *English*
Is financial assistance available for students? *No*
The program is affiliated with: *Museum(s), University(ies)*
Is instruction given in a museum? *Yes*
Do students work in a museum collection as part of the program of study? *Yes*
Do program instructors have museum experience? *Yes*
How many students begin the program each year? *15*
Are the majority of the beginning students already employed by museums? *No*
Contact person: *James Steward, Curator*
Description of program: *Course, Internship*

A one-semester **graduate/advanced undergraduate course in museum philosophy and practice**, designed to provide an introduction to work in fine arts museums and video/film archives. The course is offered each year in the spring term. Issues discussed include the history of collecting and museums, connoisseurship, conservation, collection management, recent museum development (i.e. building), philosophy of museums in contemporary culture, public access issues, funding, and ethics. The course meets as a seminar once a week for fourteen weeks and requires field work.

The University Art Museum offers two **graduate internships** and two **minority undergraduate internships** each summer for a period of ten weeks. These are open only to students at the University of California at Berkeley. These are paid internships.

Unpaid internships are available at the museum during the academic year for which up to four semester units of credit may be earned. Volunteer positions are also available. Traditionally these internships are in curatorial departments although other departments may participate on request.

92

MA Anthropology, Option in Museum Studies
Museum of Anthropology
California State University – Chico
Chico, California 95929
USA
Telephone: (916) 895 5397

The program began in: *1983*
Time required to complete program: *2 years*
Level of training provided: *Internships, Diploma, Graduate degree, Workshops, Certificate*
Areas of study: *Administration, Collection management, Exhibit design, Curatorship, Conservation*
Areas of specialization: *Anthropology, Material culture, Archeology, Museology*
Instructional opportunities provided: *Full-time study, Part-time study*
Is museum ethics a regular part of the program? *Yes*
Is the program open to international students? *Yes*
The primary language of instruction is: *English*
Is financial assistance available for students? *No*
The program is affiliated with: *University(ies)*
Is instruction given in a museum? *Yes*
Do students work in a museum collection as part of the program of study? *Yes*
Do program instructors have museum experience? *Yes*
How many students begin the program each year? *3*
How many students have completed the program since it began? *25*
What percentage of the students completing this program enter or return to museum work? *25% to 50%*
Contact person: *Keith Johnson, Director*
Description of program: *Certificate, Master's degree*

Museology Certificate: open to undergraduate and graduate students. The twenty-six-unit program is a combination of course work and on-site training. Interdisciplinary courses emphasize curatorial research, the design and installation of exhibitions, and museum management techniques. Students also create exhibitions for the anthropology museum or for the two art galleries on campus; a separate three-unit internship provides the opportunity for work-training experience in an off-campus internship, plus a graduate project or thesis. The thirty-unit program also fulfills the requirements for a **Master's degree in anthropology.**

Master of Arts in Museum Studies: open to students enrolled in an M.A. program within the Department of Anthropology. Included are seminars in archeology and museum studies, an off-campus internship, plus a graduate project or thesis. The thirty-unit program also fulfills the requirements for a **Master's degree in anthropology.**

93

University Art Museum
California State University at Long Beach
1250 Bellflower Boulevard
Long Beach, California 90840
USA
Telephone: (213) 985 5761

The program began in: *1974*
Time required to complete program: *More than 2 years*
Level of training provided: *Internships, Graduate degree, Certificate*
Areas of study: *Administration, Collection management, Exhibit design, Public programming, Curatorship, Education, Field methods*
Areas of specialization: *Fine arts, Decorative arts, Museology*
Instructional opportunities provided: *Full-time study*
Is museum ethics a regular part of the program? *Yes*
Is the program open to international students? *Yes*
The primary language of instruction is: *English*
Is financial assistance available for students? *Yes*
The program is affiliated with: *Museum(s), University(ies)*
Is instruction given in a museum? *Yes*
Do students work in a museum collection as part of the program of study? *Yes*
Do program instructors have museum experience? *Yes*
How many students begin the program each year? *12*
How many students have completed the program since it began? *120*
Are the majority of the beginning students already employed by museums? *Yes*
What percentage of the students completing this program enter or return to museum work? *More than 75%*
Contact person: *Constance W. Glenn*
Description of program: *Certificate, Master's degree*

The Art Department and the University Art Museum offer a graduate program leading to the **Certificate in Museum Studies** that provides basic orientation, training, and experience in museum work and is open to students in art history, studio art, and other disciplines related to museum careers. Each student's individual program is chosen with particular regard to preparation for internship and ultimate employment, in his or her chosen area of specialization.

Students spend at least two years in the certificate program. The provisional museum studies course includes a brief introduction to the history of museums. Seminars are devoted to museum ethics and practices and in-depth study of many aspects of museum management.

The program admits students on a provisional basis with final admission based on evaluation during the introductory semester.

The **M.A. degree in Museum Studies** and related disciplines may be pursued through the Special Master's Programs.

94

Museum Studies Program
University of Southern California
University Park
Los Angeles, California 90089-0292
USA
Telephone: (213) 743 2799

The program began in: *1980*
Time required to complete program: *More than 2 years*
Level of training provided: *Internships, Diploma, Graduate degree, Workshops, Certificate, Master's in Art History with Certificate*
Areas of study: *Administration, Collection management, Exhibit design, Public programming, Curatorship, Education, Conservation*
Areas of specialization: *Fine arts, Decorative arts, Ethics, History, Museology, Art History*
Instructional opportunities provided: *Full-time study, Scheduled lectures/seminars*
Is museum ethics a regular part of the program? *Yes*
Is the program open to international students? *Yes*
The primary language of instruction is: *English*
Is financial assistance available for students? *Yes*
Financial assistance is available in the following ways. *Scholarships, Loans, Tuition waiver, Student work program*
The program is affiliated with: *Museum(s), University(ies)*
Is instruction given in a museum? *Yes*
Do students work in a museum collection as part of the program of study? *Yes*
Do program instructors have museum experience? *Yes*
How many students begin the program each year? *7–11*
How many students have completed the program since it began? *45*
Are the majority of the beginning students already employed by museums? *No*

What percentage of the students completing this program enter or return
to museum work?   *More than 75%*
Contact person: *Selma Holo, Ph.D., Director*
Description of program: *Master's degree*

Master of Arts in Art History (Museum Studies Option): this three-year
course of study is designed to meet the special training needs of students
whose career goals are oriented toward professional work in art museums.
The degree, for students enrolled in the museum studies program, requires
a minimum of forty-four units. The program consists of four parts: the
academic core discipline, the museum studies courses, a thesis-catalog and
exhibition, and an internship in a museum. Candidates must pass reading
proficiency examinations in one language and a comprehensive examination demonstrating a thorough background in art history. Some financial
aid is available.

95

Getty Graduate Intern Program
J. Paul Getty Museum
17985 Pacific Coast Highway
Malibu, California 90265
USA
Telephone: (310) 459 7611 Ext. 254

The program began in: *1980*
Time required to complete program: *1 year*
Level of training provided: *Graduate degree*
Areas of study: *Administration, Exhibit design, Curatorship, Education,
    Conservation*
Areas of specialization: *Archives, Fine arts, Archeology, Decorative arts,
    History, Museology, Paleontology, Arts administration, Art history*
Instructional opportunities provided: *Scheduled lectures/seminars*
Is museum ethics a regular part of the program?   *No*
Is the program open to international students?   *Yes*
The primary language of instruction is: *English*
Is financial assistance available for students?   *Yes*
Financial assistance is available in the following ways: *Stipend*
The program is affiliated with: *Museum(s), Gallery(ies)*
Is instruction given in a museum?   *Yes*
Do students work in a museum collection as part of the program of
    study?   *Yes*

Do program instructors have museum experience?   *Yes*
How many students begin the program each year?   *17*
How many students have completed the program since it began?   *200*
Are the majority of the beginning students already employed by
   museums?   *No*
What percentage of the students completing this program enter or return
   to museum work?   *25% to 50%*
Contact person: *Andrew J. Clark, Intern Program*
Description of program: *Internships*

The J. Paul Getty Museum sponsors the following program for individuals currently pursuing specific degrees or who have finished degree studies no more than one year prior to application.

Graduate Student Intern Program: applicants must be candidates for an M.A. or conservation degree currently enrolled in a university program or a recent recipient of an M.A. or conservation degree. Interns are assigned to one of the departments within the Museum. The purpose of the program is to provide training and educational experiences for persons planning to enter the museum profession. Program length is nine to twelve months. Stipend of $12,462 for nine months and $18,000 for twelve months.

96

Department of Museum Studies
John F. Kennedy University
12 Altarinda Road
Orinda, California 94563
USA
Telephone: (510) 253 4371, Fax: (510) 254 0420

The program began in: *1974*
Time required to complete program: *2 years*
Level of training provided: *Courses, Internships, Graduate degree,
   Certificate*
Areas of study: *Administration, Collection management, Exhibit design,
   Public programming, Education, Conservation, Information technology*
Areas of specialization: *Archives, Material culture, Ethics, Museology*
Instructional opportunities provided: *Full-time study, Part-time study*
Is museum ethics a regular part of the program?   *Yes*
Is the program open to international students?   *Yes*

United States of America

The primary language of instruction is: *English*
Is financial assistance available for students?   *Yes*
Financial assistance is available in the following ways: *Scholarships, Loans*
The program is affiliated with: *Museum(s), University(ies)*
Is instruction given in a museum?   *Yes*
Do students work in a museum collection as part of the program of study?   *Yes*
Do program instructors have museum experience?   *Yes*
How many students begin the program each year?   *20*
How many students have completed the program since it began?   *165*
Are the majority of the beginning students already employed by museums?   *Yes*
What percentage of the students completing this program enter or return to museum work?   *More than 75%*
Contact person: *John Sobraske*
Description of program: *Master's degree, Certificate*

Located in the San Francisco Bay Area, the Department of Museum Studies at John F. Kennedy University is committed to redefining the role of museums in a multicultural and changing society. Toward this goal it offers a thorough professional training in both the practical and theoretical aspects of museum work.

The department offers a **Master's degree in Museum Studies** with three specializations: administration, collections management, and interpretation. The fifty-eight-unit program is designed to be completed in two years and includes an internship and Master's project. The one-year certificate offers specializations in collections management and interpretation.

Classes are taught in the evening by practicing museum professionals.

97

Museum Studies
California State University – San Bernardino
5500 University Parkway
San Bernardino, California 92407
USA

The program began in: *1981*
Time required to complete program: *1 year*
Level of training provided: *Certificate, Bachelor degree*

176

Areas of study: *Administration, Exhibit design, Public programming, Education*
Areas of specialization: *Anthropology, Fine arts, Decorative arts*
Instructional opportunities provided: *Full-time study, Part-time study*
Is museum ethics a regular part of the program? *Yes*
Is the program open to international students? *Yes*
The primary language of instruction is: *English*
Is financial assistance available for students? *Yes*
Financial assistance is available in the following ways: *Scholarships, Student work program, Loans*
The program is affiliated with: *University(ies)*
Do students work in a museum collection as part of the program of study? *Yes*
Do program instructors have museum experience? *Yes*
How many students begin the program each year? *5*
How many students have completed the program since it began? *50*
Are the majority of the beginning students already employed by museums? *No*
What percentage of the students completing this program enter or return to museum work? *50% to 75%*
Contact person: *Russell Barber*
Description of program: *Bachelor's degree, Certificate*

Bachelor of Arts in Anthropology (Museum Studies Concentration): the two components of the museum studies program are the museum studies track within the undergraduate program in anthropology and the **Certificate in Museum Studies.** Both programs are interdisciplinary in nature. Requirements for the track include a minimum of forty-six upper-division units in anthropology, plus an additional thirty units of course work in related fields. In addition students complete two internships at local museums (part of the forty-six anthropology units). The thirty-four units required for the certificate are distributed among internship training and such areas as administration, art, data management, and history.

98

Public History Program
University of San Diego
Alcala Park
San Diego, California 92110
USA

The program began in: *1978*
Time required to complete program: *2 years*
Level of training provided: *Internships, Graduate degree*
Areas of study: *Administration, Exhibit design, Education, Field methods, Public programming, Architectural preservation*
Areas of specialization: *Anthropology, Archives, Fine arts, Archeology, Architecture, History, Museology*
Instructional opportunities provided: *Full-time study, Part-time study*
Is museum ethics a regular part of the program? *No*
Is the program open to international students? *Yes*
The primary language of instruction is: *English*
Is financial assistance available for students? *Yes*
Financial assistance is available in the following ways: *Scholarships, Student work program, Loans*
Is instruction given in a museum? *Yes*
Do students work in a museum collection as part of the program of study? *Yes*
Do program instructors have museum experience? *Yes*
How many students have completed the program since it began? *10*
What percentage of the students completing this program enter or return to museum work? *Less than 25%*
Contact person: *Ray Brandes*
Description of program: *Courses, Internship*

The museum course work involves one component of the **Public History Program** at the University of San Diego. Within this part of the Public History Program, the student has an **internship**, and may take courses in departments outside the History Department, for example museum exhibit design in the Departments of Art or Anthropology or business courses in the School of Business. The Public History Program requires thirty units of study involving courses primarily in history. Internships may be taken at the Museum of Man, Aerospace Museum, Sports Hall of Fame, Historical Society, Zoological Society, and a number of other institutions in the region. A thesis is required and computer programming may be substituted for foreign language depending on the thesis topic. A Graduate Record Examination is not required.

99

Museum Studies Program, Classics Department
San Francisco State University
1600 Holloway Avenue
San Francisco, California 94132
USA
Telephone: (415) 338 1612

The program began in: *1987*
Time required to complete program: *2 years*
Level of training provided: *Courses, Internships, Graduate degree*
Areas of study: *Administration, Collection management, Exhibit design, Public programming, Curatorship, Education, Conservation, Information technology*
Areas of specialization: *Anthropology, Archives, Clothing, Ethnology, Fine arts, Material culture, Natural science, Archeology, Ethics, History, Museology, Paleontology, Arts economics, Education, Technology, Planetariums*
Instructional opportunities provided: *Full-time study, Part-time study*
Is museum ethics a regular part of the program? *Yes*
Is the program open to international students? *Yes*
The primary language of instruction is: *English*
Is financial assistance available for students? *Yes*
Financial assistance is available in the following ways: *Loans, Tuition waiver*
The program is affiliated with: *Museum(s), Gallery(ies), University(ies), Science center(s)*
Is instruction given in a museum? *Yes*
Do students work in a museum collection as part of the program of study? *Yes*
Do program instructors have museum experience? *Yes*
How many students begin the program each year? *15–25*
How many students have completed the program since it began? *40*
Are the majority of the beginning students already employed by museums? *Yes*
What percentage of the students completing this program enter or return to museum work? *25% to 50%*
Contact person: *Linda Ellis, Director*
Description of program: *Master's degree*

The **M.A. program in Museum Studies** at San Francisco State University offers training for all areas of professional museum employment, as well as for careers in historical societies, historic houses, private and corporate galleries, archives, auction houses, science centers and planetariums, libraries, community arts organizations, and arts commissions. San Francisco State University operates six museums (Sutro Egyptian Museum, Treganza Anthropology Museum, DeBellis Collection of Italian Civilization, Museum of Human Evolution and Anatomy, Vertebrate Museum, Entomology Museum), two archives (Labor Archives and Research Center, Print Collection and Archive), a herbarium, a planetarium, and a fine art collection of 875 works by European and American masters.

100

Museum Studies Program/University of Colorado Museum
University of Colorado
Campus Box 218
Boulder, Colorado 80309-0218
USA
Telephone: (303) 492 6165

The program began in: *1972*
Time required to complete program: *Varies*
Level of training provided: *Courses, Internships, Diploma, Graduate degree*
Areas of study: *Administration, Collection management, Exhibit design, Public programming, Curatorship, Education, Conservation, Field methods*
Areas of specialization: *Anthropology, Ethnology, Fine arts, Natural science, Archeology, History, Museology, Paleontology*
Instructional opportunities provided: *Full-time study, Scheduled lectures/seminars*
Is museum ethics a regular part of the program?   *Yes*
Is the program open to international students?   *Yes*
The primary language of instruction is: *English*
Is financial assistance available for students?   *Yes*
Financial assistance is available in the following ways: *Scholarships, Loans, Materials/supplies, Tuition waiver, Student work program*
The program is affiliated with: *Museum(s), University(ies)*
Is instruction given in a museum?   *Yes*
Do students work in a museum collection as part of the program of study?   *Yes*
Do program instructors have museum experience?   *Yes*
How many students begin the program each year?   *6–10*

How many students have completed the program since it began?   *35–45*
Are the majority of the beginning students already employed by
   museums?   *No*
What percentage of the students completing this program enter or return
   to museum work?   *25% to 50%*
Contact person: *David M. Armstrong, Director*
Description of program: *Master's degree*

Master of Basic Science (MBS) (with specialty in biology, geology, or
anthropology), or **Master of Arts in history or anthropology with
museology minor**: the Master's degree requires a minimum of twenty-four
hours plus thesis or thirty semester hours without thesis. The MBS program
requires nine to twelve hours in museology, three to six hours in museum
administration, and fifteen hours in one of the cognate sciences. The
museology minor requires eight hours in museology and the remainder in
either history or anthropology.

101

Museum Management Program
University of Colorado
250 Bristlecone Way
Boulder, Colorado 80304
USA
Telephone: (303) 443 2946
Fax: (303) 443 8486

The program began in: *1987*
Time required to complete program: *5 days*
Level of training provided: *Courses, Certificate*
Areas of study: *Administration, Collection management, Exhibit design,
   Public programming, Curatorship, Education*
Areas of specialization: *Museum management, Ethics, Museology*
Is museum ethics a regular part of the program?   *Yes*
Is the program open to international students?   *Yes*
The primary language of instruction is: *English*
Is financial assistance available for students?   *No*
The program is affiliated with: *Museum(s), University(ies)*
Is instruction given in a museum?   *No*
Do program instructors have museum experience?   *Yes*
How many students begin the program each year?   *30–40*
How many students have completed the program since it began?   *250*

Are the majority of the beginning students already employed by
museums? *Yes*
What percentage of the students completing this program enter or return
to museum work?   *More than 75%*
Contact person: *Victor J. Danilov*
Description of program: *One-week short course*

The **Museum Management Program** at the University of Colorado in
Boulder is a one-week mid-career short course for museum directors and
other senior administrators.

The program was started in 1987 to fill the need for a relatively brief
but intense interactive look at timely issues of museum management,
centered on presentations by leading museum figures.

From thirty to forty museum directors, department heads, and other
administrators normally participate in the program dealing with developments in such areas as museum planning, fiscal management, board relations,
collections management, exhibit development, education programming, fund
raising, marketing, ethics, evaluation, and personnel management.

102

Colorado Historical Society
Colorado History Museum
Ed. Dept, 1300 Broadway
Denver, Colorado 80203
USA
Telephone: (303) 866 4656

The program began in: *1982*
Time required to complete program: *Varies*
Level of training provided: *Internships*
Areas of study: *Collection management, Public programming, Education*
Areas of specialization: *Anthropology, Material culture, Ethics, History,
    Museology*
Is museum ethics a regular part of the program?   *Yes*
Is the program open to international students?   *Yes*
The primary language of instruction is: *English*
Is financial assistance available for students?   *No*
The program is affiliated with: *Museum(s)*
Is instruction given in a museum?   *Yes*
Do students work in a museum collection as part of the program of
    study?   *Yes*

Do program instructors have museum experience? *Yes*
How many students begin the program each year? *5*
Contact person: *Mary Ann McNair*
Description of program: *Internships*

High school internships: students must be nominated by a high school teacher or administrator. Interns will conduct classes on Colorado history for younger students, learn about teaching with objects, and write narratives. Approximately five positions are available each semester.

Undergraduate and graduate internships: candidates selected to become interns at the Museum will work with members of the staff in researching the Society's collections, undertake teaching assignments, and participate in producing educational materials. Applicants should be enrolled in a degree program in one of these areas: history, anthropology, fine arts, education, or museum studies.

103

Minority Internship Program
Denver Museum of Natural History
2001 Colorado Boulevard
Denver, Colorado 80205
USA

The program began in: *1993*
Time required to complete program: *9 months*
Level of training provided: *Internships*
Areas of study: *Exhibit design, Public programming, Curatorship, Collection management, Education, Conservation*
Areas of specialization: *Anthropology, Ethnology, Material culture, Archeology, Museology, Paleontology*
Is museum ethics a regular part of the program? *Yes*
Is the program open to international students? *No*
The primary language of instruction is: *English*
Is financial assistance available for students? *Yes*
Financial assistance is available in the following ways: *Salary*
The program is affiliated with: *Museum(s), University(ies)*
Is instruction given in a museum? *Yes*
Do students work in a museum collection as part of the program of study? *Yes*
Do program instructors have museum experience? *Yes*

How many students begin the program each year?   *3*
Are the majority of the beginning students already employed by
     museums?   *No*
Contact person: *Judy Rodgers*
Description of program: *Internships*

The **Minority Internship Program** is unique in that it is designed to give minority students the competitive edge when they enter the market to obtain positions in the museum field. It is a pre-professional experience. Internships are offered in education, collections, and exhibits. The placement of students includes matching Museum needs with student interest and areas of expertise. Internships are for nine months in the area of specialization. Applicants should be upper-lever undergraduate students, graduate students, or college graduates wishing to pursue a museum career.

104

Anthropology Department
University of Denver
2130 South Race Street
Denver, Colorado 80208
USA

The program began in: *1949*
Time required to complete program: *2 years*
Level of training provided: *Courses, Internships, Graduate degree,*
     Workshops
Areas of study: *Administration, Collection management, Exhibit design,*
     Curatorship, Education, Conservation
Areas of specialization: *Anthropology, Ethnology, Material culture,*
     Archeology, Ethics, Museology
Instructional opportunities provided: *Full-time study, Part-time study,*
     Scheduled lectures/seminars
Is museum ethics a regular part of the program?   *Yes*
Is the program open to international students?   *Yes*
The primary language of instruction is: *English*
Is financial assistance available for students?   *Yes*
Financial assistance is available in the following ways: *Loans, Student*
     work program, Tuition waiver, Graduate teaching assistantships
The program is affiliated with: *University(ies)*
Is instruction given in a museum?   *No*
Do program instructors have museum experience?   *Yes*

How many students begin the program each year?   *6–8*
How many students have completed the program since it began?   *8*
Are the majority of the beginning students already employed by
  museums?   *No*
What percentage of the students completing this program enter or return
  to museum work?   *25% to 50%*
Contact person: *Terry R. Reynolds*
Description of program: *Master's degree, Workshops, Internships*

Generalist training in museum studies is provided for students interested
in working in small museums or at middle-range positions in large
museums. **Specialist training in archeology or in ethnography** is provided
for students interested in curatorial positions in departments of anthropology or ethnic arts in large museums. The program's goal is not only
to train museum professionals but to provide persons interested in
museums with an understanding of the material constraints to which
human existence is subjected; of the conservation and creative interpretation of material life; of the research potential of material culture
collections from the past and the present; and of the museum's role in
image-making and ideology-building.

105

Birdcraft Museum and Sanctuary
314 Unquowa Road
Fairfield, Connecticut 06430
USA
Telephone: (203) 259 0416

The program began in: *1980*
Time required to complete program: *6 months or less*
Level of training provided: *Internships, Workshops*
Areas of study: *Collection management, Exhibit design, Curatorship,*
  Public programming, Education, Conservation
Areas of specialization: *Environmental Education, Natural science,*
  History
Is museum ethics a regular part of the program?   *No*
Is the program open to international students?   *Yes*
The primary language of instruction is: *English*
Is financial assistance available for students?   *Yes*
Financial assistance is available in the following ways: *Materials/*
  supplies, Small grants, Possible lodging

The program is affiliated with: *Museum(s), Science center(s)*
Is instruction given in a museum?   *Yes*
Do students work in a museum collection as part of the program of
   study?   *Yes*
Do program instructors have museum experience?   *Yes*
How many students begin the program each year?   *1*
Are the majority of the beginning students already employed by
   museums?   *No*
Contact person: *Alison Olivieri, Chairman*
Description of program: *Internships, Work-study*

Students can undertake **projects including cataloging collections, designing
exhibits,** and/or **education programs** in a unique natural history museum
built in 1914 adjacent to a wildlife sanctuary. Small scholarships and
school credit are available. The Museum is located near local transportation and housing is possible. It is owned and operated by the
Connecticut Audubon Society with Nature Centers in Fairfield and
Glastonbury offering other work-study programs and internships.

106

Internship Program
Wadsworth Athenaeum
600 Main Street
Hartford, Connecticut 06103
USA
Telephone: (203) 278 2670

Time required to complete program: *6 months or less*
Level of training provided: *Internships, Intern seminars*
Areas of study: *Administration, Collection management, Exhibit design,
   Public programming, Curatorship, Education, Conservation, Information
   technology*
Areas of specialization: *Archives, Clothing, Fine arts, Decorative arts,
   History, Museology*
Instructional opportunities provided: *Scheduled lectures/seminars*
Is museum ethics a regular part of the program?   *Yes*
Is the program open to international students?   *Yes*
The primary language of instruction is: *English*
Is financial assistance available for students?   *No*
The program is affiliated with: *Museum(s), University(ies)*
Is instruction given in a museum?   *Yes*

Do students work in a museum collection as part of the program of study?   *Yes*

Do program instructors have museum experience?   *Yes*

How many students begin the program each year?   *30–40*

Are the majority of the beginning students already employed by museums?   *No*

What percentage of the students completing this program enter or return to museum work?   *25% to 50%*

Contact person: *Cynthia Cormier, Assoc. Ed. Curator; Intern Coord.*

Description of program: *Internships*

The Wadsworth Athenaeum is the oldest public art museum in the country. The **internship program** is designed for undergraduate and graduate students, and is tailored to meet individual needs. In addition to a major project in one of the Athenaeum's departments, interns participate in a weekly museum studies seminar. This seminar provides the intern with an overview of the various departments and the ways in which they interact within the museum.

The spring and fall intern will work twelve hours per week or a total of 120 hours per semester. The summer intern will work twenty hours per week for eight to ten weeks. It is up to each intern to determine, with his/her advisor, what specifically is necessary to fulfill the requirement for academic credit.

A minimum of two years of undergraduate study in appropriately related course work is required. For work in the American Decorative Arts Department, a background in American history or American studies is recommended. Students are assigned to work in specific departments according to their interests and skills. Internships do not carry a stipend.

107

Smithsonian Institution – Office of Museum Programs
Smithsonian Institution
A & I. Bldg, 900 Jefferson Dr. SW
Washington, D.C. 20560
USA

The program began in: *1974*

Time required to complete program: *6 months or less*

Level of training provided: *Internships, Workshops, Fellowships*

Areas of study: *Administration, Collection management, Exhibit design, Public programming, Curatorship, Education*

Areas of specialization: *Ethics, Museology*
Instructional opportunities provided: *Scheduled lectures/seminars*
Is museum ethics a regular part of the program? *Yes*
Is the program open to international students? *Yes*
The primary language of instruction is: *English*
Is financial assistance available for students? *Yes*
Financial assistance is available in the following ways: *Scholarships, Tuition waiver, Travel for American Indian programs*
The program is affiliated with: *Museum(s)*
Is instruction given in a museum? *Yes*
Do students work in a museum collection as part of the program of study? *Yes*
Do program instructors have museum experience? *Yes*
How many students begin the program each year? *200*
How many students have completed the program since it began? *6500*
Are the majority of the beginning students already employed by museums? *Yes*
What percentage of the students completing this program enter or return to museum work? *More than 75%*
Contact person: *Bruce C. Craig, Program Manager*
Description of program: *Programs, Fellowships*

The **Smithsonian Office of Museum Programs** (OMP) strengthens museum services to diverse publics by providing training, information, and assistance in museum theory and practice. The office offers short-term, applied training directed at the needs of people already working in museums. The office also plays an important role in career counseling and training for Smithsonian Institution interns and other students. The office does not grant degrees or confer diplomas nor does it grant academic credit or continuing education units for internships or courses completed under its auspices. All program participants do receive a certificate of completion. The following programs and services respond to the needs of the museum community, both at the Smithsonian and to a national and international audience.

American Indian Museum Studies sponsor on-site workshops at different tribal communities. The program also offers internships at the Smithsonian. Both programs serve American Indian and Alaska Natives working in tribal community museums.

Fellowships in Museum Practice enable museum professionals to research museum theory and operations using resources and facilities at the Smithsonian.

Awards for Museum Leadership promote cultural diversity within the museum profession through training and professional support to people of color working in museums.

Smithsonian Staff Training in Museology offers an annual intensive curriculum in museum practice.

Intern Services provide orientation programs, museum career seminars and evaluation sessions to enhance the Smithsonian internship experience. Advisory Services offers OMP expertise and skill for individualized assistance with museum and staff development needs.

Information Services of the office include museum training videos and publications.

108

Corcoran Gallery of Art
500 17th Street NW
Washington, D.C. 20006-4899
USA
Telephone: (202) 638 3211 Ext. 321

Time required to complete program: *6 months or less, 1 year (internship)*
Level of training provided: *Internships*
The primary language of instruction is: *English*
Is financial assistance available for students?   *No*
The program is affiliated with: *Museum(s), University(ies)*
Contact person: *Education Coordinator*
Description of program: *Internships*

Ten-week summer internships, June through August, for students of art history, American art and/or American studies: program geared to undergraduates who expect to complete their junior or senior year by June; graduate students may be eligible. Interns are assigned to one museum department and complete a special project supervised by a staff member. This highly structured program also includes study assignments on the Corcoran's collection, weekly rotations to other Museum departments and field trips to Washington area art institutions. Six to eight students chosen. No stipend available, arrangements to receive school credit should be made prior to start of internship.

Academic year internships offered to graduate students in museum education, and history/museology or American studies at George Washington University and American University in Washington, D.C. Interns are assigned to a specific department where they assist with daily departmental functions. Each intern also prepares and presents weekly public introductory tours on the Corcoran's exhibitions and collections, and completes a substantial research project.

109

Internship Program
National Museum of African Art
950 Independence Avenue SW
Washington, D.C. 20560
USA
Telephone: (202) 357 3490

Time required to complete program: *6 months or less*
Level of training provided: *Internships*
Areas of study: *Administration, Collection management, Exhibit design, Curatorship, Education, Conservation*
Areas of specialization: *Anthropology, Archives, Ethnology, Fine arts, Museology*
Is museum ethics a regular part of the program? *No*
Is the program open to international students? *Yes*
The primary language of instruction is: *English*
Is financial assistance available for students? *No*
The program is affiliated with: *Museum(s)*
Is instruction given in a museum? *Yes*
Do students work in a museum collection as part of the program of study? *Yes*
Do program instructors have museum experience? *Yes*
How many students begin the program each year? *Varies*
Are the majority of the beginning students already employed by museums? *No*
Contact person: *Veronika Jenke*
Description of program: *Internships*

Undergraduate and graduate internships: full-time and part-time opportunities exist. Students may intern for one semester during the school year; internships are also available during the summer. Assignments may be procured in such areas as conservation, education, public affairs, photographic archives, registration, curatorial, exhibits, and administration. Candidates must have a background in art history, anthropology, museum studies, or a related discipline. Specific training in African art or other aspects of African culture is desirable, particularly for students wishing to intern in the education or curatorial departments.

110

National Air and Space Museum
7th and Independence Avenue, SW
Washington, D.C. 20560
USA

Time required to complete program: *Varies*
Level of training provided: *Internships, Pre- and postdoctoral fellowships*
Areas of study: *Education, Conservation*
Contact person: *Jo Hinkel, Intern Coordinator*
Description of program: *Internships, Fellowships*

Internships are offered to undergraduate and first-year graduate students for the fall, spring, and summer semesters. Full-time (forty hours per week) and part-time (twenty hours per week) positions are available. The spring and fall programs are fourteen weeks in length. Summer appointments are for ten weeks, full-time. January internships and quarterly internships are considered on a case-by-case basis. Internships are offered in many areas, including aviation history, conservation and restoration, museum education, planetary science, publications and marketing, public relations, geology, and space science. If any student accepted to this program is planning to receive academic credit from his or her university, and is paying a tuition fee to that university for such credit, the Museum asks that the tuition be waived or shared with the Smithsonian Institution on a fifty-fifty basis.

Division of Education, Telephone: (202) 786 2106 and (202) 357 1504

Through the support of the Guggenheim Foundation, the National Air and Space Museum supports a one-year resident **fellowship** for scholars interested in historical and scientific research related to aviation and space. The fellowship is open to predoctoral and postdoctoral applicants. Predoctoral applicants should have completed preliminary course work and examinations and be engaged in dissertation research. Postdoctoral applicants preferably should have received their Ph.D. within the past seven years. Predoctoral stipend $13,000. Postdoctoral stipend $21,000.

The National Air and Space Museum has established the A. Verville Fellowship, a competitive nine- to twelve-month resident fellowship intended for the analysis of major trends, developments, and accomplishments in the history of aviation or space studies. The fellowship is open to all interested candidates with demonstrated skills in research and writing. An advanced degree in history, engineering, or related fields is not a requirement. Twelve-month fellowship $26,000.

Telephone: (202) 357 1529

111

Basic Curatorial Methods Course
US Army Center of Military History
1099 14th Street, NW
Washington, D.C. 20005-3402
USA
Telephone: (202) 272 0310

The program began in: *1982*
Time required to complete program: *6 months or less*
Level of training provided: *Courses, Workshops*
Areas of study: *Administration, Collection management, Exhibit design, Curatorship, Education, Conservation*
Areas of specialization: *Material culture, Ethics, Museology*
Instructional opportunities provided: *Scheduled lectures/seminars*
Is museum ethics a regular part of the program? *Yes*
Is the program open to international students? *No*
The primary language of instruction is: *English*
Is financial assistance available for students? *No*
The program is affiliated with: *Museum(s)*
Is instruction given in a museum? *No*
Do program instructors have museum experience? *Yes*
How many students begin the program each year? *25*
How many students have completed the program since it began? *180*
Are the majority of the beginning students already employed by museums? *Yes*
What percentage of the students completing this program enter or return to museum work? *More than 75%*

Contact person: *R. Cody Phillips*
Description of program: *Course work, Workshops*

A five-day **training course** held in Northern Virginia for individuals who are new to the museum profession or the Army Museum System. This course addresses four principal subject areas: collections management (accessioning, cataloging, and accountability of historical property), conservation (routine care and preservation of artifacts), exhibition (philosophy and techniques), and educational programs. The course also includes orientation about the Center of Military History, ethics, the Institute of Heraldry, Army Art Program, and organizational history. Each class is limited to twenty-five students. Applications are reviewed based on institutional need and career potential. A registration fee is charged to defray the cost of facilities.

112

Museum Education Program
The George Washington University
2201 G Street NW #504
Washington, D.C. 20052
USA
Telephone: (202) 994 6820 or (202) 994 4960,
Fax: (202) 994 5870

The program began in: *1974–5*
Time required to complete program: *1 year*
Level of training provided: *Internships, Graduate degree, Workshops*
Areas of study: *Public programming, Education*
Areas of specialization: *Anthropology, Fine arts, Material culture, Natural science, Archeology, Architecture, Decorative arts, Ethics, History, Museology, Museum evaluation, Historic houses*
Instructional opportunities provided: *Full-time study*
Is museum ethics a regular part of the program? *Yes*
Is the program open to international students? *Yes*
The primary language of instruction is: *English*
Is financial assistance available for students? *Yes*
Financial assistance is available in the following ways: *Scholarships, Student work program, Loans, Travel subsidy*
The program is affiliated with: *Museum(s), Gallery(ies), University(ies), Science center(s)*
Is instruction given in a museum? *Yes*

Do students work in a museum collection as part of the program of study? *Yes*

Do program instructors have museum experience? *Yes*

How many students begin the program each year? *15*

How many students have completed the program since it began? *341*

Are the majority of the beginning students already employed by museums? *No*

What percentage of the students completing this program enter or return to museum work? *50% to 75%*

Contact person: *Carol B. Stapp, Ph.D.*

Description of program: *Master's degree, Internships, Workshops*

The **Museum Education Program** offered by the School of Education and Human Development is an intensive, thirty-three-credit-hour inter-disciplinary program leading to the **degree of Master of Arts in Teaching in the field of museum education.** Balancing academic study with carefully supervised fieldwork in educational sites and museums, the program is designed to prepare selected college graduates of diverse background, with or without museum experience, for positions in art, history, or science museums. Students acquire proficiency in three areas: expertise in communication and pedagogy, understanding of the museum as an educational setting and working organization, and command of a museum-related discipline and/or museology. Areas of specialization include: museum evaluation, historic house museums, accessibility, human development, and educational theory.

113

Internship Program
National Trust for Historic Preservation
1785 Massachusetts Avenue, NW
Washington, D.C. 20036
USA
Telephone: (202) 673 4120

The program began in: *1975*

Time required to complete program: *6 months or less*

Level of training provided: *Internships*

Areas of study: *Architectural preservation*

Areas of specialization: *Architecture*

Instructional opportunities provided: *Scheduled lectures/seminars*

Is museum ethics a regular part of the program? *No*

Is the program open to international students? *No*
The primary language of instruction is: *English*
Is financial assistance available for students? *Yes*
Financial assistance is available in the following ways: *Stipend*
Is instruction given in a museum? *No*
How many students begin the program each year? *20*
Are the majority of the beginning students already employed by
   museums? *No*
What percentage of the students completing this program enter or return
   to museum work? *Less than 25%*
Contact person: *Karen Peil*
Description of program: *Internships*

The National Trust for Historic Preservation, chartered by Congress in 1949, is a non-profit organization with 250,000 members nationwide. **Internship projects** vary each summer and have included researching public policy, state preservation legislation, fund raising, house museum furnishings plan, and tax incentives. Interns attend weekly seminars on the national preservation movement, the role of the National Trust, and visit local house museum properties.

114

International Summer Intern Program
US/ICOMOS
1600 H. Street, NW
Washington, D.C. 20006
USA
Telephone: (202) 842 1862,
Fax: (202) 842 1861

The program began in: *1984*
Time required to complete program: *6 months or less*
Level of training provided: *Internships*
Areas of study: *Administration, Education, Conservation, Information
   technology, Architectural preservation*
Areas of specialization: *Archives, Material culture, Archeology,
   Architecture, Decorative arts, History, Landscape Architecture,
   Preservation, Conservation*
Is museum ethics a regular part of the program? *No*
Is the program open to international students? *Yes*
The primary language of instruction is: *English*

Is financial assistance available for students? *Yes*
Financial assistance is available in the following ways: *Scholarships*
Is instruction given in a museum? *No*
How many students begin the program each year? *35*
How many students have completed the program since it began? *200*
Are the majority of the beginning students already employed by museums? *No*
Contact person: *Ellen Delage, Program Officer*
Description of program: *Internships*

US/ICOMOS International Summer Intern Programs: applications are accepted from graduate students and young professionals in the variety of disciplines that constitute the field of historic preservation, including architecture, conservation, architectural history, history, materials science, landscape architecture, and archeology. Internships are twelve weeks, June–August, with obligatory attendance at orientation and final debriefing sessions. The intern program is organized annually to promote an understanding of foreign and American preservation philosophies and techniques and to allow participants to begin a continuing professional dialogue with colleagues from abroad. Interns work directly for a public or private non-profit historic preservation organization on a special project.

Bilateral exchanges are organized each year between the United States and Great Britain; the Russian Federation; Lithuania; Poland; Israel; a specialized position at ICOMOS headquarters in Paris, France; and other countries to be announced. Participants should be 22 to 30 years of age and must demonstrate previous experience and/or academic concentration in the field of historic preservation. Stipend of approximately $3900. March 15 deadline.

115

Arts Administration Fellows Program
National Endowment for the Arts
1100 Pennsylvania Ave NW, Rm 219
Washington, D.C. 20506
USA
Telephone: (202) 682 5786

The program began in: *1973*
Time required to complete program: *6 months or less*
Level of training provided: *Certificate, Seminars*
Areas of study: *Administration, Education*

Areas of specialization: *Federal funding*
Instructional opportunities provided: *Scheduled lectures/seminars*
Is museum ethics a regular part of the program? *No*
Is the program open to international students? *No*
The primary language of instruction is: *English*
Is financial assistance available for students? *Yes*
Financial assistance is available in the following ways: *Fellowship stipend*
Is instruction given in a museum? *No*
Do program instructors have museum experience? *Yes*
How many students begin the program each year? *32*
How many students have completed the program since it began? *850+*
Are the majority of the beginning students already employed by museums? *Yes*
What percentage of the students completing this program enter or return to museum work? *Less than 25%*
Contact person: *Anya Nykyforiak, Fellowship Program Coordinator*
Description of program: *Fellowships*

Arts Administration Program: fellows are assigned to various programs within the organization depending on prior professional experience and academic background. Participants work as members of the professional staff to gain a functional view of the Endowment and to assist the program in both daily operation and special projects. Fellowship activities also include guest speaker seminars, panel meetings, and National Council on the Arts meetings. The fellowship stipend is $5500 for eleven weeks plus round-trip travel. There are three eleven-week sessions each year.

116

Arthur M. Sackler Gallery
Smithsonian Institution
1150 Independence Avenue, SW
Washington, D.C. 20560
USA
Telephone: (202) 357 4880

The program began in: *1987*
Time required to complete program: *Varies*
Level of training provided: *Internships*
Areas of study: *Administration, Collection management, Exhibit design, Public programming, Curatorship, Education, Conservation*

Areas of specialization: *Archives, Fine arts, Archeology, Museology*
Is museum ethics a regular part of the program?   *No*
Is the program open to international students?   *Yes*
The primary language of instruction is: *English*
Is financial assistance available for students?   *No*
The program is affiliated with: *Museum(s)*
Is instruction given in a museum?   *Yes*
Do students work in a museum collection as part of the program of
    study?   *Yes*
Do program instructors have museum experience?   *Yes*
How many students begin the program each year?   *15*
Are the majority of the beginning students already employed by
    museums?   *No*
Contact person: *Farar Elliott, Intern Coordinator*
Description of program: *Internships, Research grants*

Internships provide an opportunity for students to broaden their academic
programs by participating in projects relating to work in progress at
the Sackler Gallery. Students may elect to research the Asian collection, consisting of, among other items, jades, bronzes, pottery, scrolls,
calligraphy, paintings, and metal work. The Center also houses an extensive collection of Near Eastern art. Internship applications should be
accompanied by a project proposal, providing pertinent data on the
research to be undertaken. These materials will be reviewed by the director
in consultation with appropriate members of the staff. Working knowledge of one or more of the relevant Asian languages is required.

117

Freer Gallery of Art
Smithsonian Institution
1000 Independence Avenue, SW
Washington, D.C. 20560
USA
Telephone: (202) 357 4880

The program began in: *1987*
Time required to complete program: *Varies*
Level of training provided: *Internships*
Areas of study: *Administration, Collection management, Exhibit design,
    Public programming, Curatorship, Education, Conservation*

Areas of specialization: *Archives, Fine arts, Archeology, Museology*
Is museum ethics a regular part of the program?   *No*
Is the program open to international students?   *Yes*
The primary language of instruction is: *English*
Is financial assistance available for students?   *No*
The program is affiliated with: *Museum(s)*
Is instruction given in a museum?   *Yes*
Do students work in a museum collection as part of the program of
    study?   *Yes*
Do program instructors have museum experience?   *Yes*
How many students begin the program each year?   *15*
Are the majority of the beginning students already employed by
    museums?   *No*
Contact person: *Farar Elliott, Intern Coordinator*
Description of program: *Internships, Research grants*

Internships provide an opportunity for students to broaden their academic course of study by participating in projects relating to work in progress at the Freer Gallery of Art. Students may elect to work with curators of the Freer's Asian collections, which include works of art from China, Japan, India, Korea, Southeast Asia, Persia, and the ancient Near East, or with the Freer's collection of late nineteenth- and twentieth-century American art. There are also internship opportunities in the areas of exhibition design, public affairs, education, conservation, and library science. Prospective interns should submit a letter indicating areas of interest, accompanied by a résumé and/or college transcript. These materials will be reviewed by the intern coordinator in consultation with appropriate members of the staff. Working knowledge of one or more of the relevant Asian languages is helpful for students seeking curatorial internships. The Freer Gallery does not provide internship stipends.

Harold P. Stern Memorial Fund. Visiting research appointments from the fund are made to support projects that will increase the understanding and appreciation of Japanese art. Recipients spend approximately three months studying the Freer's Japanese collection, concentrating on a particular aspect of the Freer's holdings. Selection of recipients is by invitation only and is based upon outstanding scholarly achievement in the field of Japanese art.

118

Washington, Conservation Guild
PO Box 23364
Washington, D.C. 20026
USA
Telephone: (202) 387 2979

The program began in: *1970*
Time required to complete program: *1 to 3 days*
Level of training provided: *Workshops*
Areas of study: *Conservation*
Areas of specialization: *Archives, Ethnology, Fine arts, Material culture, Decorative arts*
Instructional opportunities provided: *Short-term lectures on request*
Is museum ethics a regular part of the program? *Yes*
Is the program open to international students? *Yes*
The primary language of instruction is: *English*
Is financial assistance available for students? *Yes*
Financial assistance is available in the following ways: *Partial subsidy*
Is instruction given in a museum? *Yes*
Do students work in a museum collection as part of the program of study? *Yes*
Do program instructors have museum experience? *Yes*
How many students begin the program each year? *Varies*
Contact person: *Arthur Page, President*
Description of program: *Workshops*

Professional training. The Washington Conservation Guild occasionally sponsors workshops of varying length for its members. The workshops are advertised to the membership through the Guild's newsletter. Fees vary.

119

United States Marine Corps
Marine Corp Historical Center
Building 55, Washington, Navy Yard
Washington, D.C. 20374
USA
Telephone: (202) 433 3840

Time required to complete program: *Varies*
Level of training provided: *Internships, Fellowships*
Areas of study: *Administration, Exhibit design*
Areas of specialization: *History, Military history*
Is financial assistance available for students?   *Yes*
Financial assistance is available in the following ways: *Fellowship, Stipend, Grants*
How many students begin the program each year?   *Varies*
Contact person: *Charles R. Smith, Historian*
Description of program: *Fellowships, Internships, Research grants*

Dissertation fellowships: topics in military science and military and naval history with a direct relationship to the history of the US Marine Corps will be considered. Within this context, topics may encompass wars, institutions, organization and administration policy, biography, civil affairs and civil action, as well as diplomatic, political, economic, social and intellectual trends, among others. Applicants must be enrolled in a recognized graduate school and have completed all requirements for the Ph.D. degree except the dissertation. One fellowship is offered each academic year with a stipend of $7500.

College internships: opportunities exist for qualified students to provide paraprofessional support as reference historians, research historians, historical writers' assistants, and exhibit apprentices. Assignments in other areas may be arranged. Applicants must be registered students at a college or university that will grant academic credit for work experience as interns in subject areas related to the students' course of study.

Research grants: applicants must be persons who have demonstrated ability and special aptitude for advanced study in aspects of American military history directly related to Marine Corps activities. While grants are usually made to students enrolled in a recognized graduate school as candidates for an advanced degree, they may be given to other persons who, by virtue of significant accomplishments in military historical and museum fields, have demonstrated a capability to execute advanced study projects. A grant will be given for periods of two to ten weeks in amounts of $400 to $2000 from which the recipient must meet travel and housing and all other expenses in connection with the grant.

Master's thesis fellowships: topics should be in the same categories as for Dissertation fellowships. Applicants must be enrolled in an accredited Master's degree program but do not need to have completed all course work or examinations. Three fellowships are offered each academic year of $2500 each.

120

National Museum of Natural History
Smithsonian Institution
Office of Education, Room 212
Washington, D.C. 20560
USA
Telephone: (202) 357 3045
Fax: (202) 786 2778

The program began in: *1980*
Time required to complete program: *6 months or less*
Level of training provided: *Internships*
Areas of study: *Administration, Collection management, Exhibit design, Public programming, Education, Conservation*
Areas of specialization: *Anthropology, Archives, Ethnology, Natural science, Archeology, Museology, Paleontology, Scientific illustration, Mineral science*
Instructional opportunities provided: *Scheduled lectures/seminars*
Is museum ethics a regular part of the program? *No*
Is the program open to international students? *Yes*
The primary language of instruction is: *English*
Is financial assistance available for students? *No*
The program is affiliated with: *Museum(s)*
Is instruction given in a museum? *Yes*
Do students work in a museum collection as part of the program of study? *Yes*
Do program instructors have museum experience? *Yes*
How many students begin the program each year? *40*
Contact person: *Magda Schremp, Internship Coordinator*
Description of program: *Internships*

Internships are available at various scholastic levels for both undergraduate and graduate students. Students work on a specified project with Museum staff (scholastic training, ability, and experience are taken into account). Applications are considered year-round and the term of the internship is arranged between the student and the supervisor. Interns work on their project in the Museum between twenty and forty hours per week. Some students receive college credit for their internship, but, if credit is desired, that must be arranged between the student and his or her college advisor prior to starting the internship. There is no stipend for these positions.

121

Office of Fellowships and Grants
Smithsonian Institution
955 L'Enfant Plaza, Suite 7000
Washington, D.C. 20560
USA
Telephone: (202) 287 3271

Time required to complete program: *Varies*
Level of training provided: *Internships, Fellowships*
Areas of study: *Administration, Collection management, Curatorship, Education, Information technology, Field methods*
Areas of specialization: *Anthropology, Archives, Clothing, Ethnology, Fine arts, Material culture, Natural science, Archeology, Decorative arts, Ethics, History, Museology, Earth sciences, Paleobiology*
Is museum ethics a regular part of the program?   *Yes*
Is the program open to international students?   *Yes*
The primary language of instruction is: *English*
Is financial assistance available for students?   *Yes*
Financial assistance is available in the following ways: *Fellowships, Stipends*
The program is affiliated with: *Museum(s)*
Is instruction given in a museum?   *Yes*
Do students work in a museum collection as part of the program of study?   *Yes*
Do program instructors have museum experience?   *Yes*
Contact person: *Pamela Hudson*
Description of program: *Fellowships, Internships*

The Smithsonian Institution offers in-residence **fellowships** for research and study in fields that are actively pursued by the museums and research organizations of the Institution. At present these fields are: animal behavior, ecology, and environmental science, including an emphasis on anthropology, including archeology; earth sciences and paleobiology; evolutionary and systematic biology; history of science and technology; history of art, especially American, contemporary, African, and Asian art, twentieth-century American crafts, and decorative arts; and social and cultural history and folklife of the United States.

Research and study appointments at the Smithsonian Institution are offered in the following disciplines: American history and material and folk culture, the history of art and design, anthropology and ethnic studies, the history of African art and culture, the history of science and technology, evolutionary and systematic biology, and geological science. Appointments are open to qualified undergraduate and graduate students and to recent recipients of the doctorate. All appointments require residence at a Smithsonian muscum laboratory, field station, archive, or other facility.

Predoctoral dissertation and postdoctoral fellowships are offered in most disciplines studied at the Smithsonian. Stipend of $13,000 per annum for predoctoral fellows, $21,000 per annum for postdoctoral with some related travel and research expenses furnished.

As an affirmative action measure, internship appointments are available to applicants who are members of minority groups. Assignments are available in any of the research areas of the Smithsonian. Applicants are undergraduate or graduate students. Stipends.

Graduate research fellowships: Available to students enrolled in a formal graduate program. Fellowships last ten weeks, full-time (summer and academic year). Stipend.

122

Museum Studies Program
The George Washington University
Academic Center T215
Washington, D.C. 20052
USA
Telephone: (202) 994 7030

The program began in: *1976*
Time required to complete program: *2 years*
Level of training provided: *Courses, Internships, Graduate degree*
Areas of study: *Administration, Collection management, Exhibit design, Public programming, Curatorship, Education, Conservation, Field methods, Information technology, Architectural preservation*
Areas of specialization: *Anthropology, Clothing, Ethnology, Fine arts, Material culture, Natural science, Archeology, Architecture, Decorative arts, Ethics, History, Museology, Paleontology*
Instructional opportunities provided: *Full-time study, Part-time study*
Is museum ethics a regular part of the program? *Yes*
Is the program open to international students? *Yes*
The primary language of instruction is: *English*
Is financial assistance available for students? *Yes*

Financial assistance is available in the following ways: *Student work program, Loans*
The program is affiliated with: *Museum(s), Gallery(ies), University(ies)*
Is instruction given in a museum? *Yes*
Do students work in a museum collection as part of the program of study? *Yes*
Do program instructors have museum experience? *Yes*
How many students begin the program each year? *25*
How many students have completed the program since it began? *300*
Are the majority of the beginning students already employed by museums? *No*
What percentage of the students completing this program enter or return to museum work? *More than 75%*
Contact person: *Marie C. Malaro, Director*
Description of program: *Graduate degree*

The **Graduate Program in Museum Studies** is an interdepartmental degree program leading to the degree of **Master of Arts in Museum Studies.** Students take advanced classes in their academic specialty (anthropology, art, history, natural science, etc.), and to satisfy the museum studies portion of their courses they have available to them a wide range of classes covering all major museum functions. Internship opportunities are available in over seventy museums, historical societies, or cultural agencies. Classes are taught by nationally recognized museum professionals.

123

Museum Studies Program
The George Washington University
Academic Center T215
Washington, D.C. 20052
USA
Telephone: (202) 994 7030

The program began in: *1990*
Time required to complete program: *1 year*
Level of training provided: *Courses, Internships, Certificate*
Areas of study: *Administration, Collection management, Exhibit design, Curatorship, Education, Conservation, Public programming, Information technology*
Areas of specialization: *Museology*

Instructional opportunities provided: *Full-time study*
Is museum ethics a regular part of the program?   *Yes*
Is the program open to international students?   *Yes*
The primary language of instruction is: *English*
Is financial assistance available for students?   *No*
The program is affiliated with: *Museum(s), Gallery(ies), University(ies)*
Is instruction given in a museum?   *Yes*
Do students work in a museum collection as part of the program of
   study?   *Yes*
Do program instructors have museum experience?   *Yes*
How many students begin the program each year?   *8*
How many students have completed the program since it began?   *New
   program*
Are the majority of the beginning students already employed by
   museums?   *Yes*
What percentage of the students completing this program enter or return
   to museum work?   *More than 75%*
Contact person: *Marie C. Malaro, Director*
Description of program: *Certificate*

The **Certificate Program in Museum Studies** is designed for two types of
students: the foreign museum professional, and the US student who already
holds an advanced degree. The Certificate Program allows a student to devote
one academic year to the study of functional aspects of museum work. A
student may concentrate in one of the following areas: (1) administration;
(2) collections management and care; (3) exhibition and public programs.
Eighteen credits must be taken in a mix of classes and internships.

124

National Museum of Natural History
Research Training Program
Smithsonian Institution
166 NHB
Washington, D.C. 20560
USA
Telephone: (202) 357 4548
Fax: (202) 786 2563

The program began in: *1980*
Time required to complete program: *10 weeks*

Level of training provided: *Internships, Workshops, Certificate*
Areas of study: *Collection management, Curatorship, Field methods*
Areas of specialization: *Anthropology, Natural science, Archeology,*
  Botany, Entomology, Zoology
Instructional opportunities provided: *Scheduled lectures/seminars*
Is museum ethics a regular part of the program? *Yes*
Is the program open to international students? *Yes*
The primary language of instruction is: *English*
Is financial assistance available for students? *Yes*
Financial assistance is available in the following ways:
  Materials/supplies, Housing stipend, Transportation allowance
The program is affiliated with: *Museum(s)*
Is instruction given in a museum? *Yes*
Do students work in a museum collection as part of the program of
  study? *Yes*
Do program instructors have museum experience? *Yes*
How many students begin the program each year? *24*
How many students have completed the program since it began? *202*
Are the majority of the beginning students already employed by
  museums? *No*
Contact person: *Mary Sangrey*
Description of program: *Internships*

The National Museum of Natural History (NMNH) has developed an **undergraduate summer intern program** providing opportunities for students to be directly involved in natural history research. At the NMNH young scientists are encouraged to study biodiversity through direct exposure to the diversity of organisms as well as through their involvement with outstanding staff and research facilities.

The internship program directly addresses current concerns about declining opportunities for training in systematic and organismal biology. The current movement away from traditional organismal programs in ecology and systematics and toward molecular and cellular biology preceded the more recent growing concern about the critical problems of biodiversity loss and global change.

Twenty-four interns participate in a ten-week program centered around: (1) demonstration of processes and methodologies used by researchers; and (2) hands-on research projects supervised by Museum scientists.

Interns are recruited from a diversity of institutions and cultural backgrounds. A special emphasis is placed on small institutions and colleges with predominantly minority students. Each intern is provided a travel allowance to Washington, housing for the duration of the program, and a modest stipend. Total cost per student is approximately $3000.

125

Joseph Henry Papers
Smithsonian Institution
A & I Building, Room 2188, MS 429
Washington, D.C. 20560
USA
Telephone: (202) 357 2787
Fax: (202) 786 2878

The program began in: *1967*
Time required to complete program: *6 months or less*
Level of training provided: *Internships, Workshops, Certificate*
Areas of specialization: *Documentary editing, History*
Is museum ethics a regular part of the program?   *No*
Is the program open to international students?   *Yes*
The primary language of instruction is: *English*
Is financial assistance available for students?   *No*
The program is affiliated with: *Museum(s)*
Is instruction given in a museum?   *Yes*
Do students work in a museum collection as part of the program of
    study?   *Yes*
Do program instructors have museum experience?   *Yes*
How many students begin the program each year?   *1–4*
How many students have completed the program since it began?   *36*
Are the majority of the beginning students already employed by
    museums?   *No*
What percentage of the students completing this program enter or return
    to museum work?   *Less than 25%*
Contact person: *John C. Rumm, Ph.D.*
Description of program: *Internships*

Internships are available for undergraduate and graduate students with
interests in American history, the history of science, or documentary
editing. Duties will vary according to the background and goals of the
intern and the needs of the projects. Interns are expected to work thirty
to forty hours per week during normal office hours. Applications are
considered year-round for a minimum term of two months. Academic
credit may be granted if arrangements are made in advance. No stipend.

126

National Museum of American History
Smithsonian Institution
14th Street & Constitution Ave NW
Washington, D.C. 20560
USA
Telephone: (202) 357 1606

Time required to complete program: *6 months or less*
Level of training provided: *Internships, Fellowships*
Areas of study: *Administration, Collection management, Exhibit design, Public programming, Curatorship, Education, Conservation, Field methods, Information technology, Architectural preservation*
Areas of specialization: *Anthropology, Archives, Clothing, Ethnology, Fine arts, Material culture, Natural science, Archeology, Architecture, Decorative arts, Ethics, History, Museology, Paleontology*
Is the program open to international students? *Yes*
The primary language of instruction is: *English*
Is financial assistance available for students? *No*
The program is affiliated with: *Museum(s)*
Is instruction given in a museum? *Yes*
Do students work in a museum collection as part of the program of study? *Yes*
Do program instructors have museum experience? *Yes*
Contact person: *Mary Dyer, Intern Coordinator*
Description of program: *Internships*

Internships are available within the Museum's Department of Social and Cultural History and the Department of the History of Science and Technology. The curators in these divisions provide interns with assignments that may range from organizing an exhibition to assisting in the preparation of a publication. Other Museum officers also provide internship opportunities, including the Office of Public and Academic Programs and the Office of the Registrar. On occasion, administrative offices accept an intern interested in museum administration. Stipends or college credit are not provided by the Museum. Interns should make arrangements for these with their respective colleges or universities. Programs last three to six months.

127

National Museum of American Art
Smithsonian Institution
Intern Program Officer
Washington, D.C. 20560
USA
Telephone: (202) 357 2714

The program began in: *1968*
Time required to complete program: *Varies*
Level of training provided: *Internships, Workshops*
Areas of study: *Administration, Collection management, Exhibit design,*
   Public programming, Curatorship, Education, Information technology
Areas of specialization: *Fine arts*
The primary language of instruction is: *English*
Is financial assistance available for students?   *Yes*
Financial assistance is available in the following ways: *Stipends*
The program is affiliated with: *Museum(s)*
Is instruction given in a museum?   *Yes*
Do students work in a museum collection as part of the program of
   study?   *Yes*
Do program instructors have museum experience?   *Yes*
How many students begin the program each year?   *Varies*
Contact person: *Intern Coordinator*
Description of program: *Internships*

Intern programs are offered during the fall, spring, and summer semesters
to coincide with the academic calendar. Programs are structured to meet
the needs of students seeking degrees in art history, American studies, or
studio art. Goals and interests of each intern are considered in making
placements that also take advantage of special and ongoing museum
projects. Supplementary workshops and seminars provide exposure to a
wide range of museum careers and opportunities. The National Museum
of American Art provides a stimulating environment for professional
museum training. Depending on the program, interns are assigned or may
elect to work in any of the museum's nine offices.

Advanced program: in cooperation with universities and colleges in the
United States and abroad, the museum offers an advanced program for
academic credit to students who have completed twelve hours of art history
in a graduate-level program. Exceptional students in their senior year of
college will be considered on an individual basis as will persons seeking

self-enrichment after graduation. Students may participate twenty hours per week to complete the program over two semesters, or forty hours per week to complete the program in a single semester.

Over twenty-five workshops and lectures in art history, conservation, registration, administration, budgetary procedures, and other topics are offered. An extensive required reading list supplements practical experience and workshop presentations. A comprehensive oral examination based on each intern's particular program concludes the training.

The **summer program** is open to students who are entering or have completed their senior year of college or to graduate students. Applicants must have a strong educational background in art history, studio art, or American studies, with little or no previous museum experience. In the summer program, interns concentrate on one aspect of museum work.

128

National Portrait Gallery
Smithsonian Institution
F Street at 8th, NW
Washington, D.C. 20560
USA
Telephone: (202) 357 2920

Level of training provided: *Internships*
Areas of study: *Administration, Collection management, Exhibit design,*
   Education, Conservation, Information technology
Areas of specialization: *Archives, Fine arts, History*
The program is affiliated with: *Museum(s), Gallery(ies)*
Is instruction given in a museum?   *Yes*
Do students work in a museum collection as part of the program of
   study?   *Yes*
Do program instructors have museum experience?   *Yes*
Contact person: *Harry Jackson, Curator of Education*
Description of program: *Internships*

The National Portrait Gallery offers **internships** to undergraduate and graduate students and to individuals not affiliated with academic programs who have research or museum career interests. The availability of internships is dependent upon departmental projects and staff needs, as well as the background, skills, and interests of the applicant.

129

Museum Studies Program
University of Delaware
301 Old College
Newark, Delaware 19716
USA
Telephone: (302) 451 1251

The program began in: *1972*
Time required to complete program: *2 years*
Level of training provided: *Internships, Graduate degree, Certificate*
Areas of study: *Administration, Collection management, Exhibit design, Public programming, Curatorship, Education, Conservation, Information technology, Architectural preservation*
Areas of specialization: *Archives, Fine arts, Material culture, Archeology, Architecture, Decorative arts, Ethics, History, Museology, Historic preservation, Historical editing*
Instructional opportunities provided: *Full-time study*
Is museum ethics a regular part of the program? *Yes*
Is the program open to international students? *Yes*
The primary language of instruction is: *English*
Is financial assistance available for students? *Yes*
Financial assistance is available in the following ways: *Scholarships, Tuition fellowships, Loans*
The program is affiliated with: *Museum(s), Gallery(ies), University(ies), Science center(s)*
Is instruction given in a museum? *Yes*
Do students work in a museum collection as part of the program of study? *Yes*
Do program instructors have museum experience? *Yes*
How many students begin the program each year? *15–20*
How many students have completed the program since it began? *400+*
Are the majority of the beginning students already employed by museums? *No*
What percentage of the students completing this program enter or return to museum work? *More than 75%*
Contact person: *Bryant F. Tolles, Jr, Ph.D., Director*
Description of program: *Certificate*

Awarding a certificate in combination with a graduate degree in a museum-related academic discipline, the **Museum Studies Program** of the University of Delaware blends academic theory with practical museum experience to provide its students with the opportunity to build a foundation in the museum profession. It serves as a non-degree interdisciplinary component of graduate degree programs in material culture, history, art history, art, public horticultural administration, and other pertinent areas. Students receive their primary instruction in an academic discipline, supplemented by four semester courses in museum studies, including an internship and practicums. Tuition fellowships include: Winterthur Early American Culture and Art Conservation, Hagley and Longwood Programs.

130

Longwood Graduate Program
University of Delaware
153 Townsend Hall
Newark, Delaware 19717-1303
USA
Telephone: (302) 451 2517

The program began in: *1967*
Time required to complete program: *2 years*
Level of training provided: *Courses, Internships, Graduate degree, Workshops, Certificate*
Areas of study: *Administration, Collection management, Exhibit design, Public programming, Curatorship, Education, Conservation, Architectural preservation*
Areas of specialization: *Anthropology, Archives, Clothing, Ethnology, Fine arts, Material culture, Natural science, Archeology, Architecture, Decorative arts, Ethics, History, Museology, Paleontology, Horticulture, Administration*
Instructional opportunities provided: *Full-time study*
Is museum ethics a regular part of the program?   *Yes*
Is the program open to international students?   *Yes*
The primary language of instruction is: *English*
Is financial assistance available for students?   *Yes*
Financial assistance is available in the following ways: *Fellowships*
The program is affiliated with: *Museum(s), Gallery(ies), University(ies), Science center(s)*
Is instruction given in a museum?   *Yes*
Do students work in a museum collection as part of the program of study?   *Yes*
Do program instructors have museum experience?   *Yes*
How many students begin the program each year?   *5*
How many students have completed the program since it began?   *110*

Are the majority of the beginning students already employed by
  museums? *No*
What percentage of the students completing this program enter or return
  to museum work? *25% to 50%*
Contact person: *James E. Swasey, Program Coordinator*
Description of program: *Master's degree*

The University of Delaware, in cooperation with Longwood Gardens,
offers a program in public horticulture leading to the degree of **Master
of Science in Public Horticulture Administration**. The program is appropriate for those interested in careers in management and leadership of
botanical gardens, arboreta, horticultural societies, park systems, civic
garden centers, and related institutions. In addition to academic studies,
students gain practical experience in the operation and administration of
botanic gardens by working with floral display, education maintenance,
greenhouse, and administrative units of Longwood Gardens and other
public horticultural institutions. Experience in, and knowledge of, public
horticulture, particularly that pertaining to the development, care, and use
of living plant collections, is preferred. Up to five students are accepted
annually, all on fellowships and twelve-month contracts. Stipends are
competitive.

131

Hagley Program in the History of Industrialization
University of Delaware
History Department, 413 Ewing
Newark, Delaware 19716
USA

Time required to complete program: *More than 2 years*
Level of training provided: *Graduate degree*
Areas of study: *Collection management, Exhibit design, Education,
  Conservation, Information technology*
Areas of specialization: *Material culture, Architecture, Decorative arts,
  History, Science and technology*
Instructional opportunities provided: *Full-time study*
Is museum ethics a regular part of the program? *No*
Is the program open to international students? *Yes*
The primary language of instruction is: *English*
Is financial assistance available for students? *Yes*

Financial assistance is available in the following ways: *Scholarships, Tuition waiver*
The program is affiliated with: *Museum(s), University(ies)*
Is instruction given in a museum?   *Yes*
Do students work in a museum collection as part of the program of study?   *No*
Do program instructors have museum experience?   *Yes*
How many students begin the program each year?   *2–6*
Are the majority of the beginning students already employed by museums?   *No*
What percentage of the students completing this program enter or return to museum work?   *Less than 25%*
Contact person: *Coordinator, Hagley Program*
Description of program: *Master's degree, Doctoral degree*

Hagley Museum and Library and the Department of History at the University of Delaware offer a two- or four-year course of study leading to **Master's or Doctoral degree** for students interested in careers as professionals in museums and historical agencies or as college teachers. The Hagley fellows fulfill the University's requirements for the M.A. or Ph.D. degree in American history. Within departmental guidelines, students may pursue a specific program in the history of technology. In addition to all tuition for courses at the University of Delaware and a small travel allowance, fellows receive a yearly stipend.

132

University of Delaware/Winterthur Museum
303 Old College
Newark, Delaware 19716-2515
USA
Telephone: (302) 831 8226

Time required to complete program: *More than 2 years*
Level of training provided: *Graduate degree, M.S., Ph.D.*
Areas of study: *Administration, Collection management, Exhibit design, Public programming, Curatorship, Education, Conservation, Field methods, Architectural preservation*
Areas of specialization: *Anthropology, Ethnology, Fine arts, Material culture, Archeology, Architecture, Decorative arts, Ethics, History, Museology*

Instructional opportunities provided: *Full-time study*
Is museum ethics a regular part of the program? *Yes*
Is the program open to international students? *Yes*
The primary language of instruction is: *English*
Is financial assistance available for students? *Yes*
Financial assistance is available in the following ways: *Fellowships*
The program is affiliated with: *Museum(s), Gallery(ies), University(ies)*
Is instruction given in a museum? *Yes*
Do students work in a museum collection as part of the program of
 study? *Yes*
Do program instructors have museum experience? *Yes*
How many students begin the program each year? *10 M.S., 1 Ph.D.*
Contact person: *Christine Heyrman*
Description of program: *Graduate degree*

The **Master's degree in Art Conservation** program is a cooperative effort between the University of Delaware and the Winterthur Museum. It is a three-year course leading to a Master of Science degree in art conservation and is designed to train practicing assistant conservators who will be professionally competent to perform basic conservation treatments in their area of specialization and who also possess a background knowledge in other areas of conservation. Depending on the availability of conservation faculty in any given year, major areas of study that may be offered are textiles, paper, painting, photographs, furniture, decorative, ethnographic and archeological objects, and conservation science. Practical work in conservation techniques is stressed and emphasis is place on connoisseurship and the understanding of chemical and physical properties of art materials and the scientific techniques used to characterize them. Ten fellowships are awarded annually.

Winterthur and the University of Delaware have designated funding for a **Ph.D. in History of American Civilization** track within the Winterthur Program and have begun admitting one or more fellows annually who will pursue a Ph.D. degree. Following completion of the Winterthur Program course work, Ph.D. candidates will continue their study of material culture/decorative arts in either art history or in the history of American civilization. Fellows on the Ph.D. track are able to take courses that satisfy requirements for both the Winterthur M.A. and their chosen doctoral program. Students admitted as Ph.D. candidates will receive a four-year fellowship.

133

Summer Intern Program
Historical Society of Delaware
505 Market Street
Wilmington, Delaware 19805
USA
Telephone: (302) 655 7161

Time required to complete program: *6 months or less*
Level of training provided: *Internships*
Areas of study: *Collection management, Exhibit design, Curatorship, Public programming, Education*
Areas of specialization: *Material culture, History, Museology*
Is museum ethics a regular part of the program? *Yes*
Is the program open to international students? *No*
The primary language of instruction is: *English*
Is financial assistance available for students? *Yes*
Financial assistance is available in the following ways: *Stipend*
The program is affiliated with: *Museum(s)*
Is instruction given in a museum? *Yes*
Do students work in a museum collection as part of the program of study? *Yes*
Do program instructors have museum experience? *Yes*
How many students begin the program each year? *1–3*
Are the majority of the beginning students already employed by museums? *No*
Contact person: *Paula Holloway*
Description of program: *Internships*

Summer Intern Program: one to three positions available each summer. Interns work thirty-five hours each week. Program runs from the middle of June to end of August, or negotiable. Projects may be in the library, museum, or education divisions, according to the student interest. Duties may include the maintenance and cataloging of library or museum collections, assisting in the development of educational or public programs, or research and assistance in development of museum exhibits. Graduate or undergraduate students with an identifiable interest and background in historical study, who live in the Wilmington area or have housing in Wilmington, are eligible. Modest stipends.

134

Winterthur Museum, Garden, and Library
Henry Francis duPont Winterthur Museum
Office of Advanced Studies
Winterthur, Delaware 19735
USA
Telephone: (302) 656 8591 or (302) 831 8226

The program began in: *1952*
Time required to complete program: *Varies*
Level of training provided: *Graduate degree, Fellowship*
Areas of study: *Administration, Collection management, Curatorship, Education, Conservation, Architectural preservation*
Areas of specialization: *Anthropology, Fine arts, Material culture, Archeology, Architecture, Decorative arts, History, Folklore, Food ways, Women's history*
Instructional opportunities provided: *Full-time study*
Is museum ethics a regular part of the program? *Yes*
The primary language of instruction is: *English*
Is financial assistance available for students? *Yes*
Financial assistance is available in the following ways: *Fellowships*
The program is affiliated with: *Museum(s), University(ies)*
Is instruction given in a museum? *Yes*
Do students work in a museum collection as part of the program of study? *Yes*
Do program instructors have museum experience? *Yes*
How many students begin the program each year? *Varies*
Contact person: *Katharine Martinez*
Description of program: *Fellowships, Graduate degrees*

Winterthur Research Fellowships are available to academic, museum, and independent scholars, and to support dissertation research for one to six months. Applications will be considered for study in the history, theory, or criticism of decorative arts, household furnishing, architecture, environmental design, painting, sculpture, photography, or related arts of America from the seventeenth century to the present. Stipends range from $1,000 to $2000 per month.

National Endowment for the Humanities Fellowships are available to scholars pursuing advanced research for six to twelve months' work. Stipends up to $30,000 per annum. The fellowship program is designed to promote research in the history of American art and American cultural and social history. Neither candidates for degrees nor persons seeking support to complete degrees are eligible to apply.

The Winterthur Program in Early American Culture provides a multi-disciplinary approach to the study of American material life with special emphasis on decorative arts and household furnishing. The program approaches the study of material culture through interpretation of objects and the social context in which they were made and employed. The curriculum involves course work at both the University of Delaware and the Winterthur Museum. The two-year course of study leads to a Master of Arts degree in Early American Culture from the University of Delaware. Up to ten M.A. fellowships are awarded each year.

135

Internship Program
Museum of Science and History
1025 Museum Circle
Jacksonville, Florida 32207-9053
USA
Telephone: (904) 396 7062 Ext. 233

The program began in: *1991*
Time required to complete program: *6 months or less*
Level of training provided: *Internships*
Areas of study: *Collection management, Public programming, Curatorship, Education*
Areas of specialization: *Anthropology, Material culture, Natural science, Museology*
Instructional opportunities provided: *Short-term lectures on request*
Is museum ethics a regular part of the program? *Yes*
Is the program open to international students? *Yes*
The primary language of instruction is: *English*
Is financial assistance available for students? *No*
The program is affiliated with: *University(ies)*
Is instruction given in a museum? *Yes*
Do students work in a museum collection as part of the program of study? *Yes*
Do program instructors have museum experience? *Yes*
How many students begin the program each year? *1–3*
How many students have completed the program since it began? *3*

Are the majority of the beginning students already employed by
   museums?   *No*
What percentage of the students completing this program enter or return
   to museum work?   *25% to 50%*
Contact person: *Carol S. Henderson, Director of Education*
Description of program: *Internships*

Internship Program in the Sciences and Humanities: undergraduate
positions, a maximum of three interns accepted at one time. Humanities
interns participate in researching and managing the collections, as well as
other tasks as appropriate to museum needs and intern training and
interest. Students working with the natural sciences staff care for animals.
They may also assist with exhibit preparation and development and
implementation of programs. No stipends. Students may arrange to receive
school credit.

Teen Summer Intern Program: selected 14–17-year old interns work three
days a week during the summer. Work assignments are available in the
planetarium, the early childhood programs, the physical and natural
science programs, and as demonstrators and classroom assistants. Students
must provide recommendations from a teacher and be interviewed at the
Museum. The purpose of the program is to introduce teens to museum
operations.

136

Art Internship Program
Georgia Museum of Art
University of Georgia
Athens, Georgia 30602
USA
Telephone: (404) 542 3255

The program began in: *1988*
Time required to complete program: *1 year*
Level of training provided: *Internships*
Areas of study: *Collection management, Exhibit design, Public program-
   ming, Curatorship, Education*
Areas of specialization: *Fine arts, Decorative arts*
Is the program open to international students?   *Yes*
The primary language of instruction is: *English*

Is financial assistance available for students?   *No*
The program is affiliated with: *University(ies)*
Is instruction given in a museum?   *Yes*
Do students work in a museum collection as part of the program of
   study?   *Yes*
Do program instructors have museum experience?   *Yes*
How many students begin the program each year?   *6*
How many students have completed the program since it began?   *50*
Are the majority of the beginning students already employed by
   museums?   *No*
Contact person: *William U. Eiland, Director*
Description of program: *Internships*

Undergraduate internships provide students with a general introduction
to museum operations. Students gain knowledge of departmental duties
by working in three separate areas within the Museum. Individuals with
specific museum interests may elect to work in only one department for
the duration of the internship. In addition to performing such tasks as
cataloging works of art and assisting with the handling and shipping of
objects, students are responsible for the completion of written assignments
and supplemental reading. Interns earn three to five credit hours through
the Department of Fine Arts.

137

Atlanta History Center
3101 Andrews Drive, NW
Atlanta, Georgia 30305
USA
Telephone: (404) 841 4131

Time required to complete program: *0 months or less*
Level of training provided: *Internships*
Areas of study: *Collection management, Exhibit design, Education,*
   Public programming
Areas of specialization: *Archives, History*
The primary language of instruction is: *English*
Is financial assistance available for students?   *Yes*
Financial assistance is available in the following ways: *Stipends*
Contact person: *Andy Ambrose, Education Department*
Description of program: *Internships*

High school interns participate in a concentrated program consisting of reading assignments, interpretation training, and the completion of a research project at the Tullie Smith House, one of the historic structures at the Center. Students are placed through the Fulton County's program for talented and gifted youngsters and work approximately eight weeks, five to ten hours per week, for school credit.

Undergraduate and graduate internships are also available throughout the year. Students work in a number of departments, such as the Library and Archives, Collections, Education, Public Programs, and Exhibits under staff supervision. They receive college credit but no stipends.

Stipends are provided by the **Governor's Intern Program** for qualified undergraduate and graduate students. For more stipend-related information contact the Office of the governor at (404) 656 3804.

138

Michael C. Carlos Museum
Emory University
571 South Kilgo Street
Atlanta, Georgia 30322
USA
Telephone: (404) 727 0573
Fax: (404) 727 4292

Level of training provided: *Courses, Internships*
Areas of study: *Administration, Collection management, Exhibit design, Public programming, Curatorship, Education*
Areas of specialization: *Archives, Fine arts, Archeology, Museology*
Instructional opportunities provided: *Part-time study, Scheduled lectures/seminars*
Is museum ethics a regular part of the program? *Yes*
Is the program open to international students? *No*
The primary language of instruction is: *English*
Is financial assistance available for students? *Yes*
Financial assistance is available in the following ways: *Scholarships*
The program is affiliated with: *Museum(s)*
Is instruction given in a museum? *Yes*
Do students work in a museum collection as part of the program of study? *Yes*
Do program instructors have museum experience? *Yes*
How many students begin the program each year? *Varies*
Are the majority of the beginning students already employed by museums? *No*

What percentage of the students completing this program enter or return to museum work? *Less than 25%*
Contact person: *Elizabeth Hornor, Coordinator of Education*
Description of program: *Internships*

Positions open to undergraduate and graduate students enrolled at Emory University. Interns assist with research, general operations, and also serve as tour guides. A background in art history is preferred.

139

The Columbus Museum
1251 Wynnton Road
Columbus, Georgia 31906
USA
Telephone: (706) 649 0713

Time required to complete program: *Varies*
Level of training provided: *Internships*
Areas of study: *Curatorship, Education*
Areas of specialization: *Archeology*
Is financial assistance available for students? *No*
The program is affiliated with: *Museum(s), University(ies)*
Is instruction given in a museum? *Yes*
Do program instructors have museum experience? *Yes*
Contact person: *Anne R. King or Margie Drury, Education Department*
Description of program: *Internships*

High school and undergraduate internships: positions are available within the education, curatorial, and archeology departments and are arranged on an individual basis through area high schools and Columbus College. Length of program and projects to be completed are mutually agreed upon by the student and the supervising staff member. No stipends.

140

Internships Program
Museum of Arts and Sciences
4182 Forsyth Road
Macon, Georgia 31210
USA
Telephone: (912) 477 3232

Time required to complete program: *6 months or less*
Level of training provided: *Internships*
Areas of study: *Collection management, Public programming, Education*
Areas of specialization: *Fine arts, Natural science, Museology*
Is museum ethics a regular part of the program?   *No*
Is the program open to international students?   *Yes*
The primary language of instruction is: *English*
Is financial assistance available for students?   *No*
The program is affiliated with: *Museum(s)*
Is instruction given in a museum?   *Yes*
Do students work in a museum collection as part of the program of
   study?   *Yes*
Do program instructors have museum experience?   *Yes*
How many students begin the program each year?   *1–2*
How many students have completed the program since it began?   *10–12*
Contact person: *Mary Ann Ellis, Director of Education*
Description of program: *Internships*

Placements are available at several academic levels. Programs are tailored
to meet individual requirements. Undergraduate and graduate students as
well as students enrolled in vocational/technical classes have interned at
the Museum. Assignments have included research and cataloging of work
and the creation and installation of exhibits. High school juniors and
seniors may also apply for internships. These students are usually supervised by the science director and assist with planetarium operations.

141

University of Hawaii at Manoa
Department of Art
Honolulu, Hawaii 96822
USA
Telephone: (808) 956 6888
Fax: (808) 956 9043

The program began in: *1979*
Level of training provided: *Courses*
Areas of study: *Administration, Exhibit design, Education, Public
   programming*
Areas of specialization: *Fine arts, Decorative arts, Museology*
Instructional opportunities provided: *Full-time study, Part-time study*
Is museum ethics a regular part of the program?   *Yes*
Is the program open to international students?   *Yes*

The primary language of instruction is: *English*
Is financial assistance available for students? *Yes*
Financial assistance is available in the following ways: *Scholarships, Loans, Tuition waiver, Student work program*
The program is affiliated with: *Gallery(ies), University(ies)*
Is instruction given in a museum? *No*
Do program instructors have museum experience? *Yes*
Are the majority of the beginning students already employed by museums? *No*
What percentage of the students completing this program enter or return to museum work? *Less than 25%*
Contact person: *Tom Klobe, Director*
Description of program: *Courses*

Exhibition Design and Gallery Management: undergraduate or graduate-level course. The course is an elective within the Department of Art. Prior to enrollment, students must complete one foundation studio class, and two art classes beyond freshman level. Focusing on the aims and purposes of exhibition design, the class includes instruction on technical aspects as well as administrative concerns. Space planning, color selection, and design and mounting are dealt with in relation to the exhibition theme. Lectures also center on framing, graphics, labeling, lighting, and the fabrication of special properties. This comprehensive program of study also covers the fundamentals of financial planning, security and protection, public relations, and conservation and restoration. Work-study at the Gallery is available to qualified students.

Museum Interpretation: undergraduate or graduate-level course, elective within the Department of Art. Students must have upper division standing in a course of study relevant to museum work. The class concentrates on methods of communication within the museum context emphasizing development of research and writing skills. A variety of museum situations are considered and include art galleries, historic sites, parks, and related settings. Student employment is available in the Gallery.

142

Museum Studies Program
Southern Illinois University
University Museum
Carbondale, Illinois 62901-4508
USA
Telephone: (618) 453 5388

The program began in: *1975*
Time required to complete program: *2 years*
Level of training provided: *Courses, Internships, Graduate degree, Bachelor degree*
Areas of study: *Administration, Collection management, Exhibit design, Public programming, Curatorship, Education, Field methods*
Areas of specialization: *Anthropology, Archives, Clothing, Ethnology, Fine arts, Material culture, Natural science, Archeology, Decorative arts, Ethics, History, Museology, Paleontology*
Instructional opportunities provided: *Full-time study, Part-time study*
Is museum ethics a regular part of the program? *Yes*
Is the program open to international students? *Yes*
The primary language of instruction is: *English*
Is financial assistance available for students? *Yes*
Financial assistance is available in the following ways: *Scholarships, Loans, Tuition waiver, Student work program*
The program is affiliated with: *Museum(s), University(ies)*
Is instruction given in a museum? *Yes*
Do students work in a museum collection as part of the program of study? *Yes*
Do program instructors have museum experience? *Yes*
How many students begin the program each year? *25*
How many students have completed the program since it began? *125*
Are the majority of the beginning students already employed by museums? *No*
What percentage of the students completing this program enter or return to museum work? *25% to 50%*
Contact person: *John J. Whitlock, Ph.D., Director*
Description of program: *Bachelor's degree, Museum studies, Courses*

The main focus of the **Museum Studies Program** at Southern Illinois University at Carbondale is to familiarize persons with the administrative and practical functions of museums and to enable them to pursue a professional career in a museum.

Undergraduate and graduate students may minor in Museum Studies. In addition, through the Special Major Program, undergraduates may design a special course of study leading to a baccalaureate degree in Museology.

A special graduate program is available for students with professional interests in museum administration, leading to a Master of Public Administration (MPA) degree. Students with undergraduate backgrounds in fields such as anthropology, fine arts, political science, the sciences, and history may develop personal courses of study that blend general public administration and management concerns with the specifics of museum operations.

Arrangements have been made for museum administration students to serve internships with the Southern Illinois University Museum and/or other museum-related assignments elsewhere in the country. The MPA program in museum administration is coordinated by the Department of Political Science at SIUC, in cooperation with the University Museum.

143

Art Museum Studies
Krannert Art Museum
500 East Peabody
Champaign, Illinois 61820
USA
Telephone: (217) 333 1860

Time required to complete program: *2 years*
Level of training provided: *Internships, Graduate degree, Workshops, Certificate*
Areas of study: *Administration, Collection management, Exhibit design, Curatorship, Education*
Areas of specialization: *Fine arts, Material culture, Decorative arts, Museology*
Instructional opportunities provided: *Part-time study*
Is museum ethics a regular part of the program?   *Yes*
Is the program open to international students?   *Yes*
The primary language of instruction is: *English*
Is financial assistance available for students?   *Yes*
Financial assistance is available in the following ways: *Stipend*
The program is affiliated with: *Museum(s), University(ies)*
Is instruction given in a museum?   *Yes*
Do students work in a museum collection as part of the program of study?   *Yes*
Do program instructors have museum experience?   *Yes*
How many students begin the program each year?   *20*
How many students have completed the program since it began?   *50*
Are the majority of the beginning students already employed by museums?   *No*
What percentage of the students completing this program enter or return to museum work?   *50% to 75%*
Contact person: *Maarten van de Guchte*
Description of program: *Graduate certificate program, Internships*

United States of America

The Krannert Art Museum at the University of Illinois offers a **graduate program in art museology**. The first three courses combine lectures, demonstrations by museum specialists, and supervised practice. Student experiences include field trips to important Midwestern and eastern art museums, to technical and conservation laboratories, and to art research libraries, and photographic archives. The fourth course is an internship in a specialized department of a cooperating art museum such as the Art Institute of Chicago, the Indianapolis Museum of Art, the St Louis Art Museum, or the Krannert Art Museum.

A graduate of the Art Museum Studies Program should be qualified to enter, as a useful staff member, a curatorial, educational, or registraral department in a large art museum, or to undertake broad responsibilities in one of the many small art centers and museums that are in need of trained personnel.

The Art Museum Studies Program provides four graduate units of credit and is listed under the graduate course offerings of the School of Art and Design in the College of Fine and Applied Arts. It is recommended particularly to students qualifying for the Master's degree in Art History, but it is open to graduate students with approved prerequisites who are registered as non-degree candidates in the Graduate College, or as graduate degree candidates in disciplines such as design, art education, communications, business administration, library science, and archeology. Upon completion of the Program, the student receives a Certificate in Art Museum Studies.

This Program is supported by a grant from the National Endowment for the Arts in Washington, D.C., a federal agency. Funding is provided for supervised field trips and for stipends to those having internships in museums.

144

Historical Administration Program
Eastern Illinois University
History Department
Charleston, Illinois 61920-3099
USA
Telephone: (217) 581 5943

The program began in: *1975*
Time required to complete program: *2 years*
Level of training provided: *Internships, Graduate degree*

Areas of study: *Administration, Collection management, Exhibit design, Public programming, Information technology, Curatorship, Conservation, Field methods, Education, Architectural preservation*

Areas of specialization: *Archives, Material culture, Architecture, Decorative arts, Ethics, History, Museology, Administration, Preservation, Folklife*

Instructional opportunities provided: *Full-time study, Part-time study Scheduled lectures/seminars*

Is museum ethics a regular part of the program?   *Yes*

Is the program open to international students?   *Yes*

The primary language of instruction is: *English*

Is financial assistance available for students?   *Yes*

Financial assistance is available in the following ways: *Student work program, Scholarships, Tuition waiver, Graduate assistantships, Loans*

The program is affiliated with: *Museum(s), University(ies)*

Is instruction given in a museum?   *Yes*

Do students work in a museum collection as part of the program of study?   *Yes*

Do program instructors have museum experience?   *Yes*

How many students begin the program each year?   *10–15*

How many students have completed the program since it began?   *130*

Are the majority of the beginning students already employed by museums?   *Yes*

What percentage of the students completing this program enter or return to museum work?   *More than 75%*

Contact person: *Professor Michael D. Cook*

Description of program: *Master's degree*

Master of Arts in Historical Administration: the thirty-nine credit hour program requires courses in American architecture, decorative arts, history museum exhibits, folklife, historic preservation, and local and oral history. Students also participate in seminars in administration, archival methods and editing, education and interpretation, and cultural and social history.

In addition to regular course work, students visit and observe other museums, plan and construct an exhibit, edit the department newsletter, and research and present specific projects. After completing one year of academic course work, students begin a six- to twelve-month internship. Assistantships are available and include stipends and tuition waivers.

145

Education Department
Field Museum of Natural History
Roosevelt Road at Lake Shore Drive
Chicago, Illinois 60605-2497
USA
Telephone: (312) 922 9410

Time required to complete program: *Varies*
Level of training provided: *Internships, High school program*
Is financial assistance available for students?   *Yes*
Financial assistance is available in the following ways: *Stipends*
The program is affiliated with: *Museum(s), University(ies)*
Do program instructors have museum experience?   *Yes*
Contact person: *Carolyn Blackmon, Chair of Education*
Description of program: *Internships, High school program*

Undergraduate internships: the program is conducted in conjunction with Antioch College (Ohio), Beloit College (Wisconsin), and Evergreen State College (Washington State). Internships last from six to nine months. Students work under the supervision of a curator. Four positions are available each year. Stipends.

High School Museology Program: sponsored by the Chicago Board of Education, this program is available to gifted high school students in the Chicago area. Sessions are held every Wednesday, September through June. Students receive school credit for completed assignments.

Through the **W.K. Kellogg Foundation Fellowship Program**, the Field Museum offers publications to the museum community.

146

Society of American Archivists
600 South Federal, Suite 504
Chicago, Illinois 60605
USA
Telephone: (312) 922 0140
Fax: (312) 347 1452

The program began in: *1936*
Time required to complete program: *6 months or less*

Level of training provided: *Workshops*

Areas of study: *Collection management, Public programming, Administration, Architectural preservation, Conservation, Information technology*

Areas of specialization: *Archives, Ethics*

Instructional opportunities provided: *Scheduled lectures/seminars*

Is museum ethics a regular part of the program? *Yes*

Is the program open to international students? *Yes*

The primary language of instruction is: *English*

Is financial assistance available for students? *No*

The program is affiliated with: *University(ies)*

Is instruction given in a museum? *No*

Do program instructors have museum experience? *Yes*

How many students begin the program each year? *600*

Are the majority of the beginning students already employed by museums? *Yes*

What percentage of the students completing this program enter or return to museum work? *More than 75%*

Contact person: *Jane Kenamore, Education Officer*

Description of program: *Workshops*

The Society sponsors about thirty one- and two-day **workshops** throughout the year on a variety of topics that relate to **archival management**. The curriculum includes twenty five topics in the following areas: fundamental archival theory and practice, appraisal and acquisition, description, electronic records, legal and ethical issues, management, oral history, preservation, outreach, records management, reference, and the management of special media, such as photographs, architectural drawings, sound and video recording, etc. Workshops are held in all regions of the country.

147

Campbell Center for Historic Preservation Studies
Campbell Center
203 East Seminary Street
Mt Carroll, Illinois 61053-0066
USA
Telephone: (815) 244 1173

The program began in: *1980*

Time required to complete program: *1 to 4 weeks*

Level of training provided: *Courses, Workshops*

Areas of study: *Collection management, Architectural preservation, Conservation*
Areas of specialization: *Ethnology, Fine arts, Material culture, Archeology, Architecture, Textiles, Security, Disaster mitigation*
Instructional opportunities provided: *Scheduled lectures/seminars*
Is museum ethics a regular part of the program?   *Yes*
Is the program open to international students?   *Yes*
The primary language of instruction is: *English*
Is financial assistance available for students?   *Yes*
Financial assistance is available in the following ways: *Scholarships*
Is instruction given in a museum?   *No*
Do program instructors have museum experience?   *Yes*
How many students begin the program each year?   *100+*
How many students have completed the program since it began?   *1200*
Are the majority of the beginning students already employed by museums?   *Yes*
What percentage of the students completing this program enter or return to museum work?   *More than 75%*
Contact person: *Mary Wood Lee, Director*
Description of program: *Courses, Workshops*

The Campbell Center is a private, non-profit organization that offers a **program of mid-career training** for those in the fields of **historic preservation, collections care, and conservation.** Courses are generally four or five days in length. Exceptions are the Core Curriculum for Historical Collections and the Core Curriculum for Archeological and Ethnographic Materials, each of which is four weeks in length. Some courses, including the core curricula, are offered annually and others vary from year to year. Courses are held during the summer months and the annual course catalog is available in January. Scholarships may be available for selected courses.

148

Illinois State Museum
Spring and Edwards Streets
Springfield, Illinois 60546
USA
Telephone: (217) 782 7386

The program began in: *1982*
Time required to complete program: *8 months*
Level of training provided: *Internships*

Areas of study: *Education*
Is museum ethics a regular part of the program?   *No*
Is the program open to international students?   *Yes*
The primary language of instruction is: *English*
Is financial assistance available for students?   *Yes*
Financial assistance is available in the following ways: *Stipend*
The program is affiliated with: *Museum(s)*
Is instruction given in a museum?   *Yes*
Do students work in a museum collection as part of the program of
    study?   *No*
Do program instructors have museum experience?   *Yes*
How many students begin the program each year?   *1*
How many students have completed the program since it began?   *10*
Are the majority of the beginning students already employed by
    museums?   *Yes*
What percentage of the students completing this program enter or return
    to museum work?   *More than 75%*
Contact person: *Chris Meier*
Description of program: *Internships*

One full-time **internship in museum education** is available to an individual
who possesses or is completing a Master's degree in education or museum
studies or who has a Bachelor's degree and some museum experience.
Duties include organizing special events and programs and coordinating
volunteer schedules. Stipend is provided.

149

Museum of Natural History
University of Illinois
1301 West Green Street, Room 438
Urbana, Illinois 61801
USA
Telephone: (217) 244 3179

The program began in: *1985*
Time required to complete program: *No specific length*
Level of training provided: *Courses, Internships, Workshops*
Areas of study: *Administration, Collection management, Exhibit design,*
    Public programming, Curatorship, Education, Conservation, Field
    methods
Areas of specialization: *Anthropology, Archives, Ethnology, Material*

culture, Natural science, Archeology, Ethics, History, Museology,
Paleontology, Textiles, skins and hides
Instructional opportunities provided: Full-time study, Part-time study
Scheduled lectures/seminars
Is museum ethics a regular part of the program?   Yes
Is the program open to international students?   Yes
The primary language of instruction is: English
Is financial assistance available for students?   Yes
Financial assistance is available in the following ways: Scholarships,
Student work program, Loans
The program is affiliated with: Museum(s), University(ies)
Is instruction given in a museum?   Yes
Do students work in a museum collection as part of the program of
study?   Yes
Do program instructors have museum experience?   Yes
How many students begin the program each year?   10
How many students have completed the program since it began?   80
Are the majority of the beginning students already employed by
museums?   No
What percentage of the students completing this program enter or return
to museum work?   Less than 25%
Contact person: Charles Stout
Description of program: Internships, Courses

Independent research internships are offered to qualified undergraduate
and graduate students. These individualized programs are comprised of
the following components: research and study of a specific museum topic,
curatorial training, and participation in field trips as well as practical work
assignments.

150

Mathers Museum
Indiana University
601 East 8th Street
Bloomington, Indiana 47405
USA
Telephone: Mathers Museum (812) 335 7224; Arts Administration
(812) 335 0282

The program began in: 1963
Time required to complete program: 2 years

Level of training provided: *Minor in Museum Studies*
Areas of study: *Administration, Collection management, Exhibit design, Public programming, Curatorship, Education, Conservation, Information technology*
Areas of specialization: *Anthropology, Archives, Clothing, Ethnology, Fine arts, Material culture, Archeology, Decorative arts, Ethics, History, Museology*
Instructional opportunities provided: *Part-time study*
Is museum ethics a regular part of the program?   *Yes*
Is the program open to international students?   *Yes*
The primary language of instruction is: *English*
Is financial assistance available for students?   *Yes*
Financial assistance is available in the following ways: *Scholarships, Loans, Student work program, Financial aid through Indiana University*
The program is affiliated with: *Museum(s), University(ies)*
Is instruction given in a museum?   *Yes*
Do students work in a museum collection as part of the program of study?   *Yes*
Do program instructors have museum experience?   *Yes*
How many students begin the program each year?   *5–10*
How many students have completed the program since it began?   *45*
Are the majority of the beginning students already employed by museums?   *No*
What percentage of the students completing this program enter or return to museum work?   *More than 75%*
Contact person: *Geoffrey W. Conrad or James Suelflow*
Description of program: *Bachelor's degree, Master's degree*

Minor in Museum Studies: the program is composed of courses, selected readings, and practicum projects that center on the anthropology, history, and folklore collections of the William Hammond Mathers Museum. The sequence can fulfill the minor requirement for undergraduate and graduate students enrolled in history, anthropology, fine arts, or affiliated curricula. A proposal for a graduate certificate program has been submitted to the University Graduate School.

Master of Arts in Arts Administration: this program is designed to train men and women to manage and promote arts centers, arts councils, museums, and related organizations. The curriculum consists of courses, an in-house practicum, a year-long seminar in arts administration, and a one-semester (or summer) internship. A museum training emphasis is also included, comprised of courses in museum management and methodology and a practicum.

235

151

Museum Studies Program
University of Iowa
Museum of Natural History
Iowa City, Iowa 52242
USA
Telephone: (319) 353 5893

The program began in: *1910*
Time required to complete program: *Varies*
Level of training provided: *Courses, Internships, Graduate degree, Workshops*
Areas of study: *Administration, Collection management, Exhibit design, Curatorship, Education, Conservation, Information technology*
Areas of specialization: *Anthropology, Material culture, Natural science, Museology, Science education*
Instructional opportunities provided: *Full-time study, Part-time study*
Is museum ethics a regular part of the program? *Yes*
Is the program open to international students? *Yes*
The primary language of instruction is: *English*
Is financial assistance available for students? *Yes*
Financial assistance is available in the following ways: *Student work program, Graduate teaching assistant stipend*
The program is affiliated with: *Museum(s), University(ies)*
Is instruction given in a museum? *Yes*
Do students work in a museum collection as part of the program of study? *Yes*
Do program instructors have museum experience? *Yes*
How many students begin the program each year? *6–7*
How many students have completed the program since it began? *400–500*
Are the majority of the beginning students already employed by museums? *No*
What percentage of the students completing this program enter or return to museum work? *50% to 75%*
Contact person: *George D. Schrimper, Chairman*
Description of program: *Concentration, Courses*

Master of Arts in Anthropology or **Master of Science in Science Education with a Museum Studies concentration:** both are thirty-eight-hour non-thesis programs requiring at least fifteen semester hours from the museology curriculum. Museum Studies courses provide a fundamental background in the history, philosophy, organization, operations, and

236

management of museums, affording special emphasis on exhibit design, collection management, and education outreach development. A final research project or position paper is required, the specific nature of which is determined by the student and the faculty advisory committee. An off-campus internship is also required. On-campus access to collections, galleries, and laboratories is provided by the University of Iowa Museum of Natural History, Museum of Art and Medical Museum.

152

Historical Administration and Museum Studies
University of Kansas
Museum of Anthropology
Lawrence, Kansas 66045
USA
Telephone: (913) 864 4245

The program began in: *1981*
Time required to complete program: *2 years*
Level of training provided: *Graduate degree*
Areas of study: *Administration, Collection management, Exhibit design, Public programming, Curatorship, Education, Information technology, Conservation, Field methods, Architectural preservation*
Areas of specialization: *Anthropology, Archives, Ethnology, Material culture, Natural science, Archeology, Architecture, History, Museology*
Instructional opportunities provided: *Full-time study*
Is museum ethics a regular part of the program?   *Yes*
Is the program open to international students?   *Yes*
The primary language of instruction is: *English*
Is financial assistance available for students?   *No*
The program is affiliated with: *Museum(s), University(ies)*
Is instruction given in a museum?   *Yes*
Do students work in a museum collection as part of the program of study?   *Yes*
Do program instructors have museum experience?   *Yes*
How many students begin the program each year?   *5–10*
How many students have completed the program since it began?   *30*
Are the majority of the beginning students already employed by museums?   *Yes*
What percentage of the students completing this program enter or return to museum work?   *More than 75%*
Contact person: *Alfred E. Johnson*

Description of program: *Master's degree*

The **graduate program in Historical Administration and Museum Studies** offers training for professional careers in museums or historical agencies. Its curriculum provides a basic understanding of the nature of museums and historical agencies as well as specialized training administered by the American Studies Program and the Departments of Anthropology, History, and Systematics and Ecology.

The Historical Administration and Museum Studies Program gives degree students a core of courses concerning the theories, history, techniques, and problems common to museums and historical agencies as well as the specialized operations of such institutions. Students also receive classroom and field training in methods and subject-matter in a designated area of concentration.

The course of study leading to a Master's degree comprises a minimum of forty-two semester credit hours on the graduate level. There are eighteen semester credit hours of core courses, eighteen semester credit hours of professional and subject-matter courses in the student's designated disciplinary track, and an apprenticeship in an approved museum or historical agency, part-time for two semesters, or the equivalent, for six semester hours of credit. Upon satisfactory completion of the required credit hours, a student must pass a formal examination and evaluation to be nominated for the degree of Master of Historical Administration and Museum Studies.

Admission to the program requires the student to have a baccalaureate degree and an accumulated grade-point average of B (3.0) in previous academic work.

153

Internship Program
Old Cowtown Museum
1871 Sim Park Drive
Wichita, Kansas 67203
USA
Telephone: (316) 264 0671

The program began in: *1988*
Time required to complete program: *Two semesters*
Level of training provided: *Internships*
Areas of study: *Administration, Collection management, Public programming, Curatorship, Education, Conservation*
Areas of specialization: *Material culture, History, Museology*
Is museum ethics a regular part of the program? *No*

Is the program open to international students? *Yes*
The primary language of instruction is: *English*
Is financial assistance available for students? *Yes*
Financial assistance is available in the following ways: *Scholarships, Student work program, Loans*
The program is affiliated with: *Museum(s), University(ies)*
Is instruction given in a museum? *Yes*
Do students work in a museum collection as part of the program of study? *Yes*
Do program instructors have museum experience? *Yes*
How many students begin the program each year? *1–2*
How many students have completed the program since it began? *12*
Are the majority of the beginning students already employed by museums? *No*
What percentage of the students completing this program enter or return to museum work? *25% to 50%*
Contact person: *Elizabeth D. Kennedy, Associate Director*
Description of program: *Internships*

The **Old Cowtown Museum Internship Program** is in cooperation with the Graduate Program in Public History and the Cooperative Education Department at the Wichita State University. Students receive hourly compensation and work twenty hours per week. They receive training and experience in a variety of areas including: interpretation, collections management, and administration. Each student must complete two semesters of internship at an approved site (museum, city preservation office, archives, etc.) as part of their degree requirement.

154

Basic Museum Training
University of Kentucky Art Museum
Rose Street and Euclid Avenue
Lexington, Kentucky 40506-0241
USA
Telephone: (606) 257 5716

The program began in: *1980*
Time required to complete program: *1 year*
Level of training provided: *Courses, Internships*
Areas of study: *Administration, Collection management, Exhibit design, Public programming, Curatorship, Education, Conservation*

Areas of specialization: *Fine arts, Material culture, Decorative arts, Ethics, Museology*
Instructional opportunities provided: *Part-time study*
Is museum ethics a regular part of the program?   *Yes*
Is the program open to international students?   *Yes*
The primary language of instruction is: *English*
Is financial assistance available for students?   *Yes*
Financial assistance is available in the following ways: *Scholarships, Student work program, Loans*
The program is affiliated with: *Museum(s), University(ies)*
Is instruction given in a museum?   *Yes*
Do students work in a museum collection as part of the program of study?   *Yes*
Do program instructors have museum experience?   *Yes*
How many students begin the program each year?   *6–8*
How many students have completed the program since it began?   *50*
Are the majority of the beginning students already employed by museums?   *No*
What percentage of the students completing this program enter or return to museum work?   *Less than 25%*
Contact person: *Harriet W. Fowler, Ph.D., Director*
Description of program: *Course*

Basic Museum Training: presented in conjunction with the Department of Art, the two-semester course is open to graduate students as well as upper-division undergraduates with strong art history backgrounds. Balancing the lecture/discussion format with practical experience in museum research, the course covers such topics as the history of museums, permanent collection development, museum education, records and registration, conservation, special exhibitions, exhibit design and installation. Students complete one detailed research problem each semester and concentrate for four weeks each term on one department of the museum. The course is not offered every semester.

155

J. B. Speed Art Museum Internship Program
J. B. Speed Art Museum
PO Box 2600
Louisville, Kentucky 40201-2600
USA
Telephone: (502) 636 2893

Time required to complete program: *6 months or less*
Level of training provided: *Internships*
Areas of study: *Administration, Exhibit design, Curatorship, Conservation, Information technology, Education*
Areas of specialization: *Fine arts, Decorative arts, History*
Is museum ethics a regular part of the program?   *No*
Is the program open to international students?   *Yes*
The primary language of instruction is: *English*
Is financial assistance available for students?   *No*
The program is affiliated with: *Museum(s)*
Is instruction given in a museum?   *Yes*
Do students work in a museum collection as part of the program of study?   *Yes*
Do program instructors have museum experience?   *Yes*
How many students begin the program each year?   *5*
How many students have completed the program since it began?   *20*
Are the majority of the beginning students already employed by museums?   *No*
Contact person: *Gerri Combs, Coordinator*
Description of program: *Internships*

The J. B. Speed Art Museum offers unpaid **internships** to college students who enjoy working with people and are interested in learning more about the many facets of an art museum environment. An internship acquaints students with the museum's collection and programs as well as providing the opportunity to explore a variety of career opportunities.

In general, internships will center on projects developed and monitored by museum departmental heads and/or senior staff. All internships also include some general departmental and clerical work. Assignments are determined by the needs of the department and the student's academic background, experience, and interests. Openings in the desired department may not always be available.

156

LASC Internship Program
Louisiana Arts and Science Center
Box 3373
Baton Rouge, Louisiana 70821
USA
Telephone: (504) 344 5272

The program began in: *1985*
Time required to complete program: *6 months or less*
Level of training provided: *Internships*
Areas of study: *Collection management, Exhibit design*
Areas of specialization: *Exhibitions, Collection records*
Is museum ethics a regular part of the program? *Yes*
Is the program open to international students? *No*
The primary language of instruction is: *English*
Is financial assistance available for students? *No*
The program is affiliated with: *Museum(s), University(ies)*
Is instruction given in a museum? *Yes*
Do students work in a museum collection as part of the program of
    study? *Yes*
Do program instructors have museum experience? *Yes*
How many students begin the program each year? *3*
How many students have completed the program since it began? *5–10*
Are the majority of the beginning students already employed by
    museums? *No*
What percentage of the students completing this program enter or return
    to museum work? *Less than 25%*
Contact person: *Maia Jalenak, Museum Curator*
Description of program: *Internships*

Semester and summer internships are offered for undergraduate and
graduate students enrolled in art history, art or science education, studio
art, or museum studies programs. Interns are supervised by the Museum
Curator, Art Education Curator, or Science Education Curator depending
on their area of interest. The intern learns first-hand about museum operations by working on a wide range of projects.

Internship is not paid. Students may arrange for course credit for the
internship through their department of study.

157

Historic New Orleans Collection
533 Royal Street
New Orleans, Louisiana 70130
USA
Telephone: (504) 523 4662

The program began in: *1984*
Time required to complete program: *6 months or less*

Level of training provided: *Internships*
Areas of study: *Curatorship*
Areas of specialization: *Archives, Fine arts, Architecture, Decorative arts, History*
Is museum ethics a regular part of the program? *No*
Is the program open to international students? *Yes*
The primary language of instruction is: *English*
Is financial assistance available for students? *No*
The program is affiliated with: *University(ies)*
Is instruction given in a museum? *Yes*
Do students work in a museum collection as part of the program of study? *Yes*
Do program instructors have museum experience? *Yes*
How many students begin the program each year? *3*
How many students have completed the program since it began? *35*
Are the majority of the beginning students already employed by museums? *No*
What percentage of the students completing this program enter or return to museum work? *Less than 25%*
Contact person: *Jon Kukla*
Description of program: *Internships*

Serving as a museum and research center, the Historic New Orleans Collection houses a diverse selection of materials related to the history of the Gulf South, Louisiana, and New Orleans. As part of the educational services offered to area college students, the Collection sponsors internships for qualified individuals.

The Collection co-sponsors, with the University of New Orleans and Tulane University, **internships** for undergraduate and graduate students in the curatorial, manuscripts, and publications departments. Interested students from other colleges or universities may apply. No stipends.

158

Portland Museum of Art
Seven Congress Square
Portland, Maine 04101
USA
Telephone: (207) 775 6148

Time required to complete program: *Varies*
Level of training provided: *Internships*

Areas of study: *Collection management, Exhibit design, Education, Public programming, Information technology*
Is the program open to international students? *Yes*
The primary language of instruction is: *English*
Is financial assistance available for students? *No*
The program is affiliated with: *Museum(s)*
Is instruction given in a museum? *Yes*
Do students work in a museum collection as part of the program of study? *Yes*
Do program instructors have museum experience? *Yes*
How many students begin the program each year? *Varies*
Contact person: *Danielle Vagenas, Human Resources Assistant*
Description of program: *Internships*

High school, undergraduate, and postgraduate internships: participants are exposed to the workings of a small museum. Projects are established according to the intern's background. No stipends are available.

159

Conservation Internships
The Walters Art Gallery
600 North Charles Street
Baltimore, Maryland 21201
USA
Telephone: (301) 547 9000

The program began in: *1968*
Time required to complete program: *1 year*
Level of training provided: *Internships*
Areas of study: *Conservation*
Areas of specialization: *Fine arts, Archeology, Decorative arts, Rare books and manuscripts*
Is museum ethics a regular part of the program? *No*
Is the program open to international students? *Yes*
The primary language of instruction is: *English*
Is financial assistance available for students? *No*
The program is affiliated with: *Museum(s)*
Is instruction given in a museum? *Yes*
Do students work in a museum collection as part of the program of study? *Yes*
Do program instructors have museum experience? *Yes*

How many students begin the program each year?   *2*
How many students have completed the program since it began?   *41*
Are the majority of the beginning students already employed by
   museums?   *No*
Contact person: *Terry Drayman-Weisser*
Description of program: *Internships*

Conservation internships are offered to those who are currently enrolled
in or are recent graduates of graduate-level conservation training programs,
or those individuals with equivalent experience in conservation. Interns
may specialize in paintings, objects, or books.

160

Baltimore City Life Museums Internships
Baltimore City Life Museums
800 East Lombard Street
Baltimore, Maryland 21202
USA

The program began in: *1988*
Time required to complete program: *6 months or less*
Level of training provided: *Internships*
Areas of study: *Collection management, Education*
Areas of specialization: *Archeology, History*
Instructional opportunities provided: *Part-time study*
Is museum ethics a regular part of the program?   *No*
Is the program open to international students?   *Yes*
The primary language of instruction is: *English*
Is financial assistance available for students?   *No*
The program is affiliated with: *University(ies)*
Is instruction given in a museum?   *Yes*
Do students work in a museum collection as part of the program of
   study?   *Yes*
Do program instructors have museum experience?   *Yes*
How many students begin the program each year?   *8*
How many students have completed the program since it began?   *50*
Are the majority of the beginning students already employed by
   museums?   *No*
What percentage of the students completing this program enter or return
   to museum work?   *Less than 25%*
Contact person: *Andréa Lewis*

United States of America

Description of program: *Internships*

Internships at the Baltimore City Life Museums offer students the opportunity to explore career options and work one-on-one with museum professionals. Assignments exist throughout the Museums: interns play an active role as guides and researchers in the Department of Interpretation. They assist with membership development and are assigned research projects at the Center for Urban Archeology. Students trained in registration methods are delegated such projects as accessioning objects in the collection and preparing fragile textiles for storage. Applicants should be enrolled in a college. Stipends available for some positions.

161

The Baltimore Museum of Art Summer Internship Program
The Baltimore Museum of Art
Art Museum Drive
Baltimore, Maryland 21218
USA
Telephone: (410) 396 6300, Fax: (410) 396 6562

The program began in: *1980*
Time required to complete program: *6 months or less*
Level of training provided: *Internships*
Areas of study: *Administration, Collection management, Education, Public programming, Curatorship*
Areas of specialization: *Fine arts, Decorative arts*
Is museum ethics a regular part of the program? *Yes*
Is the program open to international students? *Yes*
The primary language of instruction is: *English*
Is financial assistance available for students? *No*
The program is affiliated with: *Museum(s)*
Is instruction given in a museum? *Yes*
Do students work in a museum collection as part of the program of study? *Yes*
Do program instructors have museum experience? *Yes*
How many students begin the program each year? *5–7*
How many students have completed the program since it began? *55*
Are the majority of the beginning students already employed by museums? *No*

Contact person: *Brigid Globensky*
Description of program: *Internships*

The Baltimore Museum of Art offers a ten-week **summer internship program** for approximately five upper-division undergraduates contemplating museum careers. During the internship, students work intensively in one department within the Museum. Students also receive a general orientation to museum work through a series of in-house seminars and participate in visits to other museums in Baltimore, Washington, D.C., and Philadelphia.

162

The Walters Art Gallery
600 North Charles Street
Baltimore, Maryland 21201
USA
Telephone: (301) 547 9000 Ext. 235

Time required to complete program: *6 months or less*
Level of training provided: *Internships*
Areas of study: *Collection management, Exhibit design, Curatorship, Public programming, Education, Conservation*
Areas of specialization: *Fine arts, Decorative arts*
Is the program open to international students? *Yes*
Is financial assistance available for students? *No*
Contact person: *John Shields, Coordinator of Docents and Interns*
Description of program: *Internships*

Undergraduate and graduate internships: based on a program of supervised learning, the internships give students the opportunity to gain an understanding of how a museum works and to relate this experience to academic and/or professional goals. During the academic years, each intern serves for periods that correspond to his or her university's quarter or semester system and is required to spend a minimum of ten hours a week at the Walters. During the summer, the internships are from eight to ten weeks in length, and the interns work a five-hour day, three to four days a week. Students are responsible for arranging academic credit from their sponsoring institution. The Gallery accepts interns in the curatorial, development and public relations, and education divisions. No stipends.

163

Smithsonian Environmental Research Center
Smithsonian Institute
PO Box 28
Edgewater, Maryland 21037
USA
Telephone: (301) 798 4424

Time required to complete program: *6 months or less*
Level of training provided: *Work/learn program*
Areas of study: *Field methods*
Areas of specialization: *Environmental biology*
Is financial assistance available for students?   *Yes*
Financial assistance is available in the following ways: *Stipend*
Contact person: *Linda Chich, Internship Coordinator*
Description of program: *Work/Learn Program*

The program enables graduate and qualified advanced undergraduate students to work on research projects under the direction of the Center's professional staff and is tailored to provide the maximum educational benefit to each participant. Students work at facilities located in Edgewater, Maryland. The Edgewater facility presents the opportunity for both laboratory and field experience. Interns may conduct research in terrestrial or estuarine environmental biology. Projects usually coincide with academic semesters or summer sessions and are normally twelve weeks in duration. Interns may receive academic credit for their projects if arrangements are made between the Smithsonian Institution and the intern's college. Those working at the Edgewater facility of the Center may have living accommodation with limited cooking facilities provided on the Center's grounds. Stipends are available.

164

Goucher College
Historic Preservation
Towson, Maryland 21204
USA
Telephone: (301) 337 6000

The program began in: *1980*
Time required to complete program: *More than 2 years*

Level of training provided: *Bachelor degree*

Areas of study: *Administration, Conservation, Field methods, Architectural preservation*

Areas of specialization: *Archives, Fine arts, Material culture, Architecture, Decorative arts, History*

Instructional opportunities provided: *Full-time study*

Is museum ethics a regular part of the program? *No*

Is the program open to international students? *Yes*

The primary language of instruction is: *English*

Is financial assistance available for students? *Yes*

Financial assistance is available in the following ways: *Scholarships, Loans, Student work program*

The program is affiliated with: *Museum(s)*

Is instruction given in a museum? *No*

Do students work in a museum collection as part of the program of study? *Yes*

How many students begin the program each year? *11*

How many students have completed the program since it began? *100*

Are the majority of the beginning students already employed by museums? *Yes*

What percentage of the students completing this program enter or return to museum work? *Less than 25%*

Contact person: *Jean H. Baker*

Description of program: *Bachelor's degree*

Students are trained to enter the fields of historic preservation, archival preservation, museum work, and historic administration on a professional level. For the major, the student is normally required to take a minimum of twelve courses (thirty-six credit hours) and is urged to elect additional courses in the area of specialization. Two practicum experiences in different settings give the student practical work experience in the preservation field. Independent projects are encouraged and summer field work may be credited toward the major. Successful students earn the **Bachelor's degree in Historic Preservation.**

165

New England Museum Association
Boston National Historical Park
Charlestown Navy Yard
Boston, Massachusetts 02129
USA

The program began in: *1976*
Level of training provided: *Workshops*
Areas of study: *Administration, Collection management, Exhibit design, Public programming, Curatorship, Education*
Areas of specialization: *Ethics, Museology, Technical assistance*
Instructional opportunities provided: *Scheduled lectures/seminars*
Is museum ethics a regular part of the program? *No*
Is the program open to international students? *Yes*
The primary language of instruction is: *English*
Is financial assistance available for students? *No*
The program is affiliated with: *Museum(s)*
Is instruction given in a museum? *Yes*
Do students work in a museum collection as part of the program of study? *No*
Do program instructors have museum experience? *Yes*
Are the majority of the beginning students already employed by museums? *Yes*
Contact person: *Laura Roberts, Executive Director*
Description of program: *Workshops*

The New England Museum Association is the regional affiliate of the American Association of Museums covering Maine, New Hampshire, Vermont, Massachusetts, Rhode Island, and Connecticut, serving museums and their personnel. Facilitating the professional development of members is a primary program area, accomplished through an annual conference (fall) and one-day workshops and seminars. Programs are oriented toward developing professional capabilities and addressing issues of current interest to the field, rather than academic content. NEMA also compiles and publishes professional development listings in the quarterly newsletter.

166

Museum as a Learning Center
Wheelock College
200 Riverway
Boston, Massachusetts 02165
USA
Telephone: (617) 734 5200

The program began in: *1975*
Time required to complete program: *6 months or less*

Level of training provided: *Internships, Bachelor degree, Independent study*

Areas of study: *Public programming, Education, Field methods*

Instructional opportunities provided: *Full-time study*

Is museum ethics a regular part of the program?   *No*

Is the program open to international students?   *Yes*

The primary language of instruction is: *English*

Is financial assistance available for students?   *Yes*

Financial assistance is available in the following ways: *Student work program, Loans*

The program is affiliated with: *Museum(s), University(ies), Science center(s)*

Is instruction given in a museum?   *Yes*

Do program instructors have museum experience?   *Yes*

How many students begin the program each year?   *7–8*

How many students have completed the program since it began?   *30*

What percentage of the students completing this program enter or return to museum work?   *25% to 50%*

Contact person: *Mary Iatridis, Ph.D.*

Description of program: *Courses*

The Museum as a Learning Center: an eighteen credit hour sequence of courses focusing on the relationship of art/science/environmental concepts, child development, and teaching strategies is offered as part of a Bachelor of Science degree. Comprised of three six credit courses, including a museum internship, the program provides instruction in maximizing the effectiveness of museum visits by young children. Each course requires the completion of a project. The internship centers on teaching children of various ages in a museum environment and planning follow-up activities that can be implemented in the classroom. The program is not included in the curriculum every year. Graduate instruction is offered as independent study.

167

Boston Athenaeum
10 1/2 Beacon Street
Boston, Massachusetts 02364
USA
Telephone: (617) 227 0270
Fax: (617) 227 5266

The program began in: *1973*
Time required to complete program: *Varies*
Level of training provided: *Courses, Internships, Certificate*
Areas of study: *Collection management, Exhibit design, Curatorship,*
   Public programming, Education, Conservation, Information technology
Areas of specialization: *Archives, Fine arts, Material culture,*
   Architecture, Decorative arts, History, Library science, Visual arts/prints
Is museum ethics a regular part of the program?   *Yes*
Is the program open to international students?   *Yes*
The primary language of instruction is: *English*
Is financial assistance available for students?   *Yes*
Financial assistance is available in the following ways: *Scholarships,*
   Student work program, Stipends, Matching grants, Work-study
The program is affiliated with: *Museum(s), Gallery(ies)*
Is instruction given in a museum?   *Yes*
Do students work in a museum collection as part of the program of
   study?   *Yes*
Do program instructors have museum experience?   *Yes*
How many students begin the program each year?   *Varies*
How many students have completed the program since it began?   *100*
Are the majority of the beginning students already employed by
   museums?   *No*
What percentage of the students completing this program enter or return
   to museum work?   *25% to 50%*
Contact person: *Norman P. Tucker, Associate Director*
Description of program: *Internships, Work-study, Field work, Directed*
   study, Museum studies

The Boston Athenaeum in cooperation with various educational institutions and education programs offers **undergraduate and graduate
internships, work-study** opportunities, and **directed study** arrangements
for academic credit and projects for certification in Museum Studies
programs. Internships and other opportunities vary in length from three
months to one year. Projects may include organizing, accessioning, research
and cataloging, and preservation of art objects and visual arts materials
with the goal of accessibility for research, exhibitions, and publication.
Interns also assist in the preparation of exhibitions, related catalogs, and
other publications. Interns provide guides to collections. Project evaluations are required and papers or theses are encouraged. Some
arrangements provide scholarships and stipends while others are unpaid.
Work-study grants are matched and academic credit is arranged.

168

Art History Department
Boston University
Room 301, 725 Commonwealth Av.
Boston, Massachusetts 02215
USA
Telephone: (617) 353 2520

The program began in: *1982*
Time required to complete program: *2 years*
Level of training provided: *Courses, Internships, Graduate degree, Certificate*
Areas of study: *Collection management, Exhibit design, Curatorship, Education, Conservation, Field methods, Architectural preservation*
Areas of specialization: *Anthropology, Fine arts, Material culture, Archeology, History, Musicology, Afro-American studies*
Instructional opportunities provided: *Part-time study, Scheduled lectures/seminars*
Is museum ethics a regular part of the program? *Yes*
Is the program open to international students? *Yes*
The primary language of instruction is: *English*
Is financial assistance available for students? *Yes*
Financial assistance is available in the following ways: *Scholarships, Student work program, Tuition waiver*
The program is affiliated with: *Museum(s), Gallery(ies), University(ies)*
Is instruction given in a museum? *Yes*
Do students work in a museum collection as part of the program of study? *Yes*
Do program instructors have museum experience? *Yes*
How many students begin the program each year? *5*
How many students have completed the program since it began? *30*
Are the majority of the beginning students already employed by museums? *No*
What percentage of the students completing this program enter or return to museum work? *50% to 75%*
Contact person: *Caroline A. Jones, Director of Museum Studies*
Description of program: *Certificate*

The **Museum Studies Certificate Program** is fully integrated with the Art History Department, and offers training in museum issues and practical experience to graduate students interested in museum work or knowledge of this field. The program has a commitment to sound art historical training, rather than a purely administrative focus. The faculty of the Art

History Department and adjunct faculty from Boston museums and historical agencies oversee the program and teach the courses.

Those students wishing to pursue a museum career will want the Museum Studies Certificate, which requires four courses on museum and curatorial issues. Courses introduce students to the history, philosophy, and practices of museum work and offer an opportunity to work in area museums. They provide the necessary references and credentials to facilitate the securing of professional, entry-level positions in curation, education, registration, and other areas of museums and historic agencies.

There are three required courses in the program: Museums and Historical Agencies, Curatorship, Practicum (or internship), and one elective. The elective can be chosen from among the following: an additional practicum, an arts administration course, a preservation and conservation course, and a course on collections care at the Museum of Fine Arts. The practicum and elective allow the student to tailor the program to his or her special area of professional interest.

169

Brockton Art Museum
455 Oak Street
Brockton, Massachusetts 02401-1399
USA
Telephone: (508) 588 6000

Time required to complete program: *Varies*
Level of training provided: *Internships*
Areas of study: *Collection management, Public programming, Education*
The primary language of instruction is: *English*
Is financial assistance available for students?   *No*
The program is affiliated with: *Museum(s)*
Is instruction given in a museum?   *Yes*
Contact person: *James Keneklis, Associate Director*
Description of program: *Internships*

The Museum offers a variety of educational **volunteer internships** for upper-level undergraduate and graduate students. Interns are trained in basic and technical museum procedures. In the past, students have surveyed and researched the permanent collections; prepared exhibition graphics and brochures; assisted with the creation of teaching materials and guides, and maintained print libraries. A background in art, art history, museum education, art administration, or a related field is desirable. Most internships require one or two days per week during the semester, or eight to sixteen hours per week. After a one-month trial period, the intern is evaluated as to work performance and qualification. A decision is made at that time whether the student is acceptable for continued training.

170

Art Museum
Harvard University
32 Quincy Street
Cambridge, Massachusetts 02138
USA

The program began in: *1979*
Time required to complete program: *10 months*
Level of training provided: *Internships, Certificate, Traineeship*
Areas of study: *Administration, Information technology, Conservation*
Areas of specialization: *Fine arts, Natural science, Art history*
Is museum ethics a regular part of the program?   *No*
Is the program open to international students?   *Yes*
The primary language of instruction is: *English*
Is financial assistance available for students?   *Yes*
Financial assistance is available in the following ways: *Stipend*
The program is affiliated with: *Museum(s), University(ies), Science center(s)*
Is instruction given in a museum?   *Yes*
Do program instructors have museum experience?   *Yes*
How many students begin the program each year?   *4–6*
How many students have completed the program since it began?   *65*
Are the majority of the beginning students already employed by museums?   *Yes*
What percentage of the students completing this program enter or return to museum work?   *50% to 75%*
Contact person: *Wendy Mackey-Kydd*
Description of program: *Internships, Courses, Traineeships*

Center for Conservation and Technical Studies – Advanced Internship in Conservation: Harvard University Art Museum offers up to six advanced-level internships in conservation. The internships are divided among the three conservation laboratories (paper, painting, and objects) and the conservation science laboratory depending on the interests and needs of the intern applicants and the professional staff.

Requirements: Completion of graduate-level or equivalent apprentice-ship training in conservation preferred; minimum of a Bachelor of Arts degree with a major in arts or art history; one or more college-level chemistry courses; additional courses in material sciences and competence in a foreign language are desirable. For conservation science training the minimum of a Master of Science in the chemical or material sciences is required.

Stipend is $15,000 with an additional travel and research allowance.

Telephone: (617) 495 2392, Fax: (617) 495 9936

Fine Arts Department – Fogg Art Museum: a graduate course is offered in the examination of works of art through the study of their materials, structures, and artist's methods, with an emphasis on visual and instrumental examination techniques. Problems of original condition, authentication, and the curatorial care of collections are considered. Laboratory assignments are conducted in areas of paintings, sculpture, works of art on paper, and scientific analysis.

Harvard University Art Museum – Curatorial Training Program: trainees who have completed, or nearly completed, Ph.D. requirements work under the supervision of a senior curator in a specific Museum department. Trainees are involved in managerial duties pertaining to the department and are also responsible for the preparation of major exhibition catalogs. The program lasts three to four years, full-time. The position is salaried.

Telephone: (617) 495 2377

171

School of Management, Arts Administration Program
Lesley College
29 Everett Street
Cambridge, Massachusetts 02138
USA
Telephone: (617) 868 9600

The program began in: *1980*
Time required to complete program: *2 years*
Level of training provided: *Graduate degree*
Areas of study: *Administration*
Areas of specialization: *Visual and performing arts*

Instructional opportunities provided: *Full-time study, Part-time study, Short-term lectures on request*
Is museum ethics a regular part of the program? *Yes*
Is the program open to international students? *Yes*
The primary language of instruction is: *English*
Is financial assistance available for students? *Yes*
Financial assistance is available in the following ways: *Student work program, Loans*
The program is affiliated with: *University(ies)*
Is instruction given in a museum? *No*
Do program instructors have museum experience? *Yes*
How many students begin the program each year? *6–10*
How many students have completed the program since it began? *55*
Are the majority of the beginning students already employed by museums? *Yes*
What percentage of the students completing this program enter or return to museum work? *25% to 50%*
Contact person: *Rachel Weiss*
Description of program: *Master's degree*

The **Arts Administration Program** is a joint program offered through the School of Management and the Arts Institute of the Lesley College Graduate School. The students enroll in fifteen credits of core management courses offered by the School of Management and fifteen credits of concentrated courses offered by the Arts Institute related to the arts in educational and cultural institutions. In addition, a practicum is undertaken. The course of study is intended for individuals who are committed to careers of leadership in the management of artistic enterprises, cultural institutions, or other art-related programs.

172

Summer Fellowship Program
Historic Deerfield, Inc.
Deerfield, Massachusetts 01342
USA
Telephone: (413) 774 5581

The program began in: *1956*
Time required to complete program: *6 months or less*
Level of training provided: *Courses, Internships, Diploma*

Areas of study: *Administration, Collection management, Curatorship, Architectural preservation, Education, Conservation*
Areas of specialization: *Fine arts, Material culture, Archeology, Architecture, Decorative arts, History, Museology*
Instructional opportunities provided: *Full-time study*
Is museum ethics a regular part of the program?   *Yes*
Is the program open to international students?   *Yes*
The primary language of instruction is: *English*
Is financial assistance available for students?   *Yes*
Financial assistance is available in the following ways: *Scholarships, Materials/supplies, Tuition waiver*
The program is affiliated with: *Museum(s), University(ies)*
Is instruction given in a museum?   *Yes*
Do students work in a museum collection as part of the program of study?   *Yes*
Do program instructors have museum experience?   *Yes*
How many students begin the program each year?   *6–10*
How many students have completed the program since it began?   *300+*
Are the majority of the beginning students already employed by museums?   *No*
What percentage of the students completing this program enter or return to museum work?   *50% to 75%*
Contact person: *Kenneth Hafertepe*
Description of program: *Fellowships*

The **Summer Fellowship Program** encourages undergraduates to consider careers in museums, history, and material culture. The museum staff and visiting lecturers present various approaches to early American architecture, decorative arts, history, museum interpretation, and museum operations. The fellows participate in seminars and room studies, guide in the museum houses, visit museums such as Old Sturbridge Village, Plimoth Plantation, Colonial Williamsburg, and Winterthur, and produce a research paper on a topic utilizing the manuscript, printed, and artifact collections at Deerfield. The Fellowship covers tuition, books, and expenses on trips to other museums. Financial aid is available for room and board. Academic credit is available through the University of Massachusetts.

173

Chesterwood
Box 827
Stockbridge, Massachusetts 01262-0827
USA
Telephone: (413) 298 3579

The program began in: *1971*
Time required to complete program: *Varies*
Level of training provided: *Internships*
Areas of study: *Administration, Collection management, Exhibit design, Public programming, Curatorship, Education, Architectural preservation, Conservation, Field methods*
Areas of specialization: *Archives, Fine arts, Material culture, Architecture, Decorative arts, History, Museology*
Is museum ethics a regular part of the program? *No*
Is the program open to international students? *Yes*
The primary language of instruction is: *English*
Is financial assistance available for students? *No*
Financial assistance is available in the following ways: *Lodging*
The program is affiliated with: *Museum(s)*
Is instruction given in a museum? *Yes*
Do students work in a museum collection as part of the program of study? *Yes*
Do program instructors have museum experience? *Yes*
How many students begin the program each year? *6*
How many students have completed the program since it began? *130*
Are the majority of the beginning students already employed by museums? *No*
What percentage of the students completing this program enter or return to museum work? *50% to 75%*
Contact person: *Susan Frisch Lehrer, Assistant Director*
Description of program: *Internship*

Chesterwood Internship Program: Chesterwood, the summer estate of American sculptor Daniel Chester French (1850–1931), is a historic house museum property of the National Trust for Historic Preservation. The volunteer program provides work-learning experience for undergraduate, graduate, and postgraduate majors in architectural history, art history, museum studies, historic preservation, education, landscape architecture, horticulture, marketing, history, and design. Interns provide important support for Chesterwood's permanent staff. They assist in such museum operations as administration, interpretation, collections care, archives, and maintenance. The program stresses hands-on experience rather than formal instruction. Housing may be provided.

174

Volunteer Program
Old Sturbridge Village
1 Old Sturbridge Village Road
Sturbridge, Massachusetts 01566
USA
Telephone: (508) 347 3362
Fax: (508) 347 5375

Time required to complete program: *Varies*
Level of training provided: *Internships, Volunteers*
Is financial assistance available for students?   *No*
Contact person: *Catherine M. Eliseo, Coordinator of Volunteers*
Description of program: *Volunteer internships*

Volunteer internships at Old Sturbridge Village are available to qualified graduate and undergraduate students enrolled in degree programs and to others with the academic qualifications and professional objectives commensurate with the project to be undertaken. Intern projects in the program and research areas may include: developing training materials, assisting in the development of interpretative programs and demon-strations, studying objects in the collections, undertaking social history research with primary sources, assisting in the development of exhibits, and cataloging and processing materials in the Research Library. Other internship projects are available in the areas of marketing, visitor services, and merchandising. The length of each internship varies. Students wishing to receive academic credit should make arrangements through their college or university.

Volunteers at Old Sturbridge Village: volunteers are trained to undertake regular work assignments within the Department of Research, Collections and Library, the Department of Marketing and Publications, and the Departments of Interpretation, Museum Education, and Visitor Services. Work assignments may be ongoing volunteer positions or project-oriented.

175

Graduate Program in the History of Art
Williams College
Box 8
Williamstown, Massachusetts 01267
USA
Telephone: (413) 458 9545

The program began in: *1972*
Time required to complete program: *2 years*
Level of training provided: *Graduate degree*
Areas of study: *Collection management, Curatorship, Conservation*
Areas of specialization: *Fine arts, Architecture, Decorative arts*
Instructional opportunities provided: *Full-time study, Part-time study, Scheduled lectures/seminars*
Is museum ethics a regular part of the program? *No*
Is the program open to international students? *Yes*
The primary language of instruction is: *English*
Is financial assistance available for students? *Yes*
Financial assistance is available in the following ways: *Scholarships, Student work program, Tuition waiver*
The program is affiliated with: *Museum(s), Gallery(ies), University(ies)*
Is instruction given in a museum? *Yes*
Do students work in a museum collection as part of the program of study? *Yes*
Do program instructors have museum experience? *Yes*
How many students begin the program each year? *12–15*
How many students have completed the program since it began? *200*
Are the majority of the beginning students already employed by museums? *No*
What percentage of the students completing this program enter or return to museum work? *50% to 75%*
Contact person: *Karen Kowitz, Program Administrator*
Description of program: *Master's degree*

A two-year course of study leading to the degree of **Master of Arts in the History of Art** is offered in cooperation with the Sterling and Francine Clark Art Institute. The objective of the program is to offer a professional preparation for careers in teaching and museums and to equip graduates of the program to pursue further study and research. Independent study opportunities include exhibitions at the Clark Art Institute and the Williams College Museum of Art, conservation internships, and off-campus work-study. Financial aid is available in the form of curatorial and teaching assistantships.

176

Williamstown Regional Art Conservation Laboratory, Inc.
225 South Street
Williamstown, Massachusetts 01267
USA
Telephone: (413) 458 5741

The program began in: *1977*
Time required to complete program: *6 months or less*
Level of training provided: *Internships*
Areas of study: *Conservation*
Areas of specialization: *Archives, Fine arts, Decorative arts*
Is museum ethics a regular part of the program? *No*
Is the program open to international students? *Yes*
The primary language of instruction is: *English*
Is financial assistance available for students? *Yes*
Financial assistance is available in the following ways: *Stipends*
Is instruction given in a museum? *No*
How many students begin the program each year? *2–3*
How many students have completed the program since it began? *60*
Are the majority of the beginning students already employed by
    museums? *No*
What percentage of the students completing this program enter or return
    to museum work? *Less than 25%*
Contact person: *Doe Zottoli*
Description of program: *Conservation internships*

An **internship** at WRACL provides training experience for undergraduate apprentices and graduate-level interns, master apprentices and advanced interns. All are provided with "hands-on" experience under close supervision to both develop and refine the high level of skill that the profession requires. Interns have access to the Laboratory's extensive technical equipment and the art historical and scientific libraries of the Clark Art Institute and Williams College. Individuals are given the opportunity to attend the graduate seminar, Art and Conservation: An Inquiry into History, Methods and Materials, taught by the conservation staff. Opportunities to train with conservators of painting, paper, furniture, and objects are available.

177

Henry Ford Museum and Greenfield Village
20900 Oakwood Boulevard
Dearborn, Michigan 48121
USA
Telephone: (313) 271 1620

The program began in: *1984*
Time required to complete program: *6 months or less*
Level of training provided: *Internships*
Areas of study: *Administration, Collection management, Exhibit design, Public programming, Curatorship, Education, Conservation*
Areas of specialization: *Archives, Clothing, Material culture, Decorative arts, History*
Is museum ethics a regular part of the program? *No*
Is the program open to international students? *Yes*
The primary language of instruction is: *English*
Is financial assistance available for students? *Yes*
Financial assistance is available in the following ways: *Stipend*
The program is affiliated with: *Museum(s)*
Do students work in a museum collection as part of the program of study? *Yes*
Do program instructors have museum experience? *Yes*
How many students begin the program each year? *4–8*
Are the majority of the beginning students already employed by museums? *No*
What percentage of the students completing this program enter or return to museum work? *50% to 75%*
Contact person: *Judith E. Endelman*
Description of program: *Internships*

Senior internship: for graduate students interested in pursuing careers in history, American studies, or related fields. Most internships are completed during the summer but may occur at any time. Internships are available in collections stewardship, design and production, educational programs, and research and assess programs. Each intern is assigned to a staff member and works on a special project. In addition, interns participate regularly in the larger life of the museum. Monthly stipend. Apply by March 1 for summer internships.

Undergraduate and graduate internships: as part of a degree-granting program, students may participate in virtually any area of the museum, provided a staff sponsor and appropriate project can be identified. Internships can be a semester or longer. No stipend.

High school internship: the Museum is affiliated with several local high school mentorship and internship programs that place students in museum departments at certain times of the year.

178

Museum Studies at Michigan State University
Michigan State University Museum
Michigan State University
East Lancing, Michigan 48824-1045
USA
Telephone: (517) 355 2370

The program began in: *1992*
Time required to complete program: *More than 2 years*
Level of training provided: *Certificate*
Areas of study: *Administration, Collection management, Exhibit design, Public programming, Curatorship, Education*
Areas of specialization: *Anthropology, Clothing, Ethnology, Material culture, Natural science, Archeology, Decorative arts, History, Museology, Paleontology, Folklife*
Instructional opportunities provided: *Full-time study*
Is museum ethics a regular part of the program?   *Yes*
Is the program open to international students?   *Yes*
The primary language of instruction is: *English*
Is financial assistance available for students?   *Yes*
Financial assistance is available in the following ways: *Student work program, Graduate assistantships*
The program is affiliated with: *Museum(s), University(ies)*
Is instruction given in a museum?   *Yes*
Do students work in a museum collection as part of the program of study?   *Yes*
Do program instructors have museum experience?   *Yes*
How many students begin the program each year?   *8–12*
Are the majority of the beginning students already employed by museums?   *No*
Contact person: *C. Kurt Dewhurst or Susan Bandes*
Description of program: *Certification, Courses, Assistantships*

Students may enroll for study in the area of **museum studies certification** as part of **M.A., M.S., or Ph.D. programs.** On the graduate level, curators offer museum studies courses and graduate research guidance in several areas, including archeology, historic textiles, folklife, museum technology, and education. Graduate assistantships are available as well as undergraduate and graduate appointments in research and development positions. Students may apply for work-study.

179

Museum Studies Program
Central Michigan University
124 Rowe Hall
Mt Pleasant, Michigan 48859
USA
Telephone: (517) 774 3829

The program began in: *1974*
Time required to complete program: *2 years*
Level of training provided: *Courses, Internships*
Areas of study: *Administration, Collection management, Exhibit design, Public programming, Curatorship, Education*
Areas of specialization: *Anthropology, Ethnology, Natural science, Archeology, History, Museology*
Instructional opportunities provided: *Part-time study*
Is museum ethics a regular part of the program? *Yes*
Is the program open to international students? *Yes*
The primary language of instruction is: *English*
Is financial assistance available for students? *Yes*
Financial assistance is available in the following ways: *Scholarships, Student work program, Loans*
The program is affiliated with: *Museum(s), University(ies)*
Is instruction given in a museum? *Yes*
Do students work in a museum collection as part of the program of study? *Yes*
Do program instructors have museum experience? *Yes*
How many students begin the program each year? *8*
How many students have completed the program since it began? *50*
Are the majority of the beginning students already employed by museums? *No*
What percentage of the students completing this program enter or return to museum work? *50% to 75%*

Contact person: *Lynn N. Fauver*
Description of program: *Courses, Internship*

This program is composed of **four courses in muscum practiccs, including a museum internship**. Hands-on experience in molding and casting forms the basis of a three-credit hour museum science laboratory. The additional courses provide students with a general orientation to museum work and collection care, and instruction in the principles and procedures utilized in the interpretation field. The internship centers on administrative functions, collection policies, budgeting, and fund raising. The program is open to undergraduate and graduate students majoring or minoring in an appropriate discipline. A variety of student/staff positions are made possible through work-study programs.

180

Museum Practices Program/Museum of Art
University of Michigan
525 South State Street
Ann Arbor, Michigan 48109-1354
USA
Telephone: (313) 764 0395

The program began in: *1963*
Time required to complete program: *2 years*
Level of training provided: *Internships, Certificate*
Areas of study: *Administration, Collection management, Exhibit design, Public programming, Curatorship, Education, Conservation*
Areas of specialization: *Fine arts, Decorative arts, History*
Instructional opportunities provided: *Part-time study*
Is museum ethics a regular part of the program?   *Yes*
Is the program open to international students?   *Yes*
The primary language of instruction is: *English*
Is financial assistance available for students?   *Yes*
Financial assistance is available in the following ways: *Scholarships, Internship stipends, Federal grants*
The program is affiliated with: *Museum(s), University(ies)*
Is instruction given in a museum?   *Yes*
Do students work in a museum collection as part of the program of study?   *Yes*
Do program instructors have museum experience?   *Yes*
How many students begin the program each year?   *3–4*

How many students have completed the program since it began? *200*
Are the majority of the beginning students already employed by
  museums? *No*
What percentage of the students completing this program enter or return
  to museum work? *25% to 50%*
Contact person: *Ellen A. Plummer, Assoc. Chair, Museum Practice*
Description of program: *Certificate*

The **Certificate in Museum Practice** is awarded in conjunction with, or
after completion of, graduate programs (M.A. or Ph.D.) in a related field
of study. The program is intended primarily for students interested in
pursuing careers in art and history museums and qualified to enter graduate departments of American culture, history, or history of art. Students
of anthropology and archeology are also considered. The eighteen credit-
hour program consists of courses on connoisseurship and the history of
museums, among other topics, and an intensive eight-to-twelve-month
internship. Students must also complete a museum-related essay or project.

181

Walker Art Center
Vineland Place
Minneapolis, Minnesota 55403
USA
Telephone: (612) 375 7617

The program began in: *1965/1979*
Time required to complete program: *1 year*
Level of training provided: *Internships*
Areas of study: *Collection management, Exhibit design, Public program-
  ming, Curatorship, Education, Field methods*
Areas of specialization: *Art history, Art education, Graphic design*
Is museum ethics a regular part of the program? *Yes*
Is the program open to international students? *Yes*
The primary language of instruction is: *English*
Is financial assistance available for students? *Yes*
Financial assistance is available in the following ways: *$13,500 stipend,
  $1000 travel, and insurance*
The program is affiliated with: *Museum(s)*
Is instruction given in a museum? *Yes*
Do students work in a museum collection as part of the program of
  study? *Yes*

Do program instructors have museum experience? *Yes*
How many students begin the program each year? *2–3*
How many students have completed the program since it began? *81*
Are the majority of the beginning students already employed by
   museums? *No*
What percentage of the students completing this program enter or return
   to museum work? *More than 75%*
Contact person: *Wendy Lane, Human Resources Manager*
Description of program: *Internships*

Curatorial and education internships: the intern is selected for a twelve-month period and works with the Center's curatorial, education, and program departments on a variety of projects. The projects may relate to the permanent collections, the production of slide, tape, or video presentations, the organization of lectures, seminars, and workshops, and general curatorial assistance in the preparation of special exhibitions. Individuals with Master's degrees in Art History (particularly contemporary art) or commensurate program experience in museums are invited to apply.

Design internship: projects include designing museum catalogs, brochures, and exhibition graphics, posters for various programs, and a monthly calendar of events. Lasting twelve months, the position offers a stipend as well as funds for relocation and travel. A B.F.A. or M.F.A. degree in design is required for all individuals applying for this internship.

182

The Minneapolis Institute of Arts
2400 Third Avenue South
Minneapolis, Minnesota 55404
USA
Telephone: (612) 870 3074

The program began in: *1991*
Time required to complete program: *Varies*
Level of training provided: *Internships*
Instructional opportunities provided: *Short-term lectures on request,
   Scheduled lectures/seminars*
Is museum ethics a regular part of the program? *No*
Is the program open to international students? *Yes*
The primary language of instruction is: *English*

Is financial assistance available for students?   *No*
The program is affiliated with: *Museum(s)*
Is instruction given in a museum?   *Yes*
Do program instructors have museum experience?   *Yes*
How many students begin the program each year?   *30–50*
Are the majority of the beginning students already employed by
   museums?   *No*
Contact person: *Sheila McGuire*
Description of program: *Internships*

The Minneapolis Institute of Arts offers many **volunteer internships** for individuals considering or pursuing careers in museum work. All candidates with skills, interests, or experiences relevant to museum work are eligible for internships.

Internships may range from one to twelve months in length, with a minimum time commitment of twenty hours per week expected. Intern positions are typically project-oriented within a specific department. A monthly classroom component acquaints interns with various functions, programs, departments, and staff of the museum. Students often arrange academic credit for their internship experience through their college or university.

The availability of internships is determined by the needs of individual departments throughout the year. Within the limitations of staff and space availability, exhibition schedules, and the varying potential for challenging intern projects, candidates may consider internships in several areas of the museum, including the Curatorial, Education, Marketing and Communication, Development, and Registration departments.

183

Minnesota State Arts Board
432 Summit Avenue
St Paul, Minnesota 55102-2624
USA
Telephone: (612) 297 2603

The program began in: *1980*
Time required to complete program: *6 months or less*
Level of training provided: *Internships*
Areas of study: *Administration*
Areas of specialization: *Fine arts, Public art*
Is museum ethics a regular part of the program?   *No*

Is the program open to international students?   *Yes*
The primary language of instruction is: *English*
Is financial assistance available for students?   *No*
Is instruction given in a museum?   *No*
Do students work in a museum collection as part of the program of
    study?   *No*
Do program instructors have museum experience?   *Yes*
How many students begin the program each year?   *2–4*
How many students have completed the program since it began?   *6*
Are the majority of the beginning students already employed by
    museums?   *No*
Contact person: *Gail Swaim, Administrative Assistant*
Description of program: *Internships*

Internship applicants should have an art-related or public administration background. Project possibilities exist in several departments. Internships may be arranged during the academic year as well as the summer. Out-of-state students are encouraged to apply; however, interns must provide their own transportation and lodging.

184

Internship and Volunteer Program
Minnesota Museum of Art
75 West 5th Street
St Paul, Minnesota 55102
USA
Telephone: (612) 292 4346

Time required to complete program: *Varies*
Level of training provided: *Internships*
Areas of study: *Administration, Education*
Areas of specialization: *Fine arts*
Instructional opportunities provided: *Part-time study*
Is museum ethics a regular part of the program?   *No*
Is the program open to international students?   *Yes*
The primary language of instruction is: *English*
Is financial assistance available for students?   *No*
The program is affiliated with: *Museum(s)*
Is instruction given in a museum?   *Yes*
Do students work in a museum collection as part of the program of
    study?   *Yes*

Do program instructors have museum experience?   *Yes*
How many students begin the program each year?   *Varies*
Are the majority of the beginning students already employed by
    museums?   *No*
Contact person: *Ramona Weselmann, Personnel Supervisor*
Description of program: *Internships*

Minnesota Museum of American Art's **internship and volunteer program**
is unique because it provides a wide variety of opportunities in all areas
of museum work. Positions are available in curatorial, educational, administrative, and fund-raising departments. On occasion, openings occur in
marketing, media relations, and graphics.

185

University of Mississippi
Department of Art
University, Mississippi 38677
USA
Telephone: (601) 232 7193

The program began in: *1987*
Time required to complete program: *2 years*
Level of training provided: *Internships, Graduate degree, Bachelor
    degree*
Areas of study: *Administration, Collection management, Education,
    Field methods*
Areas of specialization: *Southern art, Decorative arts*
Instructional opportunities provided: *Part-time study*
Is museum ethics a regular part of the program?   *No*
Is the program open to international students?   *Yes*
The primary language of instruction is: *English*
Is financial assistance available for students?   *Yes*
Financial assistance is available in the following ways: *Scholarships,
    Student work program, Tuition waiver*
The program is affiliated with: *University(ies)*
Is instruction given in a museum?   *Yes*
Do students work in a museum collection as part of the program of
    study?   *Yes*
Do program instructors have museum experience?   *Yes*
How many students begin the program each year?   *1*
How many students have completed the program since it began?   *3*

Are the majority of the beginning students already employed by
  museums?   *No*
What percentage of the students completing this program enter or return
  to museum work?   *25% to 50%*
Contact person: *Margaret Gorove, Chair*
Description of program: *Master's degree, Bachelor's degree*

Master of Art History (Arts Administration emphasis): to fulfill requirements for the arts administration emphasis, students must complete the
necessary courses in art history as well as museum studies, classes in
business, law, or educational administration, and an internship at the
University's museum or at any agreed upon museum or gallery.

  Students enrolled in the undergraduate art history curriculum may also
pursue arts administration training with a business minor.

186

Museum Studies Program/Museum of Art and Archeology
University of Missouri – Columbia
Pickard Hall Dept. Art History/Archeology
Columbia, Missouri 65211
USA
Telephone: (314) 882 6711

The program began in: *1990*
Time required to complete program: *2 years*
Level of training provided: *Courses, Internships, Minor in museum
  study*
Areas of study: *Administration, Collection management, Exhibit design,
  Public programming, Curatorship, Education, Conservation*
Areas of specialization: *Archives, Fine arts, Material culture, Archeology,
  Decorative arts, Ethics, History, Museology*
Instructional opportunities provided: *Part-time study, Scheduled
  lectures/seminars*
Is museum ethics a regular part of the program?   *Yes*
Is the program open to international students?   *Yes*
The primary language of instruction is: *English*
Is financial assistance available for students?   *Yes*
Financial assistance is available in the following ways: *Scholarships,
  Tuition waiver*
The program is affiliated with: *Museum(s), University(ies)*
Is instruction given in a museum?   *Yes*

Do students work in a museum collection as part of the program of
study? *Yes*
Do program instructors have museum experience? *Yes*
How many students begin the program each year? *10*
Are the majority of the beginning students already employed by
museums? *No*
Contact person: *Morteza Sajadian, Director*
Description of program: *Courses*

The **graduate minor in Museum Studies** is offered by the Museum of Art
and Archeology and the Department of Art History and Archeology of
the University of Missouri at Columbia. Six graduate-level courses introduce the history and role of museums; philosophical, legal, and
administrative issues; collections, exhibition and preservation concerns.
The program emphasizes museum curatorial responsibilities, educational
interpretation, and management, blending academic theory with practical
museum experience to provide students the opportunity to build a foundation in the museum profession. Internships and field trips provide
additional insight. As it is an interdisciplinary minor, interested students
may arrange courses in related areas and individual courses of study.

187

Internship Program
Harry S. Truman Library
US Highway 24 and Delaware
Independence, Missouri 64050
USA
Telephone: (816) 833 1400

The program began in: *1980*
Time required to complete program: *6 months or less*
Level of training provided: *Internships, On-the-job training*
Areas of study: *Collection management, Exhibit design, Public program-
ming, Curatorship, Education, Conservation, Field methods, Information
technology*
Areas of specialization: *Archives, Clothing, Fine arts, Material culture,
Decorative arts, History, Museology*
Is museum ethics a regular part of the program? *No*
Is the program open to international students? *Yes*
The primary language of instruction is: *English*
Is financial assistance available for students? *No*

Is instruction given in a museum?   *Yes*

Do students work in a museum collection as part of the program of study?   *Yes*

Do program instructors have museum experience?   *Yes*

How many students begin the program each year?   *6*

How many students have completed the program since it began?   *25*

Are the majority of the beginning students already employed by museums?   *No*

Contact person: *Benedict K. Zobrist, Ph.D., Director*

Description of program: *Internships*

The Harry S. Truman Library offers unpaid **internships** primarily to graduate students at accredited universities who are studying in the areas of history, archives administration, or museum studies. Internships are structured to satisfy the needs of the student and the accrediting university, but they are generally of a short-term nature (six months or less). Truman Library staff members supervise the internships and provide interns with informal training and guidance in museum and/or archival practices. Interns are then assigned to accomplish specific projects that are designed to be of benefit to the Truman Library and of an instructional nature to the interns.

188

Kansas City Museum
3218 Gladstone Boulevard
Kansas City, Missouri 64123
USA
Telephone: (816) 483 8300

Level of training provided: *Internships*

Areas of study: *Collection management, Curatorship*

Areas of specialization: *Archives, Clothing, Ethnology, Material culture, Archeology, Decorative arts, History, Museology*

Is museum ethics a regular part of the program?   *No*

Is the program open to international students?   *Yes*

The primary language of instruction is: *English*

Is financial assistance available for students?   *No*

Financial assistance is available in the following ways: *Stipends when money is available*

The program is affiliated with: *Museum(s)*

Is instruction given in a museum?   *Yes*

Do students work in a museum collection as part of the program of study? *Yes*

Do program instructors have museum experience? *Yes*

Are the majority of the beginning students already employed by museums? *No*

Contact person: *Denise Morrison, Archivist*

Description of program: *Internships*

Internships available at undergraduate and graduate levels for students working toward or having completed degrees in museum studies, history or a related field. Internships last one year or less. Students may choose to perform historical research, catalog collections, help install temporary exhibitions, process archival collections, coordinate educational projects related to exhibitions. Interns work under the supervision of the Registrar, Archivist, or Curator of Education, depending on the emphasis chosen.

189

Mid-American Art Alliance
Exhibits USA
912 Baltimore, Suite 700
Kansas City, Missouri 64105
USA
Telephone: (816) 421 1388

The program began in: *1991*

Time required to complete program: *4 hour workshop or 1 day workshop*

Level of training provided: *Workshops*

Areas of specialization: *Traveling exhibitions*

Instructional opportunities provided: *Short-term lectures on request*

Is museum ethics a regular part of the program? *No*

The primary language of instruction is: *English*

Is financial assistance available for students? *No*

Is instruction given in a museum? *No*

Do program instructors have museum experience? *Yes*

Are the majority of the beginning students already employed by museums? *Yes*

What percentage of the students completing this program enter or return to museum work? *Less than 25%*

Contact person: *Edana Elder, Marketing Coordinator*

Description of program: *Workshops*

United States of America

The Mid-America Arts Alliance is a partnership of the state arts agencies of Arkansas, Kansas, Missouri, Nebraska, and Oklahoma. The **Alliance Service Program** provides training and technical assistance for museum directors and staff, as well as state and community arts agency personnel and other arts administrators within the five–state region. This organization also assists in planning and developing workshops with museum associations in member states, and a staff exchange program provides travel funds to state and community arts administrators. No fees are charged for workshops and limited travel funds are available to museum personnel.

190

The Saint Louis Art Museum
#1 Fine Arts Drive – Forest Park
St Louis, Missouri 63110-1380
USA
Telephone: (314) 721 0072 Ext. 264
Fax: (314) 721 6172

The program began in: *1991*
Time required to complete program: *Varies*
Level of training provided: *Internships*
Areas of study: *Exhibit design, Public programming, Curatorship, Education*
Areas of specialization: *Fine arts, Archeology, Decorative arts, Museology*
Instructional opportunities provided: *Scheduled lectures/seminars*
Is the program open to international students? *No*
The primary language of instruction is: *English*
Is financial assistance available for students? *Yes*
Financial assistance is available in the following ways: *Salary*
The program is affiliated with: *Museum(s), University(ies)*
Is instruction given in a museum? *Yes*
Do students work in a museum collection as part of the program of study? *Yes*
Do program instructors have museum experience? *Yes*
How many students begin the program each year? *Internship 4–5, Bearden Fellowship 1*
How many students have completed the program since it began? *40+*
Are the majority of the beginning students already employed by museums? *No*

What percentage of the students completing this program enter or return
to museum work? *50% to 75%*
Contact person: *Elizabeth Vallance, Director, Education*
Description of program: *Internships, Fellowship*

Summer internships are open to students who have completed at least
three years' college-level instruction in art history, art education, anthropology, or archeology. The intern program provides a coordinated
eight-week program of supervised work in museum education, the
curatorial departments, and the library. Each intern will work in all three
areas. Specific assignments will be tailored to interns' backgrounds and
interests. Applicants must be residents of St Louis city or county and must
be working toward an art- or museum-related career with documented
plans to return to school the following year. Stipends.

Romare Bearden Post-Graduate Fellowship: one-year paid staff appointment designed to assist Museum staff in developing programs aimed at
increasing the cultural diversity of the Museum's programs and audiences
and gradually to increase the pool of outstanding minority applicants for
art museum work. The Bearden Fellow reports to the Education Director
but may be assigned to projects in education, curatorial, or other Museum
departments as appropriate to Museum needs and Fellow's background.
Open to recent graduates in art history, art education, anthropology, archeology, area studies, museum studies, or related fields. Privately funded
through 1994–5. African-Americans are encouraged to apply.

191

Interdisciplinary Museum Studies Program
University of Nebraska – Lincoln
307 Morrill Hall
Lincoln, Nebraska 68588-0356
USA

The program began in: *1990*
Time required to complete program: *2 years*
Level of training provided: *Graduate degree*
Areas of study: *Administration, Collection management, Exhibit design,
    Public programming, Curatorship, Education, Field methods,
    Information technology*
Areas of specialization: *Anthropology, Clothing, Ethnology, Fine arts,*

Material culture, Natural science, Archeology, Ethics, History, Museology, Paleontology

Instructional opportunities provided: *Full-time study, Part-time study*

Is museum ethics a regular part of the program? *Yes*

Is the program open to international students? *Yes*

The primary language of instruction is: *English*

Is financial assistance available for students? *Yes*

Financial assistance is available in the following ways: *Scholarships, Loans, Student work program*

The program is affiliated with: *Museum(s), Gallery(ies), University(ies)*

Is instruction given in a museum? *Yes*

Do students work in a museum collection as part of the program of study? *Yes*

Do program instructors have museum experience? *Yes*

How many students begin the program each year? *18*

How many students have completed the program since it began? *15*

Are the majority of the beginning students already employed by museums? *Yes*

What percentage of the students completing this program enter or return to museum work? *50% to 75%*

Contact person: *Hugh H. Genoways*

Description of program: *Master's degree*

Students must complete thirty-six hours of course work to receive an M.A./M.S. degree. This work will include twelve hours of museum studies, nine hours in a formal minor, nine hours of internship and six hours of electives. Major institutions supporting the program include the University of Nebraska State Museum, Museum of Nebraska History, Sheldon Memorial Art Gallery, Center for Great Plains Studies Art Collection, Historic Textile and Costume Collection, Nebraska Statewide Arboretum, and Ralph Mueller Planetarium. Students receive a broad background in museums and related fields, becoming competitive for positions in museums, galleries, nature centers, arboreta, planetariums, archives, zoos, and historical societies.

192

Joslyn Art Museum
2200 Dodge Street
Omaha, Nebraska 68102
USA
Telephone: (402) 342 3300

Level of training provided: *Internships*
Areas of specialization: *Fine arts*
The primary language of instruction is: *English*
Is instruction given in a museum?   *Yes*
Do program instructors have museum experience?   *Yes*
How many students begin the program each year?   *1–4*
Are the majority of the beginning students already employed by
    museums?   *No*
Contact person: *Chief Curator*
Description of program: *Internships*

Undergraduate Internships for Art History Majors: students may work in
the collections, library, administrative, and/or public relations area. No
stipends. Minimum 150-hour commitment. Offered when space, super-
visory time, and appropriate projects are available.

Curatorial interns: applicants must have at least a Master's degree in Art
History. Interns function as research assistants in the American and
European art departments. Minimum twelve-month commitment. Full-
time salaried positions, dependent upon the availability of funding.

193

Museum Studies
University of Nevada – Reno
Departments of Art, Anthropology,
Biology, Geology, and History
Reno, Nevada 89557
USA

The program began in: *1975*
Time required to complete program.   *1 year*
Level of training provided: *Courses, Internships*
Areas of study: *Administration, Collection management, Exhibit design,*
    Public programming, Curatorship, Education, Conservation
Areas of specialization: *Anthropology, Clothing, Ethnology, Fine arts,*
    Material culture, Natural science, Archeology, Decorative arts, Ethics,
    History, Museology, Paleontology
Instructional opportunities provided: *Short-term lectures on request*
Is museum ethics a regular part of the program?   *Yes*
Is the program open to international students?   *Yes*
The primary language of instruction is: *English*

The program is affiliated with: *Museum(s), University(ies)*
Is instruction given in a museum? *Yes*
Do students work in a museum collection as part of the program of
    study? *Yes*
How many students begin the program each year? *40*
Are the majority of the beginning students already employed by
    museums? *No*
What percentage of the students completing this program enter or return
    to museum work? *Less than 25%*
Contact person: *Peter Bandurraga, Nevada Historical Society*
Description of program: *Courses, Internships*

This program consists of two interdisciplinary courses and independent
study. The fall course is team-taught by faculty from each of the departments and museums involved. It is an **introduction to museum work** and
includes behind-the-scene visits to the major museums of the Reno-Carson
City area plus a field trip to a large California city. Projects in various
museum settings are required. The second semester is an **internship in a
museum.** The Departments of Art and Anthropology provide for undergraduate minors in Museum Studies.

The program is offered with participation of the Nevada Historical
Society and the Nevada State Museum.

194

Science Center of New Hampshire
PO Box 173
Holderness, New Hampshire 03245
USA
Telephone: (603) 968 7194

The program began in: *1974*
Time required to complete program: *10 weeks*
Level of training provided: *Internships*
Areas of study: *Exhibit design, Public programming, Education, Field
    methods*
Areas of specialization: *Natural science*
Instructional opportunities provided: *Full-time study*
Is museum ethics a regular part of the program? *No*
Is the program open to international students? *No*
The primary language of instruction is: *English*
Is financial assistance available for students? *Yes*

Financial assistance is available in the following ways: *Lodging, Stipend*
The program is affiliated with: *Science center(s)*
Is instruction given in a museum?   *Yes*
Do students work in a museum collection as part of the program of study?   *Yes*
Do program instructors have museum experience?   *Yes*
How many students begin the program each year?   *6*
How many students have completed the program since it began?   *110*
Are the majority of the beginning students already employed by museums?   *No*
What percentage of the students completing this program enter or return to museum work?   *Less than 25%*
Contact person: *Dave Eder, Intern Coordinator*
Description of program: *Internships*

The **Environmental Intern Program** is offered year round to undergraduate and graduate students interested in the areas of environmental education, ecology, limnology, entomology, and general natural history. Students are trained to provide an effective interpretative program for seasonal visitors and for school groups. Special workshops in natural history interpretation, land management, and display design are available.

195

Department of Art History
Rutgers University
Voorhees Hall
New Brunswick, New Jersey 08903
USA

The program began in: *1901*
Time required to complete program: *2 years*
Level of training provided: *Internships, Graduate degree, Certificate*
Areas of study: *Administration, Collection management, Exhibit design, Public programming, Curatorship, Education*
Areas of specialization: *Anthropology, Fine arts*
Instructional opportunities provided: *Full-time study*
Is museum ethics a regular part of the program?   *Yes*
Is the program open to international students?   *Yes*
The primary language of instruction is: *English*
Is financial assistance available for students?   *Yes*

Financial assistance is available in the following ways: *Student work program, Scholarships, Loans*

The program is affiliated with: *Museum(s), Gallery(ies), University(ies)*

Is instruction given in a museum? *Yes*

Do students work in a museum collection as part of the program of study? *Yes*

Do program instructors have museum experience? *Yes*

How many students begin the program each year? *10*

How many students have completed the program since it began? *25*

Are the majority of the beginning students already employed by museums? *No*

What percentage of the students completing this program enter or return to museum work? *25% to 50%*

Contact person: *Joan Marter*

Description of program: *Certificate*

The **Graduate Program in Art History** at Rutgers University offers a Certificate in Museum Studies to students enrolled in the program. These students are also working toward a Master's degree in Art History. A unique aspect of the program is the proximity to New York City, and the use of major museums such as the Metropolitan Museum of Art and the Whitney Museum of American Art for internships.

196

Museum Studies Department
Institute of American Indian Arts
PO Box 20007
Santa Fe, New Mexico 87504
USA
Telephone: (505) 988 6281 Ext. 114

The program began in: *1971*

Time required to complete program: *2 years, 1 year intern*

Level of training provided: *Courses, Internships, Diploma, Workshops, Certificate, Associate of Arts degree*

Areas of study: *Administration, Collection management, Exhibit design, Public programming, Curatorship, Education, Conservation*

Areas of specialization: *Anthropology, Archives, Clothing, Ethnology, Fine arts, Material culture, Ethics, History, Museology*

Instructional opportunities provided: *Full-time study, Short-term lectures on request, Part-time study, Scheduled lectures/seminars*

Is museum ethics a regular part of the program?   *Yes*
Is the program open to international students?   *Yes*
The primary language of instruction is: *English*
Is financial assistance available for students?   *Yes*
Financial assistance is available in the following ways: *Scholarships, Lodging, Tuition waiver, Materials/supplies, Meals*
The program is affiliated with: *Museum(s), University(ies)*
Is instruction given in a museum?   *Yes*
Do students work in a museum collection as part of the program of study?   *Yes*
Do program instructors have museum experience?   *Yes*
How many students begin the program each year?   *12–15*
How many students have completed the program since it began?   *100+*
Are the majority of the beginning students already employed by museums?   *Yes*
What percentage of the students completing this program enter or return to museum work?   *25% to 50%*
Contact person: *Chuck Dailey, Chair, Museum Studies Department*
Description of program: *Associate's degree, Workshops*

Associate of Fine Arts Degree in Museum Training: the two-year course of study is designed to meet the growing demand for trained personnel to operate tribal visitor centers or museums across America and an equally large demand for Indian staff members at various museums in the United States. First-year courses provide instruction in theory, basic exhibition techniques, care of collections, research, and management. Second-year students are assisted by the faculty in defining their area of specialized study and are involved in major exhibition research as well as in preparing a scale model and a written proposal for a museum. Students have interned at the Heard Museum of Anthropology in Arizona, Museum of New Mexico, Smithsonian Institution (National Museum of Natural History), and the Heye Foundation, Museum of the American Indian in New York.

Workshops and consultation programs are offered on and off campus. A museum training "outreach program" is available to all tribes and includes audio-visual material, videotapes, and photographs.

197

The New York Botanical Garden
Bronx, New York 10458-5126
USA
Telephone: (718) 220 8747

United States of America

Time required to complete program: *2 years*
Level of training provided: *Internships, Diploma, Certificate, Bachelor degree, Associate degree*
Areas of specialization: *Horticulture*
Instructional opportunities provided: *Full-time study, Part-time study*
The program is affiliated with: *University(ies)*
Contact person: *Jeff Katz*
Description of program: *Diploma, Degree, Internships, Certificate, Seminar*

Diploma in Horticulture: the twenty-one-month School of Horticulture program may be taken on either a full-time or part-time basis and is designed for students who desire broad-based training in both theoretical and practical aspects of horticulture. Students work at the Botanical Garden in the Bronx and they may spend up to three months at another approved horticultural organization.

Associate Degree in Ornamental Horticulture: the two-year program, offered in conjunction with Bronx Community College of the City University of New York, is a combination of academic courses and practical work in either general horticulture, or commercial floristry, or interior landscaping.

Baccalaureate Degree in Individualized Studies with a concentration in plant studies: the program, offered in conjunction with Lehman College of the City University of New York, permits an individualized course of study in either botany or horticulture.

Certificate programs: New York Botanical Garden offers certificate programs and courses in biological illustration, botany, commercial flower arranging, gardening, interior landscaping, landscape design, horticultural theory, and other areas. Most certificates take 72–198 hours of study to complete.

Internships: from time to time, as funding permits, special applications for formal internships in the Horticulture Department will be considered. Interested students should submit particulars about their education and experience as well as reasons why they wish to work at the Botanical Garden.

198

Art Conservation Department
State University College at Buffalo
RH 230, 1300 Elmwood Avenue
Buffalo, New York 14222-1095
USA
Telephone: (716) 878 5025

The program began in: *1970*
Time required to complete program: *More than 2 years*
Level of training provided: *Graduate degree, Certificate*
Areas of study: *Conservation*
Areas of specialization: *Anthropology, Fine arts, Material culture, Archeology, Decorative arts*
Instructional opportunities provided: *Full-time study*
Is museum ethics a regular part of the program? *Yes*
Is the program open to international students? *Yes*
The primary language of instruction is: *English*
Is financial assistance available for students? *Yes*
Financial assistance is available in the following ways: *Scholarships, Loans, Tuition waiver*
The program is affiliated with: *University(ies)*
Is instruction given in a museum? *No*
Do students work in a museum collection as part of the program of study? *No*
Do program instructors have museum experience? *Yes*
How many students begin the program each year? *10*
How many students have completed the program since it began? *200*
Are the majority of the beginning students already employed by museums? *Yes*
What percentage of the students completing this program enter or return to museum work? *More than 75%*
Contact person: *Christopher Tahk, Director*
Description of program: *Master's degree with Certificate*

The program is designed to train students for professional practice in the care and treatment of works of artistic and historical significance. Emphasis is placed on the acquisition of precision skills required in conservation practice. The course of study extends over three years and consists of four semesters of classroom study and a twelve-month internship in a conservation laboratory under a senior conservator. The **Master of Arts degree** and a **Certificate of Advanced Study in Art Conservation** are awarded simultaneously at the successful completion of the program.

199

History Museum Studies
Cooperstown Graduate Program
PO Box 800
Cooperstown, New York 13326
USA
Telephone: (607) 547 2596
Fax: (607) 547 8926

The program began in: *1964*
Time required to complete program: *2 years*
Level of training provided: *Graduate degree*
Areas of study: *Administration, Collection management, Exhibit design, Public programming, Curatorship, Education*
Areas of specialization: *Material culture, Architecture, Decorative arts, History, Museology*
Instructional opportunities provided: *Full-time study*
Is museum ethics a regular part of the program?   *Yes*
Is the program open to international students?   *Yes*
The primary language of instruction is: *English*
Is financial assistance available for students?   *Yes*
Financial assistance is available in the following ways: *Scholarships, Student work program, Tuition waiver*
The program is affiliated with: *Museum(s), University(ies)*
Is instruction given in a museum?   *Yes*
Do students work in a museum collection as part of the program of study?   *Yes*
Do program instructors have museum experience?   *Yes*
How many students begin the program each year?   *15*
How many students have completed the program since it began?   *600*
Are the majority of the beginning students already employed by museums?   *Yes*
What percentage of the students completing this program enter or return to museum work?   *More than 75%*
Contact person: *Langdon G. Wright*
Description of program: *Master's degree*

Cooperstown Graduate Program is a Master's degree program co-sponsored by the State University College at Oneonta and the New York State Historical Association. It combines museum theory, practical experience, and academic training. Students take forty credit hours, including required courses in museum administration, collections management, education and interpretation, exhibits, material culture, and research.

Electives in American architecture, art, decorative arts, social history, and independent studies are also offered. Most students spend three or four semesters in residence. A continuing education option requires two non-consecutive semesters in residence. Financial aid is available.

200

Conservation Center of the Institute of Fine Arts
New York University
14 East 78th Street
New York, New York 10021
USA
Telephone: (212) 772 5848

The program began in: *1960*
Time required to complete program: *More than 2 years*
Level of training provided: *Diploma, Graduate degree*
Areas of study: *Collection management, Conservation, Field methods*
Areas of specialization: *Anthropology, Archives, Fine arts, Material culture, Archeology, Decorative arts, Ethics*
Instructional opportunities provided: *Full-time study, Scheduled lectures/seminars*
Is museum ethics a regular part of the program? *Yes*
Is the program open to international students? *Yes*
The primary language of instruction is: *English*
Is financial assistance available for students? *Yes*
Financial assistance is available in the following ways: *Scholarships, Loans*
The program is affiliated with: *University(ies)*
Do students work in a museum collection as part of the program of study? *No*
Do program instructors have museum experience? *Yes*
How many students begin the program each year? *8*
How many students have completed the program since it began? *125*
Are the majority of the beginning students already employed by museums? *Yes*
What percentage of the students completing this program enter or return to museum work? *More than 75%*
Contact person: *Margaret Holben Ellis, Chairman*
Description of program: *Master's degree, Diploma*

The Conservation Center is dedicated to the study of the technology and conservation of works of art and historic artifacts. It prepares students for careers in conservation through a four-year program that combines practical experience in conservation with art historical, archeological, curatorial, and scientific studies of the materials and construction of works of art. Students undertake research projects, laboratory work, and seminars in special areas of conservation and gain intensive conservation experience through advanced field work and the internship. Eighty points are required for the combined **Master's degree in Art History** and **Diploma in Conservation.**

201

Graduate Seminar
American Numismatic Society
Broadway at 155th Street
New York, New York 10032
USA
Telephone: (212) 234 3140

The program began in: *1952*
Time required to complete program: *6 months or less*
Level of training provided: *Courses, Certificate*
Areas of specialization: *Material culture, Archeology, History*
Instructional opportunities provided: *Scheduled lectures/seminars*
Is museum ethics a regular part of the program?   *No*
Is the program open to international students?   *Yes*
The primary language of instruction is: *English*
Is financial assistance available for students?   *Yes*
Financial assistance is available in the following ways: *Scholarships*
Is instruction given in a museum?   *Yes*
Do students work in a museum collection as part of the program of study?   *Yes*
Do program instructors have museum experience?   *Yes*
How many students begin the program each year?   *12*
How many students have completed the program since it began?   *400*
Are the majority of the beginning students already employed by museums?   *No*
Contact person: *William E. Metcalf, Chief Curator*
Description of program: *Seminars, Fellowships*

The seminar is an intensive program of study including lectures and conferences conducted by specialists in various fields, preparation and oral delivery of a paper on a topic of the student's choice, and actual contact with the coinage related to that topic. Curators of the American Numismatic Society and experts from this country and abroad will participate in the seminar. Applications are accepted from students of demonstrated competency who will have completed at least one year of graduate work in classical studies, history, art history, economic history, or related disciplines. Applications are also accepted from junior faculty members with an advanced degree in one of these fields.

Stipends of $2000 are available to qualified applicants who are citizens or permanent residents of the United States or who are affiliated with colleges and universities in the United States and Canada. The Society will endeavor to provide round-trip travel fare from each student's home institution.

Applications are also accepted from outstanding foreign students who have completed the equivalent of one year's graduate work, who are affiliated with a museum or institution of higher learning, and who are able to demonstrate fluency in English. No financial aid is offered, and it is expected that no more than two positions will be available.

Fellowships: Each year the Society awards a fellowship in support of doctoral dissertation work employing numismatic evidence. Applicants must have attended the Society's Graduate Seminar, have completed the general examination (or the equivalent) and be writing a dissertation during the coming academic year in which the use of numismatic evidence plays a significant part. The current stipend is $3500.

The Society periodically awards a fellowship in memory of Frances M. Schwartz. The fellowship is intended to educate qualified students in museum practice and to train them in numismatics, as well as to provide for curatorial assistance in the Greek, Roman, and Byzantine Departments. Candidates must have completed the B.A. or equivalent. The stipend will vary with the term of tenure (normally the academic year) but will not exceed $2000.

202

Museum Studies/City College
City University of New York
Convent Avenue at 138 Street
New York, New York 10031
USA

The program began in: *1975*
Time required to complete program: *2 years*

Level of training provided: *Courses, Internships, Diploma, Graduate degree, Workshops*

Areas of study: *Administration, Collection management, Exhibit design, Public programming, Curatorship, Education*

Areas of specialization: *Fine arts, Architecture, Museology*

Instructional opportunities provided: *Full-time study, Part-time study*

Is museum ethics a regular part of the program?   *Yes*

Is the program open to international students?   *Yes*

The primary language of instruction is: *English*

Is financial assistance available for students?   *Yes*

Financial assistance is available in the following ways: *Scholarships, Student work program, Tuition waiver, Internships, Teaching assistantships*

The program is affiliated with: *University(ies)*

Is instruction given in a museum?   *Yes*

Do students work in a museum collection as part of the program of study?   *Yes*

Do program instructors have museum experience?   *Yes*

How many students begin the program each year?   *6–8*

How many students have completed the program since it began?   *30*

Are the majority of the beginning students already employed by museums?   *No*

What percentage of the students completing this program enter or return to museum work?   *50% to 75%*

Contact person: *Harriet Senie, Ph.D.*

Description of program: *Master's degree*

Master of Arts in Museum Studies: the thirty credit program consists of two full-semester internships at a museum or related institution, a course each in museology, exhibition analysis, and thesis, seminar, elective courses (twelve to fifteen credits) in art history and museum education. In addition, students must complete a formal Master's thesis. Individuals applying for the program should have a Bachelor's degree with twelve credits in art history or a related field.

203

American Museum – Hayden Planetarium
81st Street and Central Park West
New York, New York 10024
USA
Telephone: (212) 873 1300

The program began in: *1966*
Time required to complete program: *9 months*
Level of training provided: *Internships*
Areas of study: *Exhibit design, Public programming, Education, Information technology*
Areas of specialization: *Astronomy*
Is the program open to international students?   *Yes*
The primary language of instruction is: *English*
Is financial assistance available for students?   *Yes*
Financial assistance is available in the following ways: *Salary*
The program is affiliated with: *Museum(s)*
How many students begin the program each year?   *1*
How many students have completed the program since it began?   *20*
Contact person: *William A. Gutsch, Jr, Ph.D., Chairman*
Description of program: *Internship*

The intern will work under the supervision of the Planetarium's Chairman and Education Coordinator and participate in all aspects of planetarium operation. Some of this work will include presenting live sky shows to school groups as well as show planning, script writing, sound recording, photography required for show production, and possibly teaching. The intern will work a thirty-five-hour per week schedule. The position of Planetarium Intern is for nine months with a stipend of $11,500 along with a small amount for travel to planetarium conferences. Applicants should have a strong desire to pursue planetarium work as a career, a good background in descriptive astronomy, and a Bachelor's or higher degree in a planetarium-related field. Previous planetarium experience is highly desirable.

204

Institute of Fine Arts
New York University
Academic Office, 1 East 78th Street
New York, New York 10021
USA

Time required to complete program: *More than 2 years*
Level of training provided: *Courses, Internships, Graduate degree, Certificate*
Areas of study: *Collection management, Exhibit design, Curatorship, Conservation*
Areas of specialization: *Fine arts, Archeology, Architecture*

Instructional opportunities provided: *Full-time study, Part-time study*
Is the program open to international students? *Yes*
The primary language of instruction is: *English*
Is financial assistance available for students? *Yes*
Financial assistance is available in the following ways: *Scholarships, Student work program, Loans, Tuition waiver*
The program is affiliated with: *Museum(s), University(ies)*
Is instruction given in a museum? *Yes*
Do students work in a museum collection as part of the program of study? *Yes*
Do program instructors have museum experience? *Yes*
How many students begin the program each year? *5–10*
Are the majority of the beginning students already employed by museums? *No*
What percentage of the students completing this program enter or return to museum work? *More than 75%*
Contact person: *Marian Burleigh-Motley*
Description of program: *Certificate*

Certificate of Curatorial Studies: the program is offered jointly by the Institute of Fine Arts and the Metropolitan Museum of Art. Its purpose is to prepare students for curatorial careers in specialized fields. Problems of museum education and general administration are not emphasized. The course of study normally requires 3½–4 years to include the Master's degree, successful completion of a Ph.D. candidacy interview, and the successful resolution of a curatorial studies interview. Specific requirements include a nine-month internship in a curatorial department within the Museum.

205

Museum Education
Bank Street College
610 West 112th Street
New York, New York 10025
USA
Telephone: (212) 875 4491 or (212) 875 4400

The program began in: *1978*
Time required to complete program: *More than 2 years*
Level of training provided: *Graduate degree*
Areas of study: *Administration, Public programming, Education, Field methods*

292

Areas of specialization: *Ethics, Museology*
Instructional opportunities provided: *Part-time study*
Is museum ethics a regular part of the program?   *Yes*
Is the program open to international students?   *Yes*
The primary language of instruction is: *English*
Is financial assistance available for students?   *Yes*
Financial assistance is available in the following ways: *Scholarships, Student work program, Loans*
Do students work in a museum collection as part of the program of study?   *No*
Do program instructors have museum experience?   *Yes*
How many students begin the program each year?   *6–10*
How many students have completed the program since it began?   *100*
Are the majority of the beginning students already employed by museums?   *Yes*
What percentage of the students completing this program enter or return to museum work?   *More than 75%*
Contact person: *Nina Jensen*
Description of program: *Master's degree*

Leadership in Museum Education: this program is designed for the working museum professional. Students complete the course work and supervised field work over a two-year period during which they meet one weekend a month, September through June and for one two-week institute in June of both years of the program. The central focus of the course work is the development of museum programming and administrative practice based on a knowledge of human development. Students use their jobs as their field work settings. Upon completion of the program, students receive a Master of Science in Education with specialization in museum leadership. Students complete thirty-six credits at Bank Street and six credits in a museum discipline (art history, science, anthropology, etc.) at another institution for a total of forty-two credits.

206

Kevorkian Center for Near Eastern Studies
New York University
50 Washington Square S., Suite 400
New York, New York 10012
USA
Telephone: (212) 998 8080 or (212) 998 2697

Time required to complete program: *2 years*
Level of training provided: *Internships, Graduate degree*
Areas of study: *Administration, Collection management, Exhibit design, Curatorship, Education*
Areas of specialization: *Anthropology, Fine arts, History, Museology, Near Eastern studies*
Instructional opportunities provided: *Full-time study, Part-time study*
Is museum ethics a regular part of the program?   *Yes*
Is the program open to international students?   *Yes*
The primary language of instruction is: *English*
Is financial assistance available for students?   *Yes*
Financial assistance is available in the following ways: *Scholarships, Loans, Tuition waiver, Student work program*
The program is affiliated with: *Museum(s), University(ies)*
Is instruction given in a museum?   *Yes*
Do students work in a museum collection as part of the program of study?   *No*
Do program instructors have museum experience?   *Yes*
Contact person: *Professors Jill Claster and Flora Kaplan*
Description of program: *Concentration*

Master of Arts in Near Eastern Studies with a concentration in Museum Studies: this concentration combines study of the Near East with professional training in museum studies. It is designed for those who intend to pursue careers in museums and cultural organizations, and those currently employed in the field who wish to acquire formal training. The program offers individualized internship placements, and provides a comprehensive knowledge of the contemporary theory and practice of museum work, as well as a substantive curriculum in Near Eastern studies.

207

Museum Studies Program, GSAS
New York University, FAS
19 University Place, Suite 308
New York, New York 10003
USA
Telephone: (212) 598 3461

The program began in: *1977*
Time required to complete program: *Varies*

Level of training provided: *Courses, Internships, Workshops, Certificate, Post M.A., Ph.D.*

Areas of study: *Administration, Collection management, Exhibit design, Public programming, Curatorship, Education, Field methods, Information technology, Conservation*

Areas of specialization: *Anthropology, Archives, Ethnology, Fine arts, Material culture, Archeology, Decorative arts, Ethics, History, Museology*

Instructional opportunities provided: *Full-time study, Short-term lectures on request, Part-time study, Scheduled lectures/seminars*

Is museum ethics a regular part of the program? *Yes*

Is the program open to international students? *Yes*

The primary language of instruction is: *English*

Is financial assistance available for students? *Yes*

Financial assistance is available in the following ways: *Student work program, Project employment, Loans*

The program is affiliated with: *Museum(s), University(ies), Science center(s)*

Is instruction given in a museum? *Yes*

Do students work in a museum collection as part of the program of study? *Yes*

Do program instructors have museum experience? *Yes*

How many students begin the program each year? *23*

How many students have completed the program since it began? *200*

Are the majority of the beginning students already employed by museums? *No*

What percentage of the students completing this program enter or return to museum work? *More than 75%*

Contact person: *Flora S. Kaplan, Director*

Description of program: *Certificate*

The **New York State Professional Certificate Program in Museum Studies** is a twenty-four-credit program for students who aspire to careers as curators, registrars, directors, and administrators. It also prepares those already working in museums for new responsibilities. Each student is required to complete twenty-four credits in Museum Studies, of which a minimum of eight credits will be counted toward the M.A., M.S., or Ph.D. degree by the participating department of New York University. Students must also complete an intensive period of work as an intern, for a minimum of one semester, in a museum or other suitable institution in the New York metropolitan area or elsewhere. The program is offered only to those who hold a graduate degree or who are concurrently earning a graduate degree. Non-certificate students may be admitted into courses offered by the program, although they are not eligible for supervised internships in a museum, or for certificate award.

Master of Arts in Near Eastern Studies, Master of Arts in Latin American and Caribbean Studies: the New York University offers two joint thirty-six credit Master of Arts degrees aimed primarily at foreign museum professionals. The first is a Master of Arts in Near Eastern Studies with a concentration in Museum Studies, offered jointly by Museum Studies program and the Hagop Kevorkian Center for Near Eastern Studies. The second is a Master of Arts in Latin American and Caribbean Studies.

208

Cooper Hewitt Museum
Parsons School of Design
2 East 91st Street
New York, New York 10128
USA
Telephone: (212) 860 6345

The program began in: *1982*
Time required to complete program: *2 years*
Level of training provided: *Graduate degree*
Areas of study: *Curatorship*
Areas of specialization: *Material culture, Decorative arts*
Instructional opportunities provided: *Full-time study*
Is museum ethics a regular part of the program? *Yes*
Is the program open to international students? *Yes*
The primary language of instruction is: *English*
Is financial assistance available for students? *Yes*
Financial assistance is available in the following ways: *Scholarships, Student work program, Loans*
The program is affiliated with: *Museum(s), University(ies)*
Is instruction given in a museum? *Yes*
Do students work in a museum collection as part of the program of study? *Yes*
Do program instructors have museum experience? *Yes*
How many students begin the program each year? *15–20*
How many students have completed the program since it began? *100*
Are the majority of the beginning students already employed by museums? *No*
What percentage of the students completing this program enter or return to museum work? *50% to 75%*
Contact person: *Maria Ann Conelli, Ph.D.*
Description of program: *Master's degree*

The **Master's Program in the History of Decorative Arts**: the program is offered jointly by Cooper-Hewitt, National Museum of Design, Smithsonian Institution, and Parsons School of Design. The program in the history of European decorative arts offers a comprehensive training that goes beyond connoisseurship to include critical understanding of historical and cultural issues.

The Cooper-Hewitt/Parsons program focuses primarily on European decorative arts from the Renaissance to the twentieth century, although other areas, such as Asian and American decorative arts, are included to provide a broader understanding of the arts. The curriculum fosters the examination of the formal aspects of the object within its historical and cultural context. The interpretation of the object and the effective written and oral communication of this information is also emphasized within the curriculum.

The degree of Master of Arts in the History of Decorative Arts is awarded upon completion of forty-eight credits of course work with a minimum grade point average of 3.0 and the successful completion of the Master's examination. The program may be completed in two years of full-time study or four years of part-time study.

209

Center for Studies in the Decorative Arts
Bard College
18 West 86th Street
New York, New York 10024
USA
Telephone: (212) 744 7878, Fax: (212) 744 7920

The program began in: *1992*
Time required to complete program: *2 years*
Level of training provided: *Graduate degree*
Areas of study: *Administration, Exhibit design, Curatorship, Education*
Areas of specialization: *Fine arts, Material culture, Decorative arts, History, Museology, Connoisseurship, Furniture, Ceramics*
Instructional opportunities provided: *Full-time study*
Is the program open to international students?   *Yes*
The primary language of instruction is: *English*
Is financial assistance available for students?   *Yes*
Financial assistance is available in the following ways: *Scholarships, Student work program, Fellowships*
The program is affiliated with: *Museum(s), Gallery(ies), University(ies)*

Is instruction given in a museum?   *Yes*
Do program instructors have museum experience?   *Yes*
How many students begin the program each year?   *25*
Contact person: *Veronica McNiff, Admissions Director*
Description of program: *Master's degree*

The Bard Graduate Center for Studies in the Decorative Arts is an international study and exhibition center in New York City devoted to the interdisciplinary study of the decorative arts in all cultures. Operated under the auspices of Bard College in Annandale-on-Hudson, the Center offers an intensive two-year program of study (five semesters) leading to a **Master of Arts degree in the History of the Decorative Arts**. Courses examine European and American decorative arts, as well as those of Central and Eastern Europe, Russia, Scandinavia, Asia, and South America. Students take a combination of mandatory and elective classes including material courses, historical surveys, national surveys, and interdisciplinary studies. Degree candidates must complete a minimum of sixty academic credits, a Master's seminar, and a written thesis.

Hands-on examination of materials and objects is an essential feature of this program. Field work takes place in the museums and private collections in the metropolitan New York area.

Applicants must have a Bachelor's degree or the equivalent, with reading proficiency in at least one foreign language (preferably French, German, or Italian). Because of the interdisciplinary nature of the program, there are no restrictions as to the applicant's prior field of study. The Bard Graduate Center welcomes students of all ages and backgrounds, as well as working professionals. The Center offers fellowships, scholarships, and student work programs. Aid is awarded on the basis of need and merit.

210

Museum Education
Bank Street College
610 West 112th Street
New York, New York 10025
USA
Telephone: (212) 875 4491 or (212) 875 4400

The program began in: *1975*
Time required to complete program: *1 year*
Level of training provided: *Graduate degree*

Areas of study: *Administration, Exhibit design, Education, Information technology, Public programming, Field methods*
Areas of specialization: *Ethics, Museology*
Instructional opportunities provided: *Full-time study, Part-time study*
Is museum ethics a regular part of the program?   *Yes*
Is the program open to international students?   *Yes*
The primary language of instruction is: *English*
Is financial assistance available for students?   *Yes*
Financial assistance is available in the following ways: *Scholarships, Student work program, Loans, Tuition waiver, Assistantships*
The program is affiliated with: *Museum(s)*
Do students work in a museum collection as part of the program of study?   *No*
Do program instructors have museum experience?   *Yes*
How many students begin the program each year?   *15–20*
How many students have completed the program since it began?   *200*
Are the majority of the beginning students already employed by museums?   *Yes*
What percentage of the students completing this program enter or return to museum work?   *50% to 75%*
Contact person: *Nina Jensen*
Description of program: *Master's degree*

Museum Education: this is a forty-two credit program that leads to a Master of Science in Education and New York State certification for teaching K-6. Included are both teacher education and specialized museum education courses. Concurrent field work in New York City museums and schools is individually selected to complement each student's background, experience, and career goals. The spring semester is spent three days per week in one museum with a specific focus on educational work. Areas of specialization include: child development, curriculum development, and special education. Students specialize in their museum discipline through their museum internship site and assignments. This program normally requires one academic year plus two summer sessions.

211

Museum Special Education
Bank Street College
610 West 112th Street
New York, New York 10025
USA
Telephone: (212) 875 4491 or (212) 875 4400

The program began in: *1978*
Time required to complete program: *2 years*
Level of training provided: *Graduate degree, NY teacher certification*
Areas of study: *Administration, Exhibit design, Education, Public programming, Field methods, Information technology*
Areas of specialization: *Ethics, Child development, Museology, Special education*
Instructional opportunities provided: *Full-time study, Part-time study*
Is museum ethics a regular part of the program? *Yes*
Is the program open to international students? *Yes*
The primary language of instruction is: *English*
Is financial assistance available for students? *Yes*
Financial assistance is available in the following ways: *Scholarships, Loans, Tuition waiver, Student work program, Assistantships*
The program is affiliated with: *Museum(s)*
Do students work in a museum collection as part of the program of study? *No*
Do program instructors have museum experience? *Yes*
How many students begin the program each year? *0–2*
How many students have completed the program since it began? *10*
Are the majority of the beginning students already employed by museums? *No*
What percentage of the students completing this program enter or return to museum work? *25% to 50%*
Contact person: *Nina Jensen*
Description of program: *Master's degree*

Museum Special Education: the fifty-one credit program leads to a Master's degree with dual specializations in museum education and special education. In addition to the requirements for the museum education program, students take nine credits in special education. A year of field work includes two eight-week student teaching placements and a semester internship in one museum with a specific focus on working with a wide range of special audiences. Students may have backgrounds in any museum discipline (art, science, history, etc.). Students specialize through their internship site and assignment. This is a two-year program.

212

Museum Studies
Hartwick College
The Museums of Hartwick
Oneonta, New York 13820
USA
Telephone: (607) 432 4200

The program began in: *1975*
Time required to complete program: *More than 2 years*
Level of training provided: *Courses, Internships, Workshops, Core curriculum*
Areas of study: *Administration, Collection management, Exhibit design, Public programming, Curatorship, Education, Field methods, Information technology*
Areas of specialization: *Anthropology, Archives, Clothing, Ethnology, Fine arts, Material culture, Archeology, Decorative arts, History, Museology, Corporate law, Budget management*
Instructional opportunities provided: *Full-time study*
Is museum ethics a regular part of the program?   *Yes*
Is the program open to international students?   *Yes*
The primary language of instruction is: *English*
Is financial assistance available for students?   *Yes*
Financial assistance is available in the following ways: *Scholarships, Student work program, Materials/supplies*
The program is affiliated with: *Museum(s), Gallery(ies)*
Is instruction given in a museum?   *Yes*
Do students work in a museum collection as part of the program of study?   *Yes*
Do program instructors have museum experience?   *Yes*
How many students begin the program each year?   *26*
How many students have completed the program since it began?   *200+*
Are the majority of the beginning students already employed by museums?   *Yes*
What percentage of the students completing this program enter or return to museum work?   *25% to 50%*
Contact person: *Jane des Grange, Director*
Description of program: *Bachelor's degree*

Bachelor of Arts with a Museum Studies Concentration: emphasis is placed on the acquisition of a solid background in museum administration, education, and curatorship. The core curriculum of twelve credits provides for basic instruction in exhibition techniques, interpretation, and education. The topics of museum administration and the architectural design and structure of museum buildings are also covered. Actual training in a museum environment is provided by an ongoing series of internships. An off-campus internship at the beginning of the program is followed, in the junior year, by a semester-long internship in a selected museum of national prominence. During the senior year, the student functions as an assistant curator in one of Hartwick's four major museum departments.

213

State University of New York
Oswego, New York 13126
USA

The program began in: *1972*
Time required to complete program: *2 years*
Level of training provided: *Courses, Internships*
Areas of study: *Administration, Collection management, Exhibit design, Curatorship*
Areas of specialization: *Applicable undergraduate major*
Instructional opportunities provided: *Part-time study*
Is museum ethics a regular part of the program? *Yes*
Is the program open to international students? *Yes*
The primary language of instruction is: *English*
Is financial assistance available for students? *Yes*
Financial assistance is available in the following ways: *Student work program, Loans*
The program is affiliated with: *Gallery(ies), University(ies)*
Is instruction given in a museum? *Yes*
Do program instructors have museum experience? *Yes*
How many students begin the program each year? *6*
How many students have completed the program since it began? *100*
Are the majority of the beginning students already employed by museums? *No*
What percentage of the students completing this program enter or return to museum work? *Less than 25%*
Contact person: *Coy L. Ludwig or Judith Wellman*
Description of program: *Bachelor's degree*

Bachelor of Arts with a Minor in Museum Studies Program: the twenty-four-hour interdisciplinary program provides students with a knowledge of the concepts and philosophies under which today's museums and historical agencies function. Participating students must fulfill twelve-hour core requirements of two courses. One is an introduction to museum studies and the other deals with contemporary museum issues and ethics. A six credit internship is also a part of the core. The internship lasts one semester and students work twenty hours per week in a museum away from campus. Courses, selected from such areas as art history, history, anthropology, graphic arts, business administration, computer science, or education, complete the program.

Telephone: Coy L. Ludwig, Tyler Art Gallery (315) 341 2113 or Judith Wellman, Department of History (315) 341 3110

214

Research Division
Rochester Museum and Science Center
657 East Avenue, Box 1480
Rochester, New York 14603-1480
USA
Telephone: (716) 271 4320

The program began in: *1980*
Time required to complete program: *6 months or less*
Level of training provided: *Certificate*
Areas of study: *Administration, Collection management, Exhibit design, Curatorship, Education, Conservation, Field methods*
Areas of specialization: *Anthropology, Archives, Clothing, Ethnology, Material culture, Natural science, Archeology, Museology, Paleontology*
Instructional opportunities provided: *Scheduled lectures/seminars*
Is museum ethics a regular part of the program? *Yes*
Is the program open to international students? *Yes*
The primary language of instruction is: *English*
Is financial assistance available for students? *No*
Is instruction given in a museum? *Yes*
Do students work in a museum collection as part of the program of study? *Yes*
Do program instructors have museum experience? *Yes*
How many students begin the program each year? *2*
How many students have completed the program since it began? *10*
Are the majority of the beginning students already employed by museums? *No*

What percentage of the students completing this program enter or return
to museum work? *25% to 50%*
Contact person: *Charles F. Hayes III, Research Director*
Description of program: *Career training, Fellowships*

Career training: primarily for upper-level undergraduates from Rochester,
New York, and New York area colleges and universities. Trainees attend
lectures on museum-related topics and work on semester-long projects in
such areas as interpretation, library documentation, anthropology, history
and technology, decorative arts, archeology, and audio-visual programming, among others. Credit to be determined by participating college. Fees
paid by students to RMSC.

Fellowships utilizing RMSC resources and collections in anthropology,
natural history, and history and technology for upper-level undergraduates,
graduate students, and museum professionals from colleges, universities,
and museums throughout the United States.

215

Strasenburgh Planetarium
Rochester Museum and Science Center
657 East Avenue, Box 1480
Rochester, New York 14603-1480
USA
Telephone: (716) 271 4320
Fax: (716) 271 5935

The program began in: *1970*
Time required to complete program: *1 year*
Level of training provided: *Internships*
Areas of study: *Public programming, Education*
Areas of specialization: *Natural science*
Is the program open to international students? *No*
Is financial assistance available for students? *Yes*
Financial assistance is available in the following ways: *Student work
program*
The program is affiliated with: *Museum(s), Science center(s)*
How many students begin the program each year? *1*
How many students have completed the program since it began? *21*
Contact person: *Donald S. Hall, Director*
Description of program: *Internship, Seminars*

Planetarium internship: one position available each year. The intern will pursue personal interests along with regular staff assignments that may include script preparation, public speaking, program production, photography, and visual design. Preference will be given to applicants with a Bachelor's degree and planetarium experience. Stipend given.

Planetarium Production Techniques Seminar: sessions focus on soundtracks, visuals, and special effects. The seminar lasts three days. In addition, a day-long orientation program is offered for new or inexperienced planetarium personnel. This pre-seminar introduces participants to the basics of these same areas. Registration is limited to thirty people.

216

International Museum of Photography
George Eastman House
900 East Avenue
Rochester, New York 14607
USA
Telephone: (716) 271 3361

The program began in: *1990*
Time required to complete program: *1 year*
Level of training provided: *Certificate*
Areas of study: *Administration, Collection management, Exhibit design, Curatorship, Conservation, Information technology*
Areas of specialization: *Archives, Fine arts, Material culture, History, Photographic collection care*
Instructional opportunities provided: *Full-time study, Part-time study, Scheduled lectures/seminars*
Is museum ethics a regular part of the program?   *Yes*
Is the program open to international students?   *Yes*
The primary language of instruction is.   *English*
Is financial assistance available for students?   *No*
The program is affiliated with: *Museum(s)*
Is instruction given in a museum?   *Yes*
Do students work in a museum collection as part of the program of study?   *Yes*
Do program instructors have museum experience?   *Yes*
How many students begin the program each year?   *7*
How many students have completed the program since it began?   *10*
Are the majority of the beginning students already employed by museums?   *No*

What percentage of the students completing this program enter or return to museum work? *25% to 50%*
Contact person: *Grant B. Romer*
Description of program: *Certificate*

Photograph Preservation and Archival Practice Training Program: the program is designed with working professionals in mind. The "typical" candidate is expected to be someone who is already employed or working with an institutional photograph collection and who seeks specialized graduate training in the preservation discipline. The program is designed to be completed in one calendar year, in order to minimize the time away from a job. Classes are taught at the International Museum of Photography. One of the program's strengths is that specialized courses in cataloging, duplicating, etc., are taught by adjunct faculty who are experts in their field and work on the Eastman House staff or privately in the Rochester area.

The program has an intensive course load, but is supplemented throughout by guided experience working in the Eastman House collection or on research projects at RIT's Image Permanence Institute. Students can choose the kind of experiences in these practica that best suit their needs. In addition, each student must complete a project that demonstrates mastery of one of the topics in the curriculum. Candidates who successfully complete the program will be able to manage the physical care of photographic materials and make possible their continued accessibility as an intellectual resource.

Entry requirements include a baccalaureate degree or equivalent, knowledge of basic photographic technique as indicated by course work or portfolio, computer literacy, and for international students, English language proficiency (TOEFL score of 500 or above).

217

Museum Studies Program
Syracuse University
029 Sims Hall
Syracuse, New York 13244-1230
USA
Telephone: (315) 423 4098

The program began in: *1974*
Time required to complete program: *2 years*

Level of training provided: *Graduate degree*
Areas of study: *Administration, Collection management, Exhibit design, Curatorship, Education, Conservation, Field methods, Information technology*
Areas of specialization: *Fine arts, Ethics, History, Museology*
Instructional opportunities provided: *Full-time study, Part-time study*
Is museum ethics a regular part of the program?   *Yes*
Is the program open to international students?   *Yes*
The primary language of instruction is: *English*
Is financial assistance available for students?   *Yes*
Financial assistance is available in the following ways: *Scholarships, Student work program, Loans*
The program is affiliated with: *Gallery(ies), University(ies)*
Is instruction given in a museum?   *Yes*
Do students work in a museum collection as part of the program of study?   *Yes*
How many students begin the program each year?   *10*
Are the majority of the beginning students already employed by museums?   *No*
What percentage of the students completing this program enter or return to museum work?   *More than 75%*
Contact person: *Edward A. Aiken, Ph.D., Chair, Museum Studies*
Description of program: *Master's degree*

The **graduate program in Museum Studies** at Syracuse University prepares individuals to enter the museum profession. The program of study leads to a Master of Arts degree. Courses are taught by faculty from the University and from the local museum community. In addition to classroom teaching, students gain substantial experience working in the Lowe Art Gallery and the University Art Collection. Students undertake summer internships at museums throughout the United States. Through separate application, a graduate student may pursue a concurrent program of study in another field such as art history. The University maintains a large research library and has significant computer facilities.

218

Curatorial Internship
Rensselaer County Historical Society
59 Second Street
Troy, New York 12180-3928
USA
Telephone: (518) 272 7232

Time required to complete program: *6 months or less*
Level of training provided: *Internships*
Areas of study: *Collection management, Curatorship*
Areas of specialization: *Archives, Fine arts, Material culture, Decorative arts, History*
Is museum ethics a regular part of the program? *Yes*
Is the program open to international students? *Yes*
The primary language of instruction is: *English*
Is financial assistance available for students? *No*
Is instruction given in a museum? *Yes*
Do students work in a museum collection as part of the program of study? *Yes*
Do program instructors have museum experience? *Yes*
Contact person: *Stacy Pomeroy Draper, Curator*
Description of program: *Internship*

The Rensselaer County Historical Society, an active medium-sized local history museum and library in Troy, New York, offers the opportunity for hands-on curatorial experience to undergraduate and graduate students in ten-week to six-month periods throughout the year. Students assist with a variety of collection-related and research projects in an effort to develop a broad understanding of the curatorial mission of the institution. RCHS's extensive object and library-related collections are well known in the region and will provide a diverse challenging internship experience.

219

Marine Education Internships
North Carolina Aquarium on Roanoke Island
PO Box 967, Airport Road
Manteo, North Carolina 27954
USA
Telephone: (919) 473 3493

The program began in: *1986*
Time required to complete program: *6 months or less*
Level of training provided: *Internships*
Areas of study: *Exhibit design, Public programming, Curatorship, Education, Information technology*
Areas of specialization: *Natural science, Marine and aquatic education*
Instructional opportunities provided: *Scheduled lectures/seminars*
Is museum ethics a regular part of the program? *No*

Is the program open to international students? *Yes*
The primary language of instruction is: *English*
Is financial assistance available for students? *Yes*
Financial assistance is available in the following ways: *Student work program*
The program is affiliated with: *Science center(s)*
Is instruction given in a museum? *Yes*
Do students work in a museum collection as part of the program of study? *Yes*
Do program instructors have museum experience? *Yes*
How many students begin the program each year? *5–8*
How many students have completed the program since it began? *38*
Are the majority of the beginning students already employed by museums? *No*
What percentage of the students completing this program enter or return to museum work? *25% to 50%*
Contact person: *Rhett B. White, Director*
Description of program: *Internships, Training programs*

The North Carolina Aquarium on Roanoke Island houses a public aquarium, exhibits, classroom, and laboratories. It serves as a center for public information, education, and research. Students are accepted for internships lasting from four to ten weeks. Participants are involved in all phases of operation. Students may work for school credit.

Workshops, seminars, field trips, and other programs are available to youth groups, college students, adults, and people in industries and trades involving marine and coastal resources.

220

Public History Degree Program
North Carolina State University
Department of History, Box 8108
Raleigh, North Carolina 27695-8108
USA
Telephone: (919) 515 2483

The program began in: *1982*
Time required to complete program: *2 years*
Level of training provided: *Graduate degree*
Areas of study: *Administration, Collection management, Exhibit design, Curatorship, Conservation, Field methods, Architectural preservation*

Areas of specialization: *Archives, Clothing, Fine arts, Material culture, Architecture, History, Museology, Paper and rare book conservation*
Instructional opportunities provided: *Full-time study, Part-time study*
Is museum ethics a regular part of the program? *Yes*
Is the program open to international students? *Yes*
The primary language of instruction is: *English*
Is financial assistance available for students? *Yes*
Financial assistance is available in the following ways: *Scholarships, Student work program, Tuition waiver, Special fellowships, Graduate assistantships*
The program is affiliated with: *Museum(s), Gallery(ies), University(ies)*
Is instruction given in a museum? *Yes*
Do students work in a museum collection as part of the program of study? *Yes*
Do program instructors have museum experience? *Yes*
How many students begin the program each year? *6*
How many students have completed the program since it began? *42*
Are the majority of the beginning students already employed by museums? *No*
What percentage of the students completing this program enter or return to museum work? *Less than 25%*
Contact person: *Professor John David Smith*
Description of program: *Master's degree*

Museum studies are vitally integrated into North Carolina State University's Master of Arts in **Public History program**. In addition to a required seminar in public history, museum studies students enroll in a graduate-level lecture course in history museums and complete internships at the North Carolina Museum of History and at other historic sites and museums throughout the United States. Though students may concentrate in museum studies, most students select a broad range of public history courses as they shape their public history curriculum. Other advanced classes include archival management theory, archival management practice, documentary editing, records management, historic preservation, and paper and photographic preservation. Students benefit from the program's close affiliation with the North Carolina Division of Archives and History.

221

Reynolda House, Museum of American Art
PO Box 11765
Winston-Salem, North Carolina 27116
USA
Telephone: (919) 725 5325

The program began in: *1967*
Time required to complete program: *6 months or less*
Level of training provided: *Courses, Internships*
Areas of study: *Collection management, Public programming, Education*
Areas of specialization: *Clothing, Fine arts, Architecture, History*
Instructional opportunities provided: *Part-time study, Short-term lectures
  on request, Scheduled lectures/seminars*
Is museum ethics a regular part of the program? *Yes*
Is the program open to international students? *Yes*
The primary language of instruction is: *English*
Is financial assistance available for students? *No*
The program is affiliated with: *Museum(s), University(ies)*
Is instruction given in a museum? *Yes*
Do students work in a museum collection as part of the program of
  study? *Yes*
Do program instructors have museum experience? *Yes*
How many students begin the program each year? *25*
How many students have completed the program since it began? *600*
Are the majority of the beginning students already employed by
  museums? *No*
Contact person: *Nicholas Bragg or Marjorie Northup*
Description of program: *Internships, Courses*

January **internships** are available to undergraduate and graduate students
interested in American art, music, and literature. Interns research a painting
from the collection; each painting selected is studied in relation to the
music and literature of the same period. Internships may be for any length
of time and are offered year-round; however, the January program consists
of three weeks of concentrated study.

American foundations: the purpose of the four-week summer course is to
explore how different art forms express the common experiences of
Americans during various periods of history. The original works of art in
the Reynolda House collections provide a primary source, and participants are asked to discover contemporaneous works of art in other
expressive disciplines that share similar visions. During the third week of

the course a trip to New York City is planned that includes visits to art museums and galleries. Six hours of graduate credit are offered through Wake Forest University. Twenty students are accepted. Full or partial scholarships are available.

222

Internship Program
Cincinnati Zoo and Botanical Garden
3400 Vine Street
Cincinnati, Ohio 45220-1399
USA
Telephone: (513) 559 7715
Fax: (513) 281 CATS

The program began in: *1975*
Time required to complete program: *10 weeks*
Level of training provided: *Internships*
Areas of study: *Education, Conservation*
Areas of specialization: *Natural science*
Instructional opportunities provided: *Scheduled lectures/seminars*
Is museum ethics a regular part of the program? *No*
Is the program open to international students? *Yes*
The primary language of instruction is: *English*
Is financial assistance available for students? *No*
Is instruction given in a museum? *No*
Do program instructors have museum experience? *No*
How many students begin the program each year? *40*
Are the majority of the beginning students already employed by
    museums? *No*
What percentage of the students completing this program enter or return
    to museum work? *Less than 25%*
Contact person: *Penny Jarrett Geary, Intern Program Coordinator*
Description of program: *Internships*

Cincinnati Zoo and Botanical Garden Intern Program: the purpose of the internship is to provide college students with practical hands-on experience assisting zoo personnel with the daily operations of a zoological park and botanical garden. This challenging atmosphere offers the opportunity to supplement and apply classroom knowledge. The intern program offers a wide range of experiences in areas such as animal care, horticulture/ botany, marketing and development, education, veterinary medicine, and reproductive research at the Center for Reproduction of Endangered Wildlife.

Internships are offered year round usually for ten weeks. Special arrangements can be made if necessary. Interns have the opportunity for housing within walking distance of the Zoo. Since there is no housing fee and space is limited, it is allocated on a first-come first-served basis.

An internship at the Cincinnati Zoo can further develop career goals by employing skills, motivations, and interests in a professional zoological environment.

223

Internship in Museum Education
The Cleveland Museum of Art
11150 East Boulevard
Cleveland, Ohio 44118
USA
Telephone: (216) 421 7340

The program began in: *1993*
Time required to complete program: *1 year*
Areas of study: *Public programming, Education*
Areas of specialization: *Fine arts, Museology, Art history, Museum education*
Is museum ethics a regular part of the program? *Yes*
Is the program open to international students? *Yes*
The primary language of instruction is: *English*
Is financial assistance available for students? *Yes*
Financial assistance is available in the following ways: *Stipends*
The program is affiliated with: *Museum(s)*
Is instruction given in a museum? *Yes*
Do students work in a museum collection as part of the program of study? *No*
Do program instructors have museum experience? *Yes*
How many students begin the program each year? *1*
Are the majority of the beginning students already employed by museums? *No*
Contact person: *Katherine Solender, Curator*
Description of program: *Internship in Museum Education*

Position funded by the National Endowment for the Arts. Candidates for an M.F.A. or M.A. in Art History or Studio Art or recent recipients of

B.A., B.F.A., or M.F.A. degrees are eligible. Interns will teach the Museum's collection and special exhibitions; conduct workshops for teachers; develop slide packets and brochures; teach studio art classes when applicable; attend professional meetings, and visit other Midwest museums; other projects as time allows. Send letter of application, résumé, current transcript, and three references.

224

**Case Western Reserve University/
Cleveland Museum of Art Program**
Case Western Reserve University
10900 Euclid Avenue
Cleveland, Ohio 44106-7110
USA
Telephone: (216) 368 4118
Fax: (216) 368 4681

The program began in: *1967*
Time required to complete program: *2 years*
Level of training provided: *Internships, Graduate degree*
Areas of study: *Curatorship*
Areas of specialization: *Fine arts*
Instructional opportunities provided: *Full-time study, Part-time study*
Is museum ethics a regular part of the program? *Yes*
Is the program open to international students? *Yes*
The primary language of instruction is: *English*
Is financial assistance available for students? *Yes*
Financial assistance is available in the following ways: *Scholarships*
The program is affiliated with: *Museum(s)*
Is instruction given in a museum? *Yes*
Do students work in a museum collection as part of the program of study? *Yes*
Do program instructors have museum experience? *Yes*
How many students begin the program each year? *6*
How many students have completed the program since it began? *100*
Are the majority of the beginning students already employed by museums? *Yes*
What percentage of the students completing this program enter or return to museum work? *More than 75%*
Contact person: *Jenifer Neils, Chair, Art Department*
Description of program: *Master's degree, Doctoral degree*

Case Western Reserve University/Cleveland Museum of Art **Joint Program in Art History and Museum Studies.** Students enrolled in the Master's degree and doctoral degree programs combine a two-year curriculum of academic study with semesters on connoisseurship and museum practice administered by the curators of the Cleveland Museum of Art and the Department of Art History at Case Western Reserve. Each candidate spends at least one year as an intern in the Museum, and Ph.D. candidates also conduct a scholarly project that qualifies as a doctoral dissertation. Special areas of expertise include ancient, Northern and Italian Renaissance, modern European and American, and Asian Art. All classes are held in the museum.

225

Aullwood Audubon Center and Farm
National Audubon Society
1000 Aullwood Road
Dayton, Ohio 45414
USA
Telephone: (513) 890 7360

The program began in: *1965*
Time required to complete program: *6 months or less*
Level of training provided: *Internships*
Areas of study: *Education*
Areas of specialization: *Natural science*
Is museum ethics a regular part of the program? *Yes*
Is the program open to international students? *Yes*
The primary language of instruction is: *English*
Is financial assistance available for students? *Yes*
Financial assistance is available in the following ways: *Lodging, $500 stipend for three month session*
Is instruction given in a museum? *Yes*
Do students work in a museum collection as part of the program of study? *Yes*
Do program instructors have museum experience? *No*
How many students begin the program each year? *12*
How many students have completed the program since it began? *150*
Are the majority of the beginning students already employed by museums? *No*
Contact person: *John A. Wilson, Intern Coordinator*
Description of program: *Internship*

Environmental education/interpretation internship: this 200-acre natural area and organic farm provides outstanding opportunities for "learning by doing." During this internship, participants are involved in an extensive orientation and then gradually assume the same kinds of responsibilities as full-time staff. For the most part, interns are regarded as full-time staff; however, special care is taken by staff to provide learning opportunities, guidance, and sharing sessions that will be helpful to each intern in developing professional expertise and career goals. All facets of the operation of an environmental education center are explored. Each intern works with the staff to create his or her own individualized program. In addition, completion of a special project that benefits both the intern and Aullwood is encouraged.

Interns become involved in all aspects of Aullwood's varied educational programs. Areas of involvement include on-site guided programs for children and adults, teacher workshops, volunteer training and management, seasonal events, off-site programs, land management, care of wild and domestic animals, farm management, interpretative material and program design, and day-to-day operations.

226

Master of Liberal Studies with Museum Emphasis
University of Oklahoma
1700 Asp Avenue, Suite 226
Norman, Oklahoma 73037
USA
Telephone: (405) 325 1061

The program began in: *1981*
Time required to complete program: *2 years*
Level of training provided: *Graduate degree*
Areas of study: *Administration, Collection management, Exhibit design, Public programming, Curatorship, Education, Conservation, Field methods*
Areas of specialization: *Anthropology, Ethnology, Fine arts, Material culture, Natural science, Archeology, Ethics, History, Museology, Paleontology, Education*
Instructional opportunities provided: *Scheduled lectures/seminars, Correspondence study*
Is museum ethics a regular part of the program? *Yes*
Is the program open to international students? *Yes*
The primary language of instruction is: *English*

Is financial assistance available for students?   *Yes*
Financial assistance is available in the following ways: *Scholarships,*
   Loans, Scholarships given in the middle of the program
The program is affiliated with: *University(ies)*
Do students work in a museum collection as part of the program of
   study?   *Yes*
Do program instructors have museum experience?   *Yes*
How many students begin the program each year?   *15–20*
How many students have completed the program since it began?   *44*
Are the majority of the beginning students already employed by
   museums?   *Yes*
What percentage of the students completing this program enter or return
   to museum work?   *More than 75%*
Contact person: *Barbara Wilson, Coordinator*
Description of program: *Master's degree*

Master of Liberal Studies with museum emphasis: this program is directed
to those currently employed in museums, galleries, historical societies, and
similar educational institutions, desiring academic growth and advancement, but unable to pursue study through conventional academic
programs. The degree provides a broad foundation for museum work with
its emphasis on museology studies and individualized content. The steps
of the program consist of three on-campus seminars with two years of
independent study, culminating in a thesis. The program is designed to
be completed within a two-year period of time, but students move
according to their individual motivation, ability, and time available for
study.

227

Museum Studies
Lehigh University
Chandler Hall, 17 Memorial Drive
Bethlehem, Pennsylvania 18015
USA
Telephone: (215) 861 3651

The program began in: *1976*
Time required to complete program: *More than 2 years*
Level of training provided: *Internships, Workshops, Bachelor degree,*
   Concentration/minor

Areas of study: *Collection management, Exhibit design, Public program-*
ming, Curatorship, Education
Areas of specialization: *Anthropology, Fine arts, Archeology,*
Architecture, Museology
Is museum ethics a regular part of the program?   *Yes*
Is the program open to international students?   *Yes*
The primary language of instruction is: *English*
Is financial assistance available for students?   *Yes*
The program is affiliated with: *University(ies)*
Is instruction given in a museum?   *Yes*
Do students work in a museum collection as part of the program of
study?   *Yes*
Do program instructors have museum experience?   *Yes*
How many students begin the program each year?   *2–3*
How many students have completed the program since it began?   *25–30*
Are the majority of the beginning students already employed by
museums?   *Yes*
What percentage of the students completing this program enter or return
to museum work?   *More than 75%*
Contact person: *Ricardo Viera, Director*
Description of program: *Courses, Internships, Workshops*

Undergraduate programs: courses deal with the methods and procedures
involved in researching art objects, historical sites, and documents.
Internships are available in the principal museum areas of curatorship,
conservation, exhibition, interpretation, and administration. Placements
may be arranged at the Lehigh University Art Galleries, Historic
Bethlehem, Inc., and Lehigh County Historical Society. Work-study is also
offered.
   Workshops are presented for professionals from neighboring historical
societies and museums.

228

Friends Internship
Independence National Historical Park
313 Walnut Street
Philadelphia, Pennsylvania 19106
USA
Telephone: (215) 597 7087

The program began in: *1982*

Time required to complete program: *1 year*
Level of training provided: *Post-M.A. training*
Areas of study: *Collection management, Curatorship, Conservation*
Areas of specialization: *Material culture, Architecture, Decorative arts, History*
Is museum ethics a regular part of the program?   *No*
Is the program open to international students?   *Yes*
The primary language of instruction is: *English*
Is financial assistance available for students?   *Yes*
Financial assistance is available in the following ways: *Salary, Health benefits, Travel stipends*
The program is affiliated with: *Museum(s)*
How many students begin the program each year?   *1*
How many students have completed the program since it began?   *10*
Are the majority of the beginning students already employed by museums?   *Yes*
What percentage of the students completing this program enter or return to museum work?   *25% to 50%*
Contact person: *Doris Devine Fanelli*
Description of program: *Internship*

Graduate internship in the Division of Museum Operations: the intern will work with the nine-member museum staff and specialists from other Park divisions on a wide range of curatorial, interpretation, exhibition, and collections management projects related to the Park's eighteenth- and early nineteenth-century decorative and fine arts collections and its historic buildings. The program is designed to be flexible and to give the intern staff responsibility. One twelve-month position is available at a time. Applicants must have a Master's degree in American civilization, Anglo-American history, or related field. The internship carries a stipend of $15,000, health insurance benefits, and a limited travel allowance.

229

CIGNA Museum and Art Collection
1601 Chestnut Street
Philadelphia, Pennsylvania 19192-2078
USA
Telephone: (215) 761 4907

The program began in: *1979*
Time required to complete program: *6 months or less*

Level of training provided: *Courses*
Areas of study: *Collection management, Exhibit design, Curatorship*
Areas of specialization: *Archives, Fine arts, Material culture, Decorative arts, History, Museology*
Instructional opportunities provided: *Short-term lectures on request*
Is museum ethics a regular part of the program?   *Yes*
The primary language of instruction is: *English*
Is financial assistance available for students?   *No*
Is instruction given in a museum?   *Yes*
Do students work in a museum collection as part of the program of study?   *Yes*
Do program instructors have museum experience?   *Yes*
How many students begin the program each year?   *1*
How many students have completed the program since it began?   *5*
Are the majority of the beginning students already employed by museums?   *No*
What percentage of the students completing this program enter or return to museum work?   *25% to 50%*
Contact person: *Melissa E. Hough, Director*
Description of program: *Internships*

Undergraduate and graduate program: by working on a wide range of assignments, interns learn about the unique position of a museum in a corporate environment. Students assist the professional staff with registration duties, the installation of art in offices, conservation, and exhibition development and implementation. Applicants should be of at least junior standing and enrolled in art history, material culture, or a related curriculum. Graduate students are especially encouraged to apply. Internships are for a minimum of six weeks. Students who can work 12–15 weeks or longer are preferred. School credit may be arranged. No stipend.

The internship program at the CIGNA Museum and Art Collection provides practical experience as an entry-level professional. There are no structured classes; however, work assignments can be tailored to meet goals set by college and university museum studies programs. CIGNA's previous interns have all used the internship to complete practicum requirements at their respective educational institutions.

CIGNA refers to the corporation that was created when the Connecticut General Life Insurance Company merged with the Insurance Company of North America.

230

Committee on Continuing Professional Education
American Law Institute-American Bar Association (ALI-ABA)
4025 Chestnut Street
Philadelphia, Pennsylvania 19104
USA
Telephone: (215) 243 1630

The program began in: *1973*
Time required to complete program: *2½ days*
Level of training provided: *Courses*
Areas of study: *Administration*
Areas of specialization: *Legal issues*
Instructional opportunities provided: *Scheduled lectures/seminars*
Is museum ethics a regular part of the program? *Yes*
Is the program open to international students? *Yes*
The primary language of instruction is: *English*
Is financial assistance available for students? *Yes*
Financial assistance is available in the following ways: *Scholarships*
Is instruction given in a museum? *Yes*
Do students work in a museum collection as part of the program of
    study? *No*
Do program instructors have museum experience? *Yes*
How many students begin the program each year? *200*
How many students have completed the program since it began? *5000*
Are the majority of the beginning students already employed by
    museums? *Yes*
Contact person: *Alexander Hart*
Description of program: *Course*

Legal Problems of Museum Administration: this annual course of study
is co-sponsored by the Smithsonian Institution with the cooperation of
the American Association of Museums. The purpose is to provide museum
administrators, trustees, legal counsel, and staff involved in museum operations with an awareness of legal problems and other concerns that are
unique to museums and related organizations. The course location varies
from year to year.

231

Department of History
Duquesne University
Pittsburgh, Pennsylvania 15282
USA
Telephone: (412) 434 6400

The program began in: *1981*
Time required to complete program: *1½ years*
Level of training provided: *Internships, Graduate degree, Certificate*
Areas of study: *Administration, Collection management, Exhibit design, Public programming, Curatorship, Education, Information technology*
Areas of specialization: *Archives, Material culture, Decorative arts, History*
Instructional opportunities provided: *Full-time study, Part-time study*
Is museum ethics a regular part of the program? *No*
Is the program open to international students? *Yes*
The primary language of instruction is: *English*
Is financial assistance available for students? *Yes*
Financial assistance is available in the following ways: *Scholarships, Loans, Tuition waiver, Student work program*
The program is affiliated with: *University(ies)*
Is instruction given in a museum? *No*
Do program instructors have museum experience? *Yes*
How many students begin the program each year? *12*
How many students have completed the program since it began? *100*
Are the majority of the beginning students already employed by museums? *Yes*
What percentage of the students completing this program enter or return to museum work? *25% to 50%*
Contact person: *Perry K. Blatz*
Description of program: *Master's degree, Certificate*

Duquesne University's **graduate program in Archival, Museum, and Editing Studies** provides broad-based training directed toward employment in historical museums, historical societies, and archival institutions. Amidst the diverse and vibrant urban setting of Pittsburgh, students combine courses and internships in the program's three professional areas with graduate historical study leading toward the Master of Arts degree in history. For students who already possess the Master's degree, a certificate program is available.

232

Art Education – Museum Studies Option
Penn State University
207 Arts Cottage
University Park, Pennsylvania 16802-2905
USA

The program began in: *1974*
Time required to complete program: *1 year*
Level of training provided: *Internships, Graduate degree, Bachelor degree*
Areas of study: *Administration, Education*
Areas of specialization: *Anthropology, Ethnology, Fine arts, Material culture, Decorative arts, History, Elementary and Secondary Education, Museology*
Instructional opportunities provided: *Full-time study, Scheduled lectures/ seminars*
Is museum ethics a regular part of the program? *Yes*
Is the program open to international students? *Yes*
The primary language of instruction is: *English*
Is financial assistance available for students? *Yes*
Financial assistance is available in the following ways: *Scholarships, Loans, Tuition waiver, Student work program, Teaching assistantships*
The program is affiliated with: *Museum(s), Gallery(ies), University(ies)*
Is instruction given in a museum? *Yes*
Do students work in a museum collection as part of the program of study? *No*
Do program instructors have museum experience? *Yes*
How many students begin the program each year? *6*
How many students have completed the program since it began? *55*
Are the majority of the beginning students already employed by museums? *Yes*
What percentage of the students completing this program enter or return to museum work? *50% to 75%*
Contact person: *Robert W. Ott*
Description of program: *Internships, Bachelor's degree, Master's degree, Doctoral degree*

The **Museum Studies Program** at Penn State is an option that can be elected as an undergraduate in the Art Education for Social and Cultural Agencies Program or at the Master's degree or doctoral degree levels. The emphasis on the program is upon the arts and humanities. Penn State has a long record of successful graduates at all degree levels.

Internships are in cooperation with a consortium of northeast museums. For those pursuing the undergraduate major, internships are in museums throughout the Commonwealth of Pennsylvania. Included in these sites are such museums as the Philadelphia Museum of Art and the Carnegie Museum. At the graduate degree level, museum internships are available on national and international levels. Many students have completed successful professional experiences in major world-class museums through the Penn State program.

All students enrolled complete required course work in art education inclusive of research and theory courses, a concentration in art history/American studies/anthropology/esthetics and meet the requirements of the graduate school of Penn State.

233

Historic Preservation Program
Roger Williams University
One Old Ferry Road
Bristol, Rhode Island 02809-2921
USA
Telephone: (401) 253 1040

The program began in: *1976*
Time required to complete program: *More than 2 years*
Level of training provided: *Internships, Bachelor degree*
Areas of study: *Education, Conservation, Field methods, Information technology, Architectural preservation*
Areas of specialization: *Archives, Material culture, Archeology, Architecture, Ethics, Architectural conservation*
Instructional opportunities provided: *Full-time study*
Is museum ethics a regular part of the program? *No*
Is the program open to international students? *Yes*
The primary language of instruction is: *English*
Is financial assistance available for students? *Yes*
Financial assistance is available in the following ways: *Scholarships, Student work program, Loans*
The program is affiliated with: *Museum(s), University(ies)*
Is instruction given in a museum? *Yes*
Do students work in a museum collection as part of the program of study? *Yes*
Do program instructors have museum experience? *Yes*
How many students begin the program each year? *25*

Are the majority of the beginning students already employed by
museums? *No*
Contact person: *Karen L. Jessup, Director*
Description of program: *Bachelor's degree*

Bachelor of Arts or Bachelor of Science in Historic Preservation: the goals
of the program are to introduce students to the various components of
prevention, to familiarize students with the relationship between cultural
studies and preservation, and to prepare students for both careers in preservation and continuing education. Also required is participation in the
internship/apprenticeship program, a group project in historic preservation,
and to complete a senior project of the student's choosing. Study abroad
for one semester is required.

234

Department of History of Art and Architecture
Brown University
PO Box 1855
Providence, Rhode Island 02912
USA
Telephone: (401) 863 1174

The program began in: *1992*
Time required to complete program: *1 year*
Instructional opportunities provided: *Full-time study*
Is museum ethics a regular part of the program? *No*
Is the program open to international students? *Yes*
The primary language of instruction is: *English*
Is financial assistance available for students? *Yes*
Financial assistance is available in the following ways: *Scholarships,
Loans*
The program is affiliated with: *University(ies)*
How many students begin the program each year? *8*
Are the majority of the beginning students already employed by
museums? *No*
Description of program: *Practicum*

Department of History of Art and Architecture Practicum: the two-
semester methodology course culminates in a practicum that has a museum
component. The course is required for the completion of the Master's
degree and is a prerequisite for entry into the doctoral program.

235

American Association for State and Local History
530 Church Street
Nashville, Tennessee 37219
USA
Telephone: (615) 255 2971

Time required to complete program: *6 months or less*
Level of training provided: *Internships, Workshops, Seminars*
Areas of study: *Administration, Collection management, Conservation*
Areas of specialization: *History, Topics relevant to the museum field*
Instructional opportunities provided: *Short-term lectures on request,
    Scheduled lectures/seminars*
The primary language of instruction is: *English*
Is financial assistance available for students?   *Yes*
Financial assistance is available in the following ways: *Stipend for
    internships*
Contact person: *Donna Baumgartner, Deputy Director*
Description of program: *Seminars, Workshops, Internships*

Seminars and workshops: programs are sponsored each year for paid and volunteer professionals working in historical agencies. Subjects covered include collections care and conservation, interpretation, museum management, and marketing and development for museums, as well as other topics relevant to the field. The programs are conducted at locations throughout the United States.

William T. Alderson Internship Program: the intern will be headquartered at the AASLH office in Nashville. The intern will receive an orientation to the work of the AASLH and its relationship to the field. The intern will engage in field studies, through arrangements made with historical organizations in Nashville and the mid-South and complete a special project related to the historical agency field and reflecting the intern's interests. Eligibility is limited to students currently engaged in graduate studies in history, historical agency administration, or related fields. The internship lasts ten weeks and has a stipend of $1500. Limited funds for travel to and from Nashville are also provided.

236

The Winedale Museum Seminar
Texas Historical Commission
Local History Programs, Box 12276
Austin, Texas 78711-2276
USA
Telephone: (512) 463 6100 or (409) 278 3530

The program began in: *1971*
Time required to complete program: *10 days*
Level of training provided: *Workshops, Certificate*
Areas of study: *Administration, Collection management, Exhibit design, Public programming, Curatorship, Education, Conservation*
Areas of specialization: *Material culture, Ethics, Museology*
Instructional opportunities provided: *Scheduled lectures/seminars*
Is museum ethics a regular part of the program? *Yes*
Is the program open to international students? *Yes*
The primary language of instruction is: *English*
Is financial assistance available for students? *No*
The program is affiliated with: *Museum(s)*
Is instruction given in a museum? *No*
Do program instructors have museum experience? *Yes*
How many students begin the program each year? *20*
How many students have completed the program since it began? *500*
Are the majority of the beginning students already employed by museums? *Yes*
What percentage of the students completing this program enter or return to museum work? *More than 75%*
Contact person: *Kit Neumann, Seminar Coordinator*

The **Winedale Museum Seminar** is designed to improve the quality and promote the continuing development of community and regional history museums, historical organizations, and other cultural institutions. The program is designed to meet the needs of mid- to upper-level museum administrators, curators, educators, exhibits specialists, and other staff members as well as the lone professional and experienced volunteer.

The seminar consists of sessions on a wide variety of topics, including grant proposals, fund raising, financial planning, trustee relations and board development, staff relations, volunteer management, marketing, ethics, and political survival. Other sessions are presented on object research, historical photographs, material culture, education programming, program evaluation, design and fabrication of exhibits, security, and conservation of collections.

Applicants must be professional staff members or experienced volunteers in museums or historical organizations. Enrollment is limited to twenty people.

237

Harry Ransom Humanities Research Center
Conservation Department
University of Texas
PO Box 7219
Austin, Texas 78713-7219
USA
Telephone: (512) 471 9117

The program began in: *1982*
Time required to complete program: *3 months to one year*
Level of training provided: *Internships*
Areas of study: *Conservation*
Areas of specialization: *Archives, Fine arts, Library collections, Rare books*
Is museum ethics a regular part of the program? *No*
Is the program open to international students? *Yes*
The primary language of instruction is: *English*
Is financial assistance available for students? *No*
How many students begin the program each year? *Varies*
How many students have completed the program since it began? *15*
Are the majority of the beginning students already employed by museums (libraries)? *Yes*
What percentage of the students completing this program enter or return to museum work? *More than 75%*
Contact person: *James Stroud, Chief Conservation Officer*
Description of program: *Internships*

The Harry Ransom Center provides opportunities for qualified students and practitioners of paper, photograph, and book conservation to serve **internships** in its Conservation Department. The Ransom Center collections primarily contain nineteenth- and twentieth-century literary manuscripts and archives, photographs, rare books, and works of art on paper. The Conservation Department normally does not accept interns who have limited or no training or experience. Interns participate in all aspects of the department's programs, including conservation treatment, preservation housing, and exhibition preparation. The minimum length of internship is six months, though shorter internships are available for advanced practitioners having specific objectives. Interns are accepted at the discretion of the Chief Conservation Officer. The Center does not provide financial support for Conservation Department interns. The program is not affiliated with any University of Texas educational program and no degrees, certificates, or other awards are offered on completion of the internship.

238

Harry Ransom Humanities Research Center
University of Texas at Austin
PO Drawer 7219
Austin, Texas 78713-7219
USA
Telephone: (512) 471 9119

The program began in: *1988*
Time required to complete program: *2 years*
Level of training provided: *Internships*
Areas of study: *Information technology, Collection management, Exhibit design, Public programming, Curatorship, Administration*
Areas of specialization: *Archives, Rare books*
Instructional opportunities provided: *Full-time study*
Is museum ethics a regular part of the program?   *No*
Is the program open to international students?   *Yes*
The primary language of instruction is: *English*
Is financial assistance available for students?   *Yes*
Financial assistance is available in the following ways: *Student work program, Tuition waiver*
The program is affiliated with: *University(ies)*
Is instruction given in a museum?   *Yes*
Do students work in a museum collection as part of the program of study?   *Yes*
How many students begin the program each year?   *2–3*
How many students have completed the program since it began?   7
Are the majority of the beginning students already employed by museums (libraries)?   *Yes*
What percentage of the students completing this program enter or return to museum work?   *50% to 75%*
Contact person: *Cathy Henderson, Research Librarian*
Description of program: *Internships*

The Harry Ransom Humanities Research Center offers an **internship** program that is designed to provide participants with experience in the nature and operations of a major humanities research center. The experience gained by interns will benefit them in advanced graduate studies and academic research and present to them a career option in the humanities.

In addition to providing general support for HRHRC programs and services, duties may include organizing and cataloging book and manuscript collections, answering research queries, conducting bibliographic searches in connection with the purchase of materials, preserving HRHRC collections, planning and preparing exhibitions, and doing editorial work for HRHRC's publication program.

HRHRC interns are expected to have completed an undergraduate degree and to enroll in an appropriate graduate program at the University of Texas at Austin. Successful applicants will be appointed for one year and may apply to renew the internship for a second year. Preference is given to candidates who will be enrolled long enough to complete a two-year term.

239

Panhandle-Plains Historical Museum
WTSU Box 967
Canyon, Texas 79016
USA
Telephone: (806) 656 2244

Time required to complete program: *6 months or less*
Level of training provided: *Internships*
Areas of study: *Collection management, Exhibit design, Curatorship*
Areas of specialization: *Fine arts, Archeology, History*
The primary language of instruction is: *English*
Is financial assistance available for students?   *Yes*
Financial assistance is available in the following ways: *Salary*
The program is affiliated with: *Museum(s)*
Is instruction given in a museum?   *Yes*
Do students work in a museum collection as part of the program of study?   *Yes*
Do program instructors have museum experience?   *Yes*
How many students begin the program each year?   *20–30*
Contact person: *Walter R. Davis II, Museum Director*
Description of program: *Internships*

West Texas State University undergraduates may apply for the ten to fifteen work-study positions that exist each semester. Students are paid minimum wage and assist curators with cataloging duties, collections care, and exhibition preparation.

Non-salaried internship positions are available to qualified professionals and graduate students.

240

John E. Conner Museum
Texas A & I University
PO Box 2172, Station 1
Kingsville, Texas 78363
USA
Telephone: (512) 595 2819

The program began in: *1978*
Time required to complete program: *1 semester*
Level of training provided: *Internships*
Areas of study: *Administration, Collection management, Education, Public programming*
Areas of specialization: *Archives, Clothing, Ethnology, Material culture, Ethics, History, Museology, Exhibit planning*
Is museum ethics a regular part of the program?   *Yes*
Is the program open to international students?   *Yes*
The primary language of instruction is: *English*
Is financial assistance available for students?   *Yes*
Financial assistance is available in the following ways: *Stipend*
The program is affiliated with: *Museum(s)*
Is instruction given in a museum?   *Yes*
Do students work in a museum collection as part of the program of study?   *Yes*
Do program instructors have museum experience?   *Yes*
How many students begin the program each year?   *1*
How many students have completed the program since it began?   7
Are the majority of the beginning students already employed by museums?   *Yes*
What percentage of the students completing this program enter or return to museum work?   *More than 75%*
Contact person: *Jimmie R. Picquet, Director*
Description of program: *Internship*

An **internship** at the John E. Conner Museum is designed to give the graduate student in museum studies an opportunity to participate in all phases of small museum work. Hands-on experience including: textile registration, storage, and identification; archival preservation and research; computer applications relevant to all aspects of museum work from mailing lists to collections information; writing and editing exhibit labels, newsletters, and handouts; museum management; and grant proposals.

241

Museum Science Program
Texas Tech University
Museum of TTU, Box 43191
Lubbock, Texas 79409-3191
USA
Telephone: (806) 742 2442
Fax: (806) 742 1136

The program began in: *1974*
Time required to complete program: *2 years*
Level of training provided: *Graduate degree*
Areas of study: *Administration, Collection management, Exhibit design, Public programming, Curatorship, Education, Conservation, Field methods*
Areas of specialization: *Anthropology, Archives, Clothing, Ethnology, Fine arts, Material culture, Natural science, Archeology, Architecture, Ethics, History, Museology, Paleontology*
Instructional opportunities provided: *Full-time study, Part-time study*
Is museum ethics a regular part of the program? *Yes*
Is the program open to international students? *Yes*
The primary language of instruction is: *English*
Is financial assistance available for students? *Yes*
Financial assistance is available in the following ways: *Scholarships, Loans, Stipends, Student work program*
The program is affiliated with: *Museum(s), University(ies)*
Is instruction given in a museum? *Yes*
Do students work in a museum collection as part of the program of study? *Yes*
Do program instructors have museum experience? *Yes*
How many students begin the program each year? *15–20*
How many students have completed the program since it began? *300*
Are the majority of the beginning students already employed by museums? *No*

What percentage of the students completing this program enter or return
   to museum work?   *More than 75%*
Contact person: *Gary Edson, Director*
Description of program: *Master's degree, Field work*

Master of Arts in Museum Science: the Texas Tech University program
leads to the Master of Arts degree in two years and requires a total of
forty-five semester hours to graduate. The course of study consists of a
minimum of twenty-four credit hours in the core curriculum that includes:
professional development, collection management, museology, museum
ethics, law and standards, museum administration, preventive conservation, and interpretation and communication. All students participate in
a museum forum that allows interaction with both curatorial staff and
faculty and staff from across the university. In addition to the core
curriculum, students take a minimum of fifteen credit hours in elective
courses in a discipline area relevant to their special interests. The final six
credit hours is an internship, special problem, or Master's thesis. The
museum science program offers a generalist track as well as specializations in curatorial and collection management training in anthropology,
history, clothing and textiles, and the natural sciences. Students interested
in archival training work through the Texas Tech Southwest Collection.
Those wishing to pursue a career in historic preservation work at the
Ranching Heritage Center and take support course work in the Texas
Tech College of Architecture. Financial assistance is available through
Texas Tech University.

The museum science program at Texas Tech University welcomes international students. Recent participants have been from Mexico, Costa Rica,
India, China, Korea, Taiwan, Italy, Germany, and the United Kingdom.

A summer field work program including archeological excavation
activities at the Lubbock Lake Landmark, hands-on historical research at
the Ranching Heritage Center, natural science specimen collecting, and
paleontological field work is available to students.

242

Department of Museum Studies
Baylor University
PO Box 97154
Waco, Texas 76798
USA
Telephone: (817) 755 1110
Fax: (817) 755 2673

The program began in: *1978*
Time required to complete program: *2 years*
Level of training provided: *Graduate degree, Bachelor degree*
Areas of study: *Administration, Collection management, Exhibit design, Public programming, Curatorship, Education, Conservation, Information technology, Field methods, Architectural preservation*
Areas of specialization: *Anthropology, Fine arts, Material culture, Natural science, Archeology, History, Museum administration, Marketing*
Instructional opportunities provided: *Full-time study, Part-time study, Scheduled lectures/seminars*
Is museum ethics a regular part of the program?   *Yes*
Is the program open to international students?   *Yes*
The primary language of instruction is: *English*
Is financial assistance available for students?   *Yes*
Financial assistance is available in the following ways: *Scholarships, Loans, Tuition waiver, Student work program, Graduate assistantships*
The program is affiliated with: *Museum(s), Gallery(ies), University(ies)*
Is instruction given in a museum?   *Yes*
Do students work in a museum collection as part of the program of study?   *Yes*
Do program instructors have museum experience?   *Yes*
How many students begin the program each year?   *Over 30*
How many students have completed the program since it began?   *Over 25*
Are the majority of the beginning students already employed by museums?   *Yes*
What percentage of the students completing this program enter or return to museum work?   *50% to 75%*
Contact person: *T. Lindsay Baker or Calvin B. Smith*
Description of program: *Bachelor's degree, Master's degree*

The Department of Museum Studies at Baylor University offers both **baccalaureate and master's degrees in Museum Studies.** The program leading to a B.A. or B.S. degree emphasizes the mastery of hands-on skills required for entry-level museum employment and combines a major field in Museum Studies with one in a second discipline related to the student's career goals. The M.A. degree program is designed for students already working in museums or holders of baccalaureate degrees in Museum Studies who either aspire to become museum department heads, managers, or directors or already hold such positions and desire to become more effective.

243

Internship Program
Office of Historic Alexandria
Box 178, City Hall
Alexandria, Virginia 22313
USA
Telephone: (703) 838 4554

The program began in: *1983*
Time required to complete program: *6 months or less*
Level of training provided: *Courses, Internships, Bachelor degree*
Areas of study: *Administration, Collection management, Exhibit design, Public programming, Curatorship, Education, Field methods, Information technology*
Areas of specialization: *Anthropology, Archives, Fine arts, Material culture, Archeology, Decorative arts, Ethics, History, Museology*
Is museum ethics a regular part of the program? *Yes*
Is the program open to international students? *Yes*
The primary language of instruction is: *English*
Is financial assistance available for students? *No*
The program is affiliated with: *Museum(s), University(ies)*
Is instruction given in a museum? *Yes*
Do students work in a museum collection as part of the program of study? *Yes*
Do program instructors have museum experience? *Yes*
How many students begin the program each year? *5–7*
How many students have completed the program since it began? *40*
Are the majority of the beginning students already employed by museums? *Yes*
What percentage of the students completing this program enter or return to museum work? *25% to 50%*
Contact person: *Jeen Taylor Federico, Director*
Description of program: *Internships*

The Office of Historic Alexandria offers **internship** opportunities to qualified undergraduate and graduate students. Positions exist at several historic properties throughout the city, including Gadsby's Tavern, an eighteenth-century house museum; the Lyceum, which features exhibits relating to the history of Alexandria, and Fort Ward, a military installation constructed during the Civil War for the defense of Washington, D.C., which now functions as a city museum, exhibiting artifacts of that era; Friendship Firehouse, an 1855 installation exhibiting equipment and memorabilia; the Alexandria Black History Resource Center and the city's archives and records program. Interns are also utilized by Alexandria Archeology which seeks individuals to work on research projects, plan and implement educational programs, and work with the collections. Selected graduate students, preferably from arts and management programs, learn administrative procedures by assisting with the management of the Torpedo Factory Art Center, a large complex of studios for artists and craftspeople. All of the internships are non-salaried positions. Applicants should have backgrounds in decorative arts, American history, museum studies, or a related field. School credit may be earned.

244

School of the Arts
Virginia Commonwealth University
922 West Franklin Street
Richmond, Virginia 23284-3046
USA
Telephone: (804) 367 1064
Fax: (804) 367 0102

Time required to complete program: *2 years*
Level of training provided: *Courses, Internships, Graduate degree*
Areas of study: *Administration, Collection management, Exhibit design, Public programming, Curatorship, Education*
Areas of specialization: *Archives, Fine arts, Material culture, Architecture, Decorative arts, Ethics, History, Museology*
Instructional opportunities provided: *Full-time study, Part-time study, Scheduled lectures/seminars*
Is museum ethics a regular part of the program?   *Yes*
Is the program open to international students?   *Yes*
The primary language of instruction is: *English*
Is financial assistance available for students?   *Yes*
Financial assistance is available in the following ways: *Scholarships, Student work program, Tuition waiver, Teaching assistantships*
The program is affiliated with: *Museum(s), Gallery(ies)*
Is instruction given in a museum?   *Yes*
Do students work in a museum collection as part of the program of study?   *Yes*
Do program instructors have museum experience?   *Yes*
How many students begin the program each year?   *8*
How many students have completed the program since it began?   *50*

Are the majority of the beginning students already employed by
museums? *No*
What percentage of the students completing this program enter or return
to museum work? *25% to 50%*
Contact person: *Bruce M. Koplin*
Description of program: *Master's degree*

Master of Art in Museum Studies: the two-year program in Museum
Studies stresses those attitudes and skills necessary to accomplish the major
goals of any professional museum operation: to collect, to preserve, to
exhibit, and to interpret the art and artifacts of the past and present
within an extended curriculum and professional museum environment.
The course of study also includes an internship for academic credit under
the direct supervision and professional guidance of individuals in the field.

The curriculum provides a broad educational background in art history
and, in the field, will include studies in connoisseurship, registration
methods, exhibition design, and educational programs for museums. It
also provides a more particularized experience in areas in which the student
desires to develop expertise. These areas include museum theory and
administration, historic house museum, curatorship, and contemporary
alternative space gallery.

245

School of the Arts
Virginia Commonwealth University
922 West Franklin Street
Richmond, Virginia 23284-3046
USA
Telephone: (804) 367 1064
Fax: (804) 367 0102

Time required to complete program: *More than 2 years*
Level of training provided: *Courses, Internships, Bachelor degree*
Areas of study: *Administration, Collection management, Exhibit design,
Public programming, Curatorship, Education*
Areas of specialization: *Fine arts, Material culture, Architecture,
Decorative arts, Ethics*
Instructional opportunities provided: *Full-time study, Part-time study,
Scheduled lectures/seminars*
Is museum ethics a regular part of the program? *Yes*
Is the program open to international students? *Yes*

The primary language of instruction is: *English*
Is financial assistance available for students? *Yes*
Financial assistance is available in the following ways: *Student work program*
The program is affiliated with: *Museum(s), Gallery(ies), University(ies)*
Is instruction given in a museum? *Yes*
Do students work in a museum collection as part of the program of study? *Yes*
Do program instructors have museum experience? *Yes*
How many students begin the program each year? *15*
How many students have completed the program since it began? *100*
Are the majority of the beginning students already employed by museums? *No*
What percentage of the students completing this program enter or return to museum work? *50% to 75%*
Contact person: *Bruce M. Koplin*
Description of program: *Bachelor's degree*

The Department of Art History offers its **undergraduate majors** a program of study which acquaints them with the humanistic discipline of art historical inquiry. While providing students with the opportunity for a broad education actively drawing upon the liberal arts and humanities, the department also emphasizes a close bond with the studio and performing arts, and enjoys a close relationship with the professional art school of which it is a part.

Recognizing the diverse interests of undergraduate students and the varied practical applications of art history after graduation, the department offers its majors a choice among three distinct curricula resulting in either the Bachelor of Arts or Bachelor of Fine Arts degree.

The B.A. degree provides a course of study focusing on a program with a museum studies orientation which calls upon the excellent resources in the Richmond and Virginia areas. The uniqueness of the program, as well as its strength, is the opportunity it provides the student to intern in a regional museum.

246

Arts Management
Mary Baldwin College
Department of Arts and Humanities
Staunton, Virginia 24401
USA
Telephone: (703) 887 7197

Time required to complete program: *More than 2 years*
Level of training provided: *Internships, Bachelor degree*
Areas of study: *Administration, Exhibit design, Curatorship*
Areas of specialization: *Fine arts, Architecture, Museology*
Instructional opportunities provided: *Full-time study, Correspondence study*
Is museum ethics a regular part of the program? *No*
Is the program open to international students? *Yes*
The primary language of instruction is: *English*
Is financial assistance available for students? *Yes*
Financial assistance is available in the following ways: *Student work program, Loans*
The program is affiliated with: *Museum(s), Gallery(ies)*
Is instruction given in a museum? *No*
Do program instructors have museum experience? *Yes*
How many students begin the program each year? *5*
How many students have completed the program since it began? *10*
Are the majority of the beginning students already employed by museums? *No*
What percentage of the students completing this program enter or return to museum work? *Less than 25%*
Contact person: *Marlena Hobson, Assistant Professor*
Description of program: *Bachelor's degree*

Department of Arts and Humanities: the **undergraduate in arts management** is a mixture of art courses and business courses. Students study business organization and management as well as museology, historic preservation, and art history. Each student also participates in the internship program, working for school credit in a museum, gallery, or other art-related institution.

247

Seminar for Historical Administration
Colonial Williamsburg Foundation
PO Box 1776
Williamsburg, Virginia 23187-1776
USA
Telephone: (804) 220 7211

The program began in: *1958*
Time required to complete program: *3 weeks*
Level of training provided: *Certificate*

Areas of study: *Administration, Collection management, Exhibit design, Public programming, Curatorship, Education, Conservation, Field methods, Architectural preservation*

Areas of specialization: *Anthropology, Archives, Fine arts, Material culture, Archeology, Architecture, History, Museology*

Instructional opportunities provided: *Part-time study, Scheduled lectures/seminars*

Is museum ethics a regular part of the program? *Yes*

Is the program open to international students? *Yes*

The primary language of instruction is: *English*

Is financial assistance available for students? *Yes*

Financial assistance is available in the following ways: *Minority scholarships are offered*

The program is affiliated with: *Museum(s)*

Is instruction given in a museum? *Yes*

Do students work in a museum collection as part of the program of study? *No*

Do program instructors have museum experience? *Yes*

How many students begin the program each year? *18*

How many students have completed the program since it began? *600*

Are the majority of the beginning students already employed by museums? *Yes*

What percentage of the students completing this program enter or return to museum work? *More than 75%*

Contact person: *Peggy McDonald Howells*

Description of program: *Seminar*

The **Seminar for Historical Administration** offers historical organization professionals an opportunity to prepare for leadership in their chosen field. The issues-oriented curriculum is organized around three broad themes: the historical administrator as cultural leader, as executive, and as career professional. Case studies, skills workshops, issues forums, panel discussions, and site visits are some of the methods used by the Seminar's faculty. Informal discussions and after-hours events focus on topics of current interest. Colonial Williamsburg staff, programs, and facilities are open to participants. Trends in historical scholarship, preservation, and interpretation provide a central focus for the Seminar.

The Seminar is sponsored by the American Association of Museums, the American Association for State and Local History, the Colonial Williamsburg Foundation, and the National Trust for Historic Preservation. There are no tuition charges for participants. The cost of lodgings and meals at Colonial Williamsburg for the three weeks, estimated to be $900–$1000, as well as transportation costs are to be borne by participants or participants' organizations. Financial assistance is available for minority historical professionals.

248

Museum Services
Colonial Williamsburg Foundation
PO Box 1776
Williamsburg, Virginia 23187-1776
USA
Telephone: (804) 220 7211

Time required to complete program: *Varies*
Level of training provided: *Internships*
Areas of study: *Collection management, Exhibit design*
Areas of specialization: *Archives, Architecture, History, Rockefeller Folk Art Center*
The primary language of instruction is: *English*
Is financial assistance available for students?   *No*
The program is affiliated with: *Museum(s)*
How many students begin the program each year?   *Limited number*
Contact person: *Peggy Howells*
Description of program: *Internships*

Undergraduate and graduate internships: the Colonial Williamsburg Foundation accepts a limited number of interns each year on an unpaid basis. Acceptance as an intern depends on the applicant's previous training, proposed area of work and study, and the availability of an opening in a particular department. Students have interned at the Abby Aldrich Rockefeller Folk Art Center and in the architecture, archives, records, and collections divisions. Interns have also served in the craft shops and exhibitions buildings. Internships vary in length from one month to several months. Participants are expected to bear all costs of travel and living expenses while in Williamsburg.

249

Museum Services
Colonial Williamsburg Foundation
PO Box 1776
Williamsburg, Virginia 23187-1776
USA
Telephone: (804) 220 7211

Level of training provided: *Seminars*
Areas of study: *Administration*

Areas of specialization: *Fine arts, Architecture, History*
Instructional opportunities provided: *Scheduled lectures and seminars*
The primary language of instruction is: *English*
How many students begin the program each year? *18*
Are the majority of the beginning students already employed by
  museums? *Yes*
Contact person: *Peggy Howells*
Description of program: *Professional seminars*

Annual Seminar for Historical Administration: this program provides eighteen mid-level museum professionals with a knowledge of the special nature of historical museums. It seeks to advance the participants' skills in the planning, management, and evaluation of the functions of museums. Applicants should have prior training and experience in American history, art, architectural history or allied fields, and from five to ten years of work experience with other historical agencies. The seminar is sponsored by the Colonial Williamsburg Foundation, the American Association of Museums, the American Association for State and Local History, and the National Trust for Historic Preservation.

250

Museum Education
College of William and Mary
School of Education
Williamsburg, Virginia 23185
USA
Telephone: (804) 221 2329
Fax: (804) 221 2988

The program began in: *1977*
Time required to complete program: *2 years*
Level of training provided: *Graduate degree*
Areas of study: *Administration, Collection management, Public
  programming, Education, Information technology*
Instructional opportunities provided: *Full-time study, Part-time study*
Is museum ethics a regular part of the program? *Yes*
Is the program open to international students? *Yes*
The primary language of instruction is: *English*
Is financial assistance available for students? *Yes*
Financial assistance is available in the following ways: *Loans, Student
  work program, Assistantships*

Is instruction given in a museum?   *No*
Do program instructors have museum experience?   *Yes*
How many students begin the program each year?   *10–15*
How many students have completed the program since it began?   *100*
Are the majority of the beginning students already employed by
   museums?   *Yes*
What percentage of the students completing this program enter or return
   to museum work?   *More than 75%*
Contact person: *William E. Garland, Jr.*
Description of program: *Master's degree*

Museum educators have responsibility for a wide range of tasks: recruiting
and training docents, advertising and scheduling group tours, arranging
for special lectures, creating and managing outreach educational kits, and
conducting educational programs within the museum and the community
the museum serves. Rather than attempt to encompass each aspect of the
museum educator's role in the context of a thirty-hour academic program,
the curriculum focuses on preparing candidates to build accurate, useful,
and imaginative learning programs for the constituencies served by
museums in a modern society.

251

Curatorial Methods
National Park Service
Mather Employee Development Center
Harpers Ferry, West Virginia 25425-0077
USA

Time required to complete program: *2 weeks*
Level of training provided: *Courses*
Areas of study: *Collection management, Curatorship*
Areas of specialization: *Archives, Material culture, Natural science,
   Museology*
Instructional opportunities provided: *Full-time study*
Is museum ethics a regular part of the program?   *Yes*
Is the program open to international students?   *Yes*
The primary language of instruction is: *English*
Is financial assistance available for students?   *No*
Is instruction given in a museum?   *No*
Do program instructors have museum experience?   *Yes*
How many students begin the program each year?   *30*

Are the majority of the beginning students already employed by
museums? *Yes*
Description of program: *Course work*

For comprehensive information about all National Park Service Training,
contact Emogene Bevitt, NPS, 800 North Capital Street, Washington, D.C.
20560.

252

Elvehjem Museum of Art
University of Wisconsin – Madison
800 University Avenue
Madison, Wisconsin 53706
USA
Telephone (608) 263 2246

Time required to complete program: *1 year*
Level of training provided: *Courses*
Areas of study: *Administration, Collection management, Exhibit design,
Curatorship, Education*
Areas of specialization: *Fine arts, Museology*
Instructional opportunities provided: *Full-time study*
Is museum ethics a regular part of the program? *No*
Is the program open to international students? *Yes*
The primary language of instruction is: *English*
Is financial assistance available for students? *No*
The program is affiliated with: *Museum(s), University(ies)*
Is instruction given in a museum? *Yes*
Do students work in a museum collection as part of the program of
study? *No*
Do program instructors have museum experience? *Yes*
How many students begin the program each year? *15*
Are the majority of the beginning students already employed by
museums? *No*
What percentage of the students completing this program enter or return
to museum work? *Less than 25%*
Contact person: *Russell Panczenko*
Description of program: *Course*

Department of Art History: training in exhibition preparation, research
methods, and education programming form the basis of this course. Other

aspects of museum work and the topic of connoisseurship are also examined. Collections of the University's Elvehjem Museum of Art are used to further enhance instruction. A background in art history is required.

253

Milwaukee Public Museum/Museum Studies Program
University of Wisconsin – Milwaukee
800 West Wells Street
Milwaukee, Wisconsin 53233
USA
Telephone: (414) 278 2702
Fax: (414) 223 1396

The program began in: *1972*
Time required to complete program: *2 years*
Level of training provided: *Certificate*
Areas of study: *Collection management, Exhibit design, Curatorship, Education, Conservation*
Areas of specialization: *Anthropology, Archives, Clothing, Ethnology, Fine arts, Material culture, Natural science, Archeology, Architecture, Decorative arts, Ethics, History, Museology, Paleontology*
Instructional opportunities provided: *Full-time study*
Is museum ethics a regular part of the program? *Yes*
Is the program open to international students? *Yes*
The primary language of instruction is: *English*
Is financial assistance available for students? *Yes*
Financial assistance is available in the following ways: *Scholarships, Loans*
The program is affiliated with: *Museum(s), University(ies)*
Is instruction given in a museum? *Yes*
Do students work in a museum collection as part of the program of study? *Yes*
Do program instructors have museum experience? *Yes*
How many students begin the program each year? *10*
How many students have completed the program since it began? *200+*
Are the majority of the beginning students already employed by museums? *No*
What percentage of the students completing this program enter or return to museum work? *More than 75%*
Contact person: *Claudia Jacobson or Carter Lupton*
Description of program: *Certificate*

The **Museum Studies Program** is a cooperative venture between the University of Wisconsin – Milwaukee and the Milwaukee Public Museum. It consists of five courses taught at the graduate level by museum professionals and confers a certificate upon successful completion. The program is designed to supplement a student's graduate course study and includes instruction in museum history and theory, collections management, curation, preventive conservation, and exhibition.

254

The John Michael Kohler Arts Center
PO Box 489
Sheboygan, Wisconsin 53082-0489
USA
Telephone: (414) 458 6144

The program began in: *1982*
Time required to complete program: *1 year*
Level of training provided: *Internships*
Areas of study: *Administration, Curatorship, Education*
Areas of specialization: *Arts and Industry*
Is museum ethics a regular part of the program? *Yes*
Is the program open to international students? *Yes*
The primary language of instruction is: *English*
Is financial assistance available for students? *No*
The program is affiliated with: *Museum(s), Gallery(ies), University(ies)*
Is instruction given in a museum? *Yes*
Do students work in a museum collection as part of the program of study? *Yes*
Do program instructors have museum experience? *Yes*
How many students begin the program each year? *2*
How many students have completed the program since it began? *12*
Are the majority of the beginning students already employed by museums? *No*
What percentage of the students completing this program enter or return to museum work? *50% to 75%*
Contact person: *John Johnson*
Description of program: *Internships*

The John Michael Kohler Arts Center consists of several exhibition galleries, two retail shops, a 180-seat theater, a preschool, and an arts/industry program, as well as artists' residencies, classes, Arts Day

Camp, and other related programs. Its mission is to encourage and support innovative exploration in the world of art. **Internships** are offered in administration, education, curatorial work, and arts/industry. Internships will run on the standard college semester or quarter system. There is no pay or stipend involved for the intern but if needed, housing can be found.

Yugoslavia

255

Department of Art History
University of Belgrade
Cika Ljubina 18-20
Belgrade 11000
Yugoslavia
Telephone: (11) 63 92 22 Ext. 227
Fax: (11) 63 93 56

The program began in: *1953*
Time required to complete program: *1 year*
Level of training provided: *Courses*
Areas of study: *Administration, Collection management, Exhibit design, Public programming, Curatorship, Education, Field methods, Information technology*
Areas of specialization: *Anthropology, Ethnology, Fine arts, Archeology, History, Museology*
Instructional opportunities provided: *Scheduled lectures/seminars*
Is museum ethics a regular part of the program? *Yes*
Is the program open to international students? *Yes*
The primary language of instruction is: *Serbian*
Is financial assistance available for students? *Yes*
Financial assistance is available in the following ways: *State university offers free study*
The program is affiliated with: *Museum(s), University(ies)*
Is instruction given in a museum? *Yes*
Do students work in a museum collection as part of the program of study? *No*
Do program instructors have museum experience? *Yes*

Yugoslavia

How many students begin the program each year?   *60*
How many students have completed the program since it began?   *2000*
Are the majority of the beginning students already employed by
    museums?   *No*
What percentage of the students completing this program enter or return
    to museum work?   *Less than 25%*
Contact person: *Dragan Bulatovic*
Description of program: *Course*

Museology and the Protection of Cultural Monuments: offered through
the Department of Art History, this program is obligatory for graduate
studies in art history, archeology, and ethnology. The first part of the
curriculum is organized around a series of comprehensive lectures on
museology, museography, and museum work. The second segment relates
to the theory and practice of social, legal, and technical protection of
cultural monuments. Students are acquainted with practical themes of the
program in museums, bureaus, and the computer center of the University.

PART III

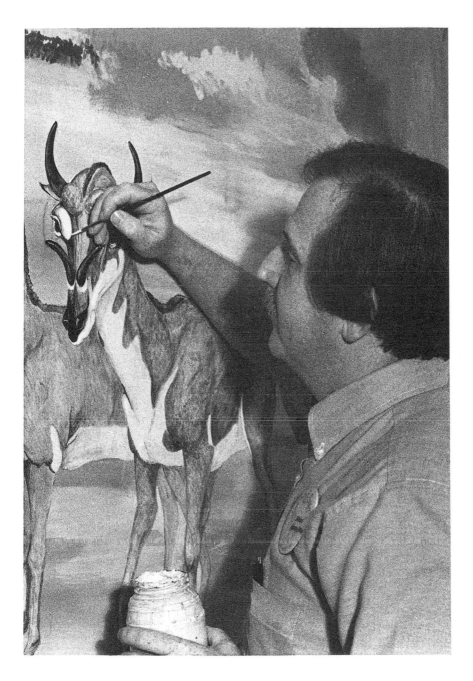

Plate 6 Museum administrator David Dean painting diorama
(photograph by Gary Edson)

Proposed standards and ethics for museum training programs

———•◆•———

(Editor's note: The following proposed Standards and Ethics for Museum Training Programs were developed by the International Committee for Training of Personnel. The proposal was introduced and reviewed at the ICTOP annual meeting in Rome (1991), distributed to the ICTOP general membership, and re-evaluated in Quebec City (1992). At that time, the Committee membership voted to forward the document to the ICOM Ethics Committee for review and action. The Ethics Committee may decide to return the Standards and Ethics proposal to ICTOP for further consideration or it may recommend the document for general acceptance. Should the latter action be decided, acceptance could be announced at the ICOM General Conference in 1995. The proposal is included in this publication as information.)

* * *

I Preamble

Standards and Ethics for Museum Training Programs provide a general statement of practices for those programs offering instruction, information, education, and training related to the museum field. These principles and guidelines apply to entry-level programs, mid-career training, seminars, and specialized instructional sessions. They shall be germane to both paid and non-paid, collection care and non-collection care training personnel and programs. Adherence to the ideals of this document is regarded as a minimum requirement for those serving the museum profession as training/education providers. Often it will be possible (if not necessary) to strengthen the contents of this document to meet particular institutional and national requirements.

The intention of this document is not to establish a single set of benchmarks with which to judge museum training programs. It is intended to define an attitude of correct action against which museum trainers can evaluate themselves and their activities.

1   Definitions

1.1   General terminology

Where possible and applicable, this document was drawn from the text of the ICOM *Code of Professional Ethics*. Often the style and wording of the original document have been altered to apply to training. In every instance this document is to reinforce the *Code of Professional Ethics* as set forth by the International Committee of Museums. Elements of this document have been drawn from other professionally oriented organizations addressing like concerns.

1.2   Museology/museography

Museology is the branch of knowledge concerned with the study of the theories, procedures, concepts, and organization of museums. Museography is the application of that thinking in the museum.

1.3   Museum training programs

Training program shall refer to any or all of the following:
1.3.1   Those instructional or educational activities designed to advance knowledge and understanding of the nature, functions, and role of museums in the service of society and of its development;
1.3.2   Those programs organized to prepare individuals for professional museum careers;
1.3.3   Those programs that provide training/education based on courses of instruction relative to the needs and requirements of the museum profession and that are responsive to the changing expectations of that profession; and
1.3.4   Those programs that provide the appropriate museum-related training/education in concert with one or more museums.

1.4   Museum trainees

1.4.1   The word trainee is used in this document to describe those persons normally called students. Trainee is inclusive of all persons receiving either formal education through an academic program or work enhancement/skill development.

1.4.2 Museum trainees are all those persons, regardless of their level of achievement, position designation, or pay status, who receive some form of training related to museological or museographical practice. They may be beginning students in museum training programs, mid-career museum workers wishing to increase their skills, or volunteers gaining new or expanded abilities to serve museums or museum visitors.

1.4.3 No individual, for reasons of age, race, gender, religion, national origin, marital status, or physical disability, shall be denied access to or participation in museum training/ educational programs.

1.5 Governing body

The governing body for museum training programs shall be a museum or museum organization, institution of higher education, or professional organization affiliated with a museum(s) and dedicated to the goal set forth in the *ICOM Statutes*, Article 3, paragraph 1, as follows:

1.5.1 To encourage and support the establishment, development, and professional management of museums of all kinds;

1.5.2 To advance knowledge and understanding of the nature, functions, and role of museums in the service of society and of its development;

1.5.3 To organize cooperation and mutual help between museums and between professional museum workers in the different countries;

1.5.4 To represent, support, and advance the interests of professional museum workers of all kinds; and

1.5.5 To advance and disseminate knowledge in museology and other disciplines concerned with museum management and operations.

1.6 Museum

A museum is defined in Article 2, paragraph 1, of the *Statutes* of the International Council of Museum as

> a non-profit making, permanent institution in the service of society and of its development, and open to the public which acquires, conserves, researches, communicates, and exhibits, for the purposes of study, education, and enjoyment, material evidence of people and their environment.

In addition to museums designated, ICOM recognizes (under Article 4 of the *Statutes*) that the following comply with the ICOM definition:

1.6.1 Conservation institutes and exhibition galleries permanently maintained by libraries and archive centers.

1.6.2 Natural, archeological, and ethnographical monuments and sites, and historical monuments and sites of a museum nature, for their acquisition, conservation, and communication activities.
1.6.3 Institutions displaying live specimens such as botanical and zoological gardens, aquariums, vivaria, etc.
1.6.4 Nature reserves.
1.6.5 Science centers and planetariums.

II Training program

2 Basic principles for training programs

2.1 Minimum standards for training programs

The governing body of the training program has an ethical duty to review, evaluate, and maintain the curriculum, finances, premises, staffing, and integral services. Above all, it is responsible to ensure the highest standard of training/education, at all levels, to meet the needs of the museum profession.

2.2 Curriculum

2.2.1 The curriculum for a basic professional museum training/educational program should include the following elements:

1 Museum history, purpose, and types;
2 Museum administration – organization, personnel, and budget;
3 Museum collections management – origin, records, maintenance, preservation, and care, including elements of both curative and preventive conservation;
4 Museum law, ethics, and standards;
5 Museum collections research and interpretation, including the theory and practice of exhibition development and implementation;
6 Museum education and communication;
7 Philosophy of museums;
8 Social and cultural role and responsibility of museums; and
9 Museum architecture, equipment, and security.

2.2.2 Hands-on work experience in a quality museum setting is a core element of the museum training process. This may include a formal internship or other form of practical experience. (Work experience is an extension of professional training, not a substitute.)

2.2.3 Mid-career and specialized training program curricula may include any of those subjects noted in 2.2.1 or may concentrate on topics of institutional, regional, or personal interest. It is imperative that the curriculum, no matter what the topic(s), be clearly defined and pertinent to the highest standards of museum practice.

2.3 Levels of training/education

2.3.1 *Entry-level* degree-granting training programs intended to prepare individuals to begin work in museums should provide instruction in all nine elements. The level of emphasis may vary. Training programs of this type are normally affiliated with institutions of higher education.

2.3.2 *Mid-career* training programs normally provide additional training/education for those persons already in the museum field. These programs include introduction to current technology, methods, and materials. The concept associated with this training is that the continuous training opportunities are an essential part of the museum training effort. It is essential that all persons, regardless of their job, educational background, and experiential level, have the opportunity to improve their museological skills.

2.3.3 *Specialized* training programs are those focusing on an area or skill that reinforces or enhances past training or experience. These programs differ from mid-career training programs in that they are sharply focused and designed to meet the need of a specialized segment of the museum workforce.

2.4 Financial requirements

Material describing the training program shall include the actual cost of such training. The trainee shall expect to pay the training institution, association, museum, or workshop organizer only the amount stated in the descriptive information. Other costs, such as associated lodging, food, books or support material, should be stated as accurately as possible.

2.5 Training personnel

2.5.1 The preferable qualifications of a museum program trainer are those of a scholar who is engaged in the discovery, evaluation, transmission, and extension of knowledge as it relates to museum practice. In addition to maintaining standards of competence, particularly those relating to scholarship and teaching ability, museum trainers are responsible for maintaining the proper attitude of objectivity, industry, and cooperation with associates within the museum profession.

2.5.2 The selection of trainers and trainees shall be the responsibility of the institution, organization or group providing the instructional program. However, all parties have the right to expect the trainers to have the necessary skills, knowledge, and qualifications to provide the described program of instruction and the trainees to have the needed background, interest, and motivation to comprehend and use the information provided.

2.6 Admission requirements

Admission to museum training programs should be based on fairness, honesty, and equal opportunity. All prerequisites for admission must be clearly stated and readily available to all prospective trainees.

2.7 Documentation

Museum training programs shall maintain proper pre-instructional documentation to provide the prospective trainee with a complete description of the course of instruction, the projected outcome, and intended benefit. Post-instructional documentation recording the name and identification number (where applicable) of the participants, the instruction content, the evaluation method, and the results of the evaluation shall become a part of the permanent record. These documents are to insure qualified acknowledgment of participants and their level of achievement.

3 Training content and method

3.1 Course descriptions

Each course shall be adequately described to provide prospective students with the necessary data to allow informed selection.

3.2 Certification, diploma, and degree requirements

3.2.1 Training programs shall clearly note in all informational material the levels of recognition provided. A precise definition shall describe the work required to receive the recognition announced. Certification and diploma program statements should include the level of training/education offered and the curriculum design.

3.2.2 At the end of the training session(s) each participant, depending on conformity with pre-defined criteria, shall receive a document stating the level and category of training, and the sponsoring organization. The document should be signed by the administrative authority of the organization or institution.

3.2.3 Degree-granting institutions shall include in their bulletin or catalog the name of the certifying agency authorizing the degree and the date of the last certification or accreditation.

3.3   Career assistance

The goal of all training programs is to prepare trainees for greater professional involvement with museums. As part of the process and as appropriate to the subject, duration, and level of training, it is a responsibility of the trainer and training organization to aid trainees in realizing their museum-related goals.

3.4   Evaluation methods

3.4.1   As part of the description of the course of study, trainers shall include the goals of the program and the method of evaluating the level of attaining those goals.
3.4.2   Trainee evaluation methods should be fair and without prejudice. There should be clearly defined goals against which trainees can rate their progress and by which trainers can determine trainee achievement.

III   Professional conduct

4   General principles

4.1   Ethical obligations for museum training personnel

Involvement in the museum training process, whether for pay or as a volunteer, involves great responsibility. Trainers have responsibilities to students, the museum profession, and to the instructional institution. These responsibilities entail facilitating the intellectual and emotional growth of students, encouraging free inquiry, and striving to create and maintain a climate of mutual respect that will enhance the free exchange of ideas. A trainer has a responsibility to recognize the varying needs and capabilities of trainees and to make every effort to insure that evaluations of a trainee's work correctly reflect the individual's level of achievement. A trainer also has the responsibility to uphold the highest scholarly standards and to encourage respect for such standards. Trainers must engage in a continual and critical study of museum-related information, to insure that instructional programs contain the most current and useful knowledge. The information provided must be consistent with the described subject as defined by pre-instructional material. The trainer must also be aware of the role of counselor, and devote a reasonable amount of time to guiding and counseling trainees. Finally, the trainer has a responsibility to maintain and expand those skills and values that insure the continuation of free and open inquiry.

4.2 Personal conduct of trainers

4.2.1   Museum training personnel shall act in a responsible manner, both legally and ethically, in all matters associated with operating a museum training program.
4.2.2   Trainers shall address, with equity, the social and cultural needs of all trainees and shall maintain an unbiased attitude toward individual customs and traditions, provided those practices do not infringe upon the rights of other trainers or trainees.
4.2.3   Trainers shall continually update their knowledge of museum practices and museum training information through reading professional journals and current publications.
4.2.4   Trainers shall not derive personal benefit, other than pre-established payment based on acceptable standards.

4.3 Personal interests

Trainers shall not engage in any business, transaction, or other activities or incur any debt of any nature that is in conflict with the proper discharge of their training duties.

4.4 Intellectual freedom

Training programs must be conducted for the common good of the museum profession. The common good depends upon the right to search for truth and its free expression. Consequently the trainer and trainee must be unrestricted to pursue intellectual inquiry without constraint and to state or publish material considered pertinent to the museum profession.

4.5 Research

4.5.1   Trainers should be encouraged to fulfill their roles as members of the museum profession by engaging in and actively pursuing a meaningful program of research and scholarly productivity.
4.5.2   Through research a trainer grows intellectually, stimulates trainee learning, and adds to the collective knowledge of the museum profession. A trainer should strive to contribute to the growth and understanding of the museum field through research and scholarship. A trainer has the added responsibility to share the results of that research by disseminating such information to trainees, colleagues, and museum professionals.

5 Trainer responsibility to trainees

5.1 Uphold professional standards

5.1.1   As teachers, trainers have responsibilities to trainees, to museology, to the museum profession, and to the museum community. These responsibilities include aiding the intellectual and emotional growth of trainees, encouraging free inquiry in museological practices, and striving to create and maintain an attitude of mutual respect.

5.1.2   Trainers may address a wide variety of social, political, artistic, and scientific issues as appropriate to the aims of the training program, if presented objectively and without prejudice. Intellectual honesty and objectivity in presentation are the duty of every trainer.

5.1.3   Trainers are responsible for maintaining the most current and professionally acceptable levels of museum methodology and technology and for making that information available to trainees.

5.1.4   Trainers are responsible for the descriptions of training courses under their supervision.

5.1.5   Trainers have the responsibility to uphold the highest museological standards and to encourage respect for such standards.

5.1.6   Trainers have the responsibility to maintain those skills and values that support free and open inquiry into museum theories and practices.

5.1.7   Trainers shall not intentionally injure the professional reputation or practice of another practitioner.

5.2 Fair and equal treatment

5.2.1   Museum training personnel shall place honesty, integrity, and cultural awareness foremost in defining the education, exhibition, interpretation, and special program content of the museums. Trainers must be certain that no intentionally hurtful or culturally demeaning attitudes or concepts are fostered.

5.2.2   Museum training personnel shall provide both opportunities and support for the intellectual growth and education of all members of the museum community.

5.3 Consistency in evaluation

5.3.1   Trainers shall recognize the diverse needs, requirements, and capabilities of individual trainees and make every effort to insure that evaluations of a trainee's work reflect that individual's level of achievement.

5.3.2   Evaluation of trainee work and/or program activity shall be without prejudice.

Proposed standards and ethics

5.4 Confidentiality

Trainers shall treat as confidential all information of a private or personal nature gained through contact with trainees. Information about trainee grades and program-related evaluations shall be treated with the utmost care and confidentiality.

5.5 Post-training assistance

5.5.1 Trainees have the right to expect a reasonable level of post-training help dependent on the scope, level, and duration of the training program. Trainers and training programs may provide solicited job advancement help, employment information, or letters of reference depending on the prevailing laws, regulations, and practices of the institution, state, region, or nation. Care must be taken so that trainees do not become excessively dependent on the training institution, or the training institution overly involved in the internal operations of the employing institution, organization, or agency. The degree of post-training assistance provided by the training institution should be clearly detailed to trainees at the beginning of the program.

6 Trainer's responsibility to colleagues

6.1 Professional relationships

6.1.1 Training programs shall strive to cooperate with each other, not compete for prospective students beyond the statement of factual information about the program of study offered.
6.1.2 Training programs shall be responsible for making all trainee financial aid and support services known to potential students.

6.2 Professional cooperation

6.2.1 As time and resources permit, the museum trainer has a responsibility to respond to requests for aid and advice, and to participate in the activities of the museum profession.
6.2.2 Trainers shall help students in other training programs seeking information or advice according to their knowledge and shall exercise reasonable discretion in describing the attributes of individual trainers or programs.

6.3 Professional service

6.3.1 Trainers have the same obligations and responsibilities as those assigned to other members of the museum profession and shall recognize

362

that, as with any profession, those duties are not limited by time or location.

6.3.2 Trainers shall participate in appropriate museum-related professional organizations, and attend meetings and conferences. They shall contribute to the goals of those organizations provided the requested services are beneficial to the museum profession.

6.3.3 When possible the trainer shall extend to the public information on acceptable museum practices.

Plate 7 Curator Mei Wan Campbell examining small collection object stored in plastic bag (photograph by Gary Edson)

Glossary of museum training terms

———•◆•———

One of the greatest problems in accessing and using information about museum training programs is semantics. In different regions, institutions, and centers of the same nation, words may convey different meanings. While they are necessary to transfer basic information, words add confusion to an otherwise simple transfer of data. Communicating across national, linguistic, and institutional boundaries compounds the issue. The process of literate comprehension is formulated on a simple truth – that words convey a valid or intended meaning. Even though the intention is honest, the cognition phase may cause difficulties.

Unfortunately there is no single vocabulary for museum training programs. To assist in the process of gaining greater information about museum training programs it is necessary to establish a basic vocabulary.

accession the process of transferring title or ownership from the providing source (field work, purchase, gift, transfer, etc.) to the museum (*entreé d'inventaire [acquisition]* FR (French), *ingreso, entrada,* or *acceso* SP (Spanish)).

accession record documentation maintained by the museum registrar recording all objects accessioned into the museum's collections (*registre des acquisitions* FR, *registro de entradas* SP).

accreditation the process of review and approval for instructional programs based on pre-established academic-oriented standards is called accreditation. Accrediting agencies vary from country to country but most are authorized agencies of the central or state government. There is no broad-based, discipline-specific accrediting agency for museum training programs. Those programs housed in academic institutions are normally accredited as part of the general institutional accreditation process (*octroi de statute de musée* FR, *acreditación* SP).

acquisition the act of gaining physical possession of an object, specimen, or sample. (*acquisition* FR, *adquisición* SP).

advisory board a board established under the authority of the host organization and charged by it with specified roles and responsibilities. Its essential role is to advise and recommend, and not to establish policy. (*conseil consultatif* FR, *patronato del museo* SP).

affective learning learning based upon emotional response to stimuli; emotional learning.

anthropology collections that address the science of humankind. Objects may be divided into as many discipline-based areas as the academy allows, i.e. cultural anthropology – the study of humans through their learned behaviors or culture; social anthropology – the systematic comparative study of social forms, etc. (*anthropologie* FR, *antropologia* SP).

appraisal the assigning of a monetary value to an object. (*évaluation* FR, valoración or apreciación SP).

archeology the study of past human life through their durable remains (*archéologue* FR, *arqueólogia* SP).

archivist a person charged with the collection and care of records and documents, including letters, maps, pictures, photographs, and film (*archiviste* FR, *archivista* SP).

artifact an object, either two- or three-dimensional, that has been selected, altered, used, or made by human effort (artefact UK, *artefact* or *objet faconné* FR, *artefacto* SP).

baccalaureate degree the first degree level beyond secondary education. The degrees awarded may be called by different names in various locations, but most are the primary professional degrees to be earned at a college or university. (*premier cycle* FR, *bachillerato* SP).

cataloging assigning an object to an established classification system and initiating a record of the nomenclature, provenance, number, and location of that object in the collection storage area (cataloguing UK, *catalogage* FR, *catalogación* SP).

certificate program describes non-degree- or diploma-granting training opportunities. The student receives specialized training in a particular subject and may be awarded a "certificate of achievement" upon successful completion of the study.

code of museum ethics a collection of standards or rules methodically arranged to define an accepted way of behavior for museums (*code de deéontologie muséale* FR, *código éthico de museos* SP).

cognitive learning knowledge based upon reasoned thought; rational learning.

collection an identifiable selection of objects having some significant commonalty. (*collection* FR, *colección* SP).

collection manager a person charged with care of a particular collection, normally working under the direction of a curator.

communication "the transfer of information and ideas with the deliberate intention to achieve certain changes, deemed desirable by the sender, in the knowledge, opinions, attitudes and/or behaviour of the receiver."[1] (*communication* FR, *comunicación* SP).

concept-oriented exhibition a presentation that is focused upon the transmission of information and in which collection objects may or may not be used to support the story rather than being the main emphasis.

conflict of interest those acts or activities that may be construed to be contrary to ethical museum practices based on knowledge, experience, and contracts gained through conditions of employment.

conservation the processes for preserving and protecting objects from loss, decay, damage, or other forms of deterioration (*conservation* FR, *conservación* SP).

conservator a person with the appropriate scientific training to examine museum objects, work to prevent their deterioration, and provide the necessary treatment and repairs (*restaurateur* FR, *conservador* SP).

controlled environment surroundings in which temperature, relative humidity, direct sunlight, pollution, and other atmospheric conditions are regulated (*contrôle de l'environnement* FR, *control ambiental* SP).

crafts for a time, the word crafts was used to describe the product of a leisure-time or utilitarian activity. As examples, basketry, most textiles and pottery making, and some metal work, along with a number of other hand-made products, were described as crafts. The connotation was that the items have different, usually lesser, value than works of art. In recent years the division between the arts of all kinds has been less clearly defined. Some locations maintain a strong tradition of crafts and use the word to describe the work of certain people or groups of people. So-called craft objects may be included in history, ethnology, anthropology, textile, or art collections (*art populaire* FR, *artesanía* SP).

cultural heritage a tradition, habit, skill, art form, or institution that is passed from one generation to the next (*patrimoine culturel* FR, *herencia cultural* SP).

cultural property the material manifestation of the concepts, habits, skills, art, or institutions of a specific people in a defined period of time (*bien culturel* FR, *propriedad cultural* SP).

curator a museum staff member or consultant who is a specialist in a particular field of study and who provides information, does research, and oversees the maintenance, use, and enhancement of collections (*keeper* UK, *conservateur* FR, *curador* SP).

deaccession the process for removing objects from a museum's collections (*retrait d'inventaire* FR, *salida* or *egreso* SP).

degree refers to a rank given by a college or university to a student for successful completion of a required course or curriculum of study (*degré* FR, *título* or *grado* SP).

designer a museum staff person or consultant who designs the exhibition, does working drawings, and coordinates fabrication and installation activities (*concepteur* FR, *diseñador* SP).

didactic meaning to teach and referring to educational (informational) material included as part of an exhibit.

diploma a document awarded by an authorized body (college, university, or other institution) to a student indicating the successful completion of a prescribed course of study (*diplôme* FR, *diploma* SP).

director the person providing conceptual leadership of the museum and charged with responsibility for policy making, funding, planning, organizing, staffing, supervising, and coordinating activities through the staff. The director is also responsible for the professional practices of the museum (*directeur* FR, *director* SP).

display the presentation of objects or information without special arrangement or interpretation based solely upon intrinsic merit (*présentation* FR, *presentación* SP).

dissertation a written essay required by many colleges and universities as partial fulfillment of a degree requirement – a thesis (*dissertation* FR, *disertación* SP).

docent normally referring to a teacher or lecturer not on the regular staff of the museum – often a volunteer gallery guide with special knowledge of a particular program or exhibit (volunteer guide UK, *guide volontaire* FR, *docente* SP).

doctoral degree the highest academic degree given in United States universities. Normally stated to be a doctor of philosophy (Ph.D.) degree awarded for academic research. Not a medical degree.

educator a museum staff person or consultant who specializes in museum education and who produces instructional materials, advises about educational content for exhibitions, and oversees the implementation of educational programs (*éducateur* FR, *educator* SP).

ethics the process of establishing principles of correct behavior that may serve as action guides for individuals or groups (*éthique* FR, *ética* SP).

ethnic used in the museum community as a non-discriminatory term referring to a division or group of people distinguishable by language, custom, or some special characteristic (*ethnique* FR, *étnico* SP).

ethnology collections of clothing, implements, and objects (cultural artifacts) of a people (*ethnologie* FR, *etnologia* SP).

evaluation report a document that sets down evaluation findings assessing an exhibition from the standpoints of meeting goals and successful development.

exhibit to present or expose to view, show, or display (*objet exposé* FR, *exhibición* SP).

exhibit policy a written document that states a museum's philosophy and intent toward public exhibitions (*politique d'exposition* FR, *política de exhibición* SP).

exhibition the presenting of collections, objects, or information to the public for the purpose of education, enlightenment, and enjoyment (*exposition* FR, *exhibición* SP).

fiduciary describes the concept of public trust associated with overseeing the property of others and defines the diligent and honest activities of a prudent person in managing public affairs. (*fiduciaire* FR, *fiduciario* SP).

financial aid any form of financial assistance given to students in the form of scholarships, loans, grants, and work subsidy. Most colleges and universities have a student assistance office that provides information on available financial aid (*subvention* FR, *subvención* SP).

finc art describes the unique work of gifted or talented persons created for primarily aesthetic reasons (*beaux-arts* FR, *bellas artes* SP).

folk art normally describing objects of a popular nature that may or may not be functional, produced by other than academically trained practitioners. This art form may include such things as quilts, weavings, decorative coverings, and furniture. It is closely aligned with ethnography and may include many of those items described as crafts (*art populaire* FR, *arte popular* SP).

gallery a room specifically designated for exhibitions (*galerie* FR, *galería* SP).

gallery guides written documents, usually brief and easy to carry, that are available for visitors to have and use to gain more information about an exhibition subject (*guide pour la visite* FR, *guía de la galería* SP).

gallery talk a presentation given in galleries usually by docents or curators talking about the exhibit (*conférence au galerie* FR, *conferencia en la galería* SP).

graduate students a term applied to those persons involved in college or university instructional programs beyond the baccalaureate degree level (*formation postuniversitaire* FR, *formación de postgraduados* SP).

guide used to describe those persons leading tours or groups through the museum. Unlike docents, guides are not necessarily instructors or program providers; instead they direct the visitor from site to site or object to object with predetermined commentary (*guide* FR, *guía* SP).

historic site a location with important historic connections usually relating to an important person or event (*lieu* FR, *sitio histórico* SP).

ICCROM International Center for the Study of the Preservation and the Restoration of Cultural Property – an intergovernmental organization created by Unesco in 1969. Its statutory functions are to collect and disseminate documentation of scientific problems of conservation; to promote research in this field; to provide advice on technical questions; and to assist in training technicians and raising the standard of restoration work. Address: ICCROM, Via di San Michele, 13, 00153 Rome, Italy.

ICOFOM International Committee for Museology – one of the standing committees of ICOM.

ICOM International Council of Museums – an international non-governmental organization of museums and professional museum workers established to advance the interests of museology and other disciplines concerned with museum management and operations. Address: ICOM, Maison de l'Unesco, 1 rue Miollis, 75732 Paris Cedex 15, France.[2] (*Conseil International des Musées* FR, *Concilio Internacional de Museos* SP).

ICOM *Statutes* adopted by the 16th General Assembly of ICOM in The Hague, September 5, 1989, the ICOM *Statutes* describe and define the ICOM organization, its role, membership, methods, and objectives.

ICTOP International Committee for Training of Personnel – one of the standing committees of ICOM.

inorganic collections referring to objects not composed of animal or vegetable material, i.e. stone, pottery, glass, metal, and other geological matter.

in-service training organized skill, technique, or informational development programs often subject-specific and normally provided by the institution of employment. Training programs of this kind are occasionally organized between institutions to take advantage of a particular staff need and accomplishment (*stage* FR, *prácticas en museos* SP).

internship a position of residency in a work-like situation intended to give the student (intern) an on-the-job experience. The position may be paid or voluntary (*stage* FR, *prácticas en museos* SP).

interpretation the act or process of explaining or clarifying, translating, or presenting a personal understanding about a subject or object (*interprétation* FR, *interpretación* SP).

inventory an itemized list of the objects included in a museum's collections (*inventaire* FR, *inventario* SP).

leisure activities activities that people engage in when they are not involved in a professional pursuit (*activités de loisir* FR, *actividades de ocio* SP).

major program of study in academia, the primary area of study (for example a "major" in anthropology with a minor in museum studies).

Master's degree that program of study above the baccalaureate degree and before the doctoral. A common advanced degree in United States colleges and universities (Master of Arts, Master of Science, etc.). May also describe an advanced non-thesis degree program in some countries (*maître* FR, *maestria* SP).

mid-career training non-degree-granting programs for training and professional development designed to serve the needs of museum personnel.

minor program of study in academia, the secondary area of study. (for example, a major in anthropology with a "minor" in museum studies).

mission statement a written document that states a museum's institutional philosophy, scope, and responsibility. It defines the underlying rationale for the institution's existence (museum philosophy UK, *philosophie des musées* FR, *filosofía de los museos* SP; museum policy US, *politique du musée* FR, *politica del museo* SP).

museography dealing with the various techniques of museum work.[3] (*muséographie* FR, *museografia* SP).

museology the branch of knowledge concerned with the study of the theories, procedures, concepts, and organization of museums (*muséologie* FR, *museología* SP).

museum a museum is a non-profit-making, permanent institution in the service of society and of its development, and open to the public which acquires, conserves, researches, communicates and exhibits, for purposes of study, education and enjoyment, material evidence of people and their environment.[4] (*musée* FR, *museo* SP).

nomenclature a system of names used to describe museum objects (*nomenclature* FR, *nomenclatura* SP).

non-profit an organization not configured or maintained for profit and where the proceeds are not distributed to owners or shareholders but used for the continued operation of the organization (*organisation á but non lucratif* FR, *organización no lucrativa* SP).

object file a careful listing of all actions or activities impacting a particular object in the museum's collections including all conservation, restoration, exhibition, loan, or other uses of the object (*documentation de l'objet* FR, *documentación del objeto* SP).

open storage the practice of placing stored collections on public view without interpretation or planned educational content (*réserve accessible* FR, *almacenamiento libre* SP).

organic collections used to designate objects derived from living organisms, e.g. fibers, fur, feathers, hair, skin, wood, bark, ivory, bone, shell, and horn.

paleontology the branch of geology that deals with prehistoric forms of life through the study of plant and animal fossils[5] (*paléontologie* FR, *paleontología* SP).

patrimony cultural property, both intellectual and real, passed from one generation to the next (*patrimoine* FR, *patrimonio* SP).

pedagogy the art or science of teaching – educational theory (*pédagogie* FR, *pedagogía* SP).

preparation arranging, attaching, supporting and other such activities that prepare an object/graphic for exhibit (*préparation* FR, *preparación* SP).

preparator may describe a person working in the exhibitions area or one involved with collections management. The person in exhibits may assist with the preparation of objects to be placed on exhibit such as framing, mounting, or organizing. The collections area person may clean, number, and containerize an object for storage (*préparateur* FR, *preparador* SP).

preventative conservation collection care to minimize conditions that may cause damage (*conservation préventive* FR, *conservación preventiva* SP).

production [technique] the combined activities of fabrication, preparation, facilities renovation, and installation of exhibitions (*technique de production* FR, *técnica de producción* SP).

project manager a staff person who oversees the whole process of exhibition development by facilitating communication and assisting in providing resources, with the goal to see the project through to its predetermined objectives.

registrar the person charged with registering objects accessioned into a museum's collections, maintaining the registration records, and assigning the accession number (keeper of documentation UK, *préposé au registre archiviste* FR, *registrador* SP).

registration assigning a permanent number to an object entering a museum's collections for the purpose of identification and collection management (*enregistrement* FR, *registro de los fondos* SP).

relic a non-specific term used to describe things from the past, sometimes applied to ethnographic or historic objects (*relique* FR, *reliquia* SP).

scholarship (1) a level of knowledge and learning demonstrated by an individual; (2) an amount of money or other financial assistance given by an individual or institution to help a student pursue a program of study (*bourse d'études* FR, *beca* SP).

security personnel persons assigned the duty and responsibility for maintaining the safety and security of both the contents of the institutions and the visitors (warding staff UK, *personnel de sécurité* FR, *personal de seguridad* SP).

seminar a supervised (organized) program of study (*séminaire* FR, *seminario* SP).

specimen an example of a particular class of objects normally used when referring to natural science collections (*spécimen* FR, *espécimen* SP).

stipend any fixed payment for services (*subvention* FR, *estipendio* SP).

study collection objects collected and organized for research or instructional use not for exhibition (*collection de recherche* FR, *colección para investigación* SP).

superorganic collections a term sometimes used to describe objects of a cultural nature that may combine organic and inorganic materials.

symposium a meeting or gathering to discuss a particular predetermined idea, concept, technique, or skill.

tactile exhibits exhibits that are designed to be touched (*exposition tactile* FR, *exposición táctil* SP).

textile referring to weaving or woven fabric. (*textile* FR, *textil* SP).

thematic exhibitions exhibitions based upon a connecting theme that directs the choice of collection objects and information content (*exposition thématique* FR, *exposición temática* SP).

trustees [board of] a body of persons charged with the responsibility of managing the affairs of an organization or institution holding property-in-trust for the public (*conseil d'administration* FR, *consejo de administración* SP).

undergraduate student commonly used term in the United States referring to persons enrolled in a first-level (baccalaureate) college or university degree program (*premier cycle* FR, *bachillerato* SP).

Unesco United Nations Educational, Scientific, and Cultural Organization. Unesco is the parent organization of ICOM.

warden a security person who guards or has charge of something; may also be called a keeper, guard, custodian, or supervisor (*gardien* FR, *vigilante* SP).

work of art an object of aesthetic importance created by a human being (*oeuvre d'art* FR, *obra de arte* SP).

workshop a gathering of persons to participate in a practice-oriented learning experience. (*atelier* FR, *taller* SP).

worldview an individual's rational model of reality; one's mental picture of the world consisting of facts, raw perceptual data, concepts, suppositions, theories, and generalizations (*perspective universelle* FR, *prespectiva universal* SP).

Notes

1   Ferree, H. (ed.) (no date) *Groot praktijkboek voor effective communicatie*, Antwerpen: Deventer, 1.3–15.
2   ICOM (1990) *Statutes*, Article 1 "Name and Legal Status," Paris: ICOM, p.1.
3   Evelyn, H. (1970) *Training of Museum Personnel*, Paris: ICOM, published with the help of the Smithsonian Institution, Washington, D.C., p. 23.
4   ICOM (1990) *Statutes*, Article 2 "Definitions," Paris: ICOM, p.1.
5   McKechnie, J. (ed.) (1977) *Webster's New Twentieth Century Dictionary* (2nd edition), Collins World Publishing Co., Inc.

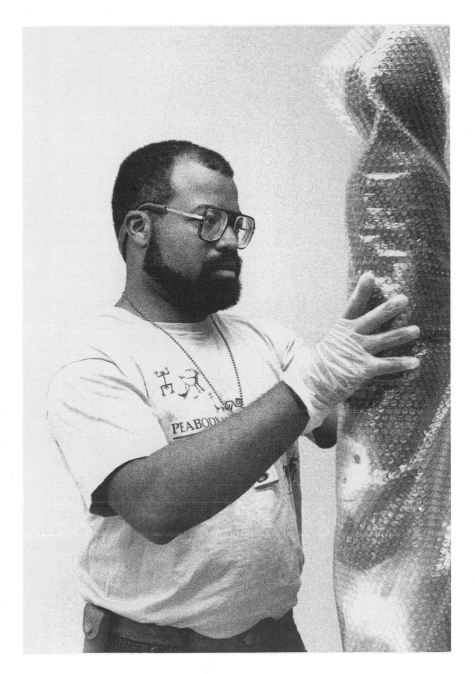

Plate 8 Museum Collections Registrar Henry Crawford preparing traveling exhibition for shipment (photograph by Gary Edson)

E I G H T

Selected bibliography (organized by discipline)

———•◆•———

The amount of information about museums and museum training has increased substantially during the past two decades. For a number of years, there was little written material available to aid museum workers or those interested in entering the museum profession in gaining greater understanding of the scope and detail of museum work. In recent years that situation has changed. Numerous publications are being produced that give detailed commentary on the general and specific workings of museums. No single book can give complete insight into this subject, and none should be viewed as providing all the answers.

To assist in the learning process, the books in this bibliography have been divided into categories. In many cases the same book applies to more than one area or occupation. In fact, knowledgeable and effective museum works have a broad base of information from which to draw. The inclusive nature of museum work cannot be overemphasized. Ongoing inquiry is an absolute necessity to stay current with museum techniques, skills, standards, and thinking. Often the most current ideas are found in journals. At the end of this bibliography is a list of museum-related journals that should be read and retained for future reference.

Museology (general)

Ambrose, T. and Paine, C. (1993) *Museum Basics*, Paris and London: ICOM in conjunction with Routledge. ISBN 0-415-05769-8 (cloth) ISBN 0-415-05770-1 (paper)

Bazin, G. (1967) *The Museum Age* (translated from French by Jane van Nuis Cahill), Brussels: Desoer S. A. Publishers. Official registration number D/1967/0038/14; UK Standard Number 85321..000..4.

Borowitz, H. and Borowitz, A. (1991) *Pawnshop and Palaces: The Fall and Rise of the Campana Art Museum* (edited by J. Lorenzo), Washington, D.C.: Smithsonian Institution. ISBN 1-56098-010-9.

Cleere, H. (1984) *Approaches to the Archaeological Heritage*, Cambridge: Cambridge University Press. ISBN 0-521-24305-X.

—— (1989) *Archaeological Heritage Management in the Modern World*, London: Unwin Hyman. ISBN 0-04-445028-1.

Danilov, V. (1990) *America's Science Museums*, Westport, CT: Greenwood Press. ISBN 0-313-25865-1.

Fennelly, L. (1983) *Museum, Archive, and Library Security*, London: Butterworths. ISBN 0-409-95058-0.

Hendon, W. (1979) *Analyzing an Art Museum*, New York: Praeger Publishers. ISBN 0-03-050386-8.

Hudson, K. (1977) *Museums for the 1980s*, London: Macmillan Press. ISBN 92 3 101435 8.

—— (1987) *Museums of Influence*, London: Cambridge University Press. ISBN 0 521 305340 9.

Impey, O. and MacGregor, A. (eds) (1985) *The Origins of Museums*, Oxford: Clarendon Press. ISBN 0-19-952108-5.

Levin, M. (1983) *The Modern Museum: Temple or Showroom*, Tel Aviv: Dvir Publishing House. ISBN 965-01-0105-5.

MacDonald, G. (1987)"The Future of Museums in the Global Village," *Museum (UNESCO)*, No. 155 (Vol. XXXIX, No. 3): 209–17. ISSN 0-304-3002.

MacDonald, G. and Alsford, S. (1989) *A Museum for the Global Village*, Hull, Quebec: Canadian Museum of Civilization. ISBN 0-660-10787-2.

Orosz, J. (1990) *Curators and Culture: The Museum Movement in America, 1974–1870*, Tuscaloosa, Alabama: University of Alabama Press, History of American Science and Technology Series. ANSI A39.48-1984.

Rahman Dar, S. (ed.) (1981) *Museology and Museum Problems in Pakistan*, Lahor, Pakistan: Newfine Printing Press. (No identification number.)

Rivière, G. (1989) *La Muséologie*, Paris: Dunod. ISBN 2-04-18706-5.

Shapiro, M. (edited with assistance of L. Kemp) (1990) *The Museum: A Reference Guide*, New York: Greenwood Press. ISBN 0-313-23686-0.

Sola, T. (1987) "The Concept and Nature of Museology," *Museum (UNESCO)*, Vol. XXXIX, No. 1: 45–9. ISSN 0304-3002.

Stowell, A. (1956) *The Living Museum*, New York: Vantage Press. Library of Congress Catalog Card Number: 56-13340.

Weil, S. E. (1983) *Beauty and the Beasts, On Museums, Art, the Law, and the Market*, Washington, D.C.: Smithsonian Institution Press. ISBN 0-87474-958-1 (cloth) ISBN 0-87474-957-3 (paper).

—— (1990) *Rethinking the Museum and Other Meditations*, Washington, D.C.: Smithsonian Institution Press. ISBN 0-87474-948-4 (cloth) ISBN 0-87474-953-0 (paper).

Wittlin, A. S. (1970) *Museums: In Search of a Usable Future*, Cambridge: MIT Press. ISBN 0-262-23039-9.

Training (general)

Aagaard-Mogensen, L. (ed.) (1988) *The Idea of the Museum, Problems in Contemporary Philosophy* Vol. 6, Lewiston/Queenston: Mellen Press. ISBN 0-88946-334-4.

Alexander, E. (1979) *Museums in Motion, An Introduction to the History and Functions of Museums* (4th printing 1986), Nashville: American Association for State and Local History. ISBN 0-910050-35-x.

—— (1983) *Museum Masters, Their Museums and Their Influence*, Nashville: American Association for State and Local History. ISBN 0-910050-68-6.

American Association of Museums (1969) *America's Museums: The Belmont Report*, Washington, D.C.: American Association of Museums. Library of Congress Catalog Card Number 74-80109.

Arinze, E. (1987) "Training in African Museum: The Role of the Centre for Museum Studies, Jos," *Museum (UNESCO)*, No. 156 (Vol. XXXIX, No. 4): 278–80. ISSN 0304-3002.

Bedebar, V. H. (1987)"The Museum Training Situation in India." *Museum (UNESCO)*, No. 156 (Vol. XXXIX, No. 4): 284–90. ISSN 0304-3002.

Betel, D. (1972) "The Training of Museum Personnel," *ICOM News* 25 (June 1972): 103–5. ISSN 0-018-8999.

Blackmon, C., LaMaster, T., Roberts, L., and Serrell, B. (1988) *Open Conversations: Strategies for Professional Development in Museums*, Chicago: Field Museum of Natural History. ISBN 0-914868-10-1.

Bloom, J. and Powell, E. (eds) (1984) *Museums for a New Century, A Report of the Commission on Museums for a New Century*, Washington, D.C.: American Association of Museums. ISBN 0-931201-08-x.

Boylan, P.(1987) "Museum Training: A Central Concern of ICOM for Forty Years," *Museum (UNESCO)*, No. 156 (Vol. XXXIX, No. 4): 225–30. ISSN 0304-3002.

Burcaw, G. E. (1969) "Museum Training: The Responsibility of College and University Museums," *Museum News*, Vol. 47 (April): 15–18. ISSN 0-027-4089.

—— (1975) *Introduction to Museum Work* (2nd edition), Nashville: American Association for State and Local History. ISBN 0-910050-69-4.

Carmago e Almeida-Moro, F. (1987) "Survey of Training for Museum Professionals in a Country that Covers a Vast Area – Brazil," *Museum (UNESCO)*, No. 156 (Vol. XXXIX, No. 4): 252–4. ISSN 0304-3002.

Evelyn, H. (ed.) (1970) *Training of Museum Personnel*, London: International Council of Museums. SBN 238-78952-7.

Fedi, F.(1987) "Postgraduate Course in Museography and Museology in the Faculty of Architecture in Milan," *Museum (UNESCO)*, No. 156 (Vol. XXXIX, No. 4): 261–4. ISSN 0304-3002.

Finlay, I. (1977) *Priceless Heritage: The Future of Museums*, London: Faber & Faber. ISBN 0-571-09107-5.

Finley, D. E. (1973) *A Standard of Excellence, Andrew W. Mellon Founds the National Gallery of Art at Washington, D.C.*, Washington, D. C.: Smithsonian Institution Press. ISBN 0-87474-132-7.

Glaser, J. (1987) "Museum Studies in the United States: Coming a Long Way for a Long Time," *Museum (UNESCO)*, No. 156 (Vol. XXXIX, No. 4): 268–73. ISSN 0304-3002.

Guichen, G. and Rockwell, C. (1987) "Training in the Conservation and Restoration of Movable and Immovable Cultural Property," *Museum (UNESCO)*, No. 156 (Vol. XXXIX, No. 4): 234–9. ISSN 0304-3002.

Hodge, J. (1987) "Museum Studies Training in Australia," *Museum (UNESCO)*, No. 156 (Vol. XXXIX, No. 4): 249–51. ISSN 0304-3002.

International Council of Museums (1990) *ICOM Statutes*, Paris: ICOM. (No identification number.)

Jisheng, L. (1987) "Museum Training in China," *Museum (UNESCO)*, No. 156 (Vol. XXXIX, No. 4): 291–5. ISSN 0304-3002.

Katz, H. and Katz, M. (1965) *Museums, U.S.A.*, Garden City: Doubleday & Company, Inc. Library of Congress Catalog Card Number 65-12364.

Kavanagh, G. (ed.) (1991) *Museum Languages*, Leicester: Leicester University Press. ISBN 0-7185-1359-2.

—— (ed.) (1991) *The Museums Profession*, Leicester: Leicester University Press. ISBN 0-7185-1387-8.

Kozlov, V. (1987) "The Training of Museum Personnel: the Ukrainian State Museum of the Great Patriotic War," *Museum (UNESCO)*, No. 156 (Vol. XXXIX, No. 4): 296–9. ISSN 0304-3002.

Lewis, G. (1983) "The Training of Museum Personnel in the United Kingdom," *Museums Journal*, Vol. 83, No. 1 (June–July): 65–70. ISSN 0-027-416X.

—— (1987) "Museum, Profession and University: Museum Studies and Leicester," *Museum (UNESCO)*, No. 156 (Vol. XXXIX, No. 4): 255–8. ISSN 0304-3002.

Masap, F. (1987) "The Balance Between Domestic Needs and International Aid to Museum Training," *Museum (UNESCO)*, No. 156 (Vol. XXXIX, No. 4): 275–7. ISSN 0304-3002.

Pearce, S. (ed.) (1989) *Museum Studies in Material Culture*, Leicester: Leicester University Press. ISBN 0-7185-1288-X (cloth) ISBN 0-7185-1391-6 (paper).

Segger, M. (1987) "Canada: Great Distances Require Distance Training . . .," *Museum (UNESCO)*, No. 156 (Vol. XXXIX, No. 4): 222–48. ISSN 0304-3002.

Sellers, C. (1980) *Mr. Peale's Museum*, New York: W. W. Norton. ISBN 0-393-05700-3.

Singleton, R. (1969) "The Purpose of Museums and Museum Training," *Museums Journal*, Vol. 69, No. 3 (December). ISSN 0-027-416X.

—— (1977) "The Future of the Profession," *Museum Journal*, Vol. 77 (December): 121–2. ISSN 0-027-416X.

—— (1987) "Museum Training: Status and Development," *Museum (UNESCO)*, No. 156 (Vol. XXXIX, No. 4): 221–4. ISSN 0304-3002.

Solinger, J. (ed.) (1990) *Museums and Universities: New Paths for Continuing Education*, New York: Collier Macmillan Publishers. ISBN 0-02-929860-1.

van Mensch, P. (ed.) (1989) *Professionalising the Muses*, Amsterdam: AHA Books. ISBN 90-5246-013-2.

Administration/management

Ambrose, T. and Runyard, S. (1991) *Forward Planning*, London: Routledge. ISBN 0-415-06482-1 (cloth) ISBN 0-415-07026-0 (paper).

George, G. and Sherrell-Leo, C. (1986) *Starting Right, A Basic Guide to Museum Planning*, Nashville: American Association for State and Local History. ISBN 0-910050-78-3.

Hodgkinson, V., Lyman, R., and Associates (1989) *The Future of the Nonprofit Sector: Challenges, Changes, and Policy Considerations*, San Francisco: Jossey-Bass Publishers. ISBN 1-55542-179-2.

Houle, C. (1990) *Governing Boards, Their Nature and Nurture*, San Francisco: Jossey-Bass Publishers. ISBN 1-55542-157-1.

Key, A. F. (1973) *Beyond Four Walls*, Toronto: McClelland & Stewart. ISBN 0-7710-4520-4.

Lord, B. and Lord, G. (1983) *Planning Our Museum (La Planification de nos musées)*, Ottawa: National Museums of Canada. Distributed by Nashville: American Association for State and Local History. ISBN 0-660-90275-3.

Miller, R. (1980) *Personnel Policies for Museums: A Handbook for Management*, Washington, D.C.: American Association of Museum. Library of Congress Catalog Card Number 80-80231.

Nelson, C. (1991) *Protecting the Past from Natural Disasters*, Washington, D.C.: National Trust for Historic Preservation. ISBN 0-89133-178-6.

O'Connell, B. (1985) *The Board Member's Book*, New York: The Foundation Center. ISBN 0-87954-133-4.

Steckel, R., Simons, R., and Lengsfelder, P. (1989) *Filthy Rich and Other Nonprofit Fantasies*, Berkeley, Calif.: 10 Speed Press. ISBN 0-89815-267-4.

Theobald, M. (1991) *Museum Store Management*, Nashville: American Association of State and Local History. ISBN 0-943063-14-7.

Tolles, B. (ed.) (1991) *Leadership for the Future*, Nashville: American Association of State and Local History. ISBN 0-942063-11-2.

Ullberg, A. and Ullberg, P. (1981) *Museum Trusteeship*, Washington, D.C.: American Association of Museums. Library of Congress Catalog Card Number 81-68741.

van Til, J. (1988) *Mapping the Third Sector: Voluntarism in a Changing Social Economy*, New York: The Foundation Center. ISBN 0-87954-240-3.

Wolf, T. (1990) *Managing a Nonprofit Organization*, New York: Prentice Hall Press. ISBN 0-13-551557-2.

Conservation/restoration

Agrawal, O. (ed.) (1972) *Conservation in the Tropics, Proceedings of the Asia-Pacific Seminar on Conservation of Cultural Property, New Delhi*, Rome: International Centre for Conservation. (No identification number.)

Ellis, M. (1987) *The Care of Prints and Drawings*, Nashville: The American Association of State and Local History. ISBN 0-910050-79-1.

Fall, F. (1973) *Art Objects: Their Care and Preservation* (A Handbook for Museums and Collections), La Jolla, CA.: Laurence McGilvery. ISBN 0-910938-55-5.

Finch, K. and Putnam, G. (1985) *The Care and Preservation of Textiles*, London: B. T. Batsford. ISBN 0-7134-4411-8.

Flury-Lemberg, M. (1988) *Textile Conservation and Research* (translated from *Textilkonservierung im Dienste der Forschung* by Pamela Leinbundgut, text; Monica Vroon, technical catalog; Dina Baars-Flury, general index; Idward Maeder, editor), Berne: Schriften der ABEGG-Stiftung. ISBN 3-905014-02 5.

Guldbeck, P. (1972) *The Care of Historical Collections, A Conservation Handbook for the Nonspecialist* (2nd edition 1976) Nashville: The American Association of State and Local History. ISBN 0-910050-07-4.

Guldbeck, P. (MacLeish, A. ed. 2nd edition) (1986) *The Care of Antiques and Historical Collections*, Nashville: The American Association for State and Local History. ISBN 0-910050-73-2.

Harley, R. D. (1970) *Artists' Pigments c. 1600–1835* (2nd edition 1982), London: Butterworth Scientific. ISBN 0-408-70945-6.

Horie, C. V. (1987) *Materials For Conservation*, London: Butterworths. ISBN 0-40801-531-4.

Hower, R. (1979) *Freeze-Drying Biological Specimens: A Laboratory Manual*, Washington, D.C.: Smithsonian Institution Press. ISBN 0-87474-532-2.

Ito, N. (chair) (1983) *The Conservation of Wooden Cultural Property*, Proceedings of the International Symposium on the Conservation and Restoration of Cultural Property, Tokyo and Saitama, Japan 1982, Tokyo: Tokyo National Research Institute of Cultural Property. (No identification number.)

Járó, M. (ed.)(1989) *Conservation of Metals*, Proceedings of the International Restorers Seminar, Veszprém, Hungary 1989. Veszprém, Hungary: István Eri Publisher. ISBN 963-555-770-1.

Keck, C. (1978) *How to Take Care of Your Paintings*, New York: Charles Scribner's Sons. ISBN 0-684-15551-6.

King, R. (1985) *Textile Identification, Conservation, and Preservation*, Park Ridge, NJ: Noyes Publications. ISBN 0-8155-1033-0.

Kühn, H. (1986) *Conservation and Restoration of Works of Art and Antiquities*, Vol. 1, London: Butterworths. ISBN 0-408-10851-7 (v. 1).

Landi, S. (1985) *The Textile Conservator's Manual*, London: Butterworths. ISBN 0-408-106624-7.

Leene, J. (ed.) (1972) *Textile Conservation*, London: Butterworths. ISBN 0-408-36750-4.

McGiffin, R. (1983) *Furniture Care and Conservation*, Nashville: The American Association of State and Local History. ISBN 0-910050-62-7.

Martin, G. and Cunha, D. (1971) *Conservation of Library Materials: A Manual and Bibliography on the Care, Repair and Restoration of Library Materials*, Vol. I, Metuchen, NJ: The Scarecrow Press. ISBN 0-8108-0427-1.

—— (1972) *Conservation of Library Materials: A Manual and Bibliography on the Care, Repair and Restoration of Library Materials*, Vol. II: Bibliography, Metuchen, NJ: The Scarecrow Press. ISBN 0-8108-0427-1.

Mills, J. and White, R. (1987) *The Organic Chemistry of Museum Objects*, London: Butterworths. ISBN 0-408-11810-5.

Mora, P., Mora, L., and Philippot, P. (1984) *Conservation of Wall Paintings*. London: Butterworths. ISBN 0-408-10812-6.

Newton, R. and Davison, S. (1989) *Conservation of Glass*, London: Butterworths. ISBN 0-408-10623-9.

Organ, R. (1968) *Design for Scientific Conservation of Antiquities*, London: Butterworths. UDC Number 7-025-3: 7-031/032.

Paine, C. (ed.) (1992) *Standards in the Museum Care of Archaeological Collections*, London: Museums and Galleries Commission Publication. ISBN 0-948630-15-9.

Pearce, D. (1989) *Conservation Today*, London: Routledge. ISBN 0-415-00778-X (hard back) 0-415-03914-2 (paper).

Pearson, C. (ed.)(1987) *Conservation of Marine Archaeological Objects*, London: Butterworths. ISBN 0-408-10668-9.

Perkins, J. (ed.), Boyer, C. and Paterson, E. (asst. eds) (1985) *Computer Technology for Conservators: Proceedings of the 11th Annual IIC-CG Conference Workshop, Halifax, Canada*, The Atlantic Regional Group of the International Institute for Conservation of Historic and Artistic Works, Halifax: Canadian Group Publisher. ISBN 0-9691347-1-1.

Plenderleith, H. and Werner, A. (1956) *The Conservation of Antiquities and Works of Art* (2nd edition 1974) London: Oxford University Press. ISBN 0-19-212960-0.

Stolow, N. (1986) *Conservation and Exhibitions*, London: Butterworths. ISBN 0-408-01434-2.

Thomson, G. (ed.) (1963) *Recent Advances in Conservation* (contributions to the IIC Rome conference, 1961), London: Butterworths. UDC Number 7-025-3/4.

Timmons, S. (ed.) (1976) *Preservation and Conservation: Principles and Practices*, Proceedings of the North American International Regional Conference, Washington, D.C.: Preservation Press and Smithsonian Institution Press. ISBN 0-89133-029-1.

Waterer, J. (1972) *A Guide to the Conservation and Restoration of Objects Made Wholly or in Part of Leather*, London: G. Bell & Sons. ISBN 0-7135-1822-7.

Working Group of the International Committee for Conservation (1987) "The Conservator-Restorer: A Definition of the Profession," *Museum (UNESCO)*, No. 156 (Vol. XXXIX, No. 4): 231–3. ISSN 0304-3002.

Curator/collection manager

Alderson, W. and Low, S. (1987) *Interpretation Of Historic Sites*, (2nd edition revised), Nashville: The American Association for State and Local History. ISBN 0-910050-73-2.

Allen, B. and Montell, W. (1981) *From Memory to History*, Nashville: The American Association of State and Local History. ISBN 0-910050-51-1.

Appelbaum, B. (1991) *Guide to Environmental Protection of Collections*, Madison: Sound View Press. ISBN 0-932087-16-7.

Bachmann, K. (ed.) (1992) *Conservation Concerns – A Guide for Collections and Curators*, Washington, D.C.: Smithsonian Institution Press. ISBN 1-56098-174-1.

Bandes, S. (project director) (1984) *Caring for Collections*, Washington, D.C.: American Association of Museums. (No identification number.)

Baum, W. (1977) *Transcribing and Editing Oral History*, Nashville: The American Association of State and Local History. ISBN 0-910050-26-0.

Cantwell, A., Griffin, J., and Rothschild, N. (eds.) (1981) *The Research Potential of Anthropological Museum Collections*, Annals of the New York Academy of Sciences, Vol. 376, New York: The New York Academy of Sciences. ISBN 0-89766-141-9 (cloth) ISBN 0-89766-142-7 (paper).

Cleere, H. (ed.) (1989) *Archaeological Heritage Management in the Modern World*, London: Unwin Hyman. ISBN 0-04-445028-1.

Fleming, D. and Higginson, R. (1984) "Collections Management – An Independent Approach," *Museum Journal*, Vol. 84, No. 2 (September): 87-91. ISSN 0-027-416X.

Genoways, H., Jones, C., and Rossolimo, O. (eds) (1987) *Mammal Collection Management*, Lubbock, TX: Texas Tech University Press. ISBN 0-89672-157-5 (cloth) ISBN 0-89672-156-6 (paper).

Hudson, K. (1971) *A Guide to the Industrial Archaeology of Europe*, Madison, WI: Fairleigh Dickinson University Press. ISBN 0-8386-1001-3.

—— (1976) *Industrial Archaeology*, London: John Baker (Publishers). ISBN 0-212-97014-3.

—— (1976) *A Pocket Book for Industrial Archaeologists*, London: John Baker (Publishers). ISBN 0-212-97018-6.

Jeudy, H. (sous la dir.) (1990) *Patrimoines en Folie*, Collection Ethnologie de la France, Cahier 5, Paris: Editions de la Maison des Sciences de l'Homme. ISBN 2-7351-0352-8.

Kavanagh, G. (1990) *History Curatorship*, Leicester: Leicester University Press. ISBN 0-7185-1305-3.

Lewis, R. (1976) *Manual for Museums*, Washington, D.C.: National Park Service, US Department of Interior. (No identification number.)

Lord, B., Lord, G., and Nicks, J. (1989) *The Cost of Collecting, Collection Management in UK Museums*, London: Her Majesty's Stationery Office. ISBN 0-11-290476-9.

Mayo, E. (1984) *American Material Culture*, Bowling Green, OH: Bowling Green State University Popular Press. ISBN 0-87972-303-3.

Rains, A. (chair) (1966) *With Heritage So Rich*, A Report of a Special Committee on Historic Preservation under the auspices of the United States Conference of Mayors with a grant from the Ford Foundation. New York: Random House. Library of Congress Catalog Card Number 66-17835.

Research and Education Association (1982) *Handbook of Museum Technology*, New York: Research and Education Association. ISBN 0-87891-540-0.

Selected bibliography

Shelley, M. (1987) *The Care and Handling of Art Objects*, New York: The Metropolitan Museum of Art. ISBN 0-87099-318-6.
Tarrant, N. (1983) *Collecting Costume: The Care and Display of Clothes and Accessories*, London: George Allen & Unwin. ISBN 0-04-746017-2.
Taylor, L. (1987) *A Common Agenda for History Museums*, Conference Proceedings, Nashville: The American Association for State and Local History, and Washington, D. C.: The Smithsonian Institution. (No identification number.)
Thompson, J. M. A. (ed.) (1984) *Manual of Curatorship, a Guide to Museum Practice* (2nd edition 1992), London: Butterworth Heinemann. ISBN 0-7506-0351-8.

Education/interpretation

Alfrey, J. and Putnam, T. (1992) *The Industrial Heritage*, London: Routledge. ISBN 0-415-04068-X (hard cover) ISBN 0-415-07043-0 (paper).
Anderson, H., Davey, G., and McKenry, K. (1987) *Folklife: Our Living Heritage*, Report of the Committee of Inquiry into Folklife in Australia, Canberra: Australian Government Publishing Service. ISBN 0-664-06710-1.
Blatti, J. (ed.) (1987) *Past Meets Present, Essays About Historic Interpretation and Public Audiences*, Washington, D.C.: Smithsonian Institution Press. ISBN 0-87474-272-2.
Hooper-Greenhill, E. (1983) "Some Basic Principles and Issues Relating to Museum Education," *Museum Journal*, Vol. 83, No. 2/3 (September/December): 127–9. ISSN 0-027-416X.
—— (1991) *Museum and Gallery Education*, Leicester: Leicester University Press, ISBN 0-7185-1306-1.
—— (1992) *Museums and the Shaping of Knowledge*, London: Routledge. ISBN 0-415-06145-8 (cloth) ISBN 0-415-07031-7 (paper).
Isar, Y. (ed.) (1984) *The Challenge to Our Cultural Heritage*, co-sponsored by United Nations Educational, Scientific, and Cultural Organization (Unesco) and Smithsonian Institution in cooperation with the United States Committee of the International Council on Monuments and Sites (US/ICOMOS) and the National Trust for Historic Preservation, Washington, D.C.: Smithsonian Institution Press. ISBN 0-87474-543-8.
Karp, I. and Lavine, S. (eds.) (1991) *Exhibiting Cultures: The Poetics and Politics of Museum Display*, Washington, D.C.: Smithsonian Institution Press. ISBN 1-56098-020-6 (cloth) ISBN 1-56098-021-4 (paper).
Karp, I., Kreamer, C., and Lavine, S. (eds.) (1992) *Museums and Communities: The Politics of Public Culture*, Washington, D.C.: Smithsonian Institution Press. ISBN 1-56098-164-4 (cloth) ISBN 1-56098-189-x (paper).
Loomis, R. (1987) *Museum Visitor Evaluation: New Tool for Management*, Vol. 3, AASLH Management Series, Nashville: The American Association for State and Local History. ISBN 0-910050-83-x.
Loor, L. (1987) *El museo como instrumento de aprendizaje*, Cuenca: Banco Central del Ecuador. (No identification number.)
Museum Education Roundtable (1992) *Patterns in Practice*, Washington, D.C.: Museum Education Roundtable. ISBN 1-880437-00-7.
Nichols, S. (ed.) (1984) *Museum Education Anthology 1973–1983*, Museum Education Roundtable, Washington, D.C.: American Association of Museums. (No identification number.)
Pearce, S. (ed.) (1990) *Objects of Knowledge*, London: The Athlone Press. ISBN 0-485-90001-7.

Uzzell, D. (ed.) (1989) *Heritage Interpretation*, Vol. I *The Natural and Built Environment*, London: Belhaven Press. ISBN 1-85293-077-2.
—— (ed.) (1989) *Heritage Interpretation*, Vol. 2 *The Visitor Experience*, London: Belhaven Press. ISBN 1-85293-078-0.

Exhibits design/preparation

Belcher, M. (1991) *Exhibitions in Museums*, Leicester: Leicester University Press. ISBN 0-87474-913-1.
Brill, T. (1980) *Light – Its Interaction with Art and Antiquities*, New York and London: Plenum Press. ISBN 0-306-40416-8.
Burstein, D. and Stasiowski, F. (1982) *Project Management for the Design Professional*, London: Whitney Library of Design, an Imprint of Watson-Guptill Publication. ISBN 0-8230-7434-x.
Communications Design Team of the Royal Ontario Museum (1976) *Communicating with the Museum Visitor: Guidelines for Planning*, Toronto: ROM. ISBN 0-88854-193-7.
Finn, D. (1985) *How to Visit a Museum*, New York: Harry Abrams. ISBN 0-8109-2297-5.
Fondation de France/ICOM (1991) *Museums Without Barriers*, Paris: Fondation de France/ICOM in conjunction with Routledge Press. ISBN 0-415-05454-0 (cloth) ISBN 0-415-06994-7 (paper).
Hall, M. (1987) *On Display: A Design Grammar for Museum Exhibitions*, London: Lund Humphries. ISBN 0-85331-455-1.
Kanikow, R. (1987) *Exhibit Design*, New York: PBC International. ISBN 0-86636-001-8.
Klein, L. (1986) *Exhibits: Planning and Design*, New York: Madison Square Press. ISBN 0-942604-18-0.
Miles, R. (1988) *The Design of Educational Exhibits* (2nd revised edition), London: Unwin Hyman. ISBN 0-04-445078-8.
Neal, A. (1969) *HELP! for the Small Museum, Handbook of Exhibit Ideas and Methods*, Boulder, CO: Pruett Publishing. Library of Congress Catalog Card Number: 70-75438.
—— (1976) *Exhibits for the Small Museum*, Nashville: The American Association for State and Local History. ISBN 0-910050-23-6.
Reeve, J. (1986) *The Art of Showing Art*, Tulsa, OK: HCE Publications and Council Oak Books. ISBN 0-933031-04-1.
Reinwardt Academie (1983) *Exhibition Design as an Education Tool*, Amsterdam: Reinwardt Academie. (No identification number.)
Serrell, B. (1985) *Making Exhibit Labels*, Nashville: The American Association for State and Local History. ISBN 0-910050-64-3.
Vehoor, J. and Meeter, H. (1987) *Project Model Exhibitions*, Amsterdam: Reinwardt Academie. (No identification number.)
Velarde, G. (1988) *Designing Exhibitions*, London: The Design Council. ISBN 0-85072-223-3.
Witteborg, L. (1981) *Good Show! A Practical Guide for Temporary Exhibitions*, Washington, D.C.: Smithsonian Institution Traveling Exhibition Service. ISBN 0-86528-007-x.

Facilities/security

Howie, F. (ed.) (1987) *Safety in Museums and Galleries*, London: Butterworths (in association with the International Journal of Museum Management and Curatorship). ISBN 0-408-02362-7.

International Committee on Museum Security (1986) *A Manual of Basic Museum Security*, London: International Council of Museums. ISBN 0-85022-209-5.

Jones, B. (1986) *Protecting Historic Architecture and Museum Collections from Natural Disaster*, London: Butterworths. ISBN 0-409-90035-4.

Olkowski, W., Doar, S., and Olkowski, H. (1991) *Common-Sense Pest Control*, Newton, CT: The Taunton Press. ISBN 0-942391-63-2.

Schröder, H. (1981) *Museum Security Survey*, Paris: International Council of Museum. (No identification number.)

Thompson, G. (1978) *The Museum Environment*, London: Butterworths. ISBN 0-408-70792-5.

Tillotson, R. (chair, International Committee on Security) (1977) (D. Menkes (ed.) and translated from French by Martha de Moltke), *La Sécurité dans les musées* (*Museum Security*), Paris: International Council of Museums. Library of Congress Catalog Card Number 77-74644.

Zycherman, L. (ed.) (1988) *A Guide to Museum Pest Control*, Washington, D.C.: Association of Systematics Collections. ISBN 0-942924-14-2.

Fund raising

Lauffer, A. (1984) *Strategic Marketing for Not-for-Profit Organizations*, New York: The Free Press. ISBN 0-02-918260-3.

Quigg, H. (ed.) (1986) *The Successful Capital Campaign*, Washington, D.C.: The Council for Advancement and Support of Education.

Ross, David (ed.) (1981) *Understanding and Increasing Foundation Support*, San Francisco: Jossey-Bass. ISBN 87589-836-X.

Seltzer, M. (1987) *Securing Your Organization's Future*, New York: The Foundation Center. ISBN 0-87954-190-3.

Stolper, C. and Hopkins, K. (1989) *Successful Fundraising for Arts and Cultural Organizations*, Phoenix, AZ.: The Onex Press. ISBN 0-89774-539-6.

Law/ethics/standards

Association of Art Museum Directors (1981) *Professional Practices in Art Museums, Report of the Ethics and Standards Committee*, Savannah, Georgia: Association of Art Museum Directors. Library of Congress Catalog Card Number 81-66765.

Gathercole, P. and Lowenthal, D. (eds) (1990) *The Policies of the Past*, London: Unwin Hyman. ISBN 0-04-445018-4.

Greenfield, J. (1989) *The Return of Cultural Treasures*, Cambridge: Cambridge University Press. ISBN 0-521-333199.

Kluwer, B. (1989) *Monument Protection in Europe*, Amsterdam: Deventer. ISBN 90-268-1107-1.

Malaro, M. (1985) *A Legal Primer on Managing Museum Collections*, (2nd edition 1987) Washington, D.C.: Smithsonian Institution Press. ISBN 0-87474-656-6.

Marion, J. (1989) *The Best of Everything*, New York: Simon & Schuster. ISBN 0-671-66783-1.

Merryman, J. and Elsen, A. (1987) *Law, Ethics, and the Visual Arts* (2nd edition, Vols I and II), Philadelphia: University of Pennsylvania Press. ISBN 0-8122-8052-2 (set).

Messenger, P. (ed.) (1989) *The Ethics of Collecting Cultural Property*, Albuquerque, NM: University of New Mexico Press. ISBN 0-8263-1167-9.

Meyer, K. (1973) *The Plundered Past*, New York: Atheneum. ISBN 0-689-1-522-3.

Phelan, M. (1982) *Museums and the Law*, Vol. 1, AASLH Management Series, Nashville: The American Association for State and Local History. ISBN 0-910050-60-0.

Williams, S. (1977) *The International and National Protection of Movable Cultural Property, A Comparative Study*, Dobbs Ferry, NY: Oceana Publications. ISBN 0-379-20294-8.

Public relations/outreach

Adams, G. D. (1983) *Museum Public Relations*, Vol. 2, AASLH Management Series, Nashville: The American Association for State and Local History. ISBN 0-910050-65-1.

Agustí, L. (ed.) (1973) *Friends of the World's Museums: Proceedings of the 1st International Congress, Barcelona*, Barcelona-14: Pasaje Solona, s/n. (No identification number.)

Benington, J. and White, J. (eds) (1988) *The Future of Leisure Services*, London: Longman House. ISBN 0582-02637-7.

French, Y. (1991) *The Handbook of Public Relations*, London: The Museum Development Company. ISBN 1-873114-03-6.

International Council of Museums (1986) *Public View, The ICOM Handbook of Museum Public Relations*, Paris: The International Council of Museums. ISBN 92-9012-107-6.

Merriman, N. (1991) *Beyond the Glass Case*, Leicester: Leicester University Press. ISBN 0-7185-1349-5.

Pearce, S. (ed.) (1991) *Museum Economics and the Community*, London: Athlone Press. ISBN 0-485-90002-5.

Phillips, C. and Hogan, P. (1984) *A Culture at Risk, Who Cares for America's Heritage?*, Nashville: The American Association for State and Local History. (No identification number.)

Quimby, M. (ed.) (1978) *Material Culture and the Study of American Life*, New York: W. W. Norton. ISBN 0 393 05661-9 (cloth) ISBN 0-393-05665-1 (paper).

Roberts, D. (1990) *Terminology for Museums*, Cambridge, UK: The Museum Documentation Association. ISBN 0-905963-62-8.

Trenbeth, R. (1986) *The Membership Mystique*, Rockville, MD: Fund Raising Institute/Taft Group. ISBN 0-930807-01-4.

Registration/documentation

Beibel, D. (1978) *Registration Methods for the Small Museum*, Nashville: The American Association of State and Local History. ISBN 0-910050-37-6.

Selected bibliography

Chenhall, R. (1978) *Nomenclature for Museum Cataloging*, Nashville: The American Association of State and Local History. ISBN 0-910050-30-9.

Dudley, D., Wilkinson, I., et al. (1981) *Museum Registration Methods* (3rd edition revised), Washington, D.C.: American Association of Museums. Library of Congress Catalog Card Number: 79-52058.

Eri, I and Vegh, B. (eds-in-chief) (1986) *Dictionarium Museologicum* (compiled by the ICOM International Committee for Documentation (CIDOC) Working Group on Terminology), Budapest: Hungarian Esperanto Association. ISBN 963-571-1743.

Light, R., Robert, D., and Stewart, J. (eds) (1986) *Museum Documentation Systems*, London: Butterworths. ISBN 0-408-10815-0.

Pederson, A. (ed.) (1987) *Keeping Archives*, Sydney, New South Wales: Australian Society of Archivists Incorporated, Museums Association of Australia. ISBN 0-9595565-9-1.

Salaman, R. (1977) *Dictionary of Tools* [used in the woodworking and allied trades, c. 1700–1970], London: George Allen & Unwin. ISBN 0-04-621020-2.

Museum journals

Curator
Published quarterly by the American Museum of Natural History, *Curator* (ISSN 0-011-3069) is a means of publishing papers, essays, and book reviews by museum professionals.
American Museum of Natural History
Central Park West at 79th Street
New York, New York 10024
USA

ICOM News
The bulletin of the International Council of Museums (ISSN 0-018-8999), is published quarterly in English, French, and Spanish.
International Council of Museums
Maison de l'UNESCO
1 rue Miollis
75732 Paris Cedex 15
France

Muse
The quarterly journal of Canadian Museums, *Muse* (ISSN 0-820-0165) is published in English and French by the CMA.
Canadian Museums Association
280 Metcalfe Street
Suite 400
Ottawa, Ontario
Canada K2P 1R7

Museum Journal
The *Museum Journal* (ISSN 0-027-416X), published monthly by the Museum Association, aims to present a wide range of news, views, and opinions in order to encourage informed debate on issues of importance to the museum and gallery community.

Museum Journal
42 Clerkenwell Close
London EC1R 0PA
United Kingdom

Museum News
Museum News (ISSN 0-027-4089), is published bimonthly by the AAM.
American Association of Museums
1225 Eye Street N.W.
Suite 200
Washington, D.C. 20005
USA

Museum (UNESCO)
Museum (UNESCO) (ISSN 0-027-3996) is published quarterly by the United
Nations Educational, Scientific, and Cultural Organization in Paris. It is an
international forum of information and reflection on museums of all kinds. It
is designed to enliven museums everywhere. The English edition is published in
Oxford; French and Spanish editions are published in Paris, the Arabic edition
in Cairo, and the Russian edition in Moscow.
Subscriptions Department
Marston Book Service
PO Box 87
Oxford OX2 0DT
United Kingdom

Plate 9 Museum Security personnel Antonio Garcia on duty at the reception desk (photograph by Gary Edson)

Museum training survey

—•◆•—

A great deal of time was spent gathering and editing the information included in this publication. However, the directory of training programs is incomplete. The survey mailing list was compiled from a number of sources but there is an obvious lack of information from several areas of the world. In some cases agencies chose not to be included in the directory. Other institutions were simply missed. Exclusion is not intentional and all programs are invited to send information for the next edition of *International Directory of Museum Training*.

Unavoidably this edition has a heavy emphasis on the United States, Canada, and parts of western Europe. This prominence is the result of the available mailing lists and does not reflect program quality or availability. All institutions on the mailing lists were sent a letter and survey requesting input. Surveys were also distributed at two international meetings and one national conference. Several programs received second mailings followed by telephone contacts. Persons having information about training programs in the Middle and Far East, North Africa, and eastern Europe are encouraged to send names and addresses to:

Gary Edson, Executive Director
Museum of Texas Tech University
Box 43191
Lubbock, Texas 79409-3191
USA
Telephone: 1 (806) 742 2442   Fax: 1 (806) 742 1136

The international museum training community has an opportunity and a responsibility to share information. The ICOM *Code of Professional Ethics* includes the following statement on page 34, paragraph 8.2, "Professional Co-operation":

The training of personnel in the specialized activities involved in museum work is of great importance in the development of the profession and all should accept responsibility, where appropriate, in the training of colleagues. Members of the profession who in their official appointment have under their direction junior staff, trainees, students and assistants undertaking formal or informal professional training, should give these the benefit of their experience and knowledge, and should also treat them with the consideration and respect customary among members of the profession.

The International Directory of Museum Training provides easy reference for trainers as well as for those seeking training. To be an effective and useful publication it must provide more than a simple listing of names and locations. Future editions will stress the importance of national identity, that is training programs designed to meet the needs of a particular nation or region while simultaneously supporting an international view. This focus will include museum training planned to support national and/or economic growth. Future editions will also try to include more input from national committees and greater diversity in defining the needs of the museum profession.

Museums have an increasingly significant role to perform in many areas of society. The mission may vary from nation to nation but the needs, opportunities, and responsibilities are global. To respond, those working in or entering the museum profession will have to increase their skills and knowledge. Information exchange, shared technology, and international cooperation are essential elements in the effective training of museum personnel at all levels. Central to this concept is the belief that all people and nations must be honestly and equitably represented in all aspects of the museum community. Museum training is essential to the development of museums and to the preservation, study, and interpretation of world cultural, scientific, and natural heritage. It is a shared responsibility.

* * *

International Directory of Museum Training

Survey of Museum Training Programs

The *International Directory of Museum Training* is an important communication link with those beginning or expanding their knowledge and/or
skills to better serve the museum community. It is also a valuable reference for all members of the museum profession. To provide as much
information as possible, an up-dated listing is essential. Please complete
this survey to the best of your ability and return it to the address on the
following page. Return the survey even if some questions are unanswered
or inappropriate to the program with which you are affiliated. On a separate piece of paper, you may provide a short descriptive statement of no
more than 100 words about your program and its primary attributions.

1 Name of program: ....

2 Address of program: ....
Institution

....
Address or PO box no.   City

....
State. province, or territory   Mailing code   Country

....
Telephone number   Fax number

3 The year the program began: ....

4 The length of time required to complete the program:

   6 months or less ❏   1 year ❏   2 years ❏   More than 2 years ❏

   Other (specify): ....

5 Levels of training available to students (check all appropriate boxes):

   Course work   ❏   Workshops   ❏
   Internships   ❏   Baccalaureate degree   ❏
   Diploma   ❏   Graduate degree   ❏
   Certificate   ❏   Other (specify): ....

6 Areas of study included in the program (check all appropriate boxes):

   Administration   ❏   Curation   ❏
   Education   ❏   Collection management   ❏
   Exhibition design   ❏   Conservation   ❏
   Public programming   ❏   Field methods   ❏
   Fund raising   ❏   Information technology   ❏
   Public relations   ❏   Architectural preservation ❏

7   Areas of specialized training included in the program (check all appropriate boxes):

Anthropology	❏	Archeology	❏
Archives	❏	Architecture	❏
Clothing	❏	Decorative arts	❏
Ethnology	❏	Ethics	❏
Fine arts	❏	History	❏
Marketing	❏	Material culture	❏
Museology	❏	Natural sciences	❏
Paleontology	❏	Public policy	❏

Other (specify): ....

8   Which of the following describes the instructional opportunities provided by this program? Check all appropriate boxes:

Full-time study in regularly scheduled classes   ❏

Part-time study in regularly scheduled classes   ❏

Short-term lectures offered in response to requests   ❏

Lectures/seminars offered on an announced schedule   ❏

Workshops as requested   ❏

Correspondence study   ❏

9   Is the study of museum ethics a regular part of the program of study?

       yes ❏   no ❏

10 Is the program open to international students?   yes ❏   no ❏

11 What is the primary language of instruction?......................................

12 Is financial assistance available for students?   yes ❏   no ❏

13 What kind of financial assistance is available?
(check all appropriate boxes):

Scholarships	❏	Student work program	❏
Loans	❏	Materials/supplies/books	❏
Lodging	❏	Tuition/registration waiver	❏

Other (specify): ....

14 Is the training program/workshop/seminar affiliated with the following? Check all appropriate boxes:

Archives ❏   Conservation center(s) ❏

Museum(s) ❏   University(ies) ❏

Gallery(ies) ❏   Science center(s) ❏

15 Is instruction given in a museum, archives/conservation center?
yes ❏   no ❏

16 If the answer to question number 15 is "yes," do students work in the collections as part of the program of study?   yes ❏   no ❏

17 Do instructors have museum experience?   yes ❏   no ❏

18 How many students begin the program each year? ....

19 Approximately how many students have completed the program since it began? ....

20 Are the majority of the students in your program already employed by a museum, archive, conservation center, zoo, or similar institution?
yes ❏   no ❏

21 Approximately what percentage of the students completing your program return to or enter employment in museums?

Less than 25%   ❏   25% to 50%   ❏

50% to 75%   ❏   More than 75%   ❏

22 Name of contact person: ....

23 Is the contact person or the program providing organization, institution, museum, archive, conservation center, zoo, or similar agency currently a member of ICOM?   yes ❏   no ❏

24 Please provide the names and addresses of other museum training programs that have not been included in this directory. World-wide investment in museum training is of major importance. Your contribution adds to the completeness of the data.

....
....
....
....
....
....

25 On a separate page describe the characteristics of the program (please limit comments to no more than 100 words).

Return completed survey to: Gary Edson, Director
                               Museum Science Program
                               Museum of Texas Tech University
                               Box 43191
                               Lubbock, Texas 79409-3191 USA
Telephone: 1 (806) 742 2442 Fax: 1 (806) 742 1136

Plate 10 Collections Manager Nicky Ladkin conducting anthropology field work (photograph by Nicky L. Olson)

TEN

Museum training indices

———•◆•———

The numbers used in these indices refer to the Directory No. shown at the top of each program entry above the institution's name.

Training levels index

Certificate program 9, 14, 18, 20–2, 30, 32, 35, 40, 43, 45, 46, 53–5, 57–9, 61, 65, 77, 88, 92–7, 101, 115, 123–5, 129, 130, 143, 167, 168, 170, 178, 180, 195–8, 201, 204, 207, 214, 216, 231, 236, 247, 253.
Correspondence courses 6, 7, 20–2, 24, 27, 35, 60, 226, 246.
Diploma programs 1–3, 5, 8, 14, 20, 27, 38, 44, 45, 47, 52, 55, 56, 60, 63–5, 67, 77, 83, 84, 86, 92, 94, 100, 172, 196, 197, 200, 202.
Bachelor's degree programs 1, 2, 13, 15, 16, 19, 26, 41, 44, 62, 64, 65, 68, 71, 75, 97, 142, 164, 166, 185, 197, 227, 232, 233, 242, 243, 245, 246.
Graduate degree programs 1, 2, 4, 7, 10, 11, 16, 19, 25, 28, 36, 38, 42, 44, 47, 55, 60, 64–6, 68, 72, 74–6, 78–84, 88, 92–6, 98–100, 104, 112, 122, 129–32, 134, 142–4, 151, 152, 168, 171, 175, 185, 191, 195, 198–200, 202, 204–6, 208–11, 217, 220, 224, 226, 231, 232, 241, 242, 244, 250.
Internships 10, 18–20, 24–7, 31, 36, 38, 45, 48, 50, 61, 64, 65, 68, 70, 73, 74, 76, 77, 79, 80, 83, 85–7, 89, 91–4, 96, 98–100, 102–110, 112–14, 116, 117, 119, 120–30, 133, 135–40, 142–5, 148, 149, 151, 153–62, 166–70, 172–4, 176, 177, 179–88, 190, 192–7, 202–4, 206, 207, 212, 213, 215, 216, 219, 221, 222, 224, 225, 227, 231–3, 235, 237–40, 243–6, 248, 254.
Workshops 6, 14, 17, 19, 23, 25, 26, 30, 31–7, 40, 45, 46, 48, 51, 59, 65, 68, 69, 71, 73, 76, 80, 83, 92, 94, 104, 105, 107, 111, 112, 118, 124, 125, 127, 130, 143, 146, 147, 149, 151, 165, 189, 196, 202, 207, 212, 227, 235, 236.

Discipline index

Administration 1, 3, 5–10, 13, 14, 16–22, 24, 27, 28, 32–6, 38, 40–8, 51, 55, 56, 60, 61, 63–5, 67, 75, 76, 78, 80–4, 88, 89, 91–101, 104, 106, 107, 109, 111, 114–17, 119–23, 126–30, 132, 134, 138, 141–4, 146, 149, 150–5, 161,

Financial aid index

Training agency index